PENGUIN BOOKS

THE COST OF CHAOS

Peter Bergen is a vice president at New America in Washington, DC, as well as national security analyst for CNN, where he writes a weekly online column. He is also a professor and codirector of the Center on the Future of War at Arizona State University and has held teaching positions at the Kennedy School of Government at Harvard University and at the School of Advanced International Studies at Johns Hopkins University.

Bergen is the author of seven books about national security, including three *New York Times* bestsellers and four *Washington Post* nonfiction books of the year. In 1997, as a producer for CNN, Bergen produced Osama bin Laden's first television interview, in which bin Laden declared war against the United States for the first time to a Western audience.

He lives in Washington, DC, with his wife, documentary producer Tresha Mabile, and their children, Pierre and Grace.

ALSO BY PETER BERGEN

The Rise and Fall of Osama bin Laden

United States of Jihad

Manhunt

The Longest War

The Osama bin Laden I Know

Holy War, Inc.

Drone Wars (coeditor)

Talibanistan (coeditor)

THE COST OF CHAOS

THE TRUMP ADMINISTRATION
AND THE WORLD

PETER BERGEN

Previously published as Trump and His Generals

PENGUIN BOOKS

PENGUIN BOOKS
An imprint of Penguin Random House LLC
penguinrandomhouse.com

First published in the United States of America as *Trump and His Generals*
by Penguin Press, an imprint of Penguin Random House LLC, 2019
Published in Penguin Books 2022

Library of Congress record available at https://lccn.loc.gov/2019957273

ISBN 9780525522416 (hardcover)
ISBN 9780525522430 (paperback)
ISBN 9780593652893 (ebook)

Printed in the United States of America
1st Printing

BOOK DESIGN BY LUCIA BERNARD

For Tresha, Pierre, and Grace

Our politics, religion, news . . . have been transformed into congenial adjuncts of show business, largely without protest or even much popular notice. The result is that we are a people on the verge of amusing ourselves to death.

AMUSING OURSELVES TO DEATH:
PUBLIC DISCOURSE IN THE AGE OF SHOW BUSINESS

—NEIL POSTMAN, 1985

From this day forward, a new vision will govern our land. From this moment on, it's going to be America first!

INAUGURAL ADDRESS OF THE
FORTY-FIFTH PRESIDENT OF THE UNITED STATES

—DONALD J. TRUMP, JANUARY 20, 2017

If you asked Babe Ruth how he hit home runs, he was unable to tell you. I do things by instinct.

—DONALD TRUMP TO THE *NEW YORK TIMES* IN 2004

We are all enrolled in Trump University now.

—TOM TOLES, *WASHINGTON POST* CARTOONIST,
NOVEMBER 11, 2016

A certain grasp of military affairs is vital for those in charge of general policy.

—CARL VON CLAUSEWITZ, *ON WAR*

— CONTENTS —

A NOTE ON SOURCING   *xiii*

PROLOGUE   *xv*

Chapter 1
THE WAR ROOM   *1*

Chapter 2
IN THE BEGINNING   *17*

Chapter 3
ALL THE BEST PEOPLE   *43*

Chapter 4
ENTER MCMASTER   *79*

Chapter 5
THE TRAVEL BAN   *93*

Chapter 6
ASSAD AND ISIS   *109*

Chapter 7
THE LONGEST WAR   *125*

Chapter 8
HOUSE OF SAUD, HOUSE OF TRUMP   *165*

Chapter 9

THE MURDER OF JAMAL KHASHOGGI   *199*

Chapter 10

FROM "FIRE AND FURY" TO "LOVE"   *211*

Chapter 11

PISSING OFF ALLIES, EMBRACING PUTIN   *223*

Chapter 12

REVOLT OF THE GENERALS   *235*

Chapter 13

WITHDRAWAL   *257*

Chapter 14

THE "INVASION"   *269*

Chapter 15

THE PLANES WERE LEAVING   *277*

Chapter 16

COMMANDER IN CHIEF   *285*

Chapter 17

THE FINAL YEAR   *303*

ACKNOWLEDGMENTS   *321*

BIBLIOGRAPHY   *325*

NOTES   *331*

INDEX   *395*

A NOTE ON SOURCING

This book is based on some one hundred interviews with current and former officials in the Trump administration, current and former senior US military officers, senior officials of foreign countries, and others who have worked with or interacted with Trump administration officials. Most of those interviews were recorded. The interviews were largely conducted on background because of the sensitive nature of the topics, although some interviewees did go on the record. A number of individuals were interviewed on multiple occasions, while others kept contemporaneous notes, diaries, and emails that were useful in establishing timelines and the details of meetings. All quotes in the book are based on at least one person's account of a meeting or event. In a number of cases, I spoke to multiple people who were at the same meeting or event.

Much of the action of this book takes place in Washington, DC. I also reported from some of the key countries that are discussed in the book such as Afghanistan, Iraq, Qatar, and Saudi Arabia, each of which I was able to visit at least twice during the course of my reporting. I also read some seventy books related to the Trump phenomenon. The notes at the end of this book reference the books and articles that I have drawn upon. Otherwise, all the information in the book comes from the interviews that I performed.

Prologue

On the twentieth anniversary of the 9/11 attacks, Donald Trump returned to his hometown to mark the solemn occasion. Trump skipped the official memorial ceremonies at the World Trade Center, which were attended by President Joe Biden, instead visiting a police station in Manhattan. Even as he was memorializing the anniversary with a group of New York City police officers, Trump couldn't help regaling the cops with his long-debunked claim that the 2020 presidential election was "rigged" against him. This was a lie: more than fifty lawsuits by Trump or his surrogates challenging those election results had already been dismissed in federal and state courts, while Trump's own election security officials had publicly stated that the 2020 election was "the most secure in American history."

The same day that Trump was in Manhattan, former president George W. Bush was attending a memorial service for the passengers and crew on United Flight 93, which had crashed in Shanksville, Pennsylvania, on 9/11. During the service, Bush took a thinly veiled swipe at Trump and the violent forces he had unleashed with his constant lies about the presidential election, which had culminated in the January 6, 2021, storming of the US Capitol by hundreds of enraged Trump supporters, some of whom fought pitched battles with police officers.

In Shanksville, Bush, who rarely made public statements now that he was out of office, said, "There is little cultural overlap between violent extremists abroad and violent extremists at home, but in their disdain for pluralism, in their disregard for human life, in their determination to defile national symbols, they are children of the same foul spirit, and it is our continuing duty to confront them." A Republican former president publicly calling out Trump's supporters on the anniversary of 9/11 for defiling the US Capitol quickly generated a forest of headlines.

Back at the Manhattan police station, Trump slammed the Biden administration for its ignominious departure from Afghanistan the previous month. That same day, half a world away, the Taliban raised their distinctive white flag over the presidential palace in Kabul, which was their way of memorializing the twentieth anniversary of 9/11.

The Taliban's seizure of Afghanistan was one of Trump's most significant foreign policy legacies. President Biden certainly deserved blame for claiming that he was bound by Trump's 2020 "peace" deal with the Taliban, which was really a "surrender agreement" in the mordant words of H. R. McMaster, Trump's former national security advisor. And Biden also deserved blame for the botched execution of the US withdrawal from Afghanistan during the summer of 2021. Some Afghans were so desperate to flee the Taliban that they hung on to the fuselage of a US military plane taking off from Kabul Airport; two of them dropped to their deaths. Thirteen US service members and 170 Afghans were also killed at the airport by the Afghan branch of ISIS as the Americans hurriedly withdrew. The chaos and tragedy made the US pullout from Saigon in 1975 look like a dignified retreat.

But it was Trump, not Biden, who had laid the groundwork for the Taliban takeover of Afghanistan. In 2018, Trump authorized his secretary of state, Mike Pompeo, to begin negotiations with the Taliban. US ambassador Zalmay Khalilzad led the effort, making an agreement with the Taliban that, in exchange for a total US withdrawal from Afghanistan, they would break with al-Qaeda and engage in genuine peace talks with the Afghan government. Despite these agreements, the Taliban maintained close ties with al-Qaeda and prepared for a major military offensive against the Afghan government. Meanwhile, the Trump administration agreed to pressure the Afghan government to release five thousand Taliban prisoners, some of whom rejoined their old comrades on the battlefield once they were released.

Trump often asserted he was a great dealmaker, but his administration's agreement with the Taliban was one of the worst deals in American diplomatic history. The Taliban received everything that they wanted without offering anything substantive in return, other than an agreement not to attack US forces as they withdrew from Afghanistan. Since the Taliban's main goal in their negotiations with the United States was a total American withdrawal—which would also precipitate the withdrawal of thousands of allied NATO forces, as well as more than fifteen thousand contractors, many of whom were supporting the Afghan air force and army—this was an easy concession for the Taliban to make. A total American withdrawal would then help pave the way for their complete victory over the Afghan government.

The week before the twentieth anniversary of 9/11, the Taliban had appointed Sirajuddin Haqqani, a member of al-Qaeda's leadership, to a top cabinet position in their new government. Haqqani was appointed acting interior minister, a job analogous to running the US Department of Homeland Security and the FBI. The Taliban peace negotiations initiated by Trump ended up leading to the takeover of Afghanistan by the Taliban and ensured that al-Qaeda would play a role in the leadership of the country.

And so it went with many other of Trump's foreign policy initiatives. Trump believed that by dint of his personal charm he could persuade the North Korean dictator Kim Jong Un to give up his nuclear weapons. American presidents going back to Bill Clinton had tried to persuade the nuclear-armed hermit state to rein in its weapons program, and all of them had failed. Trump met with Kim three times as president, first in Singapore in 2018, and a year later in Hanoi and then at the border between North and South Korea. Each meeting generated a media frenzy, giving Kim and the US president equal billing on the world stage, which was a huge coup for the dictator of a country whose GDP was similar to that of the state of Vermont.

At the Singapore meeting, Trump unilaterally gave a key concession to Kim—canceling joint US–South Korea military exercises, which had been a longtime cornerstone of containing the North Korean rogue state—and got nothing in return. Trump didn't consult any members of his cabinet before telling Kim the exercises would be canceled, blindsiding the Pentagon. Trump told Kim that North Korea was doing the US a big favor because canceling the exercises "saved the United States a lot of money." When Trump made this remark, Kim was smiling broadly, laughing from time to time. The jovial dictator had correctly pegged Trump as an easy mark. It was the same negotiating strategy that the Trump administration would later employ with the Taliban, giving away major concessions and getting nothing in return.

Trump and Kim also exchanged twenty-seven letters, publicly described by Trump as "love letters." Yet, these summits and exchanges yielded nothing. While Trump was in office, the North Koreans continued producing fissile material and tested short-range ballistic missiles in contravention of UN Security Council prohibitions, in addition to developing hard-to-detect submarine-launched missiles.

While Trump's efforts to constrain North Korea's nuclear program failed, his erratic diplomacy encouraged Iran's nuclear ambitions. Trump regularly castigated Obama's 2015 nuclear agreement with the Iranians as the "worst deal in history." But unlike Trump's peace agreement with the Taliban, the Iranians were observing their end of the nuclear deal, according to Trump's own intelligence agencies. Yet, Trump was determined to get out of Obama's Iran agreement, which he did in 2018. As a result, by the time that Trump left office in January 2021, the Iranians were planning to enrich uranium up to 20 percent purity, far above the 4 percent purity agreed to in their deal with the Obama administration. While 20 percent is well short of the 90 percent purity needed for a nuclear bomb, the Iranians had accumulated enough fissile material by the time Biden assumed office that they were within a few months of having enough for a nuclear weapon. The Iranian nuclear program took a large step forward as a result of Trump's ham-handed approach.

Throughout his presidency, Trump embraced Russian strongman president Vladimir Putin while regularly taking potshots at key American allies such as the British, French, and Germans. What was the strategic benefit of all this geopolitical trumpery to the United States? It was never clear, although it was certainly a key aim of Putin's to weaken the

NATO alliance. Rather than seeing NATO as a mutual self-defense alliance that served American interests very well, Trump saw it as a constellation of countries that were ripping off the United States. Trump often told his key advisers that he wanted to pull out of NATO, which his own defense secretary, Jim Mattis, described as the most successful alliance in history. Luckily, Trump never followed through, but by the time he left office, Trump was largely despised by ordinary British, French, and German citizens whose countries were at the core of NATO.

Trump, who had a fascination with autocrats, also embraced the dictatorial Saudi crown prince Mohammed bin Salman, the de facto ruler of the Saudi kingdom, known as MBS. The headstrong prince embroiled his country in a war in neighboring Yemen that precipitated one of the worst humanitarian crises in the world. Rather than extirpating Iranian influence in Yemen, which was a key goal of the Saudi war, Iran's influence in Yemen was amplified as its alliance with the anti-Saudi Houthi rebels deepened. MBS also jailed innocuous Saudi dissidents, such as women who had demanded the right to drive, and his goons murdered the Saudi writer Jamal Khashoggi in Istanbul in 2018. None of this advanced American interests, yet Trump bragged that he'd shielded MBS after Khashoggi's murder, and he also vetoed a bill attempting to end US military assistance for the Saudis' war in Yemen.

Trump's embrace of dictators overseas was of a piece with his attempts to undermine democratic processes and norms at home in the United States, which was exemplified by his continued refusal to accede to the will of the people in the 2020 presidential election and his support of his followers storming the US Capitol. As a result, two-thirds of Republicans believed that the 2020 election was rigged against Trump, despite all evidence to the contrary. That statistic underlined how polarized American society had become, a polarization greatly intensified by Trump himself.

Trump also tuned out the baleful effects of a warming planet, pulling the United States out of the Paris climate agreement. The evidence for accelerating climate change during the Trump presidency was plain to see, from the vast forest fires in the American West to the NASA analysis, which found that 2020 was the hottest year since record keeping began.

But it was, above all, in his mishandling of the COVID pandemic that Trump revealed his many weaknesses as a leader.

On February 28, 2020, as Americans first became aware of the threat from the coronavirus, Trump said that cases of the virus would go down to zero "within a couple of days." He also claimed that the coronavirus was no more dangerous than the seasonal flu. The following month, Trump said that "anybody that wants a test can get a test" at a time when there were only seventy-five thousand tests for 330 million Americans. Trump then said that come Easter Sunday on April 12, 2020, the US should be "opened up" because he "just thought it was a beautiful time."

The Trump administration abdicated its responsibilities by not issuing a mandate to wear masks and also never developed a nationwide COVID-19 testing strategy. After the expiration on April 30, 2020, of a voluntary forty-five-day federal advisory to "slow the spread," the Centers for Disease Control and Prevention (CDC) guidance on how to reopen carefully in phases was ignored in many states. As Trump pressed for states to reopen, social distancing often went out the window. In defiance of CDC guidelines on large gatherings, Trump held a large indoor rally in Tulsa, Oklahoma, on June 20, 2020, which likely contributed to a spike of cases there. One of the attendees at the Tulsa rally was Republican governor Kevin Stitt, who subsequently became the first US governor to test positive for the virus. By prioritizing "reopening" over public health, the Trump administration chose to accept that hundreds of thousands of Americans could die of COVID-19.

In late April, Trump suggested that injecting bleach might prove to be a treatment for the virus. A month later, Trump said that he was taking the drug hydroxychloroquine, an antimalarial. In June 2020, the Food and Drug Administration revoked "emergency use" of hydroxychloroquine for COVID-19 patients because it could cause heart problems.

When testing became more widespread in July 2020, Trump claimed that the only reason coronavirus cases were rising in the US was not because of rapid community spread, but because there was more testing.

And Trump publicly denigrated his top infectious disease expert, Dr. Anthony Fauci, as an "alarmist."

For Trump, the buck never stopped at his desk. Trump tried labeling the virus the "China virus," the "Wuhan virus," and even the "kung flu." But those diversionary efforts fell flat. A poll released in July 2020 by the Associated Press found that Trump's approval rating on his handling of the virus had fallen to an all-time low of 32 percent.

Occasionally, Trump officials made sensible decisions, such as when, on January 31, 2020, they barred non-US citizens who had recently visited China from entering the United States and also imposed two-week quarantines on Americans who had visited Hubei province, where the virus had originated. But these good calls were far outweighed by the procession of bad policy choices made by Trump. Before effective vaccines, there were two tools that worked to stop the spread of the virus: social distancing and wearing a mask in public. Trump denigrated mask wearing and almost invariably refused to wear a mask himself.

He explained it was all about the optics: "Somehow sitting in the Oval Office behind that beautiful Resolute Desk, the great Resolute Desk. I think wearing a face mask as I greet presidents, prime ministers, dictators, kings, queens—I don't know, somehow, I don't see it for myself. I just, I just don't." Trump turned masks into political footballs rather than symbols of sound public health policy. He also convened events at the White House with large numbers of guests mingling without masks, such as the celebration of the nomination of Amy Coney Barrett to the Supreme Court on September 26, 2020.

By August 2020, eighteen American states had set records for their numbers of confirmed coronavirus cases, and there were more than four million confirmed cases in the US, a quarter of the total number of known cases in the world, though Americans made up just over 4 percent of the global population.

Trump's falsehoods and cavalier behavior had other impacts. A Cornell University study released in October 2020 found that mentions of Trump made up 37 percent of the overall "misinformation conversation" about the coronavirus based on a sample analysis of thirty-eight million articles in English from around the world. Even when Trump had the chance to make a public statement that might have made a difference to the scope of the pandemic, he failed to do so. He and his wife, Melania, were vaccinated at the White House during the closing days of his presidency. Any leader with the slightest regard for his own people would have allowed the media to cover this event, especially given the prevalence of vaccine hesitancy in the United States. Trump chose instead to be vaccinated in secret.

More than four hundred thousand Americans died from COVID-19 during Trump's final year in office, which was more than the American death toll in wars going back to World War II. Many of those deaths could have been avoided with better leadership; COVID mortality in the US was 40 percent higher than the average of other advanced nations such as Canada, France, Germany, Italy, Japan, and the United Kingdom. The first duty of the commander in chief is the protection of US citizens, and Trump clearly was derelict in this duty. In short, Trump was the most incompetent president in modern American history. This book is an attempt to tell the story of how that happened.

Chapter 1

THE WAR ROOM

Gentlemen, you can't fight in here! This is the War Room!

—*President Merkin Muffley in the movie* Dr. Strangelove

T he day began well enough. Six months into his young presidency, Donald Trump arrived at the front steps of the Pentagon on a muggy Thursday morning in late July. Alighting from "the Beast," the heavily armored presidential limo, Trump was greeted by his favorite general, Secretary of Defense James "Mad Dog" Mattis. Mattis didn't care for this nickname, but Trump, whose experience of the military was limited to a stint at a military-style boarding school, reveled in the four-star generals on his team, especially the "killers." Trump respected the raw power embodied by the US military.

As Trump ascended the front steps of the Pentagon on the morning of July 20, 2017, a reporter shouted, "Mr. President: Are you sending more troops to Afghanistan?" An intense and largely hidden battle was then consuming Trump's war cabinet about precisely this question.

At the top of the Pentagon steps, flanked by an honor guard and towering over his secretary of defense, the president responded with one of his favorite lines, saying, "We'll see."

Trump was at the Pentagon for a briefing that was planned by Mattis; Trump's chief strategist, Steve Bannon; Trump's national security adviser, Lieutenant General H. R. McMaster; the secretary of state, Rex Tillerson; and Trump's chief economic adviser, Gary Cohn. They all felt it would be useful for Trump—the first American president not to have served in public office or the military—to receive a briefing about what *exactly* the United States was doing around the globe as well as its economic relationships and security arrangements. They also wanted Trump to understand the tools at his disposal as the commander in chief, from the eleven US aircraft carriers to American nuclear weapons capabilities.

Trump's key advisers all had quite different goals for the briefing. Bannon was the standard-bearer of Trump's "America First" populism and he hoped that the briefing would show Trump how overextended and overcommitted the United States was overseas. Mattis and Tillerson wanted to make the case for the United States' alliances that had shaped the world order since World War II. Those alliances, in their view, had benefited the United States tremendously, not only by hastening the peaceful implosion of the Soviet Union, but also more recently when a US-led NATO force had formed after 9/11 to oust the Taliban from power in Afghanistan. Cohn wanted to make the case for the economic rules-based international order that was built on free trade and had created unprecedented prosperity around the world.

On the surface, Bannon and Mattis didn't have much in common. A laconic, publicity-shy general and lifelong bachelor, Mattis had enlisted in the US Marines when he was eighteen and had spent his entire career in the military. Bannon, a voluble ringmaster of a man who had landed on the cover of *Time* for his role in guiding the Trump administration's strategy, had served an eight-year stint in the navy and then gone to work at Goldman Sachs and later as a Hollywood producer. More recently he had run the far-right media site *Breitbart News*.

Despite their different temperaments and experiences, both men shared a love of books and military history. If Bannon wasn't discussing American politics, he was almost a different person talking knowledgeably about Asia, financial markets, and Alfred Thayer Mahan, the American historian who was the most influential naval strategist in the world in the run-up to World War I.

A four-star general was likely to move around some two dozen times during the course of a long career. Typically, the general would move his family and household effects from one posting to the next. General Mattis instead moved his books—all seven thousand of them. In 2003 during the Iraq War, Mattis explained in an email to a fellow officer why deep reading about the history of warfare could help to save American lives on the battlefield: "By reading, you learn through others' experiences—generally a better way to do business—especially in our line of work where the consequences of incompetence are so final for young men."

Bannon met with Mattis and two of his top aides, senior adviser Sally Donnelly and chief of staff retired rear admiral Kevin Sweeney, in Mattis's Pentagon office at 7:00 am on Saturday, June 24, to discuss the United States' military posture around the world. During the course of a several-hour discussion, Bannon said to Mattis, "We're talking about putting in Special Operations Forces from North Africa to the Saudi Peninsula to Asia. You're all over the place. And there's no strategy to back it up. It feels like we're in something like seventy-three countries. We've got to pull the camera back and we've got to set a strategic framework."

Bannon was obsessed by the long-term threat posed by China. He drew a diagram on a piece of paper for Mattis and his staff showing how China posed a rising challenge to American global supremacy, in particular, because of its ambitious "One Belt, One Road" policy that was designed to build transportation infrastructure that intertwined China deeply with the Middle East, Africa, and Europe.

The solution, Bannon said, was to build up "the Quad," which was an emerging alliance between the democratic Pacific powers: Australia, India, Japan, and the United States.

Bannon kept a dog-eared, marked-up copy of *Unrestricted Warfare*, a treatise that was published by two Chinese army colonels in 1999. It laid out a surprisingly prescient strategy about how China could undercut the militarily far-superior United States through economic warfare and information operations. Bannon gave a copy of the book to Trump. At the White House, Bannon also handed out copies of Michael Pillsbury's 2015 book *The Hundred-Year Marathon: China's Secret Strategy to Replace America as the Global Superpower*. A longtime scholar of China, Pillsbury argued that the Chinese were stealthily and patiently building up their economic, political, and military power with the ultimate aim to take their "rightful place" as the world's sole superpower, but they were doing it in such a way that they weren't, for the moment, directly challenging the United States.

Bannon also diagrammed for Mattis other key threats that he believed were in the ascendant, such as Iran. As he sketched out these threats, Bannon said, "Look, this is the dark valley. This is the 1930s all over again, right?"

In college, Bannon had studied the historian Arnold Toynbee, who argued that history was an endless cycle of the rise and decay of civilizations. Was the United States going to be the next hegemon in the also-ran category? An obscure tract published in 1997 also influenced Bannon, *The Fourth Turning: An American Prophecy—What the Cycles of History Tell Us about America's Next Rendezvous with Destiny*. It was a work of pseudohistory purporting to have found the secret to the ebbs and flows of American history, and it prophesied a looming catastrophe for the United States. *The Fourth Turning* helped to confirm Bannon's belief that the United States, and indeed the entire West, was in a phase of deep civilizational decay and was on the road to ruin until Trump had come along to save it.

Bannon was raised as a devout, orthodox Catholic and he believed strongly that "Judeo-Christian civilization" was under attack. Bannon's apocalyptic *vision du monde* was underlined in an address he delivered via Skype to a group of conservative Catholics who were meeting at the Vatican during the summer of 2014. To the group at the Vatican, Bannon asserted, "We're at the very beginning stages of a very brutal and bloody conflict, of which if the people in this room, the people in the church, do not bind together and really form what I feel is an aspect of the church militant, to really be able to not just stand with our beliefs, but to fight for our beliefs against this new barbarity that's starting, that will completely eradicate everything that we've been bequeathed over the last two thousand five hundred years."

Back in Mattis's vast office at the Pentagon, Bannon said that Trump should be briefed on all of America's global commitments from "the Pacific, all the way to the Gulf, to NATO. And let's talk about the commercial relationships, the capital markets, the trade deals, the military-security alliances, and what we have as far as weapons, manpower, and bases."

Bannon suggested that they do these presentations in "the Tank," a bland conference room deep in the bowels of the Pentagon where the chiefs of the various branches of the military conducted their most important, classified business.

Bannon told Mattis that Trump "loves the Tank, because that's where FDR and General Marshall ran World War II. It's very historic."

Mattis replied, "That's a great idea."

A day before the July 20 briefing in the Tank, Mattis went to see Tillerson in his seventh-floor conference room at the State Department to prep for the meeting with Trump. Neither Mattis nor Tillerson was a Trump guy. Both in their midsixties and outsiders in Trumpland who had never met Trump before they started working for him, they had formed a tight alliance that was cemented over a weekly breakfast that took place on Thursdays in the magnificently appointed formal reception rooms on the top floor of the State Department. Both cabinet secretaries were concerned that the United States was pulling back from the world. Already Trump had pulled the country out of the Paris climate agreement and the Trans-Pacific Partnership, the trade deal between a dozen Pacific countries that was designed in part to contain the rise of China. Trump was also questioning the value of having a large military footprint overseas, whether it was in Europe or Asia. Mattis and Tillerson wanted to give Trump a primer about what the United States was doing around the world and how it benefited America's security and kept international trade flowing.

For the briefing in the Tank, they sat Trump, of course, at the head of the conference room table. Sitting next to him was Mattis, and close to him was General Joseph Dunford, chairman of the Joint Chiefs of Staff, the top military adviser to the president and the most senior officer in the US military. During the American invasion of Iraq in 2003, then-colonel "Fighting Joe" Dunford and then-major general Mattis had worked closely, leading their marines in the fight to seize Baghdad.

Because the briefing was also going to outline American trade deals and financial commitments, in attendance were Cohn and Treasury Secretary Steve Mnuchin, who were both enormously rich veterans of

Goldman Sachs. Sitting on the "backbenches" around the wall of the room were Bannon, who placed himself close to Trump, and Trump's son-in-law, Jared Kushner, as well as a slew of senior military and national security officials.

Not present to discuss this overview of American national security was the national security adviser, H. R. McMaster, who was taking some rare time off for a family vacation.

This absence suited Tillerson, who barely spoke to McMaster. When McMaster was presiding over a "principals" meeting of Trump's war cabinet, Tillerson would routinely "table-drop" documents at the last minute that hadn't been circulated ahead of time to cabinet officials, which was Tillerson's not-so-subtle way of trying to take control of the meeting and to sideline McMaster.

McMaster's absence also suited Mattis, who pointedly referred to him as "Lieutenant General McMaster" in meetings. This was understood by officials at those meetings to be an intentional reminder that Mattis was an exalted, retired four-star general, while McMaster was an uppity officer of more junior rank. Also, Lieutenant General McMaster remained in uniform while he was the national security adviser so, in a sense, the secretary of defense *was* his boss. Mattis's experience of being micromanaged by the Obama White House while he ran Central Command (CENTCOM) also seemed to have influenced his thinking about the role that the national security adviser should play in managing the Pentagon, which in his view was as little as possible.

For his part, McMaster felt that Mattis "slow rolled" any of the president's priorities he disagreed with, such as providing a range of options for potential military strikes against North Korea.

McMaster began referring to Mattis and Tillerson as the "Club of Two."

Both Tillerson and Mattis refused to send State Department and Pentagon officials to work for McMaster, a tactic that seemed designed to weaken the National Security Council, an unprecedented effort to undermine it since it was routine in every administration for Foreign Service officers and Pentagon officials to be detailed to work there.

Trump also found McMaster—a brilliant officer with a history PhD and a penchant for making multiple carefully constructed, professorial points about any given topic—to be something of an irritant. If McMaster presented on the Middle East to Trump, he might begin with the Ottoman Empire, showing scant instinct for his audience's zone of interest or aptitude.

Bannon had warned McMaster before he took the job as national security adviser, "Whatever you do don't be professorial. Trump is a game-day player. Trump is a guy who never went to class. Never got the syllabus. Never bought a book. Never took a note. He basically comes in the night before the final exams after partying all night, puts on a pot of coffee, takes your notes, memorizes what he's got to memorize. Walks in at eight o'clock in the morning and gets whatever grade he needs. That's the reason he doesn't like professors. He doesn't like being lectured to."

For Bannon and McMaster it was even simpler; they held each other in considerable mutual contempt. Bannon described McMaster as a "fucking globalist and a professor," while McMaster could never figure out exactly what Bannon's deal was. What was Bannon actually trying to accomplish? Bannon was the smartest and most well-read of the America First faction in the Trump administration, while McMaster was the smartest and most well-read of the internationalist bloc. The arguments between them about the United States' proper role in the world would in many ways define the debates about American foreign policy and national security strategy during Trump's presidency.

In the Pentagon Tank, Mattis prefaced his "laydown" of US troop deployments around the world by telling Trump, "The greatest gift of the greatest generation is the post-war, liberal, international rules-based order."

It was Mattis's and Tillerson's firmly held view that the United States had greatly benefited from the post–World War II order that it had largely created. One of the legacies of that order was a substantial

American troop presence in countries around the globe, from Afghanistan to Germany and from Iraq to Japan.

Using two giant screens as aids, Mattis laid out American military commitments in Europe, the Middle East, Asia, and the Pacific. Mattis also touched on American nuclear weapons strategy, speaking for about half an hour. Tillerson followed with an explanation of America's alliances. Cohn emphasized the strategic importance of strong trading relationships with allies in challenging regions such as South Korea, Saudi Arabia, and Kuwait.

Trump was uncharacteristically silent during these presentations, asking no questions and making no comments. When Cohn finished, Trump finally spoke up. His voice rising to a shout, Trump harangued his cabinet, "You guys have just walked through exactly what we're not gonna do! We're not doing this! The whole thing is on our shoulders. We're everywhere. It's our dollars! We're going bankrupt! If NATO is so afraid of Russia, somebody must stand up and write some checks! Show me an ally. Get me an ally. Get me a guy that's really pulling their weight. You got Israel, and you got UAE, right?"

For Trump, mutual defense alliances such as NATO were largely worthless. The real estate developer from New York City saw relations with other countries as transactions in which there could only be a winner and a loser, and he fervently believed that the United States was getting stiffed by some of its closest allies.

It was a strongly held belief that Trump had nurtured for at least three decades. In 1987, Trump had even paid for a full-page open letter in the *New York Times* in which he claimed, "For decades, Japan and other nations have been taking advantage of the United States. . . . Make Japan, Saudi Arabia, and others pay for the protection we extend as allies." That same year, Trump gave a speech at a Rotary club in Portsmouth, New Hampshire, asserting that Japan and Saudi Arabia were "ripping us off" and should pay off the United States' then-$200 billion deficit.

Trump believed that the United States had taken upon itself a mandate to maintain world order instead of looking after the well-being of

Americans. The United States had ended up solving everybody else's problems by opening up its markets and by taking on security commitments that were well beyond its ability to pay for, and ultimately had created a world in which America was providing benefits to many other countries but was getting very little in return. It was unfair, Trump thought, and he resented it.

Trump was correct that many American allies were indeed "free-riding" on the United States in the era of Pax Americana. After World War II, which had devastated much of Europe and Asia, the United States accounted for about half of all global economic output. By the time that Trump met with his cabinet in the Tank, the United States produced just under a quarter of global output. This didn't mean that the United States was producing fewer goods and services, but rather that Europe and Asia were now producing far more after they had rebuilt their war-torn economies. Britain, France, Germany, and Japan were all now economic powerhouses, yet it was the United States that continued to be the world's policeman.

President Obama had privately pushed for NATO allies to spend at least 2 percent of their GDP on defense, which few did. Of the twenty-nine countries in NATO in 2017, only six hit this target: Estonia, Greece, Poland, Romania, the United Kingdom, and the United States. NATO European countries collectively spent around $250 billion on their own defense while the United States spent around $700 billion. Trump publicly berated NATO allies to spend 2 percent or more of their GDP on defense.

In the Pentagon Tank, Trump then turned on Cohn, who had spent his career at institutions predicated on the belief that free markets and free trade ineluctably led to greater American prosperity. Trump was having none of it. He railed against the United States' large trade deficits with countries like China.

Gesturing to the charts on the screens that showed American trade with the world, Trump said, "Look at this, Gary. We're upside down everywhere! I don't get your stuff about how trade deficits don't count. Let's assume these minus numbers count! They're ripping us off, right?"

The businessman from Queens was just asking the same kind of questions that many of those who had elected him were asking.

If there was a core tenet of a "Trump Doctrine," it was that economic power wasn't just about prosperity, it was also a form of hard, national power, which is why Trump often focused on trade issues. Trump told his advisers, "Look, national security is a function of two things. It's the military stuff, and I'm rebuilding the military, but it's also economics. It's trade. It's finance."

For the first twenty minutes of Trump's tirade in the Tank, Bannon was silent. He'd never been prouder of Donald J. Trump than now. Bannon later told White House colleagues, "Fuck, this guy was so good. Their fucking heads were blowing up."

When he saw an opening, Bannon lit into the treasury secretary, Steve Mnuchin, who would be responsible for implementing financial sanctions on Iran if, as seemed very likely, Trump decided to pull out of the Iranian nuclear deal that had been painstakingly negotiated by the Obama administration.

Bannon told Mnuchin, "The Iran deal, you know he's ripping this fucking thing up. As soon as he puts sanctions on Iran, I want you to name me one fucking European country that is with us."

Mnuchin tried to respond, but Bannon interrupted him, saying, "They're not allies, they're protectorates. Name me one meaningful country. Give me a country that's going to support us on Iran, in particular on sanctions. Name me one country. They're making money hand over fist in Iran. They're supposed to be allies. Give me one name. Well, they're not there. Fuck you. They're not going to be there."

This was not the kind of discussion FDR had presided over in the Tank during World War II.

Trump turned on Tillerson, who was visibly uncomfortable with the discussion of the Iranian nuclear agreement, which he was trying to preserve.

Trump said, "I told you, Rex: I want that fucking thing redone. Rex, you're a globalist."

In Trump's lexicon, a globalist meant somebody who was undercutting the America First campaign that he had run on.

Tillerson, who had made a vast fortune by striking agreements with countries around the world as the global CEO of Exxon, was discombobulated by Trump's attack. A systems-oriented engineer who had spent four decades at Exxon, Tillerson considered Trump to be quite undisciplined, and he was puzzled that the president didn't like to read briefing books or to get into the details of things.

As Trump continued to harangue him, Tillerson conceded defeat, leaning back in his chair and saying in his broad Texas accent, "It's your deal." At this point, Tillerson wasn't even looking at Trump. "It's your deal, if that's what you want. It's your deal, just tell me what to do."

During these heated discussions Vice President Pence kept his mouth shut. National security issues were not his deal either. When it came to foreign policy, Pence only really cared about one issue, which was the persecution of Christians in the Middle East.

Trump didn't directly attack Mattis, the only member of his cabinet that he then seemed to truly respect, but he did criticize American military commitments overseas, saying, "General, I disagree with all of this."

By now, after six months on the job, many of the "principals" in the cabinet knew the kind of roller-coaster ride they could be on with Trump, but this ride was about to get a whole lot stranger.

Trump started yelling, "Generals, I love you, but you don't know business, you don't know economics. We're getting crushed. Look at this. We're upside down. We're fucking bleeding. Look at the fucking Chinese. They're making money hand over fist. They're fucking us." Referring to the Afghan War, Trump demanded to know from General Dunford, the chairman of the Joint Chiefs, "Why don't we win anymore? Why are we not winning?" Three years earlier Dunford had been the commander of the Afghan War, a fact that Trump either didn't know or didn't care about.

Taking on General Dunford in the Pentagon was like haranguing the Pope in the Vatican; a certain decorum and a great respect for rank prevails at the Pentagon, and the Tank was regarded as a sacred space. Yet here was the commander in chief ripping into the nation's top military officer in front of some two dozen of the nation's most senior military and national security officials. It was hardly the Pentagon's fault that some 190,000 American soldiers were deployed around the world, or that the United States was party to all sorts of global trade deals. These were the legacies of more than seventy years of bipartisan American policy making.

After a couple of hours, the meeting in the Tank ended. Trump left the room to pose for some happy snaps with a group of smiling servicemen and servicewomen who were waiting for him outside the room. Trump then left for the White House, as did Bannon, Kushner, and Trump's chief of staff, Reince Priebus.

In the car back to the White House, Bannon was euphoric, telling Kushner and Priebus, "This is Lincoln and his generals." A Civil War buff, Bannon thought that Trump had just fired the first volley to force his generals to follow his lead, just as President Lincoln had exerted increasingly more control over his generals as the war against the Confederacy had ground on. The meeting in the Tank marked Trump's decisive break with the "axis of adults" such as Mattis and Tillerson who were, in Bannon's view, constraining Trump.

The mood in the Tank after Trump left was funereal. The president had just launched a cruise missile through seven decades of American national security policy and trade agreements.

Remaining in the Tank were Mattis, Pence, and Tillerson. To no one in particular, Tillerson said, "That guy's a fucking moron."

A version of this observation would soon leak to the media, and it was only a matter of time before Tillerson would be fired.

In the Tank, there was a desultory discussion of redoing the briefing, which everyone agreed was a fiasco. It should have been a predictable fiasco because Trump loathed being lectured to and he also hated getting managed in any way. Trump's professional experience before becoming president was running a relatively small family real estate company in which he was the sole and unquestioned boss. The cabinet officials briefing Trump in the Tank had treated the president like he was a schoolkid who needed remedial coaching.

Cohn walked back into the White House complex, where he found Bannon. "Well, that was pleasant," Cohn observed drily.

Bannon replied, "When are you prepared to get real and drop all this crazy shit you believe on this free trade bullshit? Gary, the day that I can convince you and convert you about the reality of trade and what deficits really mean is the day I'll support you to be chairman of the Federal Reserve."

Bannon thought, "This guy has never seen a factory in his life. For him, trade deficits don't matter."

Trump and Bannon went to the Oval Office, where they savored their victory at the Pentagon.

Trump told Bannon, "Steve, that was spectacular. We had them on the ropes. Rex is a globalist. Rex didn't have any idea what to say."

Bannon replied, "He'll never get it, Mr. President. He's totally establishment in his thinking."

"Totally establishment," Trump agreed. "That's the perfect way to put it: completely and totally establishment. Everyone in the room was completely and totally establishment."

Trump then needled Bannon about not speaking up earlier during the meeting in the Tank, saying, "Where the fuck were you when I was getting clobbered? Where were you, tough guy?"

Bannon replied, "Hey, you had it handled. It didn't look like you needed any help. I didn't want it to be an unfair fight."

The Tank meeting was one of the most important moments of Trump's presidency. Trump had for the first time laid down a marker in front of pretty much his entire cabinet that an isolationist, protectionist America First policy really was the Trump Doctrine.

No modern president had ever appointed so many generals to cabinet posts. Trump had never served in the military or in political office and so he needed the cover of senior officers around him with plenty of fruit salad on their chests. But Trump's romance with his generals would eventually turn disastrously sour and the meeting in the Tank marked the beginning of the end of that romance.

Trump was now six months on the job and he had heard all the highly classified briefings about national security that he needed, and he wasn't going to get railroaded by the establishment Council on Foreign Relations types anymore. They were part of the problem, not the solution. From now on, Trump was just going to be Trump.

The "axis of adults" would just have to go along for the ride. Or be thrown off the bus.

Chapter 2

IN THE BEGINNING

Just before the fifth anniversary of the operation that had killed Osama bin Laden, President Barack Obama was sitting at the head of the conference room table in the White House Situation Room. This author asked Obama, "Donald Trump: What are your thoughts, if he was to be sitting in this chair, about how he would be handling these decisions?"

Obama replied: "Well, I don't have those thoughts. Because I don't expect that to happen."

He doesn't have a birth certificate, or if he does, there's something on that certificate that is very bad for him. Now, somebody told me— and I have no idea if this is bad for him or not, but perhaps it would be—that where it says "religion," it might have "Muslim."

—*Donald Trump on* The Laura Ingraham Show
discussing President Obama, March 30, 2011

I wouldn't believe Donald Trump if his tongue was notarized.

—*Manhattan hotelier Leona Helmsley in 1990*

I n the beginning was the lie. And it was a brutally effective one: that the first African American president of the United States wasn't an American and was born outside of the States, which made him ineligible to be the president. He was also a secret Muslim.

The lie achieved several purposes for the billionaire reality TV show host. First, and above all, it brought Trump what he always craved: attention! The lie also positioned him as a political player. Suddenly Trump was the toast of a growing ecosystem on the right consisting of Fox News and talk radio, and to the right of them, the emerging "alt-right" movement. The lie also played well into American fears of "the Other," in particular, of Muslims, a fear that could only be understood in the context of the 9/11 attacks, one of the hinge events of American history.

The 9/11 attacks were the backdrop for Trump's ascension to the presidency. A large majority of Americans considered them the most memorable events of their lives, just as an earlier generation was haunted by the assassination of President John F. Kennedy. The fear of another 9/11 helped to explain the anxiety that grew up around Muslims in the United States in the years afterward. Just under 60 percent of Republicans polled had negative views of Muslims, and among respondents of all political persuasions, Muslim Americans polled less favorably than Americans of any other faith.

Another poll, from 2015, found that nearly a third of Americans, including almost half of Republicans, believed President Obama to be a Muslim, despite all evidence to the contrary. A virulent minority also believed that Obama was seeking to populate his administration with members of the Muslim Brotherhood as part of a secret plan to bring sharia law to the United States.

Trump's presidential campaign brought these prejudices and conspiracy theories into the mainstream of American politics. During the campaign, Trump claimed that he had watched "thousands" of Muslims cheering the 9/11 attacks from their rooftops in New Jersey. There was, of course, no evidence for this.

The prejudices that Trump played on were amplified by the rise of ISIS, which took place as his campaign started to gather steam. The story of ISIS's rise out of the simmering mess of post-invasion Iraq and the wider instability of the Middle East after the Arab Spring was a narrative that Trump would weaponize to great effect.

In 2011, then-secretary of state Hillary Clinton had pushed for US intervention in Libya, and ISIS later gained a significant foothold there following the anarchy that engulfed the country after the fall of the Libyan dictator Muammar el-Qaddafi.

The collapse of the Libyan state following the ouster of Qaddafi greatly influenced President Barack Obama's subsequent approach to Syria, which was to do little. Obama said that the Libyan intervention was the foreign policy decision he most regretted. Clinton proposed a robust plan to combat the Syrian dictator Bashar al-Assad, including a no-fly zone aimed at Assad's air force, but Obama overruled her.

Obama believed that Iran was going all-in in Syria to prop up their ally Assad and using their proxy force, Hezbollah, which had fought in Lebanon for thirty years, while those who favored arming the "moderate" Syrian opposition were wasting time on a fantasy that involved turning a bunch of carpenters, dentists, and farmers into a major fighting force. And what would happen the day after Assad fell in the unlikely event that he was overthrown? Would it replicate the brutal civil wars in Iraq after Saddam Hussein was deposed, or the chaos in Libya after the fall of Qaddafi? Obama's view of overseas adventures in the Middle East was best encapsulated in his pungent aphorism "Don't do stupid shit."

The rise of ISIS was partly a result of Obama's unwillingness to intervene in a decisive manner in the Syrian war and also of his haste to disengage from Iraq at the end of 2011, which helped pave the way for a vacuum in the country into which ISIS inserted itself three years later. It was in the chaos of the deepening Syrian civil war that the group that became ISIS was able to gain battlefield experience, which the terrorist army then put to good use in Iraq.

During 2014, seemingly out of nowhere, ISIS's terrorist army stormed across Syria and Iraq, seizing territory the size of Portugal and lording over some eight million subjects—more than the population of Bulgaria. ISIS declared its caliphate in Mosul, the second largest city in Iraq, in July 2014. A month later, the group videotaped its beheading of the American journalist James Foley and broadcast it around the globe. According to a *Wall Street Journal*-NBC News poll, the murders of Foley and other American hostages held by ISIS was the most widely followed news story of any kind during the previous five years in the United States. Those murders provoked widespread outrage among Americans.

Trump's presidential campaign took place during a wave of mass-casualty terrorist attacks in the West directed or inspired by ISIS. On November 13, 2015, ISIS-trained terrorists launched attacks at several locations in Paris, killing 130 people.

The night before the ISIS terrorists attacked in Paris, Trump had addressed a raucous campaign rally in Iowa, where he explained his plan to defeat ISIS: "I have a plan, but I don't want to tell ISIS what it is. . . . So I was on one of the shows, and I said, 'ISIS is making a tremendous amount of money because of the oil that they took away, they have some in Syria, they have some in Iraq.' I would bomb the shit out of them."

Two weeks after the Paris attacks, sixty miles east of Los Angeles, Syed Rizwan Farook and his wife, Tashfeen Malik, stormed into a holiday party hosted by the San Bernardino County health department. Wearing military-style clothing and black masks and wielding assault rifles, the couple unleashed a barrage of bullets, killing fourteen people. Just before the shootings, Malik had pledged her allegiance to ISIS's leader, Abu Bakr al-Baghdadi, in a post on Facebook. She and her husband then carried out what was, at the time, the most lethal terrorist attack in the States since 9/11. Two days after the attacks, an ISIS radio station embraced Farook and Malik as "supporters."

The massacres in San Bernardino and Paris presented an opportunity for Trump's campaign to lock up the Republican nomination. Five days after the San Bernardino attack, Trump called for a "total and complete shutdown" of Muslim immigration to the States. Trump also asserted that many Muslims have "great hatred towards Americans." Other Republican presidential candidates condemned Trump's call. Jeb Bush tweeted that Trump was "unhinged," while Senator Lindsey Graham said that Trump's rhetoric was "putting our troops serving abroad and our diplomats at risk."

Bush and Graham had unwittingly stumbled into a well-laid trap. According to Trump's campaign manager, Corey Lewandowski, "We wanted none of the other candidates to move to the right of us on immigration." This stratagem worked. Polling in early 2016 showed that half of all Americans supported banning Muslims from traveling to the United States and more than two-thirds of Republican voters supported it. Among Trump supporters, more than 80 percent backed the ban.

Worries about terrorism continued to help propel the Trump campaign during the spring of 2016. Early in the morning of June 12, 2016, a 911 operator in Orlando received a strange call. The caller said, "My name is 'I pledge allegiance to Abu Bakr al-Baghdadi.'" The mysterious caller was Omar Mateen, and this was his way of announcing to the world that he was systematically murdering patrons at Pulse, a nightclub that catered to Orlando's gay community. During his three-hour rampage, Mateen killed forty-nine and wounded fifty-three people. It was not only the worst terrorist attack on American soil since 9/11, at the time, it was also the deadliest mass shooting in the United States to date.

Later that same morning, Trump tweeted, "Appreciate the congrats for being right on radical Islamic terrorism, I don't want congrats, I want toughness & vigilance. We must be smart!" This self-congratulatory tweet didn't mention the many victims of the Orlando massacre.

A day after the Orlando attack, Trump gave a speech in New

Hampshire that his campaign billed as a major statement on counterterrorism. Trump renewed his call for a travel ban, saying, "I will suspend immigration from areas of the world where there is a proven history of terrorism against the United States, Europe, or our allies." He also accused Hillary Clinton, his Democratic opponent, of having a plan to bring in hundreds of thousands of refugees every year from the Middle East with "no system to vet them," a false claim that Trump frequently made during the campaign. In fact, Clinton planned to admit sixty-five thousand Syrian refugees, who were overwhelmingly women and children, out of a total of some five million Syrians who had fled their country. Syrian refugees were already subject to the most intense vetting of any group coming to the United States, a screening process that could take as long as two years.

During a campaign speech in Florida in August, Trump even accused Obama and Clinton of playing on the same team as ISIS: "ISIS will hand her the most valuable player award. Her only competition is Obama, between the two of them."

During the final months of the presidential campaign, terrorist attacks continued across the West. On July 14, 2016, an ISIS-inspired terrorist in Nice, France, used a truck as a weapon to kill eighty-four people. Two months later Ahmad Khan Rahami of Elizabeth, New Jersey, set off a bomb in the Chelsea neighborhood of Manhattan, injuring thirty-one bystanders. ISIS terrorists then killed twenty-six people at Istanbul Airport. All of these attacks received exhaustive TV news coverage.

Many Americans felt threatened by these terrorist attacks, which could occur seemingly anywhere without warning, and Trump channeled their fears far better than any other politician. During the presidential campaign, just over half of Americans said they were "very" or "somewhat" worried that they, or a member of their family, would be victims of terrorism. This was the largest number to feel this way since just after 9/11.

Even though Trump was adept at exploiting the fears that many Americans had about terrorism, he had a major electoral problem compared to Clinton, a former secretary of state, which was his complete lack of experience on the world stage. When Americans elect a president, they are also electing their commander in chief. Could enough Americans really see Trump in that role?

This uncertainty was compounded by the appearance of the "Never Trump" movement. This consisted of more than one hundred Republican national security officials and prominent Republican thinkers who warned that Trump would make an appalling commander in chief. The Never Trumpers were led by Eliot Cohen, who was a senior State Department official in the George W. Bush administration. They published an open letter in early March 2016, charging Trump with being "wildly inconsistent and unmoored in principle. He swings from isolationism to military adventurism within the space of one sentence. . . . He is fundamentally dishonest. Evidence of this includes his attempts to deny positions he has unquestionably taken in the past, including on the 2003 Iraq war." Signatories to the letter included Republican national security heavyweights such as Frances Townsend, George W. Bush's top counterterrorism adviser; Michael Chertoff, Bush's secretary of homeland security; and Michael Mukasey, Bush's attorney general. No other serious contender for the presidency had ever received such a public thrashing from his own party elders.

The Trump campaign realized it had a problem. It needed to get some national security experts on board, and *fast*. At a meeting with the *Washington Post* editorial board on March 21, 2016, Trump pulled out a list of his national security advisers, who were revealed to the world for the first time. Trump told the *Post* editorial board that his team included "Walid Phares, who you probably know, PhD, adviser to the House of Representatives. He's a counterterrorism expert. Carter Page, PhD. George Papadopoulos. He's an oil and energy consultant. Excellent guy. The honorable Joe Schmitz, inspector general at the Department of Defense. General Keith Kellogg."

The reaction that national security experts had to this list was, *Huh?* It was, at best, a group of figures on the margins and, at worst, a bad joke. Kellogg had commanded the storied Eighty-second Airborne Division, but that was during the pre-9/11 period and he was now long retired. Before he was tapped by the Trump campaign, Kellogg wasn't doing much of anything. Phares was a Fox News talking head, but he had no experience working in government. Papadopoulos had highlighted his representation of the United States at the Model UN in Geneva in 2012 as one of his achievements on his LinkedIn page. It was the sort of qualification a college student applying for an internship on Capitol Hill might list.

Bannon called Trump's campaign manager, Corey Lewandowski. "Corey, what the fuck did you just do?"

Lewandowski replied, "Well, we had to put up some names. We're getting heat."

Bannon said, "Corey, it's better not to put up something than to show the world you don't know anybody. I never heard of most of these clowns. Joe Schmitz, I knew Joe, the IG [inspector general] for the army. This is the biggest guy you've got? Fuck."

The striking absence of serious players on Trump's national security team and the large number of Republican national security heavyweights who came out as Never Trumpers explained why retired lieutenant general Michael Flynn became so vitally important to the Trump campaign. Unlike anyone else on Trump's campaign team, Flynn was a genuine war hero, with the blood of the Afghan and Iraq Wars on his hands. If a recently retired three-star general such as Flynn backed Trump, that helped considerably with those voters who were wavering on the commander-in-chief issue. Bannon told Trump, "All we need to do is give people permission to vote for you as commander in chief."

Trump and Flynn made an unlikely pair. One was the son of a multimillionaire real estate developer from New York City who had avoided service in Vietnam and whose knowledge of the military and national security was close to zero. The other was one of nine children who had grown up in a one-bathroom house in Middletown, Rhode Island, who went on to run intelligence for the Joint Special Operations Command (JSOC), which includes the Navy's SEAL Team Six and the Army's Delta Force. But Trump and Flynn found common cause in their worries that "radical Islam" was in the ascendant, and they shared a deep contempt for the Obama administration and Hillary Clinton. Flynn also looked the part. Flynn's aquiline features gave him the air of a Roman senator, and his buzz cut and ramrod bearing were those of a battle-tested officer.

During his military career, few could have predicted the path that Flynn would eventually take. As a colonel in charge of intelligence for JSOC, Flynn was a well-loved, effective team leader and an intensely hardworking officer who deployed constantly to Iraq and Afghanistan. Flynn used to joke that he lived at the JSOC base in Balad, Iraq, and took his vacations at the JSOC base in Bagram, Afghanistan.

Flynn prided himself on being a maverick and an out-of-the-box thinker. His peers found that he would generate ten ideas, nine of which were kind of nutty and one that was absolutely brilliant. In the JSOC environment, Flynn had a team to vet these creative ideas, which was not the case after he left military service.

The hours working for JSOC were brutal—seventeen-hour days every day of the week—but the mission was clear. Flynn and his boss, then-major general Stanley McChrystal, understood by 2005 that the United States was losing the war in Iraq and that JSOC wasn't configured at all well to destroy the industrial-strength insurgency it was facing, which was led by Al-Qaeda in Iraq.

Al-Qaeda in Iraq wasn't a traditional military opponent operating with a top-down bureaucratic hierarchy, but rather was a loose network of like-minded jihadists. McChrystal's mantra became "It takes a network to defeat a network." To become a network, JSOC would have to get much flatter and more agile, not qualities often associated with the bureaucratic hierarchy prevalent in the US military. McChrystal and Flynn reconfigured JSOC so it communicated more seamlessly with all the components of the intelligence community and it also more quickly processed the intelligence gathered on raids so other raids could be immediately launched based on what was gleaned from the initial operation. The results were startling; JSOC went from doing only a handful of raids a month to doing hundreds of raids every month. Al-Qaeda in Iraq took a huge beating.

When McChrystal was tapped by Obama in 2009 to run the war in Afghanistan, he flew into the country with now-major general Mike Flynn, whom he had selected to be his top "intel" officer. Also on the same flight was Colonel Charlie Flynn, Mike Flynn's brother, whom McChrystal had appointed to be his executive officer.

The McChrystal team agreed to a request from a *Rolling Stone* reporter, Michael Hastings, to do a story about their work. Hastings spent months profiling McChrystal and his team in Afghanistan. When the article finally appeared under the headline "The Runaway General," it was studded with unflattering, anonymous quotes about Obama's cabinet by members of McChrystal's staff.

Obama immediately summoned McChrystal back to Washington. Obama felt strongly that President George W. Bush had given a blank check to the military and to officers such as General David Petraeus when he was the commander in Iraq. He also felt that the military had boxed him in early in his first term by leaking a tightly held assessment overseen by McChrystal that described the deteriorating situation in Afghanistan. Obama felt that the leaked assessment had helped to force his hand to send tens of thousands of additional troops to the country. Obama wanted to send a clear message that the civilians were now back in control of the Pentagon.

The Flynn brothers were watching TV together in Kabul on June 23, 2010, as Obama walked out of the White House to the Rose Garden to make an announcement. Obama said that he had just accepted McChrystal's resignation. The brothers were stunned. Charlie and Mike Flynn both revered McChrystal; they had fought in combat together and they had buried soldiers together. Mike Flynn and his wife, Lori, had recently celebrated Stan and Annie McChrystal's thirty-third wedding anniversary on a rare night off in Paris. Flynn was a registered Democrat, but the firing of his friend and mentor sparked his increasing disenchantment with the Obama administration.

Three years later, after tours at CENTCOM and the Office of the Director of National Intelligence, Flynn, now promoted to lieutenant general, was appointed to run the Defense Intelligence Agency (DIA).

Pentagon officials who had worked with Flynn admired his passion when he was a colonel in JSOC, but were concerned about his propensity to flit from subject to subject in a superficial manner. One of them warned colleagues at DIA that they should "buy neck braces" because Flynn was going to swivel from one topic to another topic in meetings and he wasn't going to be an effective manager.

Flynn wanted to turn DIA into something more like JSOC, with more of its officials deployed "forward" in the war zones. This was an excellent idea; after all, if you were supposed to be providing intelligence on a war, it would help if you were not working in an office six thousand miles away from where the conflict was actually happening.

The DIA desk jockeys pushed back against Flynn and his plans to deploy many of them to the war zones. DIA wasn't JSOC. Unlike JSOC, whose soldiers and sailors had to follow orders, DIA was a largely civilian organization. DIA was also a bureaucratic behemoth of some seventeen thousand employees that was ten times larger than JSOC. Most DIA employees were quite content living in the Washington, DC, area as opposed to, say, working at Bagram Air Base in the windswept, mountainous deserts of central Afghanistan.

Flynn had never commanded a giant organization like DIA. The first rule of bureaucratic politics is if you want to make big changes, you need to enlist folks to help, and Flynn didn't make much of an effort to do that at DIA, which ruffled bureaucratic feathers and irritated his bosses at the Pentagon and in the intelligence community.

At DIA, Flynn also began developing some eccentric notions. Flynn became convinced that the jihadist attack against the US consulate in Benghazi in Libya in 2012 in which four Americans were killed was orchestrated by Iran. On the face of it this made little sense since the Shia regime in Iran rarely cooperated with Sunni militants. There was also no evidence for this fanciful notion, but Flynn pushed his analysts at DIA to find a link. Flynn's failure to distinguish between conjecture and truth led analysts at DIA to coin the term "Flynn facts."

Flynn also became convinced that the Obama national security team was only selectively publicly releasing documents recovered in the May

2011 SEAL raid at the Pakistani compound where Osama bin Laden was killed. Flynn thought that the Obama team was only releasing those documents that portrayed al-Qaeda and its affiliates as on the ropes and was not releasing documents that showed that leaders of al-Qaeda were living in Iran.

In fact, there was a more prosaic reason for the disclosures that were made and when they were made, according to the director of the National Counterterrorism Center, Nick Rasmussen, who served in that role for both President Obama and President Trump: if any of the documents still had some operational utility to the CIA, they were not released.

When Flynn was running DIA, the Obama administration's view of the terrorism threat was best encapsulated by Obama's statement to *New Yorker* editor David Remnick in January 2014 that the group that would evolve into ISIS was merely a "jayvee" team.

Flynn had a far less sanguine view, warning that the global jihadist movement was not waning in the wake of bin Laden's death, as was then the conventional analysis. Flynn made this case publicly in congressional testimony on February 11, 2014. Oklahoma Republican senator James Inhofe asked him if al-Qaeda was indeed on the run, as the Obama administration was claiming.

"They are not," testified Flynn.

A few months later, Flynn made a similar public statement at the Aspen Security Forum, a conference held annually in July in the pleasant, green mountains of Aspen, Colorado, that attracted top US national security officials and the journalists who covered them, all happy to have fled the sweltering swamp of Washington, DC, at the height of summer.

CNN's Evan Perez asked Flynn, "Are we safer today than we were two years, five years, ten years ago?"

"My quick answer is we're not," Flynn replied.

Flynn went on to say that focusing only on the declining fortunes of "core" al-Qaeda, the group that had attacked the States on 9/11, was to gloss over the fact that jihadist ideology was in fact "exponentially growing."

As ISIS conquered much of Iraq during the summer of 2014 and imposed its brutal totalitarian rule, it was clear that Obama and his national security team had underestimated the strength of ISIS, while Flynn had understood the threat better than many of his peers. But Flynn had angered his two bosses, Michael Vickers, the overall head of intelligence at the Pentagon, and James Clapper, the director of national intelligence. Vickers and Clapper thought that Flynn's efforts at trying to shake things up at DIA were sabotaging morale at the agency. They decided to force Flynn out of office a year early. Vickers summoned Flynn to his Pentagon office, where he was joined by Clapper; together they told Flynn he had to go. Flynn understood that when you are a general officer and your civilian bosses tell you it's over, you salute and move on.

Flynn was bitter and embarrassed about the way he had been fired. In his own mind, he was forced out because he wasn't playing along with the Obama administration line that the war on terror was largely over. For Vickers and Clapper, it was much simpler: they fired him because he was a bad manager. Either way, Flynn, a highly decorated officer with thirty-three years of service in the army, much of it in special operations, at the age of fifty-five had his career abruptly terminated, and in an inglorious manner to boot.

Perhaps by way of compensation, once he was out in the civilian world, Flynn aimed to be a rainmaker. Flynn set up Flynn Intel Group, which took on all manner of clients. Out of some combination of naiveté and arrogance, Flynn, the maverick who came out of the insular world of Joint Special Operations Command, did not play by the rules when it came to the lobbying work he did for his foreign clients, for which he was supposed to register as an agent of a foreign government.

Flynn also began dipping his toe into politics. In August 2015, what was supposed to be a half-hour meeting with Trump turned into a ninety-minute discussion. Flynn came away deeply impressed. He found Trump to be a good listener who asked smart questions and seemed truly worried about the direction that the country was heading.

Flynn became a prominent presence on the Trump campaign and a vocal critic of Obama's supposedly "weak" policies on ISIS. This, of course, dovetailed very neatly with what Trump was saying. Flynn's support of Trump was all the more important because he was the only person on Trump's campaign team with any battlefield experience of America's post-9/11 wars grinding on at various levels of intensity in Afghanistan, Iraq, Libya, Pakistan, Somalia, Syria, and Yemen.

Like Trump, Flynn thought that the United States could work with Putin and sat next to the Russian president at a black-tie gala dinner in Moscow in December 2015 that celebrated the tenth anniversary of Russia Today (RT), the Kremlin-sponsored TV network, an appearance for which Flynn was handsomely paid. Flynn later said that he wasn't paid by the Russians for the speech. This was true only in a jesuitical sense because the Russians paid Flynn's speaking agency, which deducted its standard commission and then paid Flynn $33,750.

Flynn also sat down for an interview with an RT anchor and critiqued Obama's plan to defeat ISIS. Flynn later told a *Washington Post* reporter that this wasn't a big deal as RT was similar to CNN, a bizarre claim given that RT was effectively an arm of the Kremlin.

In the spring of 2016, Trump started to seriously consider Flynn to be his running mate. The three-star general would certainly help on the commander-in-chief issue. At the time, the leading candidates to be Trump's running mate were former House Speaker Newt Gingrich,* New Jersey governor Chris Christie, and Flynn. Indiana governor Mike Pence was seen as only a distant possibility for the number two slot on the ticket.

Flynn made his major debut on the public stage when he made a fiery speech of support for Trump at the Republican convention in Cleveland on July 19, 2016. Flynn angrily charged Obama and Clinton with endangering the United States and even lying about the nature of the terrorist threat: "Tonight, Americans stand as one with strength and confidence to overcome the last eight years of the Obama-Clinton failures such as bumbling indecisiveness, willful ignorance, and total

---

* Of a possible Trump-Gingrich ticket, the Republican strategist Ed Rollins remarked drily, "It'd be a ticket with six former wives, kind of like a Henry VIII thing. They certainly understand women."

incompetence. . . . Because Obama chose to conceal the actions of terrorists like Osama bin Laden and groups like ISIS, and the role of Iran in the rise of radical Islam, Americans are at a loss to fully understand the enormous threat they pose against us."

As he spoke, Flynn led the crowd in chants of "U-S-A! U-S-A!" and incited them to "Get fired up! This is about this country!"

Flynn declared, "I have called on Hillary Clinton to drop out of the race because she put our nation's security at extremely high risk with her careless use of a private email server."

The crowd started chanting, "Lock her up! Lock her up!"

Hesitating only slightly, Flynn added his voice to the chants, declaring, "Lock her up, that's right! Damn right, exactly right. And you know why we're saying that? We're saying that because if I, a guy who knows this business, if I did a tenth of what [Clinton] did, I would be in jail today."

Generals who had served with Flynn were dismayed by this performance, which went against their code not to take such clearly partisan positions, even in retirement. McChrystal watched Flynn on a TV monitor at an airport. McChrystal had heard what Flynn was saying at Trump's rallies, but now, watching Flynn at the convention rail against Clinton with such a level of vitriol, it felt like his old companion-in-arms had crossed a Rubicon in front of a large, national TV audience. The angry man onstage didn't seem like the Mike Flynn that McChrystal knew so well. A SEAL Team Six officer who had served with Flynn watched Flynn's performance with a similar mix of shock, confusion, and dismay.

Some of his peers felt Flynn had succumbed to a case of "Obama derangement syndrome" after he was fired from running the Defense Intelligence Agency. That might have been a partial explanation for Flynn's impassioned rhetoric against Obama and Clinton, but it is also clear that in the years after he was pushed out of the military, Flynn became increasingly enamored of leading neoconservatives as well as right-wing conspiracy theories.

Flynn coauthored a book, *The Field of Fight: How We Can Win the*

Global War Against Radical Islam and Its Allies, with Michael Ledeen, an academic who was a longtime, bitter critic of the Iranian regime. In *Field of Fight*, which was published just before the 2016 Republican convention, Flynn claimed that the United States was in a "world war" with "radical Islam," a war that "we're losing," that could last "several generations," and he asserted that "political correctness forbids us to denounce radical Islamists." Flynn also claimed that American Islamists were trying to create "an Islamic state right here at home" by pushing to "gain legal standing for Sharia." Flynn cited no evidence for this claim, which was a common right-wing conspiracy theory.

Flynn also wrote for the *New York Post* about a supposed "enemy alliance" that included Cuba, Iran, North Korea, and Venezuela, as well as al-Qaeda, ISIS, and the Taliban. This was George W. Bush's "axis of evil" on steroids and even less convincing since ISIS and Iran were at war, as were al-Qaeda and ISIS, and none of these terrorist groups had any relationship with the North Koreans or with the leftist regimes in Latin America.

Flynn became increasingly gripped by conspiracy theories. In August 2016, Flynn claimed in a speech that Democratic members of the Florida legislature were trying to install sharia law in their state. This was nonsense. Flynn also tweeted that fear of Muslims was "rational," and in another speech Flynn said that Islam was really a "political ideology" rather than a religion. When he was in uniform, Flynn had never made these kinds of assertions about Muslims and Islam.

Flynn's inability to distinguish easily between facts and obvious falsehoods seemed to worsen as the presidential campaign went on. Flynn claimed in a radio interview in August 2016 that there were Arabic signs along the United States–Mexico border to guide potential terrorists into the States and that he had seen evidence of these signs. Flynn said, "I have personally seen the photos of the signage along those paths that are in Arabic. They're like waypoints along that path as you come in. Primarily, in this case the one that I saw was in Texas and it's literally, it's like signs, that say, in Arabic, 'this way, move to this point.' It's unbelievable." It was unbelievable because it was completely false.

Flynn's son Michael, who was Flynn's chief of staff during the presidential campaign, passed on false news on Twitter that claimed that Clinton and her campaign chairman, John Podesta, were running a child sex ring out of the basement of the Comet Ping Pong pizzeria in northwest Washington, DC.

This patently absurd story prompted twenty-eight-year-old Edgar Welch of Salisbury, North Carolina, to travel to Washington to "self-investigate." On December 5, 2016, Welch walked into the popular pizza restaurant carrying an assault rifle and started firing shots. He pointed the firearm in the direction of a restaurant employee, who fled and called the police, which arrested Welch in short order. Welch told investigators that he had come armed to help rescue the abused children. He also told a reporter, with masterful understatement, "the intel on this wasn't 100 percent."

After the shooting incident, Michael Flynn Jr. tweeted, "Until #Pizzagate proven to be false, it'll remain a story. The left seems to forget #PodestaEmails and the many 'coincidences' tied to it." This proved too much for the Trump team and the younger Flynn was quietly fired.

During the campaign, Flynn forged a strong connection with the TV pundit Sebastian Gorka. Of British-Hungarian extraction, Gorka styled himself an "irregular warfare strategist." It was never clear what this meant as the only wars that Gorka fought in were on television, as a frequent, bombastic guest on Fox News. Gorka's full goatee, three-piece suits, and braying English accent gave him the look and feel of a villain from a Victorian melodrama.*

Gorka insisted on being called "Dr. Gorka" because of his doctorate from Corvinus University, a college in Hungary so obscure that it didn't

---

* Fox didn't seem to value Gorka much; in 2016, despite his appearances on the network, they paid him only $4,320. By contrast, they paid John Bolton more than $500,000 a year for a similar gig.

appear on *US News & World Report*'s list of the 1,250 universities that it tracked around the world. Gorka's PhD about terrorism would never have been granted at an American university because it was a glorified clip job with no original research. Per Google Scholar, which tracks all citations of work by scholars—the currency of the realm in academia— no expert has ever cited Gorka's PhD on terrorism. Compare this to the work of terrorism scholar Marc Sageman, who published the book *Understanding Terror Networks* three years before Gorka published his PhD: other experts have cited Sageman's book more than three thousand times.

Gorka submitted his dissertation under the name Sebestyén L. v. Gorka. The "v." was a nod to the fact that Gorka was associated with the *Vitézi Rend*, a Hungarian far-right group that was aligned with the Nazis during World War II. Despite Gorka's association with such a group, which could have led him to be denied entry to the United States by immigration authorities, Gorka subsequently secured a post teaching at Marine Corps University. Thomas A. Saunders III, a major Republican donor, funded his chair there. It later emerged that Saunders and Gorka were related by marriage, although Saunders claimed he didn't intervene in Gorka's hiring.

The FBI funneled more than $100,000 to Gorka's consulting firm between 2012 and 2016 for counterterrorism training he gave FBI employees, but the bureau abruptly terminated the arrangement when FBI officials determined that Gorka's classes included diatribes against Muslims, whom he described as either already radicalized or soon to be radicalized. Gorka also left a post at the National Defense University in Washington, DC, a branch of the Pentagon, that hosted many foreign midcareer military officers who would go on to become generals in their home countries. Officials at the National Defense University felt that Gorka's views about Muslims did not represent the US military and government well.

During the fall of 2015, Gorka wrote position papers for the Trump team about terrorism, for which he was paid $8,000. Gorka also published a book during the campaign that sounded many of the same themes as Flynn's *Field of Fight* and echoed some of Trump's positions on terrorism. Gorka's book, *Defeating Jihad: The Winnable War*, was not much more than a pamphlet that bizarrely reprinted both the entire text of George Kennan's famous "Long Telegram," which provided much of the intellectual basis for the strategy of containment of the Soviet Union, as well as the text of NSC-68, the Truman administration's blueprint for how to roll back the Soviets, as if to suggest that Gorka was providing a similar, groundbreaking blueprint for defeating jihadism.

Defeating Jihad also made spurious claims, such as that Saddam Hussein had operational ties to al-Qaeda, a claim that had been exhaustively debunked by the Senate Intelligence Committee following the 2003 invasion of Iraq. Gorka also claimed that ISIS posed "a direct existential threat to America and the whole of Western civilization." Two years after the publication of Gorka's book, that existential threat to the West was largely out of business. Gorka also advocated for vague measures such as fighting an "ideological war" against ISIS without saying how exactly that would be accomplished.

The books by Flynn and Gorka were long on slogans and short on solutions, but both men made frequent appearances on TV and on social media amplifying one of Trump's core messages, that the United States was purportedly losing the war against the terrorists because Obama and Clinton wouldn't name the enemy as "radical Islam" because of their "political correctness," and that by failing to do so they were doomed to wage an ineffective war against ISIS and similar groups.

Obama responded to this line of argument by saying that his administration had made a great deal of progress against ISIS. While Obama's administration was slow to recognize the rising ISIS threat, during the summer of 2014 it had surged on the problem with a vengeance. According to Lieutenant General Sean MacFarland, who was the ground commander for the fight against ISIS under Obama's watch, by August 2016, five months before Obama stepped down as president, the US-led coalition had killed an estimated forty-five thousand ISIS fighters. Also, Obama asserted that expressly linking the religion of Islam with terrorism was counterproductive and actually helped ISIS's narrative that the United States was engaged in a "war against Islam."

One of the strangest episodes of the strangest of presidential campaigns was the furor surrounding the Gold Star Khan family. Humayun Khan was a Muslim American captain in the US Army who was killed by a car bomb in Iraq in 2004. Khan was posthumously awarded a Bronze Star for bravery because he shielded his fellow soldiers from the blast. His father, Khizr Khan, made a rousing speech memorializing his son at the Democratic convention in Philadelphia on July 28, 2016.

With his wife standing beside him wearing a blue headscarf, Khan said, "If it was up to Donald Trump, [Humayun] never would have been in America. Donald Trump consistently smears the character of Muslims. . . . Have you ever been to Arlington Cemetery? Go look at the graves of the brave patriots who died defending America—you will see all faiths, genders, and ethnicities."

Brandishing a copy of the Constitution, Khan addressed Trump directly, charging, "You have sacrificed nothing. And no one."

Trump wasn't going to take this lying down, even if the target of his ire was a Gold Star dad and mom who would surely always hold the moral high ground in a contest in which it was well known that he had taken five deferments from serving in the Vietnam War. Trump had even joked with Howard Stern on his radio show that his own personal Vietnam was avoiding contracting a venereal disease when he was playing the field during the eighties. Bronze Star–level heroism this surely was not.

On ABC News, Trump claimed that Khizr Khan had delivered the speech because his wife had been silenced, saying, "If you look at his wife, she was standing there, she had nothing to say, she probably—maybe she wasn't allowed to have anything to say, you tell me."

In fact, Mrs. Khan didn't speak because she was so overcome by emotion when she saw a giant photograph of her son on a TV screen at the convention.

During his ABC News interview, Trump went on to say that he had made his own sacrifices to the country: "I think I've made a lot of sacrifices. I've worked very, very hard. I've created thousands and thousands of jobs."

Comparing the sacrifice of losing a son in combat to building a business that he had inherited from his enormously wealthy father was jarring for many Americans, who were horrified by this attack on a Gold Star family. Trump didn't apologize.

A week after Trump had his spat with the Khans, a second public letter appeared from the Never Trumpers and it was even harsher than the first. John Bellinger III, a product of St. Albans, Princeton, and Harvard Law School who had served as the legal adviser both to George W. Bush's National Security Council and the Bush State Department, took the lead in recruiting key members of the Republican establishment to sign on to a letter decrying Trump.

Bellinger's family had a long record of public service; his father was an army officer and his mother a CIA analyst, while Bellinger himself had worked in government beginning in the Reagan administration. Bellinger had stewed about Trump since the fall of 2015, growing increasingly concerned about his verbal attacks on Muslims and his musings that the family members of terrorists should be killed.

Trump's view contrasted with that of Bellinger's former boss, President George W. Bush, who had visited the main mosque in Washington, DC, a week after the 9/11 attacks and had declared there, "The face of terror is not the true faith of Islam. That's not what Islam is all about. Islam is peace. These terrorists don't represent peace. They represent evil and war."

Bellinger wrote a letter stating that if elected, Trump "would be the most reckless president in American history" and "would put at risk our country's national security and well-being." He then recruited senior Republicans to join him in signing the letter.

At the annual summer meeting of the Aspen Strategy Group in Aspen, Colorado, Steve Hadley, George W. Bush's national security adviser, argued to fellow Republicans gathered there that signing this letter would be a mistake because it would play into the hands of Trump supporters campaigning against the foreign policy elite. Signatories would also be eliminating their ability to serve in or influence a Trump administration should candidate Trump be elected president.

In the end, fifty leading Republicans signed the letter, which included many of the signatories of the first Never Trump letter, while additional national security heavyweights also added their names such as General Michael Hayden, who was George W. Bush's CIA director.

The same month that the second Never Trump letter appeared, Trump's campaign manager Paul Manafort was forced to resign when a story in the *New York Times* revealed he had secretly taken millions of dollars from a pro-Russian Ukrainian politician. Trump was now down seven percentage points from Clinton in the polls with only three months before Americans cast their votes. The Trump campaign looked like it was in a death spiral.

Into the vacuum left by Manafort's abrupt departure stepped Steve Bannon, who would run the campaign for the next three months until Election Day. Bannon had served in the navy and his daughter was a graduate of West Point who had served in Iraq. His first piece of advice to Trump was to stop picking fights with the Khan family. Waging a war with a Gold Star dad and mom was unseemly; their son was buried in Arlington National Cemetery. Trump agreed with Bannon, saying, "We're going to move on to another topic."

Every September, the United Nations General Assembly (UNGA) brings pretty much every head of state and foreign minister from around the world to Manhattan. At first, Bannon was reluctant to have Trump attend UNGA on the basis that he only had to make one fuckup— Trump didn't know the name of an obscure foreign leader—and the media was going to jump on him for being unprepared. But then Bannon learned that Clinton was planning to take off valuable time from the campaign trail to go to Manhattan for several days to attend UNGA and hold court there with a variety of foreign leaders as the presumptive president of the United States.

Bannon said, "Fuck, this is not going to look good. They're all going to sit there going 'She's fabulous.' And Trump is a reality TV guy running around Ohio."

In the end, Trump went to UNGA and met with foreign leaders such as Israeli prime minister Bibi Netanyahu to burnish his image as a possible commander in chief.

Bannon counseled Trump not to worry about what the media was portraying as the death spiral of his campaign, telling him that the two most significant polling numbers were actually working in his favor: "Don't forget two-thirds of the country still thinks we're on the wrong track. Seventy percent of the American people for the first time think that the country is in decline and this is the key point; the working class and middle class will follow someone they think will turn America towards its former greatness. Voters liked Obama, but they didn't think he delivered the change the country needed."*

Bannon continued, "All we're going to do starting tomorrow is we're going to compare and contrast Clinton as a representative of a corrupt and incompetent elite and you are the tribune of the people. You are the spokesman for the country, the little guy. And we're just going to compare and contrast how venal she is and how corrupt the Clintons are and also her warmongering foreign policy."

Bannon explained that the Trump campaign would stay relentlessly on message around three themes: "Number one, we're going to stop massive illegal immigration and limit legal immigration to get our sovereignty back and protect our workers. Number two, we're going to bring manufacturing jobs back from China. And number three, we're going to get out of these pointless foreign wars. That's the mantra."

Trump didn't need much prodding about any of these topics. They were among the key issues that he hammered repeatedly on the campaign trail, both before and after Bannon's arrival as his campaign manager.

---

* Bannon had derived these polling insights from the veteran pollster Pat Caddell. Caddell's polling in the years before the 2016 election showed that a nontraditional candidate like Trump could win the White House because of the widespread sentiment among ordinary Americans that the elites in both political parties had failed to deliver for them.

Exit polling during the presidential election found that terrorism was one of the top four issues that voters cared about. Many voters clearly trusted that what Trump termed his "secret plan" to defeat ISIS trumped Hillary Clinton's many years of experience as secretary of state.

That Mike Flynn never really expected Trump to win the election was strongly suggested by an article he wrote that appeared in *The Hill* newspaper the morning after Trump's election triumph. In it, Flynn compared Fethullah Gulen, a Turkish cleric living in exile in Pennsylvania, to Ayatollah Khomeini. For the government of Turkish president Recep Tayyip Erdogan, Gulen was an obsession. It had fingered Gulen for purportedly masterminding a botched military coup in Turkey in the summer of 2016. Flynn's article suggested that Gulen, who had very good reasons to fear for his safety if he ever returned to Turkey, should not be allowed to remain in the United States.

No one who really expected that he would be the next US national security adviser would have published a provocative piece in a relatively obscure publication the same day that his candidate was just elected to the most powerful job in the world. The article also was likely to draw attention to the fact that Flynn's consulting firm had been paid more than half a million dollars by a company close to the Erdogan government. Flynn hadn't registered as an agent of a foreign government as required by law, which was an issue of particular significance for retired senior military officers. And Flynn's alignment with the Turks seemed to affect his policy choices. During the presidential transition, Flynn had pushed back against a plan that the Obama administration was developing to partner with Kurdish forces in Syria to fight ISIS. This was also the position of the Turks, who opposed the United States partnering with Kurdish forces that they regarded as terrorists.

Two days after Trump was elected president, Obama sat down with Trump in the Oval Office and warned him that the biggest national security problem he would face was the mercurial, nuclear-armed regime of North Korea. Obama also warned Trump against hiring Flynn in any senior role. A week after meeting with Obama, Trump offered Flynn the key job of national security adviser. He would not be in the position long.

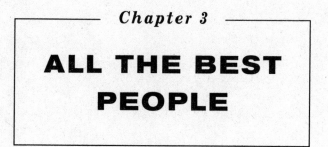

Chapter 3

ALL THE BEST PEOPLE

I'm going to surround myself only with the best and most serious people.

—*Presidential candidate Donald Trump, August 8, 2015*

Who do you talk to for military advice right now?

—*Chuck Todd, NBC News, August 2015*

Well, I watch the shows. I mean, I really see a lot of great—
you know, when you watch your show and all of the
other shows and you have the generals.

—*Candidate Donald Trump*

The day after the presidential election, on Wednesday, November 9, a dozen or so officials from the Trump transition team showed up at Trump Tower in Manhattan. Clutching multiple binders in their hands, they went to the fifth floor, where they spent the first two days in a conference room, doing nothing.

For the past seven months, Governor Chris Christie of New Jersey had managed a traditional transition process. Trump had paid no attention to the transition planning, believing superstitiously it was "bad juju" to make any plan for what might happen in the event that he won the presidency. The planning for the transition was, however, mandated by federal law, and it was a large effort; there were more than four thousand positions to fill. Hundreds of those jobs were the most senior positions in the government, and the candidates for those jobs, in particular, needed to be extensively vetted.

It was only when Trump read in the newspaper that Christie was raising money to pay for the transition that he focused on the effort. Trump thought it was not only courting bad luck to focus on the transition but he worried it might divert resources away from his campaign. He asked Christie how much money he had raised for the transition. Christie told him that it wasn't much more than a million dollars. Trump asked Christie if he could close down the transition effort. Christie explained that federal law mandated that the campaigns prepare and pay for their own transitions in preparation for the moment when one of them took over the government. Bannon, who had heard Trump talking about the transition with Christie, pointed out that if Trump closed down the transition team, it would look like he wasn't running a serious campaign. Trump allowed the transition planning to proceed.

Christie and his team had assembled short lists of candidates for cabinet-level and senior staff positions. They also prepared rollout plans for how to repeal Obamacare, implement tax cuts, and overhaul infrastructure. All this planning was contained in some two-dozen binders. For Trump's national security adviser, Christie had short-listed General Peter Pace, the former chairman of the Joint Chiefs, and Admiral Bill McRaven, the architect of the raid that had killed bin Laden five years earlier. Christie considered Flynn to be a loose cannon and was adamantly opposed to his taking a senior role in Trump's cabinet. The Christie transition team had also short-listed a number of other heavy hitters for cabinet posts, such as the former governor of Indiana, Mitch Daniels, and Wisconsin governor Scott Walker.

For all his diligence in planning for the transition, by the final weeks of the Trump campaign, Christie was on the outs with Trump and his inner circle. On October 7, 2016, an *Access Hollywood* video from 2005 leaked, on which Trump boasted that his fame was such a magnet that he could grab women by their genitals. Christie, who was the first major Republican politician to endorse Trump, appeared on a New York radio station and said of the *Access Hollywood* video, "It's completely indefensible, and I won't defend it, and haven't defended it." This earned Christie no plaudits in Trumpworld.

On the morning of November 10, Bannon summoned Christie to his office on the fourteenth floor of Trump Tower. Bannon was concerned that Christie was pitching a bunch of Never Trumpers for senior jobs. Bannon told Christie, "We decided to make a change."

Christie replied, "Good. What are we changing?"

"You," said Bannon.

Bannon went on: "The vice president is going to be the new chairman of the transition and you're out. Going forward, you have no position of any kind in the transition, and we do not want you in the building anymore."

Christie realized he wasn't just being fired; he was being vaporized.

That evening, Rick Dearborn, the chief of staff for Senator Jeff Sessions, a close Trump ally, went to the conference room where the Trump transition officials were gathered, closed the door, and said, "I don't know what you guys are doing, but I'm going to need you here all night. It's not yet public but Chris Christie is out. The vice president is in. I am taking over as executive director. I need to look at everything that's going on."

Trump's son-in-law, Jared Kushner, had shoved a shiv in Christie's back because more than a decade earlier Christie was the federal prosecutor in New Jersey who had put Kushner's father in jail for two years for tax evasion and witness tampering.

In an episode that seemed lifted from *The Sopranos*, Jared's father, Charles Kushner, was convicted of witness tampering because he had arranged for his brother-in-law to be secretly videotaped while having sex with a prostitute. Kushner Sr. then sent the tape to his sister and her husband, who were cooperating with the feds who were investigating him for tax evasion and illegal campaign contributions. Welcome to Jersey!

With Christie gone, all the planning for an orderly transition was thrown out with him. The two dozen binders were literally consigned to the garbage. David Bossie, deputy campaign manager of the Trump campaign, said, "Everything that Chris had done was thrown out. There was no 'Hey, let's evaluate it.' It was 'Let's start from scratch.'"

The jockeying for power and position at Trump Tower was intense. "It really felt like a mix of *Survivor* meets *Big Brother* meets *The Apprentice*, because it was highly competitive," a transition official recalled. As he chose his cabinet, Trump drew on many of the tropes of reality TV that he knew so well. Trump presided over a beauty pageant of men and women contestants who looked the part and who all had to walk the gauntlet of TV cameras in the lobby of Trump Tower before they ascended to Trump's aerie high above Central Park to audition for some of the most powerful jobs on the planet. This was the same building where *The Apprentice* had been filmed, which had turned Trump from a blowhard local businessman well known to the readers of the gossipy *New*

York Post into a national celebrity who hired and fired aspiring moguls on network television.

Just as on *The Apprentice*, as Trump made his cabinet picks there were celebrations of the winners and the ritual humiliations of the losers. The former Republican presidential candidate Mitt Romney, who was auditioning to be secretary of state, even subjected himself to the ultimate reality TV convention of a candlelit dinner with Trump at the Trump International Hotel in Manhattan that played out for the cameras. Romney, who had called Trump a "fraud" during the campaign, didn't make the cut.

Frances Townsend, who was George W. Bush's top counterterrorism adviser, was one of the most prominent Republicans who had signed a public letter on behalf of the Never Trump campaign. Townsend was a serious contender for the key post of secretary of homeland security. When she spoke with Trump for about an hour at his Trump Tower office, the president-elect never mentioned Townsend's opposition to his presidential run. Instead, Trump was charming and asked a number of sharp questions about national security, presenting quite a different persona than the boorish tycoon known to the public. Townsend decided to bow out of consideration for the job because of personal reasons.

Mattis wasn't Trump's first choice to be "Sec Def," nor even his second. Mattis was his third choice. Trump loved "killers," and if ever there was a real killer, it was retired four-star general Stanley McChrystal, who led JSOC during the Iraq War. McChrystal had turned "Jay-sock" into one of the most efficient killing machines in history.

McChrystal seemed to be the ideal candidate to run Trump's Pentagon; not only had he overseen the final moments of uncounted thousands of jihadist militants, he had also resigned as the commander of the Afghan War in 2010 for disparaging remarks that some officers on his staff had made to a *Rolling Stone* reporter about top Obama administration officials.

The fact that McChrystal had to resign when he was working for President Obama was a huge plus for Trump. McChrystal had also worked closely with Lieutenant General Michael Flynn when they were both serving in Afghanistan and Iraq. Flynn was now the de facto leader of the Trump national security transition team.

Eight days after Trump won the election, on the afternoon of November 16, 2016, McChrystal was taking the train from Washington, DC, to Manhattan when his phone rang.

On the line was a Trump transition official. "We want you to come over to Trump Tower now. The president-elect is very excited to meet you and talk to you about the secretary of defense job."

McChrystal replied, "Listen, I've been watching the campaign, and I don't think I'd be a good fit for the president-elect's team. I don't think I'd be happy. Also, I'm not sure you'd be happy in the end."

After a long silence, the Trump official asked, "Are you *sure?*"

"I'm absolutely sure," McChrystal replied.

McChrystal wasn't making his views publicly known, but he was disgusted by Trump's rhetoric and conduct during the campaign and felt that he would likely serve as a president with much the same characteristics.

Around the same time that McChrystal took himself out of consideration to run the Pentagon, Vice President-Elect Mike Pence called Jack Keane, another retired four-star general and a frequent Fox News talking head, telling him, "The president-elect is very interested in you being secretary of defense."

Keane's wife, Terry, had died only a few months earlier. Terry Keane had had Parkinson's for the past decade and a half, and Keane had taken care of her. Keane told Pence, "I'm not able to do that because of my wife's recent death."

Pence replied, "Well, I'm fairly confident that when I tell them this, he still is going to want to talk to you."

Keane met with Trump on November 17 at his Trump Tower office, overlooking Central Park.

Trump said, "I understand about your wife passing away. How long were you married?"

Keane replied, "Fifty-one years. I was actually with her for fifty-five years. We met when we were both eighteen."

Trump pushed himself back in his chair. "Oh my, you are really going through something."

Keane went on, "I'm not in a position to do this emotionally and even financially. I had issues with my wife's long-term health care. To go back and live on a government salary right now is not possible."

Trump asked Keane, "Who do you think should be the secretary of defense?"

Keane asked Trump if he was insisting on a former senior military officer for the role. Keane believed that the United States was long past the Eisenhower and Marshall era when it made much sense for top generals to play in the political arena. Trump indicated that a retired four-star general was still his preference.

"What do you think of Jim Mattis?" Trump asked.

"Jim Mattis is somebody who could do the job," Keane replied.

Retired now for three years, Mattis was volunteering at the Tri-Cities Food Bank in his hometown of Richland, Washington, when he received an unexpected call from a man who said, "Hi. It's Mike Pence. I'd like to talk to you about coming and having a conversation about secretary of defense."

Mattis told Pence: "Well, I'm doing food bank stuff. Can I call you back?"

On November 19, Mattis traveled to Trump's golf club in Bedminster, New Jersey, to talk to the president-elect about the Defense job. They quickly had two important disagreements. On the campaign trail, Trump had campaigned on the promise of bringing back torture for suspected terrorists and had even talked about killing the families of terrorists.

Mattis had a very different view of how to interrogate terrorists. In real life, he told Trump, "you can get more with a pack of cigarettes and a cup of coffee."

During the campaign, Trump had also repeatedly dumped on the NATO alliance, deeming it "obsolete." Again, Mattis begged to differ, telling Trump, "If you didn't have NATO, you'd have to build it." Their disagreement about NATO would linger and intensify over time.

An issue that Trump and Mattis were in total agreement about was the need to *annihilate* ISIS. Asked if he could destroy ISIS in a year, Mattis said yes. "If you let us off the chain, we can do it."

After the meeting, Trump came out to talk to the press. Framed by the white columns of his golf club, he and Mattis posed for pictures. Reporters shouted questions at the president-elect about whether Mattis was being considered for a cabinet job.

"He's just a brilliant, wonderful man," Trump replied. "What a career! We're going to see what happens, but he is the real deal."

In picking Mattis to be his secretary of defense, Trump said, he had found his "General George Patton." That label did not capture what made Mattis a distinctive choice. Mattis's "call sign" on the battlefield was "Chaos" in part because of his ferocity in battle and his colorful aphorisms, such as "Be polite, be professional, but have a plan to kill everybody you meet." After the 2003 invasion of their country, Mattis told Iraqi military leaders, "I come in peace. I didn't bring artillery. But I'm pleading with you, with tears in my eyes: If you fuck with me, I'll kill you all." But he was also an intellectual, a general who easily quoted the Roman stoic Marcus Aurelius as well as Eliot Cohen, the Republican military historian who was a leader of the Never Trump movement.

Mattis had worked with General David Petraeus on the 2006 counterinsurgency manual that helped to revolutionize the US approach to the Iraq War by emphasizing that fighting insurgents required assuming greater risks for American troops, who had to get out of their massive bases and live among the Iraqi people if they were to have a chance of really understanding and ultimately defeating the Iraqi insurgency.

In the summer of 2010, soon after Mattis took charge of CENTCOM, which oversees all American military operations in the Middle East, President Obama asked him what his top priorities were. Mattis said that he had three: "Number one Iran. Number two Iran. Number three Iran."

A year later, an Iranian jet shot at an American drone flying in international air space over the Gulf. Mattis wanted permission to shoot down any Iranian aircraft that was attacking American drones. This permission was denied. Obama wanted to initiate the talks that eventually led to the Iran nuclear deal, and an attack on an Iranian target would surely undercut that. The Obama team forced Mattis to retire from the military early because of his hostility to Iran.

Mattis first learned about his defenestration when he was passed a note by one of his aides telling him that the Pentagon was announcing his replacement as the commander of CENTCOM. Neither the White House nor the Pentagon had bothered to give Mattis notice of his termination.

Mattis joined Flynn in that select category of senior generals whose careers were cut short by the Obama administration who would join Trump's cabinet. Obama officials didn't push General John Kelly out of office early, but he did occasionally clash with them when he was the commander of Southern Command (SOUTHCOM). Kelly championed the expansion and renovation of the prison camp at Guantanamo, which was in SOUTHCOM's area of operations, at a time when the Obama administration was trying to close the prison. Kelly would serve as Trump's secretary of homeland security and later his chief of staff.

Shortly after Trump's surprise victory, Kelly was at home on a Saturday afternoon watching college football with his wife, Karen, when the phone rang. On the phone was Reince Priebus—the man that Kelly would later supplant as White House chief of staff—who told Kelly, "Mr. Trump would like to have an opportunity to talk to you about maybe going into the administration."

After serving forty-five years in the marine corps, General Kelly was only eight months into his retirement. Kelly consulted with his wife about the possible offer from the Trump team. Karen said, "If we're anything, the Kelly family is a family of service to the nation. If they think they need you, you can't get out of it." She added jokingly, "Besides, I'm really tired of this quality retired time we're spending together."

Kelly met with Trump, who told him, "I'd like you to take the hardest, and what I consider to be the toughest, job in the federal government." Trump said he was asking him to run the Department of Homeland Security. Kelly was surprised by the offer: he didn't know Trump at all and he didn't know anyone who knew Trump. Kelly took the job because he felt it was his civic duty to do so. If Hillary Clinton had won the presidency and made him a similar offer, he would have worked for her.

Running the Department of Homeland Security (DHS) was indeed one of the toughest jobs in the government. DHS was an ungainly giant of twenty-two federal departments and agencies that merged together in the wake of 9/11; it was made up of 240,000 employees who handled everything from hurricanes to cybersecurity to border security to terrorism. Illegal immigration was an issue with which Kelly was quite familiar, as his last job in uniform was as the four-star general in charge of SOUTHCOM, which was focused on Central and Latin America and protecting the southern border.

When Jack Keane turned down the secretary of defense job, Trump had pressed him for advice about his national security team and the type of security challenges that his administration would be confronting. It was an advisory role that Keane was quite comfortable with. Keane, a Vietnam vet who had served as the vice chief of staff of the army, had played a key role in advocating the measures that had changed the course of the Iraq War, which the United States was clearly losing three years after Saddam Hussein was removed from power. In December 2006, Keane, recently retired, had gone to the White House to advise President George W. Bush that he needed to adopt a counterinsurgency approach to fighting the war, as well as surging the number of American troops in Iraq and selecting General David Petraeus to be the war's new commander. Bush implemented all of those suggestions, and within three years the tide of the war had turned in favor of the American military.

Keane was determined to give honest counsel to the president-elect. He told Trump that he wasn't the first commander in chief with scant foreign policy or national security experience: "Most post–World War II presidents have not had a significant background in these areas. George

H. W. Bush is probably the exception to that. All presidents are quick studies, but it's critical what you're doing now in selecting leaders who understand that world."

Keane grew up in a housing project in Manhattan and he connected easily with Trump as a fellow New Yorker. Keane went on, "You'll start spending more and more time with the national security team because the world has a way of intervening regardless of what your domestic agenda is. So pick the team not only for their experience and knowledge, but pick them because you're comfortable being around them; you're going to spend a lot of time with them."

Trump started sounding Keane out about the long wars he would soon be inheriting. Trump observed, "We have been in the Middle East for a long time. And we've lost thousands of soldiers and it's cost trillions of dollars." Keane acknowledged that this was true.

Trump asked, "Is the situation worse now or better?"

Keane said, "It's worse."

Trump asked, "Why?"

Keane replied, "The Middle East is the most dangerous neighborhood in the world. It is very challenging. But we did make it worse when we forced Mubarak out of Egypt and we got a Muslim Brotherhood government followed by a military coup; when we pulled all US troops out of Iraq and we got ISIS who established a sanctuary in Syria and invaded Iraq; we failed to help the Syrian moderate forces in any consequential way, and the war raged on resulting in a humanitarian crisis; we deposed Qaddafi in Libya but failed to help the elected regime that followed, and the radicals destroyed the US consulate, killed our ambassador and three other Americans, and forced the closure of the US embassy; and we made a bad deal with Iran where they received billions of dollars to fuel their malign aggressive behavior. Yes, it's worse."

Keane continued, "The alternative is that we could just pull away and leave it to themselves. I think about the 1930s in Europe. And you look at what leaders in Europe did by ignoring what was happening in Germany. They helped light a match to the greatest calamity in the history of mankind, which was World War II."

Keane said that there was now "this ideology that sits inside the Middle East, and it's a breeding ground for radicalism worldwide. We have the radicalism of Iran, which is trying to achieve regional hegemony. And they have two objectives to achieve that—one is to drive the United States out of the region, and the other is to destroy the state of Israel."

Trump talked about the massive US trade deficit with the Chinese. Keane then shifted the focus to China's rising military power, saying, "President Xi intends to replace the United States as the world's global leader. They have a brilliant asymmetric strategy to take away some of the military and technology advantages the United States has in air and maritime power. I think the Obama administration did not take on the challenges that China was presenting, despite the fact that we were supposedly pivoting to Asia to do that very thing, but you couldn't see that in the Obama military defense budget. We need new airplanes, missiles, and ships and also improved ground fighting capability. We can't do this for just a year or two. This is a five- to six-year minimum investment to dig us out of this big hole."

Shifting to Afghanistan, Trump observed, "No one can win there."

Keane disagreed. "No, Mr. President, this is not true. That's a myth: that somehow thirty thousand Taliban soldiers that used to run a brutal regime are now going to take it back. You've got to understand something: eighty-five percent of the people don't want the Taliban to be in charge. That's been true for all the years we've been there." Trump indicated that this was news to him.

Keane said, "I don't want to take too much of your time, but I did a lot of assessments in Afghanistan." Keane observed that it was Obama who had sabotaged the Afghan War by publicly announcing in 2009 a premature withdrawal date of the forces that he had surged into the country. "That decision doomed us to a protracted war in Afghanistan."

The foreign policy issues Keane discussed with the president-elect that day would indeed prove to be some of the biggest and most contentious questions Trump's national security team would wrestle with in the months to come.

The Trump team was casting around for a confirmable nominee for secretary of state. One possibility was former New York City mayor Rudy Giuliani, but his consulting company had dealings with countries and businesses around the world and presented many potential conflicts of interest; it would likely make for a messy confirmation process.

Keane saw that Trump was struggling to find the right candidate for secretary of state. Keane thought that David Petraeus, the retired four-star general with a history PhD from Princeton who had turned around the faltering Iraq War and was now working for the global investment bank KKR, would be excellent as the country's top diplomat.

Keane made the case first to Kushner and then to Trump about why Petraeus was so well qualified to run State.

Trump asked Keane, "Is he a Democrat?"

Keane replied, "I don't have a clue. Petraeus and I have something in common: neither of us votes."

Trump seemed surprised. "You don't vote?"

Keane responded, "Because we want to stay out of politics."

Henry Kissinger had also told senior Trump transition officials, "You've got to take a hard look at Petraeus."

On November 28, Petraeus took the well-trodden path to Trump's office on the twenty-sixth floor of Trump Tower where he met with the president-elect, Bannon, Kushner, and Priebus. Both Trump and Petraeus had brought lists of questions to the meeting to ask each other. It was the first time that the two men had met, and they were feeling each other out.

Trump asked the general, "Should we build a wall?"

Petraeus replied, "Sure, we should build a wall if it's part of a comprehensive approach to improving border security, such as relationships with the Mexicans, better intel-sharing between the intel agencies."

Petraeus asked Trump, "Mr. President-Elect, you are not against trade? You are just against unfair trade, right?"

Trump replied, "Yeah."

Everybody at the Trump Tower meeting was blown away by Petraeus, who gave a cogent tour d'horizon of the world and had a strong command presence. After their friendly meeting, Trump tweeted, "Just met with General Petraeus—was very impressed!"

If Trump selected Petraeus to be secretary of state, retired generals would now have a lock on all of his key national security cabinet posts, with Mattis at the Pentagon, Kelly at Homeland Security, and Flynn as the national security adviser.

Trump's top advisers didn't think it was much of an issue that Petraeus had handed over classified materials to his biographer and mistress, Paula Broadwell, which had led to his resignation as Obama's CIA director in 2012. But when they consulted Mattis and Kelly about whether Petraeus should head the State Department, they both gave an emphatic, hard no. They said selecting Petraeus as secretary of state would send a terrible signal to the officer corps that mishandling classified materials and extramarital affairs could be glossed over.

Two days later Kelly met with Trump at Trump Tower and told him, "Cannot happen. I think it would have real morale issues for the non-field-grade officers." The next day Mattis also made the same points to Trump in person. Within three days of his meeting with Trump, Petraeus's possible nomination as secretary of state was over.

Robert Gates arrived at Trump Tower on December 2. Gates had served as secretary of defense for both George W. Bush and Barack Obama and had worked in Washington going back to the time of the Lyndon Johnson administration. The Trump team saw Gates as a "Bush guy." Even though he hadn't signed a Never Trump letter, the fact that he was a Bushie was a major strike against him, as was his service in the Obama administration. The Obama team had nicknamed Gates "Yoda," after the diminutive Star Wars character who was both wise and powerful. Gates was certainly the wisest of the wise men in the Republican Party, which was why he was at Trump Tower to advise Bannon, Kushner, Priebus, and the president-elect.

Trump asked Gates to evaluate each of the candidates he was considering for secretary of state—Giuliani, Petraeus, and Senator Bob Corker, the chairman of the Senate Foreign Relations Committee. Gates didn't give ringing endorsements for any of them. Trump asked Gates who he would suggest as most qualified if he were starting with a clean sheet of paper.

Gates replied, "A guy with experience in a couple of administrations and who understands the Defense Department because Defense is such a big part of what the State Department is now. Knows the Hill. Knows intelligence."

Was Gates—also a former CIA director—making a pitch to be Trump's secretary of state?

Gates added half jokingly, "If I can humbly say, it's someone like myself."

There was dead silence. Trump just sat there and didn't say anything. The silence went on for almost a minute; it seemed like an eternity.

Finally, Gates pivoted to a new subject. "Of course, I don't need another job! I've talked extensively with Condi [George W. Bush's secretary of state, Condoleezza Rice]. And we think a guy to look at is Rex Tillerson, the CEO of Exxon." Gates said Tillerson was a tough negotiator and he already knew a lot of leaders around the world. Trump seemed intrigued.

Pence called Tillerson and asked him to come to meet the president-elect. Tillerson asked if he could skip the gauntlet of cameras that were always staking out the Trump Tower lobby and meet with Trump discreetly. Tillerson was whisked from a private entrance in Trump Tower to Trump's office, where Bannon, Kushner, and Priebus were waiting with the president-elect.

Tillerson owned the room. The silver-haired Texan came off like a head of state. And in a sense he was. ExxonMobil had revenues exceeding $250 billion a year; if it were a country, it would be the forty-first largest economy in the world, putting it on par with Pakistan.

Tillerson had spent decades working in the Middle East and in Russia and he could speak with great knowledge about them. When he was a young oil engineer, Tillerson had lived in Yemen! Exxon was the largest taxpayer in Saudi Arabia! Tillerson had known Russian president

Vladimir Putin for almost two decades! For his work developing oil fields in Russia, Putin had given Tillerson an Order of Friendship award!

Tillerson dazzled Trump and his inner circle. On the spot, Trump offered Tillerson the secretary of state job.

Bannon looked at Tillerson, asking him, "You're surprised?"

Tillerson replied, "Yeah. I already have a job."

Trump observed, "Yeah, but you're going to retire soon, aren't you?"

Indeed, Tillerson was supposed to retire to his Texas ranch in a few months, where he would get to spend time with his grandkids. He said he would have to discuss the job offer with the Exxon board and his family.

Back at home, Tillerson's wife said to him, "I told you God's not through with you."

Kushner told colleagues that his father-in-law's best cabinet choice was tapping Tillerson to be secretary of state. That halo would soon dim.

Although Trump made his cabinet choices relatively quickly, below that level the key national security agencies were dealing with the most chaotic transition in memory. At the State Department and the Pentagon, the Trump "landing teams" that were supposed to come in to ease the transition from one administration to the next barely showed up. At the State Department, no one in the counterterrorism bureau had any contact with the Trump transition team, despite the fact that Trump had made the fight against terrorism such a key part of his campaign. Similarly, at the Pentagon, few of the members of the Trump landing team held top-secret clearances, which meant that most of the team could not be briefed on the key programs at the Department of Defense.

A civil servant who worked at Obama's National Security Council for a year and then for Trump's NSC for several months summarized the transition from Obama to Trump as a "shitshow." Another NSC staffer who worked for both Obama and Trump was even blunter, describing the transition as a "a total goat fuck."

It wasn't supposed to have been this way. Susan Rice, Obama's national security adviser, summoned an all-staff NSC meeting in the spring of 2016, at which she declared, "The Bush team gave us a very good transition and our role is to meet and exceed that bar that they set for us. You NSC staffers are going to work very hard for the next eight months in setting up the incoming team, whoever that may be." Over the following months, NSC staffers churned out memos for a variety of scenarios, such as what a war might look like on the Korean Peninsula.

The morning after Election Day, some Obama staffers were weeping openly in the halls of the West Wing and the adjoining Eisenhower Executive Office Building, the massive gray, wedding-cakelike nineteenth century building where the National Security Council staff is housed. Staffers who had worked for many hundreds of hours on Obama initiatives such as the Iran nuclear deal or the Paris climate change agreement knew that all their work was likely to go up in smoke.

Obama consoled his staff, telling them, "The people have spoken. We need the best possible transition." But nobody from the Trump team showed up at the NSC during the month of November. By early December there were a couple of meetings between Trump staffers and NSC staffers. It was an oddly quiet holiday season at the White House.

An early indicator of the likely trajectory of Trump and his inner circle was the dumping of former congressman Mike Rogers from the Trump transition team. Rogers, who had chaired the House Intelligence Committee, was one of the first serious players in Congress to endorse Trump, but he was deemed to have been insufficiently zealous in his prosecution of then-secretary of state Hillary Clinton during the Benghazi hearings. Meanwhile, the star of Representative Mike Pompeo rose because Pompeo had filed his own blistering report about the Benghazi attack and had publicly claimed that the Benghazi matter was "worse" than Watergate. Pompeo would be tapped to be CIA director.

Another early indicator about where the Trump administration was headed was the dual appointment of the head of the Republican National Committee, Reince Priebus, as chief of staff and Steve Bannon as "chief strategist" in the White House. Those appointments signaled that Trump would sometimes heed the establishment types and at other times the ideologues in his administration. It also created a White House with major competing power centers. This was compounded by the large portfolio that Jared Kushner accorded to himself, taking responsibility for relations with China, Mexico, and the Middle East, which effectively made him the shadow secretary of state.

The chaos of the transition was so profound and the Trump administration had so few of its senior officials in place when it assumed office that to keep the national security apparatus running with a semblance of order, the Trump administration asked a handful of senior Obama administration officials to stay on. Among them was Nick Rasmussen, who ran the National Counterterrorism Center, which coordinated counterterrorism strategy and intelligence across the government. In this, the Trump administration was following an honorable post-9/11 bipartisan tradition when it came to counterterrorism. Rasmussen had previously served in the George W. Bush and Obama administrations in senior White House counterterrorism roles. Joshua Geltzer, the senior director for counterterrorism at the White House for Obama, was also asked to stay on in that role by the Trump administration, as was Brett McGurk, who oversaw the Global Coalition to Defeat ISIS at the Department of State.

It was clear, however, that any contender for a senior job in the Trump administration was subject to a litmus test: you would not be considered for a role if you had criticized Trump in the past. This meant that many qualified candidates were passed over by the Trump team, and certainly the many dozens of leading Republican foreign policy experts who made up the Never Trumpers. This set up some immediate conflicts between the Trump White House and Mattis, who didn't want Trump loyalists who were either amateurs or weirdos serving at the Pentagon.

Mattis wanted Michèle Flournoy to be his top deputy. Flournoy, a Democrat who had worked in defense policy in Washington for decades, would likely have been tapped to be Hillary Clinton's secretary of defense if Clinton had won the election. Flournoy would have been the first woman to serve in that position. Flournoy knew the Pentagon and its massive bureaucracy well because she had served in the key role of undersecretary for policy in Obama's Pentagon.

Flournoy was torn about taking the job. Her father had served in World War II, her husband was a naval officer, and she was the mother of a soon-to-be naval officer. She felt it was her duty to serve, and she and Mattis were close. But then there was Trump and his treatment of women and his demonization of refugees, immigrants, and Muslims. Added to that was his complete lack of understanding of the United States' historical role as the leader of a rules-based international order and the unique strategic value of America's alliances. For Trump, every country seemed to be judged only through the narrow lens of its bilateral trade balances with the United States. Not least, there was Trump's impulsiveness, which Flournoy found deeply worrisome in a commander in chief. Flournoy went to meet with a couple of officials on the Trump transition team at Trump Tower in Manhattan, but in the end she decided to drop out of consideration for the job given all of her misgivings.

To fill the important job of undersecretary for policy, Mattis wanted to bring on Anne Patterson, a recently retired career diplomat. The White House nixed Patterson because when she was US ambassador to Egypt, she had performed typical ambassadorial functions with the democratically elected Islamist government of Mohamed Morsi. This made Patterson suspect in the eyes of some Trump officials and supporters. They thought she was some kind of closet Muslim Brotherhood fan, when in reality Patterson was a seasoned diplomat simply doing her job.

At the State Department, Tillerson faced some of the same issues Mattis did. Tillerson wanted Elliott Abrams, a sharp observer of the Middle East who had worked in Republican administrations going back to Reagan, to serve as his number two. Abrams hadn't signed any of the Never Trump letters, but he had written an opinion piece in the *Weekly Standard* with the self-explanatory title "When You Can't Stand Your Candidate" after Trump had clinched the Republican nomination. Tillerson felt he needed someone seasoned like Abrams to help him navigate Washington's tricky shoals. Kushner and Republican senator Tom Cotton of Arkansas, who was closely allied with Trump, also pushed for Abrams.

Tillerson brought Abrams to meet Trump at the White House and they had a cordial exchange. Trump wasn't happy about appointing Abrams but went along with it because Tillerson wanted him.

Trump later watched Tucker Carlson on Fox who was interviewing the isolationist senator from Kentucky, Rand Paul, who railed against Abrams saying, "He said that the chair that Washington and Lincoln sat in, that Trump was not fit to sit in it. . . . Elliott Abrams is one of the key architects of the Iraq War. We don't need people with the failed policies back in. Donald Trump does represent something new and different, I think a welcome relief from the neocons. So I hope he doesn't appoint someone who doesn't really agree with him."

Trump called Tillerson saying, "Fire your buddy."

Tillerson said, "I can't do that. I just offered the job. The city will go nuts. We told everybody."

Trump replied, "He's fired. You get rid of him."

In mid-November 2016, Obama ordered a full review of the Russian meddling in the election to be finished before Trump's inauguration on January 20, 2017. Media reports soon emerged that the CIA had concluded in a secret assessment that Russia had intervened in the election to help Trump win the presidency, rather than merely to spread doubts about the American electoral system. The intelligence agencies also had identified individuals with connections to the Russian government who had provided WikiLeaks with thousands of hacked emails from the Democratic National Committee, which WikiLeaks published for maximum effect on July 22, 2016, just before the Democratic convention.

Around Christmas, the Trump transition team dismissed these findings in a statement: "These are the same people that said Saddam Hussein had weapons of mass destruction. The election ended a long time ago in one of the biggest Electoral College victories in history. It's now time to move on and 'Make America Great Again.'" Trump was famously unpersuaded that the Russians were behind the hacking, saying, "I don't believe they interfered . . . it could be Russia. And it could be China. And it could be some guy in his home in New Jersey." This put him in the unusual position of rejecting the findings of the CIA even before he took office.

There were also significant differences between the CIA's weapons-of-mass-destruction fiasco a decade and a half earlier and the evidence that was offered by the American intelligence community about the Russian hacking. Unlike the Iraqi WMD case, which relied on dodgy defectors and shaky circumstantial evidence, the evidence in the election hacking case was based on "digital fingerprints" that pointed definitively to Russian involvement.

In late December, the FBI and Department of Homeland Security took the unusual step of publicly releasing an account of the Russian hacking efforts (code-named by the US government GRIZZLY STEPPE), which went into detail about how and when the hacking was accomplished. The report portrayed a sophisticated set of spear-phishing campaigns that began in the spring of 2015 that targeted the Democratic National Committee. The report said that spear-phishing emails "tricked recipients into changing their passwords" and through the harvesting of those credentials the Russians were "able to gain access and steal content, likely leading to the exfiltration of information from multiple senior party members."

On December 29, 2016, Obama sanctioned top Russian officials for their role in the election meddling in the States, ejected thirty-five Russian diplomats who were alleged to be intelligence operatives, and denied the Russians access to some of their diplomatic facilities in New York and Maryland. It was the most robust response the United States had ever made to a cyberattack.

Trump reacted to the news of the Russian sanctions and expulsions with nonchalance, saying, "It's time for our country to move on to bigger and better things." Trump seemed unable to separate his narcissistic fears that the Russian hacking might tarnish his presidential victory from the very real problem that the Russians had successfully undermined one of the bedrock principles of the nation, its ability to have free and fair elections unhampered by outside interference. Trump's intransigence set the stage for what was shaping up to be the most serious crisis of any presidential transition in memory, pitting the CIA, FBI, and National Security Agency (NSA) against the incoming president.

The showdown was set to climax with CIA director John Brennan, Director of National Intelligence James Clapper, NSA director Admiral Mike Rogers, and FBI director James Comey all briefing the president-elect at Trump Tower on January 6, 2017, about the Russian hacking. In the days leading up to this meeting, Trump sent out a number of tweets, including one that quoted Julian Assange of WikiLeaks, an archenemy of the US intelligence community because of his role in the leaking of tens of thousands of classified US government documents. Trump tweeted that "Julian Assange said, 'a 14-year-old could have hacked Podesta'—why was DNC so careless? Also said Russians did not give him the info!" In an interview with the *New York Times*, Trump said, not for the first time and certainly not for the last, that he was the victim of a "political witch hunt."

Trump also claimed that he had "secret" intelligence he would soon reveal about the hack. He also took time out from dissing the intelligence community to dis the new star of *Celebrity Apprentice* who had replaced him on the show, tweeting, "Wow, the ratings are in and Arnold Schwarzenegger got 'swamped' (or destroyed) by comparison to the ratings machine, DJT."

By now, senior members of Trump's national security team were seriously worried that Trump might come out of the briefing and say or tweet something that would irretrievably harm his relationship with the CIA, FBI, and NSA and also render the future president suspect among anyone who took the nation's security seriously.

At the intelligence briefing, Brennan, Clapper, Comey, and Rogers laid out for Trump the case that the Russians had seriously meddled with the election. In an extraordinary unclassified version of the briefing that the CIA, FBI, and NSA released immediately after Trump was briefed, they said that the hacking was personally ordered by Putin "to undermine public faith in the US democratic process, denigrate Secretary Clinton, and harm her electability." They also said that the Russians had developed a clear preference for President-Elect Trump and that Putin's animosity against Clinton sprang from the belief that she was to blame for the mass protests against his regime five years earlier and also because he nursed a grudge against her for some unflattering comments that she had made about him.

The US intelligence community concluded that Russian intelligence had gained access to the Democratic National Committee networks and had harvested a large amount of data from the personal email accounts of Democratic Party officials. US intelligence officials also laid out the close links between WikiLeaks, which had released the hacked emails, and the Russians. They also explained the key role that the Russia Today (RT) television network had played in an information warfare campaign against Clinton. This latter point must surely have discomfited Mike Flynn, given his friendly relationship with RT. The classified version of the intelligence report said that senior Russian officials were caught on phone intercepts cheering Trump's victory, including some of the officials who knew of the secret hacking campaign.

After the Trump Tower briefing, Trump released his most conciliatory statement about the issue to date: "I had a constructive meeting and conversation with the leaders of the Intelligence Community this afternoon. . . . While Russia, China, other countries, outside groups and people are consistently trying to break through the cyber infrastructure of our governmental institutions, businesses and organizations including the Democrat [sic] National Committee, there was absolutely no effect on the outcome of the election. . . . Whether it is our government, organizations, associations or businesses we need to aggressively combat and stop cyberattacks. I will appoint a team to give me a plan within 90 days of taking office."

This statement was enough to head off a complete rupture between Trump and the intelligence community, but it was far from the end of the story. Four days after the Trump Tower briefing, CNN broke the news that a classified annex to Trump's briefing contained uncorroborated information from a trusted former British intelligence officer that the Russians had acquired significant derogatory information about Trump, including that he had allegedly consorted with prostitutes on a business trip to Moscow in 2013. There were also allegations that officials in the Trump campaign had conspired with the Russians to undermine Clinton's campaign and that as a quid pro quo Trump would not criticize Putin for his annexation of parts of Ukraine, and would also attack NATO in his public statements.

From Trump's point of view, the Democrats were simply going to use Russia to explain why they lost the election, and he didn't appreciate that one bit. Trump did not want his presidency to be understood as the fruit of a foreign intelligence operation rather than a historical achievement of extraordinary consequence. This also colored how he viewed the US intelligence and law enforcement communities, as well as the measures taken by the Obama administration against the Russians. All this had created such a negative environment that Trump thought that his ability to engage personally with Putin was going to be severely limited. Trump resented all of this.

The "lead pens" on Trump's inaugural address were Steve Bannon and Stephen Miller. They were Trump's America First brain trust. They had both spent key parts of their lives in the uber-liberal Los Angeles enclave of Santa Monica on the Pacific Ocean. As a teenager, Miller had rebelled against what he thought was the knee-jerk liberalism being rammed down his throat at Santa Monica High School. At the same time that Miller was railing against liberalism at his school, from his own perch in Santa Monica, Bannon was producing conservative, nationalist films with titles such as *In the Face of Evil* about Reagan's struggle with communism, which Bannon connected to America's post-9/11 struggle with "radical Islam."

A key message that Trump wanted in the inaugural address was that the fight against ISIS wasn't going to take a generation. As commander in chief Trump would take down their physical caliphate as quickly as feasible and would "eradicate completely from the face of the Earth . . Radical Islamic Terrorism."

As they were writing the speech, Bannon told Trump, "This is an inaugural address. People are going to be talking about this a hundred years from now, right? You're saying eradicate radical Islamic terrorists from the face of the earth. This is one they're going to hold you accountable. This is a declarative sentence. This is much bolder than Kennedy's address."

In his bleak inaugural speech, Trump painted the United States as a crime-ridden economic basket case that he had come to rescue. Trump declared, "This American carnage stops right here and stops right now." In fact, crime was at a twenty-year low and the economy was at an eight-year high. Trump went on to trumpet: "From this day forward, a new vision will govern our land. From this moment on, it's going to be *America First!*"

After the speech, Miller told Bannon, "You know, it was just perfect. Just perfect."

"There's only one problem," Bannon replied. "We should have turned the podium around and had it face the group of assholes on the platform."

The irony appeared to be lost on Bannon that the inaugural address, a manifesto of America First populism working in the service of the common man, was delivered by a multibillionaire and cowritten by a multimillionaire many times over and the scion of a wealthy Santa Monica family.

Following his inaugural address, at a lunch on Capitol Hill, Trump pointed to his new secretary of defense Jim Mattis and said, "This is central casting. If I was doing a movie, I pick you, general." Mattis certainly "looked the part," which was a matter of crucial importance to Trump, the former reality TV star and beauty pageant impresario.

The day after he was installed as president, Trump traveled from the White House to CIA headquarters just across the Potomac River in Langley, Virginia. The visit was intended to build bridges to the CIA, but Trump squandered the opportunity by bragging (falsely) about the size of the crowd at his inauguration, a speech that he made in the CIA's main lobby in front of the Memorial Wall of stars, representing all the CIA officers who have died in the line of duty.

Former CIA director John Brennan, who had stepped down from his post a day earlier, dispatched an aide to NBC News to say that he was "deeply saddened and angered at Donald Trump's despicable display of self-aggrandizement in front of CIA's Memorial Wall of Agency heroes." The bridge building was clearly still a work in progress.

Four days after his inauguration, Trump hung a portrait of President Andrew Jackson in his office. The choice was significant. Bannon found that he could talk to Trump through history. Bannon told Trump, "You are a historical figure, a transformational figure—you are Andrew Jackson. You're an outsider, fucking tough as boot leather. Women love you, you've got animal magnetism, and you've got charisma. You're Jackson and, trust me, the fucking elite hated Jackson and they hate you."

The first foreign leader to visit the newly inaugurated President Trump at the White House was British prime minister Theresa May. As they were discussing over lunch what was happening in Ukraine, May asked Trump, "Have you spoken with Putin?"

Trump said, "No, I haven't."

Mike Flynn leaned in and said, "Sir, we're arranging that call now. President Putin called several days ago, but we haven't been able to get it on your calendar yet."

Trump looked down the table and said, "Are you kidding me? Vladimir Putin tried to call me, and you didn't put him through? What the hell were you thinking?"

Flynn replied, "Well, sir, you know, you have a lot of calls coming in, and we're trying to manage who you talk to."

The president said, "Vladimir Putin is the only man on earth who can destroy us, and you didn't put the call through?" Trump realized that this was not the discussion to have in front of Theresa May, so he changed the subject.

After the lunch, Trump called his senior staff together, asking them, "What kind of bullshit is this? How is it possible that Putin calls me and you don't put the call through? I don't know what you guys are doing." Then the president stormed out of the room.

A week into his presidency, Trump signed a National Security Presidential Memorandum that gave Bannon a full seat on the National Security Council. The same order also bizarrely removed the director of national intelligence and the chairman of the Joint Chiefs from having a permanent seat on the NSC. They could only attend the NSC on an ad hoc basis rather than as a "principal" such as Bannon. Not having the leading intelligence official and the top military officer attend every NSC meeting as a matter of course was unprecedented.

Bannon later said he was appointed to the NSC to keep an eye on the national security adviser. "I never went to one NSC meeting. I was just kind of there to keep an eye on things and make sure crazy shit didn't happen," Bannon recalled.

The Obama White House had a well-deserved reputation for micromanaging military operations from the West Wing. Sometimes this made sense to ensure a thorough process to consider the risks of any operation, but combat commanders generally understood what was happening on the ground far better than officials in the White House, and waiting for West Wing approval for an operation could be time-consuming.

Bannon told Flynn, "We are de-operationalizing the NSC. We need to go to the [former national security adviser Brent] Scowcroft model, which is the curation of an interagency process that gives the president a wide range of options. We ain't running any fucking wars out of the West Wing. That's over. We're devolving those powers back to combatant commanders with the Joint Chiefs of Staff, and particularly Mattis. Mattis is on board to eradicate ISIS."

Bannon and Flynn were both surprised by how bloated the NSC staff had become. Flynn asked Bannon, "How many guys do they have at the NSC?"

Bannon said, "I don't know, one hundred, max?"

Flynn told him, "Four hundred and fifty."

"We're going to get rid of all the Obama appointees and detailees out of here ASAP and get our own people in," Bannon responded.

While he was national security adviser, Flynn never sent out an all-staff email, and he didn't hold his first all-staff meeting until two weeks into his brief tenure. At the all-staff, Flynn gave a rambling speech that included the observation, "If you get out in the country, and I know because I have been traveling the country with the president throughout the campaign, you just know things are really messed up." Flynn's speech sounded like a Trump campaign rally. If the national security adviser had a substantive view about how he would go about implementing the president's vision, he didn't speak to it.

At the meeting, a State Department detailee to the NSC asked Flynn, "What about the president's attack on the media and the 'deep state'? Any advice for those of us conducting relations with other countries that are cracking down on their media? How should we deal with this?"

Flynn replied, "Well, that's how our republic works, and the president won. Civil servants who don't like it should get out."

Another NSC staffer asked Flynn, "What does an 'America First' foreign policy look like?"

There was a long pause. A couple of hundred key foreign policy and national security officials waited for an answer. Suddenly, it became painfully obvious that the national security adviser of the United States couldn't explain what the Trump administration's foreign policy actually was. This was quite surprising. Even alarming.

Flynn turned to the deputy national security adviser, K. T. McFarland. "K. T., do you have an answer?"

McFarland was a longtime Fox News talking head who had been out of government since she had worked as a speechwriter in the Reagan administration. Flynn appointed her to be the deputy national security adviser despite scant relevant expertise or experience.

McFarland didn't answer the question directly. Instead she addressed the room. "Wow! Look at all these people! I didn't know there were so many people on the NSC staff. Together we are gonna Make America Great Again!"

NSC staffers found McFarland to be charming, but unversed in substantive issues. McFarland told the staffers that she wanted instructions about what to do in meetings at the White House. "I am a TV person," she said. "Give me the script and tell me what to say. Tell me what to do at two minutes, what I do at five minutes, and what I do at ten minutes."

McFarland did attempt to bring some order to the first chaotic weeks of the new administration, calling the first "deputies" meeting of sub-cabinet officials in the Trump administration to focus on North Korea. She also was able to interpret Trump well, warning the NSC team that getting Trump to commit to the war in Afghanistan was not going to be easy.

Adding to the overall sense of confusion about the national security policy-making process, parallel to the NSC, Bannon headed up something called the Special Initiatives Group (SIG), which also involved fellow Breitbart alumnus Sebastian Gorka. Gorka grandiosely described his work to CNN as "doing long-range initiatives of real import to the president." But it wasn't at all clear what the SIG's actual role was. A senior White House official described it as not much more than "two people going to lunch." After a few months, the SIG simply faded away.

Now that he was without a real role, Gorka spent much of his time on television pontificating about the "new sheriff in town" and asserting that "the alpha males are back." Meanwhile, at the White House, those with the most sensitive clearances stayed away from Gorka and didn't invite him to meetings about counterterrorism, his supposed specialty, because they found him to be an uninformed blowhard. Other White House officials deemed Gorka to be "harmless." Most NSC staffers could never figure out what Gorka actually *did*.

Flynn, who had the reputation of building smart teams when he was an army officer, appointed a group of NSC officials who were deeply knowledgeable in three areas key to American national security interests: China, the Middle East, and Russia. The top NSC official on Asia was Matthew Pottinger, who spent many years in China working as a Mandarin-speaking reporter for the *Wall Street Journal*. After leaving the *Journal*, Pottinger joined the marines and served as a captain in Afghanistan, which is where he met Flynn. Together they wrote an influential paper, "Fixing Intel," which made the entirely reasonable case that

American intelligence agencies had to do a better job of getting "outside the wire" if they really wanted to understand what was happening in countries such as Afghanistan. The paper's publication in 2010 by a Washington, DC, think tank caused quite a ruckus, especially as it was published outside of normal government channels.

Pottinger became a key architect of the Trump administration's more skeptical approach to China. He had experienced the authoritarianism of the Chinese firsthand during his seven-year stint as a reporter in China. When Pottinger was reporting on the sale of Chinese nuclear fuel, he was confronted by a government goon in a Starbucks in Beijing, who punched him in the face.

During the Obama administration, China was largely framed as a "frenemy." Under Trump, the framing shifted to focus more on the "enemy" side of that equation. Indicative of where Trump was going to take the relationship with China was the phone call he had during the transition with the president of Taiwan, Tsai Ing-wen. The Chinese were panicked by the call because they regarded the island of Taiwan as part of "One-China" and here Trump was treating them as if they were a separate country. Top Chinese foreign policy official Yang Jiechi flew over to New York immediately to meet with Kushner, Flynn, Bannon, and Priebus. Yang told Trump's top advisers, "Would you mind if we say something at the beginning? The territorial integrity and sovereignty of China will not be questioned." He then spent the next hour lecturing them in perfect English about the history of China and its various humiliations by Western powers over the past century and a half.

Flynn appointed Colonel Joel Rayburn as the NSC senior director for Iraq, Iran, Lebanon, and Syria. An intelligence officer and historian who had served in Iraq as an adviser to General David Petraeus, in 2014 Rayburn published *Iraq after America*, a must-read book for anyone who wanted to understand how Iraq had descended into chaos following the American troop withdrawal three years earlier. Michael

Bell, a retired colonel with a PhD who had served as the head of Petraeus's internal advisory group when he was the commanding general in Iraq, was appointed to oversee the Gulf States and Yemen. The NSC's top official on Russia was Fiona Hill, a frequent critic of Vladimir Putin who had worked as a US intelligence officer focused on Russia under President George W. Bush and President Obama.

The overall director for the Middle East at the NSC was retired colonel Derek Harvey, an intense intelligence officer who had served as the head of the US military cell examining the insurgency in Iraq in 2003. Harvey concluded after talking with a number of insurgent leaders that the decisions by the Bush administration to disband the Iraqi military and to fire tens of thousands of members of the Baath Party were pivotal to fueling the insurgency, as the military and Baath Party were dominated by Sunni Iraqis who largely ran the country under Saddam Hussein. Their abrupt dismissal had flipped the social, economic, and political order on its head, creating a large group of disenfranchised men willing to take up arms against the new rulers of Iraq. It was Colonel Harvey who first laid out for President George W. Bush at the White House in the winter of 2004 the real scale and nature of the Sunni insurgency at a time when the Bush administration wouldn't use the word "insurgency," as it implied that they were facing something much more serious than the "dead enders" that Vice President Dick Cheney was then publicly talking about. Later CENTCOM's intelligence chief under Obama, Harvey came to feel strongly that the Obama administration's dominant narrative after the death of bin Laden that al-Qaeda was on the run was dangerously out of whack with the growing and metastasizing jihadist threat that he was observing in the Middle East.

Bell, Harvey, and Rayburn were all protégés of General Petraeus, with whom they had worked closely during the Iraq War, and they all brought much experience and expertise to their new jobs. An understandable bias they shared was their visceral disdain for Iran, forged during the Iraq War, which saw hundreds of American soldiers die as a result of sophisticated Iranian-supplied roadside bombs or fighting against Iran-backed Shia militias.

Flynn also brought on Christopher Costa, a retired US Army intelligence colonel with extensive special operations experience in the field in Afghanistan, for the crucial role of running counterterrorism at the White House. Costa largely kept in place a consummately professional counterterrorism directorate at the NSC that he had inherited from Jen Easterly, a retired army lieutenant colonel and Rhodes scholar who had worked for the National Security Agency in Iraq, and who had directed counterterrorism during the Obama administration. Costa made a point of avoiding the bluster of typical incoming senior administration officials, who often took the position that the previous administration had gotten it all wrong and the new team was coming in to fix everything. Costa understood that in the CT (counterterrorism) realm, the tactics and personnel he was inheriting from the Obama team were sound.

During the first days of the Trump administration, senior national security officials immediately had to make a tough call about a possible SEAL Team Six raid in Yemen. Joint Special Operations Command, of which SEAL Team Six is a key component, had launched only two previous ground raids in Yemen. There were good reasons for that. Yemen was in the grip of a brutal civil war and pretty much every adult male was armed with an AK-47, so ground operations in the country were quite risky. The two previous JSOC raids in Yemen were both in 2014 and authorized only when the lives of American hostages held by the local al-Qaeda affiliate seemed to be at risk. In the first operation, eight Yemeni, Saudi, and Ethiopian hostages were freed, while in the second raid, both Luke Somers, an American photojournalist, and Pierre Korkie, a South African citizen, were killed during a botched rescue attempt.

In part because of the risks of ground operations, Obama had vastly expanded the CIA drone program in Yemen targeting Al-Qaeda in the Arabian Peninsula (AQAP), a branch of al-Qaeda that was quite capable. AQAP had tried to bring down an American passenger jet over Detroit during the first year of Obama's first term, deploying a suicide bomber wearing an "underwear bomb." The device didn't detonate properly, but the threat posed by AQAP was an intense preoccupation for the remainder of the Obama administration.

During the waning weeks of Obama's second term, the planning for a third SEAL ground raid in Yemen was quite advanced, including rehearsals by the SEAL Team Six operators who would eventually deploy for the mission. But Obama didn't authorize the operation because the first moonless night in Yemen came on January 28, a week after he would be out of office. A moonless night gave the SEALs, kitted out with night vision equipment, a great advantage.

On January 25, Bannon and Kushner attended a dinner at the White House where the decision to authorize the Yemen operation was weighed with President Trump. Also at the dinner were Mattis, Joint Chiefs chair Joseph Dunford, and Flynn.

Trump asked the group, "Why are you coming to me with this decision? General Mattis can decide if this goes ahead or not."

During the Obama administration, decisions about even relatively small-scale but risky ground operations in countries such as Yemen were decided by the White House. Trump was serious when he said he was going to empower his commanders to make their own decisions rather than micromanaging them. Typically, a decision about a ground operation involving significant risks would be weighed in the White House Situation Room, but Trump wasn't going to be running a typical administration. Trump gave a verbal okay to the mission at the dinner and signed the order for the operation the following morning.

On a moonless night in the early morning hours of January 29, some thirty SEALs along with a group of Emirati special forces raided a well-defended al-Qaeda complex in a remote area of western Yemen, their target an al-Qaeda leader. The SEALs encountered heavy resistance, and during a firefight Chief Petty Officer William "Ryan" Owens was killed, three SEALs were wounded, and a $75 million Osprey helicopter that took a "hard landing" had to be destroyed. Ten children and six women were also killed. One of the victims was the eight-year-old daughter of the militant Yemeni American cleric Anwar al-Awlaki, who was killed six years earlier in a US drone strike. Their target either evaded capture or hadn't been there.

When news of the raid became public, White House press secretary

Sean Spicer said, "It's hard to ever call something a complete success, when you have the loss of life or people injured," but he concluded, "It is a successful operation by all standards."

The Pentagon released a video made by AQAP that was recovered by the operators on the ground in Yemen to make the case for the valuable "intel" that was supposedly recovered by the SEALs. It quickly emerged that the video was about a decade old and could be easily found online.

Joshua Geltzer, senior director for counterterrorism at the National Security Council at the time, says, "It's obviously insufficient to use an already-public video to make the case that an operation with those costs is a success. The bar for me is very, very high when you lose a US service member to call something a success."

A senior US military officer shared that assessment of the operation, saying, "It didn't yield what we had wanted it to do, and of course we paid a heavy price for it and lost a helicopter and ended up killing civilians and losing a valued operator on the ground." A senior special operations officer also lamented, "The SSE [Sensitive Site Exploitation] intel: We hoped for a bigger take." This wasn't a successful operation; it was a failed mission.

Owens's body was transported back to the United States, to Dover Air Force Base in Delaware. President Trump was there to pay his respects, but Owens's father refused to meet the president. Bill Owens felt that the Yemen operation was badly botched and certainly wasn't worth his son's life.

The trip to Dover unsettled Trump. It was the first time that as commander in chief he had to confront the death of a serviceman that he had sent into harm's way. There would be no more casual greenlighting of such operations over dinner. Trump thought the generals had presented him with an in-and-out operation in Yemen that wasn't a big deal. Now he realized that the generals weren't always right.

Famously, President Harry Truman kept a sign on his desk in the Oval Office saying "The buck stops here." For Trump the buck stopped somewhere else. Trump told Fox News, "This was a mission that was started before I got here. This was something [the generals] wanted to do. They came to me, they explained what they wanted to do—the generals—who are very respected. . . . And they lost Ryan." All of which was true, but Trump was commander in chief and so he was ultimately responsible for all the military operations on his watch.

A month after the botched raid in Yemen, Trump invited Owens's widow, Carryn, to sit in the audience during his first address to Congress. Trump lauded Owens and his sacrifice, saying, "Ryan was part of a hugely successful raid that generated large amounts of vital intelligence that will lead to many more victories in the future." Owens's weeping widow received several standing ovations during Trump's peroration.

Trump's speech was great TV, so effective that even Van Jones, a CNN commentator and frequent Trump critic, praised the president, saying, "He became President of the United States in that moment, period." Trump, ever the showman, had taken a failed special operations raid and refashioned it into the emotional highlight of his young presidency.

Chapter 4

ENTER MCMASTER

Above all President Johnson needed reassurance. He wanted advisers who would tell him what he wanted to hear . . . those that expressed views counter to his priorities would hold little sway.

—H. R. McMaster, *Dereliction of Duty: Lyndon Johnson, Robert McNamara, the Joint Chiefs of Staff, and the Lies that Led to Vietnam*

Mike Flynn was only twenty-four days on the job as national security adviser when he was forced to resign because he had lied to Vice President Mike Pence. Flynn told Pence during the transition that he hadn't discussed lifting Obama-era sanctions against Russia with the Russian ambassador to the United States when, in fact, he had. Misled by Flynn, Pence then went on CBS's *Face the Nation* and asserted that Flynn hadn't discussed lifting sanctions with the ambassador. In an interview at the White House, Flynn also lied to FBI agents about the same issue.

Bannon told Trump that he liked Flynn, but Flynn had to go as he wasn't "salvageable."

No American national security adviser had served as briefly as Mike Flynn. Losing Flynn was a bitter pill for the president; it was his first experience with how his own law enforcement agencies could hurt him.

Retired vice admiral Bob Harward, who was Mattis's top deputy when he was the CENTCOM commander, was Trump's first choice to replace Flynn as national security adviser. Appointing Harward as the national security adviser would have given Mattis a close ally inside the White House. But Harward, who was making serious money for the first time in his life in a senior job with Lockheed in the United Arab Emirates, declined, citing family reasons to White House officials. He took a look at the chaos then unfolding at the White House and pronounced it "a shit sandwich" to a friend.

Trump officials flirted with the idea of offering the national security adviser position to Petraeus, but having had Harward already turn down the job, they were not looking to have the news cycle dominated by another bad story. They already knew that Petraeus had turned over classified materials to his biographer, Paula Broadwell. Now Broadwell suddenly popped up on CNN, where she observed to Anderson Cooper that Petraeus was still reporting to a probation officer, having pled guilty to a misdemeanor about his handling of classified materials.

For the time being, Trump appointed retired lieutenant general Keith Kellogg to be acting national security adviser. Trump started seriously considering offering the retired general the top national security job. Kellogg, seventy-two, was a Trump favorite. Kellogg was one of the five obscure national security advisers Trump had announced a year earlier during the campaign and Trump valued his loyalty. Where others on the campaign had started abandoning what looked like a sinking ship a month before the presidential election when the *Access Hollywood* tape had aired, Kellogg had kept the faith.

After the election, Bannon had asked Kellogg to join the National Security Council staff in a senior role as the chief of staff for the council. Kellogg regularly traveled around the country with Trump on Air Force One, keeping the president company and shooting the shit with him. Kellogg didn't read briefing papers, but neither did the president.

NSC staffers found Kellogg to be lazy, uninformed, and not smart. The national security adviser's office had a peephole and staffers would look through it to see if Kellogg needed something, but he would be asleep at his desk. If he wasn't napping, Kellogg was watching Fox News. To the extent that he had firm foreign policy views, Kellogg was an isolationist.

Kellogg also had the reputation of being a loose cannon who catered to Trump's worst instincts. During one Oval Office meeting, when Trump was receiving the highly classified President's Daily Brief, he expressed some concern about what to do about the Syrian dictator Bashar al-Assad. Kellogg told the president, "Just bomb his fucking compound." Since bombing Assad's residence would contravene longstanding American laws about assassinating the leaders of other countries, another official gently steered the discussion in a different direction, saying, "You know, you should really look at taking out Assad's infrastructure or military installations."

Concerned about Kellogg's competence and inclinations, a small group of NSC staffers decided they would slow roll anything of substance getting to Kellogg. They tried to reduce the amount of times that Kellogg could get in to see Trump in the Oval Office, and they cut back on his calls with senior foreign officials, figuring there was no way that Kellogg would be tapped for the key role of national security adviser and the best way to mitigate any damage he might cause was to keep him as much out of the loop as possible.*

The Trump White House was now in full scramble mode to find a new national security adviser as soon as feasible to tamp down the multiplying stories of White House chaos. Candidates for the job were summoned to Mar-a-Lago, Trump's Florida estate, over the weekend of February 18 and 19, 2017. They included Lieutenant General Robert Caslen, the superintendent of West Point; John Bolton, a neoconservative who had served in Republican administrations since the Reagan era; and Lieutenant General H. R. McMaster, who was recommended by Republican senator Tom Cotton of Arkansas, a veteran of the Iraq War and a key early supporter of Trump. When McMaster received the call from the White House to go to Mar-a-Lago, he was preparing to retire from the military.

Caslen came for his interview with Trump straight from central casting, dressed in his full dress uniform and looking like Clint Eastwood. Trump told aides that Caslen was "the best gunfighter in the US Army. This guy's a soldier's soldier." But Caslen dealt himself out of consideration, telling the president, "Look, I've spent one tour in Washington and it's really not my deal."

Jared Kushner urged his father-in-law to move fast on the decision,

---

* Kellogg was eventually appointed to be national security adviser to Vice President Pence, where he could do little damage as Pence was largely uninterested in national security issues.

telling him, "We're getting so much heat in the media because we don't have a national security adviser. We're getting lit up on *Morning Joe*."

Up next was McMaster, who was wearing a suit, not his dress uniform. Trump asked the general, "Can you stay in uniform, or do you have to retire?"

McMaster explained that if he remained active duty in the role, it wouldn't set a precedent: Colin Powell had served as Ronald Reagan's national security adviser when he was an army lieutenant general.

Trump chatted with McMaster for twenty minutes and concluded by saying, "You're terrific. I love my generals, so it's good to meet you."

After the interview, Trump turned to Bannon, asking him, "Is that guy really a general?"

Bannon assured the president that McMaster was indeed "a very highly decorated general. Silver Star."

Trump focused on the cut of McMaster's suit, saying, "He looks like a beer salesman."

The final candidate was John Bolton, a ferocious bureaucratic infighter who had worked in the Washington swamp since the era when Olivia Newton-John's "Physical" was America's number one song. Bolton was a frequent Fox News talking head, memorable for his distinctive, massive walrus mustache. Trump, always hung up on appearances, didn't appreciate the mustache. Trump was also concerned about Bolton's proclivity to call for preemptive wars against enemies of the United States, as he had recently advocated for publicly with both Iran and North Korea.

Trump told Bolton during their interview, "John, there are huge problems everywhere, but, John, you can't be bombing everywhere, John."

Despite his qualms about McMaster's suit, Trump appointed him to be his next national security adviser. White House press secretary Sarah Sanders talked to Trump about doing an official announcement in the Oval Office when he returned to Washington.

Trump said, "Well, how about we just do it right now? We'll pull this couch over here."

Trump started directing staff to rearrange the furniture in one of the grand reception rooms of Mar-a-Lago. Sitting next to McMaster, who was now in his dress uniform, Trump said he was "a man of tremendous talent and tremendous experience."

McMaster wasn't a surprising choice for national security adviser. After all, he was arguably the most capable military officer of his generation. McMaster had led American victories on the battlefields of both the 1991 Gulf War and the Iraq War more than a decade later, and he had also served in Afghanistan, running an anticorruption task force.

During the Gulf War, then-captain McMaster had led a US tank troop in what became known as the Battle of 73 Easting on February 26, 1991. McMaster's armored forces, acting as scouts, suddenly encountered a large force of the Iraqi army. McMaster could see the enemy with his naked eye; they were at very close range. In a battle that lasted only twenty-three minutes, McMaster's force destroyed more than thirty Iraqi tanks, some twenty personnel carriers, and more than thirty trucks. Young US military officers continue to study this battle as the exemplary case study of high-intensity conventional combat.

After the shooting was over, McMaster suddenly became aware of how filthy he was; he hadn't bathed in six days. McMaster stood naked on the back deck of his tank and took a crude bath with a washcloth in front of a group of Iraqi prisoners that his tank troop had captured. McMaster recalled, "The prisoners, from a culture which imbues them with physical modesty, were visibly shocked by my behavior."

McMaster's tank troop had taken no casualties. McMaster and his soldiers offered prayers of thanks to God. "We did not gloat over our victory," recalled McMaster.

According to McMaster, the lesson of that victory was "there are two ways to fight the United States military: asymmetrically and stupid. Asymmetrically means you're going to try to avoid our strengths. In the 1991 Gulf War, it's like we called Saddam's army out into the schoolyard and beat up that army."

Almost a decade and a half later, McMaster was back in Iraq. This time he wasn't fighting the orderly tank regiments of Saddam Hussein's conventional army, but instead the guerrilla forces of Al-Qaeda in Iraq, which had taken over much of western Iraq and were proving to be a far harder nut to crack than Saddam's military. Al-Qaeda had also learned from the Gulf War and wasn't fighting "stupid," it was fighting "asymmetrically" and not engaging the US military in a conventional war.

In 2005, then-colonel McMaster led the first successful full-scale battle against al-Qaeda in the western Iraqi city of Tal Afar, a city of two hundred thousand people. McMaster recalled that al-Qaeda had turned Tal Afar into a living hell: "All the schools were closed because of violence; all the marketplaces were closed. There was no power. There was no water. The city was lifeless. People lived in abject fear."

McMaster established twenty-nine small outposts in the city. His regiment lived among the Tal Afar population and partnered with tribal elders to offer protection against al-Qaeda. The citizens began to trust the Americans and provided them with intelligence on al-Qaeda's movements. Within a few months, al-Qaeda had retreated from Tal Afar.

McMaster's approach was the exact opposite of the dominant US strategy of the time, which was to hand over ever more control to the Iraqi army and withdraw the bulk of American soldiers to massive bases. Instead of reducing the American footprint, McMaster pursued a strategy in Tal Afar of *increasing* the US military presence there in an effort to tamp down the intensifying Iraqi civil war and to undermine al-Qaeda. McMaster also implemented "clear, hold, and build" counterinsurgency operations.

McMaster's Tal Afar campaign was considered by many military experts to be the classic example of counterinsurgency tactics during the Iraq War. His work there would become a model for the George W. Bush administration's new military strategy in Iraq. In October 2005, Bush's secretary of state Condoleezza Rice in congressional testimony said that "our political military strategy has to be to clear, hold, and build. To clear areas from insurgent control, to hold them securely, and to build durable national Iraqi institutions." This approach would also soon be codified in the US military's new counterinsurgency manual, written by General Petraeus with an assist from General Mattis.

A key to McMaster's thinking was his 1997 book, *Dereliction of*

Duty: Lyndon Johnson, Robert McNamara, the Joint Chiefs of Staff, and the Lies That Led to Vietnam. Published two decades before McMaster assumed his role as national security adviser and when he was only a major, *Dereliction of Duty* caused something of a sensation in the US military because it took the Pentagon's leaders to task for their derelictions of duty during the Vietnam War. McMaster painted a devastating picture of the Joint Chiefs, who told President Lyndon Johnson only what he wanted to hear about how the Vietnam War was going. He described how they went along with Johnson's ill-considered attempt to find a middle ground between withdrawing from Vietnam and fighting a conventional war there that—divorced from on-the-ground realities—had no chance of success. The Joint Chiefs never provided Johnson with useful military advice about what it might take to win the war. Instead, they accepted Johnson's preference for what the president termed "graduated pressure" against the North Vietnamese. This took the form of a gradually escalating bombing campaign that did not bend the North Vietnamese to American will and instead confused activity—bombing raids and body counts—with progress on the battlefield.

The major problem Johnson and his military advisers had was that they went to war in Vietnam without a strategy. McMaster explained: "The war in Vietnam was not lost in the field, nor was it lost on the front pages of the *New York Times* or on the college campuses. It was lost in Washington, D.C."

Despite McMaster's record of battlefield success in two wars as well as his groundbreaking book about the Vietnam War, the army in 2006 and again in 2007 passed him over for promotion from colonel to the rank of one-star general. McMaster wasn't the typical army officer that promotion boards favored. McMaster was a wounded war hero with a PhD, but some of his superior officers whispered that he "wasn't a team player." It took the intervention of General Petraeus, who was then the commander of the Iraq War, for McMaster to be promoted to brigadier general. Petraeus traveled from the Middle East to the United States to chair the army's 2008 promotion board that awarded McMaster his first star.

After Trump announced McMaster as his national security adviser, *Dereliction of Duty* became an instant bestseller on Amazon. Its lessons weighed on McMaster as he entered the White House. The problem with Johnson, in McMaster's mind, was that he wanted a Vietnam policy that conformed to his domestic political priorities. As a result, there was never an examination of a broad range of options about what to do in Vietnam, nor was there an exploration of the advantages and disadvantages associated with different courses of action.

McMaster was determined not to make the same set of mistakes. He always aimed to present multiple options to Trump, and he believed that the president was ill served if those on whom he relied for advice didn't tell him what they really thought. This was all driven home for McMaster the first day he arrived at his new White House office; it was exactly the same office where Johnson's national security adviser, McGeorge Bundy, had once sat and coordinated the policies that ultimately led to the failures in Vietnam.

McMaster quickly moved to make Trump's National Security Council a more professional institution. Bannon was removed from his permanent seat on the NSC because it gave the appearance that politics would play a role in national security decision-making. Another NSC official McMaster sidelined was Deputy National Security Adviser K. T. McFarland. She was offered the consolation prize of ambassador to Singapore, but McFarland withdrew her nomination after it stalled in the Senate because of misleading answers she gave to lawmakers about the Russia investigation.

McFarland's farewell party from the NSC was a warm affair. Jared Kushner spoke and gave a homily about the nature of the US government. "This morning I was meeting with these congressmen and a bunch of them had Texan accents and some of them had California accents and some of them had New England accents and I was just like, this country is so amazing! This is how the Congress works. They come from all corners." NSC staffers, most of whom were longtime civil servants, found

Kushner's sermon faintly amusing: *Whad'ya know*—congressmen come from all corners of the country!

The day after he started as national security adviser, McMaster called an all-hands staff meeting in the basement auditorium of the Eisenhower Executive Office Building, which adjoins the White House and is where most of the White House staff work. McMaster held up a copy of Peter Rodman's book *Presidential Command* and urged everyone to read it. Rodman was a longtime Republican national security official who had made a deep study of how to make the NSC function well. McMaster aimed to follow the "Scowcroft Model." Brent Scowcroft, the only national security adviser to have served in two administrations in that role, saw his job as acting as an honest broker between key departments such as the Pentagon and State Department with an eye toward teeing up a good range of policy options for the president to choose from.

McMaster told the group that he wanted to end the use of the pejorative term "holdovers" employed by some Trump staffers to refer to putative Obama-era "deep state" enemies of the Trump project who were working at the NSC. In fact, the vast majority of the NSC staffers were not political appointees. They were intelligence officials, military officers, or career civil servants who were detailed to the NSC from the CIA, Pentagon, and State Department.

In his address to the NSC staffers, McMaster cited Sir Halford Mackinder, the British geographer who more or less invented the modern concept of geopolitics with a paper he published in 1904, "The Geographical Pivot of History," which explained that whoever controlled the Eurasian landmass controlled the world. McMaster said the two revisionist powers of Russia and China were the key strategic problems the United States faced, notwithstanding the continuing threat posed by transnational terrorists.

"We're not going to call it radical Islamic terrorism," McMaster told the NSC staff, "because what that does, it just plays into their hand. This terrorism is not Islamic. It's irreligious; a perverted interpretation of Islam to justify criminal acts mainly against their own people." McMaster preferred the term "*Islamist* terrorism," which underlined that the terrorists were espousing "Islamism," a thoroughly politicized version of Islam that was not fundamental to Islam.

Sebastian Gorka, however, remained on a jihad to name the threat "radical *Islamic* terrorism." And when Trump gave his speech to the joint session of Congress five weeks after taking office, he pointedly said that his administration was taking steps to protect the nation from "radical Islamic terrorism." Even as Trump was still speaking, Gorka tweeted triumphantly, "'RADICAL ISLAMIC TERRORISM!' Any questions?" The day after Trump's speech, Gorka tweeted, "After 8 years of obfuscation and disastrous Counterterrorism policies those 3 words are key to Victory against Global Jihadism."

It was unclear why Gorka believed that using different terminology would in itself be crucial to the defeat of ISIS. The defeat of ISIS in Iraq and Syria was actually accomplished by tens of thousands of Iraqi special forces soldiers and Kurdish fighters, advised by American special forces, all backed up by considerable US airpower, in a concerted effort that began in the summer of 2014, two and a half years before Trump had assumed office.

McMaster beefed up the NSC, appointing a top deputy for strategy, Egyptian-born Dina Powell, who had served in the George W. Bush administration, spoke Arabic, and had worked at Goldman Sachs. Powell was widely respected; she was also close to Ivanka Trump and Jared Kushner.

McMaster also brought on defense expert Nadia Schadlow to write the Trump administration's national security strategy. Schadlow had recently published a book, *War and the Art of Governance*, which examined how to turn "combat success into political victory," a relevant question as ISIS was beginning to crumble and the Trump administration started planning for what the "day after" ISIS looked like in Iraq.

As McMaster settled into his job, he told NSC staffers they needed to adapt to the style of the commander in chief. Trump was not going to read seventy-page briefing papers. He might read one-pagers, but even so, the staff should aim to fit an issue onto an index card. The NSC wasn't a faculty lounge; it had to compress complex issues into an elevator pitch. And when a "decision package" about a particular national security issue was sent up to the president, it would be smart to include some suggested tweets.

NSC staffers found McMaster refreshing. He had done his homework and he had strategic ideas about the world beyond the sloganeering of Make America Great Again. He also wasn't obsessed with some supposed "deep state" conspiracy that was purportedly undermining the Trump administration as some of the more conspiracy-minded Trump officials were, and he quickly went about creating a solid process to bring some order to the chaos that had engulfed the White House during its first month. Emblematic of that chaos was the rollout of the travel ban.

Chapter 5

THE TRAVEL BAN

For every complex problem there is an answer
that is clear, simple, and wrong.

—*H. L. Mencken*

It's not a Muslim ban, but we were totally prepared.
It's working out very nicely. You see it
at the airports, you see it all over.

—*President Trump on January 28, 2017,
a day after the travel ban went into effect*

A week after Trump's inauguration, on January 27, 2017, Jim Mattis was ceremonially sworn in as the twenty-sixth secretary of defense of the United States at the Pentagon's Hall of Heroes, a hallowed space that memorializes the names of every service member awarded the Medal of Honor, the highest award for valor in the nation.* Vice President Pence administered the oath of office to Mattis, after which President Trump remarked, "Mattis is a man of honor, a man of devotion, and a man of total action. He likes action."

After Mattis was sworn in, Trump used the backdrop of the Hall of Heroes to sign an executive order for the set of measures known as the travel ban. As he signed the order, Trump said new vetting would be instituted "to keep radical Islamic terrorists out of the United States of America—we don't want them here. . . . We only want to admit into our country those who will support our country and love, deeply, our people."

It was the first time a president had employed the Hall of Heroes as a political prop, much less in the context of the swearing-in ceremony of a new secretary of defense. As the commander in chief, Trump could do pretty much as he liked at the Pentagon, but it was an odd display as far as Mattis was concerned, though he kept his views largely to himself. Mattis strongly believed that the military needed to remain apolitical because that's how you maintained the trust of the public. If the military

* Mattis was officially sworn in on Inauguration Day at a small ceremony at the White House complex so that he could assume office immediately in the event of any crisis.

was seen as a political pawn of a particular administration, you chipped away at that crucial public trust.

One of Trump's signature ideas on the campaign trail, of course, had been a ban on Muslim immigrants from countries that were known to harbor terrorists. During the presidential transition, Abdul Razak Ali Artan, an ISIS-inspired terrorist, rammed a car into a group of students at Ohio State University, injuring eleven. Artan was a legal permanent US resident originally from Somalia. Days later, Trump spoke at a massive victory rally in Des Moines. He said the Ohio State attack was "yet one more tragic reminder that immigration security is now national security. No more games, folks, no more games. A Trump administration will always put the safety and security of the American people first."

Following an attack in Germany by an ISIS supporter at a Christmas market in Berlin that killed twelve, Trump made remarks at Mar-a-Lago that appeared to again call for a crackdown, telling reporters who asked him about his proposals to ban Muslim immigration, "You know my plans. All along I've been proven to be right. One hundred percent correct."

The executive order that Trump signed on January 27 banned the entry of any Syrian refugees into the United States indefinitely. It was widely pointed out that it was highly unlikely that there were terrorists among the few Syrian refugees who were then settling in the United States. The United States had accepted only a very small number of Syrian refugees: at the time Trump signed the order, the United States had taken in only around fifteen thousand Syrian refugees, the large majority women and children, less than 1 percent of the total number of Syrian refugees, estimated to be nearly five million people. It was also widely noted that not only were these Syrian refugees not terrorists, they were fleeing the brutal state-sponsored terrorism of the Syrian dictator Bashar al-Assad as well as the brutal nonstate terrorism of ISIS. These refugees were the victims of terrorism, not its perpetrators.

Any ISIS terrorist with an ounce of common sense was quite unlikely to try to infiltrate the United States posing as a Syrian refugee. Officials from the Department of Homeland Security, FBI, National Counterterrorism Center, Pentagon, and State Department scrutinized any Syrian refugee trying to get into the United States. They also had to give up their biometric data—scans of their retinas, for instance—submit their detailed biographic histories, and undergo lengthy interviews. These refugees were also queried against a number of government databases to see if they might pose a threat. The whole process could take two years, sometimes more.

Leon Rodriguez, a top US immigration official, testified at a 2015 hearing of the Senate Homeland Security Committee that of all the tens of millions of people who were trying to get into the United States every year, "refugees get the most scrutiny and Syrian refugees get the most scrutiny of all." By contrast, Syrian refugees fleeing to Europe did not go through anything like the rigorous process experienced by those who were coming to the States, and the volume of Syrians fleeing to Europe was orders of magnitude larger than it was to the United States.

Along with the ban on Syrian refugees, the Trump executive order also suspended travel from seven Muslim-majority countries for a period of three months: Iran, Iraq, Libya, Somalia, Sudan, Syria, and Yemen. Nationals of those countries would be subjected to what Trump described as "extreme vetting." Many of these countries didn't have US embassies, either because the situation on the ground was too dangerous, as with Yemen, or because they didn't have diplomatic relations with the United States, as with Iran, so enforcing a higher degree of scrutiny on the citizens of those countries was sensible.

As a counterterrorism measure, however, it didn't make sense. None of the terrorists who had conducted deadly jihadist attacks in the United States since 9/11 had emigrated from or were born into a family that had emigrated from a country that was the subject of the Trump administration's travel ban. Indeed, all of the post-9/11 terrorists in the United States who had carried out lethal attacks were "homegrown" American citizens or legal permanent residents. Of the twelve terrorists who carried out these lethal attacks between 9/11 and when Trump assumed office, three were African Americans, three were from families that hailed originally from Pakistan, two came from Russia as children, one was born in Virginia to a family that had emigrated from the Palestinian Territories, one emigrated from Egypt and carried out an attack a decade after arriving, and one each had families that originally came from Kuwait and Afghanistan. None of these countries was on the travel ban list. The travel ban was, in short, a solution in search of a problem that didn't exist. No matter, it was a campaign promise, and the Trump administration moved quickly to implement it.

The execution of the travel ban order was a textbook case of how not to govern because it caught the agencies that were supposed to implement it completely by surprise. National Security Council staffers received a copy of the executive order on the morning of Tuesday, January 24, and were given forty-five minutes to send in their comments. For any such order to be successful, it needed to be vetted carefully by all the departments and agencies affected by it, which is why such orders are usually months in the making. Steve Bannon and Stephen Miller, Trump's thirty-one-year-old domestic policy director, largely drafted the executive order, and Gorka reviewed it. Between them they had scant experience about how the government actually operated. The order was simply dumped on the departments and agencies that would have to make it work.

The executive order completely blindsided the counterterrorism directorate at the NSC because it included Iraq as one of the countries that was subject to the ban, despite the fact that Iraqi soldiers were leading the fight against ISIS.

Joshua Geltzer, the senior director for counterterrorism at the White House, recalled, "The inclusion of Iraq seemed crazy. We feared what then actually happened, which is that the Iraqis would be baffled and deeply insulted by this." The United States' key allies in the fight against ISIS were being treated like potential terrorists.

The rollout of the ban was a fiasco. It was publicly announced on the afternoon of Friday, January 27, and the Department of Homeland Security, the key agency in charge of enforcing the ban, was barely consulted about it. Even John Kelly, the secretary of homeland security, had almost no time to review the executive order. Kelly was on a coast guard plane flying from Miami to Washington and had dialed into a White

House conference call to discuss the order as a work in progress. One of the officials on the call looked up at the TV in his office and saw that Trump was already signing the order at the Pentagon. "The president is signing the executive order we're discussing," said the official.

When he was in uniform, Kelly had served on Capitol Hill as the liaison between the marines and Congress. Kelly knew you didn't just surprise senators and representatives with this kind of new directive; you briefed them ahead of time.

There was a great deal of confusion initially about who exactly was covered by the ban and whether green card holders were also included in it. When the order came down, planes were already in the air carrying the citizens of countries on the list. Chaos swiftly unfolded at airports around the United States, scenes that were carried on live TV.

Foreign leaders were flummoxed by the travel ban. British foreign secretary Boris Johnson called up Stephen Miller to tell him, "I've got an Iranian who has lived in the UK for thirty-five years, and he's the world's greatest expert on electromagnetic conduction. And he's trying to get to Harvard for a conference, and you guys won't give him a visa? Can you fix this for me?"

At the White House the day after the ban was announced, Trump claimed that everything was, in fact, going to plan, asserting, "It's not a Muslim ban, but we were totally prepared. It's working out very nicely. You see it at the airports, you see it all over."

None of the normal government stuff had been done to lay the groundwork for the ban, such as informing the various countries around the world that would be affected by it. Four days after the order was issued, some one thousand State Department officials signed an unusual "dissent channel" cable protesting it. The channel had been set up during the Vietnam War so that diplomats could protest foreign policy decisions they opposed without fear of retaliation. It was the largest number of State Department officials ever to sign on to a dissent cable.

Senior Trump officials saw the dissent cable as a deeply unprofessional response to the unexpected transfer of power, which many Foreign Service officers didn't handle well. Trump's advisers felt that State

Department officials just couldn't get over the trauma of the former secretary of state, Hillary Clinton, not having won the election. It was not an auspicious start to the relationship.

The sense of chaos was magnified when the acting attorney general, Sally Yates, announced that she was advising Department of Justice lawyers not to defend the ban. Yates's reasoning was based in part on a Trump comment that he favored the entrance of Christians from the banned countries, implying that the ban was what Trump had promised all along during his campaign: a ban on Muslims from entering the United States, which seemed to contravene the bedrock constitutional principle of freedom of religion.

Trump immediately fired Yates and found someone more compliant to act in her stead, but a few days later a federal judge stayed the executive order approving the ban, which meant that the Department of Homeland Security could no longer enforce it. Trump, without regard for the separation of powers, immediately attacked the judge on Twitter, writing, "The opinion of this so-called judge, which essentially takes law-enforcement away from our country, is ridiculous and will be overturned!" Trump also tweeted that "many very bad and dangerous people may be pouring into our country. A terrible decision."

Trump's call during his campaign for a "total and complete shutdown of Muslims entering the United States" hung over his advisers' attempts to craft a ban that could withstand legal scrutiny. Miller was the most hard-core of Trump's advisers on immigration, telling another White House official at one point, "I would be happy if not a single refugee foot ever again touched American soil." Miller often claimed in meetings that refugees were an economic burden on the United States. In fact, an interagency review of the issue had found that refugees contributed more to the US economy than they took out.

Miller instructed Trump administration officials working in press relations to look for stories about immigrants involved in crimes and promote them to the media. Miller admonished the press relations officials: "You comms people need to get us more stories of immigrants doing bad things. You need to highlight the criminality. You're not doing enough to get those stories out."

The US intelligence community was asked to fix the intelligence so that it meshed with the travel ban policy and to "deliver an ex post facto intelligence justification for that which we had already decided to do," according to a senior US intelligence official.

Again, the problem was that the intelligence actually showed that terrorist attacks in the United States didn't involve anyone from the countries targeted by the travel ban and instead were the work of second-generation immigrants or green card holders who had largely arrived in the country as children. The terrorism problem was caused by "home-grown" American militants who were radicalizing in the United States, not by the infiltration of foreign-born terrorists from overseas as had happened on 9/11. (The ban wouldn't have stopped the 9/11 attacks either, since the perpetrators were mostly Saudis or from other Arab countries that were not targeted by the ban.)

This senior intelligence official worried that he would be called to testify to defend the travel ban, but to his relief that never happened. The Republicans, then in control of both houses of Congress, were not eager to call witnesses who might impugn the administration's line that the travel ban was going to make the United States safer, as opposed to a pointless exercise at best.

A Department of Homeland Security internal report that leaked in February 2017 showed that the department that was supposed to enforce the ban also found that it made little sense. The report stated that citizens of the travel ban countries were "rarely implicated in U.S.-based terrorism."

Kellyanne Conway, the counselor to the president, who coined the memorable term "alternative facts," defended the travel ban on MSNBC on February 2 by pointing to "the Bowling Green massacre" that had been carried out by two Iraqi refugees in Kentucky. Conway added, "Most people don't know that because it didn't get covered." There was a good reason for the lack of coverage of this "massacre." It never happened. There was, in fact, plenty of media coverage of what actually *did* happen, which was that the two Iraqi refugees in Bowling Green had attempted to send money and weapons to Al-Qaeda in Iraq in 2011, for which they were arrested and given long prison sentences.

To help sell the travel ban, the Trump administration continued pushing the story line that the media wasn't giving enough coverage to terrorism. Three days after Conway's "Bowling Green massacre" remarks, on a visit to the key US military base overseeing the war on ISIS—Central Command in Tampa, Florida—Trump claimed that the media wasn't reporting on terrorism for "reasons" the president didn't elaborate upon. Trump told the CENTCOM audience, "You've seen what happened in Paris and Nice. All over Europe, it's happening. It's gotten to a point where it's not even being reported. And in many cases, the very, very dishonest press doesn't want to report it. They have their reasons, and you understand that."

To "prove" that the media wasn't covering terrorism adequately, the Trump administration, still fighting in court to reinstate the travel ban, released a list of seventy-eight "major" anti-Western terrorist attacks since September 2014, claiming that "most have not received the media attention they deserved." The only problem with this line of argument was that the list of terrorist attacks, which was "declassified" by the Trump administration, was itself *based on media reports.*

In fact, the total number of media hits in the Nexis media database for the seventy-eight terrorist attacks was more than eighty thousand, or an average of slightly more than one thousand media mentions per incident. And those numbers understated how much coverage the media had given these incidents because a Nexis search can only display a maximum of three thousand media citations for any given search. There were sixteen terrorist attacks on the White House list of purportedly undercovered attacks that each elicited more than three thousand media mentions. The terror attacks in Paris and Nice that Trump had cited in his CENTCOM speech, for instance, each received more than three thousand media mentions.

The terrorist attacks that didn't get as much coverage were the ones where there were no deaths, or that took place in countries such as Saudi Arabia, where there was little independent media reporting.

The White House's terrorism list underlined the arbitrary nature of the travel ban because, by the White House's own account, the countries that were generating the most significant number of terrorists threatening the West were *from the West*. Conspicuous by their absence on the White House list of terrorists carrying out major attacks against Western targets were Iraqis, Somalis, Sudanese, and Yemenis, four of the seven Muslim countries from which the Trump administration was seeking to suspend travel.

Of the total of ninety terrorists on the White House list, at most nine were from travel ban countries. Fifty of the terrorists—more than half—were from Christian-majority countries in the West. The countries with the most terrorists carrying out or plotting anti-Western attacks were Belgium, France, and the United States, according to the White House's own terrorism list.

Attorney General Jeff Sessions, an immigration hard-liner and a mentor to Stephen Miller, who had worked for Sessions when he was a senator, was one of the key officials pushing for the travel ban. Mary McCord, a career prosecutor who was running the National Security Division at the Justice Department that oversaw all terrorism cases, told Sessions, "Our terrorism statistics don't support a heightened threat from the seven countries that are on the travel ban list." McCord told Sessions that the real threat coming from overseas was the many hundreds of French and Belgian citizens who had been recruited by ISIS over the past couple of years. McCord said, "They can come here easily because they're from France and Belgium. That's honestly where I see a threat." Because they were from European "visa waiver" countries, these ISIS recruits could enter the United States with little or no scrutiny.

This point didn't seem to have any impact on Sessions, who had a deep distrust of immigrants and anyone who was from a Middle Eastern country. When he was briefed on a terrorist investigation, the first question Sessions would ask was "Where is this person from?" The next question was "Where are his parents from?"

The inclusion of Iraqis on the travel ban list was particularly galling to those in the administration who had served in Iraq. Mattis pushed back against the travel ban on the Iraqis. He well understood the key role that Iraqi forces were playing in the fight against ISIS. Sessions was adamant about the need to keep the Iraqis on the travel ban list.

The idiocy of the Iraqi travel ban was underlined when Lieutenant General Talib Shaghati, the commander of the Iraqi special forces division known as the Counter-Terrorism Service that was spearheading the military operations against ISIS, couldn't get a visa to visit his family members living in the United States.

McMaster asked Kelly, Mattis, Tillerson, and Sessions and all of their "plus-ones" to come into his office to discuss the Iraq travel ban issue. The backbenchers filled up the sofas on the perimeter of the room, while the principals sat around a small table.

Since Sessions was leading the charge to apply the travel ban to the Iraqis, McMaster explained to the attorney general that American soldiers were fighting alongside Iraqi soldiers against ISIS in Iraq, and the travel ban was an affront to many of these Iraqis. It was an affront that could engender bad blood between the Americans and the Iraqis and therefore put US service members in a potentially dangerous situation.

Tillerson's view was that his country team in Iraq and other specialists from the State Department could get the visa system for Iraqis brought up to the right standard so that any potential threat from those applying to travel from Iraq to the United States would be dealt with.

Sessions said, "I'm not impressed."

In response, McMaster pulled a photograph off the wall, the only personal item in his office, and put the photo in front of Sessions and said, "Let me tell you about this man." When McMaster had led the anti-al-Qaeda fight in Tal Afar, Iraq, in 2005, he had grown close to the mayor of the city, Najim al-Jubouri. The photograph was of Jubouri, surrounded by a sea of smiling Iraqi children, taken shortly after McMaster's regiment had liberated their city from al-Qaeda in 2005.

McMaster told the crowd of officials in his office the story of Jubouri, how the McMaster family had sponsored him and his family on a special visa to move to the States, where he had taken a job in DC and bought a home in Northern Virginia. When ISIS seemed poised to seize all of Iraq, Jubouri had volunteered to go back to fight ISIS and was now a major general in the Iraqi army. To keep his green card status, Major General Jubouri had to return every quarter to the United States, and when he came back under the proposed travel ban, he was going to get hassled every time.

Sessions finally relented. "All right. All right. I'll support taking Iraq off."

In parallel, a furious Mattis went to the White House to confront Bannon in his office about the Iraqi travel ban, telling him, "We should take Iraq off the list because these guys are fully in the fight against ISIS."

Bannon was noncommittal. "Okay. We'll go into the Oval. The president is going to be upset because he wants to stick to this, as we should. And we'll win in the courts with this."

Mattis and Tillerson met with Trump in the Oval Office and made a compelling case that the Iraqis were full allies in the takedown of ISIS. Trump didn't like anything that suggested that the list wasn't 100 percent aboveboard, but he was willing to change his mind in the name of the fight against ISIS. "Okay," Trump said, "if this is what we need to win, I'll take them off."

Trump bitched and moaned about this decision later. He would always feel that he should have gone with the first version of the travel ban.

On February 28, during the same speech to the joint session of Congress in which Trump had lauded the sacrifice of the Navy SEAL Ryan Owens, the president also claimed that "the vast majority of individuals convicted of terrorism and terrorism-related offenses since 9/11 came here from outside of our country." This was beyond fuzzy math; it was nonsense. The only way Trump could make his figures work is if they included individuals who had come to the United States as children, those who were naturalized citizens, and terrorists who had been extradited to the United States. The real problem was no longer foreign-born terrorists entering the United States, as had happened on 9/11, it was now American citizens and legal residents who were watching ISIS propaganda online and becoming radicalized in the United States.

On March 6, the Trump administration put forward a new executive order banning travel for three months from six Muslim countries, but not Iraq, a victory for Mattis and McMaster. Two days later the state of Hawaii filed a motion to block the travel ban on the grounds that it was discriminatory.

In early June, shortly after news broke about a terrorist attack in London, President Trump tweeted: "We need to be smart, vigilant and tough. We need the courts to give us back our rights. We need the Travel Ban as an extra level of safety!"

On September 24, 2017, Trump issued a third version of the travel ban, updating the policy to apply travel restrictions to the citizens of eight countries: Chad, Iran, Libya, North Korea, Somalia, Syria, Venezuela, and Yemen. As with the two earlier versions of the travel ban, this version would not have prevented a single death from jihadist terrorism in the United States since 9/11, but by adding Chad, North Korea, and Venezuela to the list of countries facing travel restrictions, the administration was adding non-Muslim majority countries. The number of North Korean visitors to the United States was negligible, and the Venezuelan ban affected only a relatively small number of the country's government officials and their families, but the inclusion of non-Muslim majority countries would likely shore up the legal defense of the travel ban working its way to the Supreme Court.

A reminder of what constituted the actual jihadist terrorist threat to the United States came on October 31, 2017, when Sayfullo Saipov plowed a vehicle into pedestrians walking on a crowded bike path in Manhattan not far from the World Trade Center, killing eight people. Saipov was a legal US resident who had emigrated from a non–travel ban country, Uzbekistan, seven years earlier and had radicalized while living in the United States. Saipov had downloaded thousands of ISIS images on his cell phone.

Trump said he was considering sending Saipov to Guantanamo, then changed his mind, tweeting, "Would love to send the NYC terrorist to Guantanamo but statistically that process takes much longer than going through the Federal system . . ." The Guantanamo military tribunal system was indeed a complete mess. The operational commander of 9/11, Khalid Sheikh Mohammed, known as KSM, had been captured in Pakistan in 2003. Fourteen years later, KSM's trial at Guantanamo had yet to begin.

On June 26, 2018, the Supreme Court would uphold the third version of the travel ban. The decision was not entirely surprising since the judiciary tended to be quite deferential to the executive branch when it came to matters of national security. That same year, the Trump administration admitted only sixty-two Syrian refugees to the United States. It was estimated that some five million Syrians had been forced to flee their homes in one of the worst humanitarian crises of the modern era.

Nine decades earlier, one desperate migrant, Mary Anne MacLeod, left the quasi-medieval world of the Outer Hebrides islands in Scotland, one of the poorest regions in Europe, to find work as a servant in New York. Mary would have passed the Statue of Liberty; she may even have been familiar with the promise of the United States written on its base, from the Emma Lazarus poem: "Give me your tired, your poor, your huddled masses yearning to breathe free." Mary later married Fred Trump. They had five children, including a son named Donald. The United States has not traditionally been the cramped, frightened country of Trump's travel ban.

Chapter 6

ASSAD AND ISIS

Fear, honor, and interest.

—Thucydides on why nations go to war

I know more about ISIS than the generals do. Believe me.

—Donald Trump campaigning in Iowa in 2015

In the early morning hours of April 4, 2017, dozens of civilians were killed in a suspected chemical weapons attack in Khan Sheikhoun, a town in northwestern Syria held by rebel forces. The attacks were carried out by Assad's air force.

The first meeting with Trump about what to do in response took place in the Oval Office. It was clear that this was a mass-murder attack by the Assad regime, but it wasn't clear what weapons had been used, though accounts by eyewitnesses suggested that the planes had dropped a powerful nerve agent.

The CIA gathered more intelligence and also examined social media postings made after the attack. The French intelligence service also weighed in. The Trump administration concluded that Assad had used sarin, a nerve agent of the type that had been banned by international treaty for almost a century.

Trump was angered and upset by the attack, particularly when he watched images of children who were dying and were taking their last gasp of breath. Trump told staffers in the Oval Office that Assad was "a sick son of a bitch." The president wondered aloud, "What do you do when you've got animals like this running a country?"

Trump blamed Obama for not enforcing his own "red line" on Assad's use of chemical weapons five years earlier. Trump told the staffers, "I'm having to enforce 'red lines' he drew and then wouldn't enforce himself."

Trump met with his war cabinet in the White House Situation

Room. Bannon was known to be a skeptic of military action, and Trump told him, "You got to speak up."

Bannon said, "Look. First off, I don't buy it. You got to show me much more evidence than this. Also, if this is our new standard—children being abused—let's start in sub-Saharan Africa and work our way north. If we want to go do this, we can go do it all over the world. Guess what? The world's a bad place. A lot of bad shit happens."

The NSC developed a range of options for Trump. The "low end" option was diplomatic protests, but this relative inaction carried its own risks in the views of both Secretary of State Rex Tillerson and McMaster, who made the case that the Obama administration had been paralyzed by the risks of doing something in Syria but were at the same time blind to the risks of inaction.

Obama's unenforced red line helped to explain why impressive veterans of America's post-9/11 wars such as Mattis and McMaster were willing to work for Trump. They collectively felt that Obama had failed to manage the growing problems of the Middle East, epitomized by his not enforcing his own red line, and that the world was a less safe place as a result. In their view, Obama's dithering over Syria was weakness that Putin took advantage of when he moved Russian forces into Syria in 2015 to prop up the Assad regime, secure in the knowledge that the Obama administration wouldn't do much of anything to push back. Similarly, Iran had sent its forces into Syria to bolster Assad and was now the dominant regional player in the Middle East.

Now, McMaster emphasized to Trump the importance of deterring the future use of chemical weapons, saying, "This isn't just about Syria. We're on the hundredth anniversary of World War I. This hasn't been used since then and if this becomes normalized, what happens? It's a threat to all the civilized world."

The "high end" option that the NSC prepared included attacks against targets associated with Assad himself as well as against Assad's chemical warfare unit. McMaster, Tillerson, and Trump pushed for aggressive action against the Assad regime, but Mattis wanted to ensure that any attack didn't inadvertently kill any of the Russian forces in Syria that were propping up the Assad regime. Mattis argued against military operations that would get the United States "pulled into a war."

Derek Harvey, the retired colonel who oversaw the Middle East at the NSC, pushed for a consequential strike against Assad rather than just the pinprick of eliminating a fraction of Assad's air force, which was one of the options on the table. Harvey advocated for taking out a larger target set of Assad's air force and helicopter fleet as this would dramatically curtail the dictator's ability to bomb his population at will.

Bannon confronted Harvey outside of the Situation Room and told the retired colonel, "We don't want you fucking neocons starting a war."

Mattis called McMaster, scolding him, "You let this get too far down the road."

McMaster spoke with Reince Priebus, Trump's chief of staff, about the timing of the strikes, the optimal moment for which in McMaster's view happened to be soon after Trump arrived at Mar-a-Lago, where he was hosting a long-planned summit with Chinese president Xi Jinping. Soon after Trump touched down in Florida on April 6, the president along with Kushner, Mattis, McMaster, and Priebus all entered into a dark blue tent that was pitched inside one of the rooms in the palatial Mar-a-Lago building. The ultrasecure tent had noise-making devices and opaque sides to prevent anyone eavesdropping on what was happening inside. The tent was connected to the White House Situation Room on an encrypted video line.

In the tent, Trump and his national security team talked over the options on the table, joined remotely by the officials in the Situation Room. After hearing the options, Trump said, "Okay, I'll let you know in a few minutes."

Trump selected the strike option that would take out about a fifth of Assad's air force. This had two goals: to restore deterrence against the use of chemical weapons and also to diminish the Syrian regime's capacity to launch more chemical weapons attacks from the air.

Trump told Mattis, "Do it, General."

Mattis went to his room, where there was a mobile SCIF set up, a Sensitive Compartmented Information Facility, a secure facility that was hardened against electronic surveillance. From the SCIF, Mattis oversaw the operation in Syria as it unfolded half a world away.

At 5:30 pm, Mattis called CENTCOM, ordering, "Go ahead: option one. Execute."

Because the Russians had tens of thousands of servicemen in Syria propping up Assad's regime, CENTCOM sent them a warning about the strike that was about to take place at the Shayrat Airbase, which was where the Syrian planes that had carried the chemical weapons for the April 4 attack had taken off.

As the fifty-nine cruise missiles targeting the Syrian airbase "spun up" in their tubes, Trump and his team went to the formal welcome dinner for Xi. At one point an aide handed a note to McMaster that read, "The strikes occurred." McMaster walked to Trump and gave him the note. As Xi was eating a piece of chocolate cake, Trump leaned over to him and told him about the strikes.

There was some concern that the Russians might use their sophisticated surface-to-air S-300 missiles that they had deployed in Syria, but they didn't. The Syrians did deploy their own air defenses, which consisted of older Russian missile systems, but they were entirely ineffectual.

Afterward, in a distant echo of the famous photo of President Obama and his national security team watching the US Navy SEAL operation that killed Osama bin Laden in Pakistan in 2011, a photograph was taken of Trump and his national security team as they listened to an after-action report about the effects of the strikes in Syria. The reports were that all the targets were hit. The mood in the room was sober.

Trump's announcement that he had ordered the cruise missile attacks in Syria was one of his best speeches. Visibly moved, Trump said, "My fellow Americans, on Tuesday, Syrian dictator Bashar al-Assad launched a horrible chemical weapons attack on innocent civilians. Using a deadly nerve agent, Assad choked out the lives of helpless men, women, and children. It was a slow and brutal death for so many. Even beautiful babies were cruelly murdered in this very barbaric attack. No child of God should ever suffer such horror. Tonight, I ordered a targeted military strike on the airfield in Syria from where the chemical attack was launched. It is in this vital national security interest of the United States to prevent and deter the spread and use of deadly chemical weapons. There can be no dispute that Syria used banned chemical weapons, violated its obligations under the Chemical Weapons Convention, and ignored the urging of the U.N. Security Council. Years of previous attempts at changing Assad's behavior have all failed, and failed very dramatically. As a result, the refugee crisis continues to deepen and the region continues to destabilize, threatening the United States and its allies. Tonight, I call on all civilized nations to join us in seeking to end the slaughter and bloodshed in Syria."

Even his critics showered Trump with praise for the strikes. Fareed Zakaria, the CNN host who frequently took Trump to task, gave him a rousing endorsement, saying, "I think Donald Trump became president of the United States. . . . For the first time really as president, he talked about international norms, international rules, about America's role in enforcing justice in the world. It was the kind of rhetoric that we have come to expect from American presidents since Harry Truman."

It was the brutality that Assad had unleashed against his own citizens, symbolized by his use of nerve agents against them, that had played a key role in the rise of ISIS. Al-Qaeda in Iraq had largely been defeated by 2010, but it lingered on in a vestigial form, and after Assad started violently attacking Arab Spring protesters in 2011, members of the Sunni militant group slipped from Iraq into Syria to fight Assad's brutal rule.

Assad emptied his prisons of jihadists in order to justify his war against his own people as a war against supposed "terrorists." Over time, this became a self-fulfilling prophecy as the released prisoners then joined Sunni armed groups. Eventually Al-Qaeda in Iraq morphed into ISIS, which was essentially a marriage of convenience between Iraqi Baathist military officers and militant jihadists burning with zeal to oust Assad and what they saw as a "Shia" government in Baghdad. By 2014, ISIS was a terrorist army that had formed its own quasi state across great swaths of Syria and Iraq.

On the campaign trail, Trump said that within thirty days of taking office he would task the generals fighting ISIS to come up with a new plan to defeat the group. During the campaign, Trump also suggested that he would fire the generals who were then leading the campaign against ISIS.

If that were the case, the first to go would have been General Joseph Votel, who had led the ISIS fight as the commander of CENTCOM since early 2016. Votel had previously commanded JSOC, Joint Special Operations Command, the umbrella group for all US special operations forces, including the SEAL team unit that had killed bin Laden. Votel, a lanky six foot two, whose black glasses and earnest demeanor gave him the look of a very fit Clark Kent, had also spent more than a decade fighting ISIS and its precursor groups such as Al-Qaeda in Iraq, and he well understood what was needed to defeat them.

As CENTCOM commander, Votel was effectively the American proconsul in the Middle East, flying across the region in his modified C-17 with his political adviser, who was a senior diplomat, and a bevy of colonels who kept him on schedule. On his C-17, which was the size of a large passenger jet, Votel worked and slept inside an Airstream trailer that was bolted to the floor of the plane; it was specially modified so that he could stay in touch with his commanders spread out over the twenty countries in the Middle East and Central Asia, his area of operations, as well as his headquarters in Tampa. When working in his small but comfortable cabin, Votel could be found hunched over a couple of classified computers monitoring the war against ISIS.

When ISIS started seizing large chunks of territory in Iraq during the first half of 2014, initially the Obama administration dithered. There was a debate at the White House about whether to carry out airstrikes to support the Iraqi army. The debate went on for many weeks until ISIS fighters surrounded ten thousand Yazidi civilians on a mountain in western Iraq. It was the height of summer and ISIS's genocidal fanatics now seemed poised to wipe out the Yazidis, a religious sect that ISIS deemed to be infidels. Obama authorized CENTCOM to carry out airstrikes to prevent the massacre of the Yazidis. In retaliation, the terrorist group murdered the American journalist James Foley, which galvanized the Obama administration to ramp up the fight against ISIS.

The Votel-led campaign against ISIS resulted in the deaths of many ISIS leaders in Iraq and Syria and also of tens of thousands of ISIS fighters. A critical ally in Votel's campaign against ISIS was Iraqi lieutenant general Abdul-Wahab al-Saadi, who was virtually unknown outside Iraq but was a hero in his own country. When the three-star general walked into the lobby of a guesthouse in Baghdad in late 2017, well-wishers who wanted to take selfies with him quickly surrounded him. Saadi, a tall, thin man with deep, dark circles under his eyes that were a testament to his long years of fighting against ISIS, was a key to the campaign that defeated ISIS. It was his storied Golden Division of Iraq's Counter-Terrorism Service, the Iraqi version of US special operations forces, which did much of the fighting and dying to defeat ISIS.

Indeed, Iraq's US-trained Counter-Terrorism Service and its elite Golden Division played a key role in the defeat of ISIS, while the wider Iraqi army ignominiously fled from the ISIS militants who seized much of Iraq in 2014. Saadi explained why that was, "We have zero tolerance for sectarianism." Iraq's minority Sunni population had long viewed the Iraqi security services as one big armed Shia group with a deeply sectarian agenda. The Counter-Terrorism Service, which consisted of about ten thousand soldiers, also demanded continuous training for its soldiers, unlike the Iraqi army, which required only basic training. The prestige of the CTS could be gauged by the fact that when the Iraqi government launched a recruitment drive in May 2017, three hundred thousand men applied to be part of the force. Only around one thousand would end up being accepted into training at a joint US-Iraqi facility.

Saadi said American logistical and intelligence support and US airpower accounted for "fifty percent of the success of the battle" against ISIS. American bombs inflicted heavy casualties on ISIS and were a morale booster for Saadi's troops. Another important factor was the training of the CTS by US special forces. It was arguably one of the most successful training missions that the US has ever conducted.

Saadi led the Golden Division into battle in key phases of the war against ISIS, liberating first Iraq's key oil refineries in Baiji in June 2015 and then significant Iraqi cities such as Fallujah, Ramadi, and Tikrit. It was, above all, his role in the fight for Mosul that cemented Saadi's reputation among Iraqis. The fight for Mosul was never going to be easy. The second largest city in Iraq, the old section of the city in western Mosul was a warren of narrow medieval-era streets and buildings. The battle for Mosul lasted nine months—in part, Saadi said, because Iraqi forces didn't want to level the city: "We were very careful to preserve the infrastructure and also the lives of innocents remaining in the city."

The fight in Mosul was also complicated because ISIS deployed more than one thousand VBIEDs—vehicle-borne improvised explosive devices—cars and trucks driven by suicide bombers. These VBIEDs were greatly feared by the Golden Division troops. Also, many of ISIS's most competent fighters, numbering around ten thousand, decided to make their last stand in Mosul where ISIS's self-styled caliphate was first proclaimed in 2014 by Abu Bakr al-Baghdadi, the elusive leader of ISIS. Mosul finally fell to Iraqi forces in July 2017. Five months later, the Iraqi military released a statement saying Iraq was "fully liberated" from ISIS's reign of terror. Three years earlier, ISIS had controlled 40 percent of the country.

In the waning months of the Obama administration, as the US-backed Iraqi forces moved closer to wresting control of Mosul from ISIS, Votel was already deep in the planning for striking the heart of the terrorist group's "caliphate," the Syrian city of Raqqa.

Votel, a native of Minnesota and a big Vikings fan, explained, "The importance of Raqqa is that is where ISIS plans their external [terrorist] operations. That is what is driving us to get on this as quick as we can, because this is where the plotting takes place. That doesn't mean we necessarily know that there is a specific plot we are trying to disrupt now or in a couple of weeks, but Raqqa is recognized as the financial, leadership and external ops center of the Islamic State."

Both Mosul and Raqqa were the major objectives in the American military strategy to defeat ISIS's terrorist army in the Middle East.

Rather than committing substantial land forces, the Obama administration and later the Trump administration provided special forces, intelligence resources, and airpower to Iraqi and Syrian fighters on the ground. The last time the United States had used this approach in a substantial manner was a decade and a half earlier in Afghanistan, where a similar combination of US special forces working with their Afghan allies on the ground combined with large-scale American airpower led to the overthrow of the Taliban in Afghanistan in the months after 9/11.

Mattis told Trump, "If you want to take down the physical caliphate, we have to take down the physical caliphate. There will be a lot of destruction. And there will be civilian casualties." Trump and Mattis agreed that the goal was not to "defeat" ISIS as it was under Obama, but to "annihilate" the terrorist army. This was something of a distinction without a difference, since defeating ISIS would surely entail destroying it. Nor was "annihilate" a conventional military doctrinal term, but the Pentagon certainly got the point that Trump wanted to destroy ISIS's caliphate as soon as feasible.

Ten days before Trump's inauguration, Brett McGurk, who oversaw the Global Coalition to Defeat ISIS, and his deputy, retired lieutenant general Terry Wolff, went to the Trump transition headquarters in Washington to meet with Mike Flynn and Keith Kellogg, also both retired lieutenant generals, and Tom Bossert, Trump's homeland security adviser. Using a couple of maps as aids to describe where ISIS was positioned in Iraq and Syria, McGurk and Wolff explained, "There is an opportunity for Team Trump in the first six months or so. You guys can speed this up a little bit if you are willing to allow everyone to do things a little faster, without coming back and asking 'Mother, may I?' all the time." McGurk and Wolff laid out a plan that would speed up the tempo of operations against ISIS. The trio of top Trump national security advisers was enthusiastic.

A week after he was inaugurated, Trump issued National Security Presidential Memorandum 3, which mandated an updated campaign plan against ISIS within thirty days. The new plan was largely the Obama plan to defeat ISIS, but it focused on a faster tempo of operations and devolved the authority to conduct operations down to the combatant commands, which in this case was CENTCOM commander General Votel, who no longer needed to check in with the White House when he was launching operations.

Two weeks after his inauguration, on February 6, 2017, Trump visited CENTCOM headquarters at the MacDill Air Force Base in Tampa. Special Operations Command (SOCOM), which supported the largely special operations forces–led fight against ISIS, also had its headquarters at MacDill. Trump was there to be briefed about the fight against ISIS as well as the war in Afghanistan. At CENTCOM, General Votel and the SOCOM commander, General Raymond "Tony" Thomas, gave Trump and some of his top national security officials—including his as-yet-to-be-fired national security adviser, Mike Flynn—a high-level, one-hour briefing about US military operations in the greater Middle East using a large map of the region.

To emphasize the strategic importance of the region, Votel pointed to the Strait of Hormuz between Oman and Iran, the key choke point for oil coming out of the Middle East. A third of the world's sea-borne oil transited the Strait of Hormuz.

Trump told the generals, "The next time Iran sends its boats into the Strait blow them out of the water! Let's get Mad Dog on this."

The generals let that one slide. CENTCOM was not about to launch a preemptive strike against Iran without a direct legal order from the commander in chief.

About ten minutes into the briefing, Trump asked the generals, "Shouldn't we have taken the oil when we were in Iraq the last time?"

Trump believed that Iraq's oil should have been used to compensate the United States for the money it had spent invading and occupying the country.

The generals also let that one slide, as plundering another country's resources was a crime under international law. It would have also played into the common conspiracy theory that the United States had invaded Iraq in 2003 "for the oil." Also, the Iraqis hadn't exactly asked for the American invasion of their country that had precipitated a brutal civil war that had lasted in one form or another for the past decade and a half.

There tended to be very little difference between what Trump said in public and what Trump said in private when it came to his key obsessions, and the missed opportunity to seize Iraq's oil was one of them. It would be a common refrain.

The Trump administration made a substantial shift in the fight against ISIS in Syria. The Obama administration was so concerned about "mission creep" in Syria that it had put tight limits on what US commanders could do there. One limit was that there could be only three American helicopters in Syria at any given moment. This severely constrained the Pentagon's ability to support the Syrian forces fighting ISIS. McMaster removed this restriction. The Obama administration had also capped the number of US soldiers in Syria at five hundred special forces trainers.

In the waning months of Obama's second term, his war cabinet had debated about whether to arm the Kurds in northern Syria with light weapons. The Kurds would be key to taking Raqqa back from ISIS, but arming them, even only with light weaponry, would anger neighboring Turkey, with its large and sometimes restive Kurdish minority. It was the least bad option on the table, however, since without an effective ground force there was no way to retake a city the size of Raqqa from ISIS. Obama's national security team also debated whether to employ Apache attack helicopters in Syria to support the relatively small number of American troops there.

The Obama team debated these options for so long that it eventually ran out of time to implement them. Three days before he left office, on January 17, 2017, Obama directed that the plans be given to the Trump team, so they could make their own decisions. (President George W. Bush had done something similar when he left office at the end of his second term: his war cabinet had developed plans for a surge of troops into Afghanistan, but he left the decision about its implementation to President Obama.)

In May 2017, Trump approved a plan to arm the tens of thousands of Kurdish forces fighting ISIS in Syria with rifles, machine guns, and lightweight mortars. The Trump plan also lifted Obama-era caps on the size of the US military presence. During Trump's first two years in office, American forces in Syria would rise to two thousand troops.

At the same time that the Trump administration was ramping up the fight against ISIS, it also deftly defused an ISIS plot to slip hard-to-detect bombs disguised in laptops onto flights bound for the United States, bombs that would then be detonated personally by the terrorists on those flights. Israeli government hackers had learned of ISIS's plans when they had hacked into a cell of ISIS bomb makers in Syria. Israeli spies then passed on this intelligence to their American counterparts.

In March, the Department of Homeland Security announced that eight Middle Eastern and African countries that had direct flights to the States could not allow passengers to carry on electronic devices larger than a cell phone. DHS also announced enhanced security measures at all 208 airports around the world that had direct flights into the States, including greater scrutiny of electronic devices and the use of more bomb-sniffing dogs. In late July, the laptop ban was lifted following the implementation of enhanced security procedures at airports in the eight affected countries.

On October 20, 2017, US-backed forces announced that Raqqa was liberated from ISIS. No American soldiers were killed during the liberation of Raqqa. As Raqqa was falling, President Trump took a victory lap during an interview, claiming that ISIS hadn't been defeated earlier because "you didn't have Trump as your president."

Was this claim true? Yes and no. In August 2016, Lieutenant General Sean MacFarland, who was the ground commander for the fight against

ISIS, said the US-led coalition had killed an estimated forty-five thousand ISIS fighters. About a year later, at the Aspen Security Forum in July 2017, the commander of Special Operations Command, General Raymond "Tony" Thomas, said that an estimated sixty thousand to seventy thousand ISIS fighters had been killed since the campaign against the terror group began. According to these senior US military officials, by the summer of 2017 the bulk of ISIS fighters had been killed during the pre-Trump period.

This wasn't surprising since the campaign to eradicate ISIS first began two and a half years before Trump assumed office, when Obama had ordered ISIS positions to be bombed during the summer of 2014. The operation to take back Mosul, the second-largest city in Iraq where ISIS had first declared its "caliphate," began in October 2016 while Obama was still in office, and was long planned. Under Obama, ISIS also lost significant Iraqi cities such as Fallujah, Ramadi, and Tikrit.

Saadi, the Iraqi special forces commander, seemed genuinely puzzled when asked if he had noticed any changes in American support during the more than two years that he had led the Iraqi fight against ISIS. Saadi said, "There was no difference between the support given by Obama and Trump."

There was certainly considerable continuity between the Obama plan against ISIS and the Trump plan in Iraq, but Trump did push down to his military commanders the authorities for taking action against ISIS so that they were no longer micromanaged by the White House, as was often the case under Obama. Also, the Trump administration did away with the self-imposed limits that the Obama team had put on military action in Syria.

So Trump could certainly take credit for hastening the demise of ISIS's geographical "caliphate," but ultimately both presidents approached the ISIS problem in the same essential way. First, they didn't commit large numbers of American boots on the ground in either Iraq or Syria. Second, using US special forces as trainers and advisers, they operated "by, with, and through" local forces. In Iraq, those forces were the Counter-Terrorism Service and its elite Golden Division, while in Syria it was the largely Kurdish fighters of the Syrian Democratic Forces (SDF). American fighters and helicopters provided significant air support to both of these local ground forces. During the five-year campaign against ISIS that began in 2014, the largely Kurdish Syrian Democratic Forces lost eleven thousand soldiers, while seventeen American servicemen were killed in Iraq and Syria.

Trump tended to define any course of action that he took as being markedly different from Obama, but in the case of the anti-ISIS campaign, there were more similarities than differences between the two presidents' approaches.

ISIS once attracted an estimated forty thousand militants from around the world eager to join its so-called caliphate in Syria and Iraq. The Obama and Trump campaigns against ISIS pushed that number close to zero. No one wanted to join the losing team.

The geographical defeat of ISIS in Iraq and Syria did not end the influence of ISIS, however. In a January 2019 report to Congress, the director of national intelligence, Dan Coats, wrote that "ISIS still commands thousands of fighters in Iraq and Syria, and it maintains eight branches, more than a dozen networks, and thousands of dispersed supporters around the world, despite significant leadership and territorial losses."

Three months after Coats's report was published, a Sri Lankan jihadist group inspired by ISIS carried out multiple suicide bombings across the country in churches packed with worshippers who were celebrating Easter Sunday. They also attacked luxury hotels frequented by foreigners, killing at least 250 people. It was one of the most lethal terrorist attacks since 9/11. Any reports of ISIS's demise were premature.

Chapter 7

THE LONGEST WAR

Let's get out of Afghanistan. Our troops are being killed
by the Afghanis we train and we waste billions there.
Nonsense! Rebuild the USA.

—*Tweet from Donald Trump in 2013*

The first, the supreme, the most far-reaching act of
judgment that the statesman and commander have to make
is to establish the kind of war on which they are embarking;
neither mistaking it for, nor trying to turn it into,
something that is alien to its nature.

—*Carl von Clausewitz,* On War

During his campaign, Trump repeatedly complained about the purported "six trillion dollars" that the United States had spent on its post-9/11 wars in the greater Middle East. Trump made it quite clear that he wanted to extricate the US from foreign entanglements such as Afghanistan. On the one hand, Trump was advocating pulling America out of its wars—an Obama position and one of the several commonalities on national security that existed between the two presidents once you got beyond Trump's rhetoric—and on the other hand, Trump was also advocating for a more powerful Pentagon with more funding to fight an unconstrained war against terrorists.

Shortly after Trump was elected, Afghan president Ashraf Ghani called to congratulate him and to make him a pitch about American interests in Afghanistan. Ghani, a savvy technocrat with a PhD in anthropology from Columbia University, told Trump that the Chinese were exploiting Afghanistan's vast potential mineral wealth, thinking that this might capture Trump's attention. Ghani calculated that dangling Afghanistan's minerals might change Trump's calculus about Afghanistan. Trump was intrigued: perhaps the United States could be repaid for its hundreds of billions of dollars of investment in the Afghan War, which was already long past the point of being America's longest war. Estimates of the size of Afghanistan's mineral wealth went as high as one trillion dollars; it was rich in copper, gold, iron ore, and rare earth elements.

Trump tasked commerce secretary Wilbur Ross to look into it. Ross wrote a memo to the president that poured a great deal of cold water on the notion of exploiting Afghanistan's minerals, citing the continuing violence in the country and its rudimentary infrastructure that made extracting the minerals a tricky business proposition. A decade earlier, China had made an expensive effort to exploit Afghanistan's minerals, purchasing with great fanfare a $3 billion long-term lease on a massive copper mine in eastern Afghanistan, but by the time Trump assumed office it still hadn't produced any copper owing to the poor security conditions around the mine.

The need to make a decision about what to do in Afghanistan loomed large. In his first months in office, when Trump encountered a national security problem, he tended to ask the same five questions: "Why do we care?" "Why does it matter to the American people?" "Why can't others do it?" "Who's paying for it?" "Why can't others pay?" On Afghanistan, he asked a further question: "Why are we there sixteen years later?" These were all very good questions. They were also unsettling questions for many in the foreign policy and national security establishment in Washington because they hadn't been asked in a long time.

The simple answer as to why the United States was still at war in Afghanistan was that the only thing worse than staying in Afghanistan was leaving and letting the country revert into a brutal civil war in which the Taliban would take over ever-larger chunks of the country and would then play host to a wide range of jihadist groups, some of which might plot against the United States. After all, ISIS already had a foothold in the country.

Leaving Afghanistan ran the risk of repeating what Trump and his top advisers saw as the big mistake Obama had made in Iraq, which was to not maintain some kind of enduring American military presence there when the Obama administration ended its Iraq mission in the winter of 2011. At that time, General Mattis was the CENTCOM commander overseeing all US military operations in the Middle East. Mattis had advocated leaving eighteen thousand soldiers in Iraq, but he was over-ruled. Together with his hawkish position on Iran, this made Mattis an outlier among the generally dovish Obama national security team.

McMaster had also been concerned in 2011 that the withdrawal of

US troops from Iraq would provide an opening for al-Qaeda. He had forwarded to the chairman of the Joint Chiefs an intelligence assessment that predicted that al-Qaeda was going to come back in a new form and would take over large swaths of territory.

If there was one argument that Trump often found a winner, it was to do the opposite of his predecessor. Trump had already pulled out of the Trans-Pacific Partnership (TPP)—the trade deal with a dozen nations in Asia that was designed to contain the rise of China—as well as the Paris climate accord. Now he could buck his predecessor by reversing the drawdown of troops in Afghanistan instigated by Obama, but this also ran the risk of doing something that Trump hated, which was admitting in some shape or form that his campaign rhetoric about the wasteful wars in the greater Middle East was wrong.

In 2015, Obama had seriously considered completely withdrawing all US troops from the country. After all, Obama himself had run on a promise of drawing down from America's expensive overseas wars. Susan Rice, Obama's national security adviser, saw her role as executing Obama's vision to get the United States out of Afghanistan and to leave only a vestigial American military presence there to guard the massive US embassy in Kabul.

However, once you got into the details, that plan didn't make much sense. American troops were needed to protect the vital Kabul International Airport and also to support US counterterrorism operations, including CIA drones that continued to deploy to Pakistan's Federally Administered Tribal Areas along the border with Afghanistan to hunt for members of al-Qaeda and Taliban leaders who had found safe haven there.

Also, always in the background of the discussion of the Afghan drawdown in the Obama White House was the fiasco that had unfolded in Iraq after all US troops there were pulled out of the country at the end of 2011. This had contributed to a vacuum in Iraq that ISIS had taken great advantage of during the summer of 2014. No one wanted a replay of that in Afghanistan.

The rise of ISIS across the greater Middle East and the fall of the northern Afghan city of Kunduz to the Taliban in late September 2015, which held the city for two weeks, as well as the extended political crisis between the Afghan president Ashraf Ghani and his political rival, Afghan chief executive officer Abdullah Abdullah, had made Obama realize that going to zero troops could be very destabilizing. Obama might then get blamed for "losing" Afghanistan, just as he was blamed for pulling out of Iraq four years earlier.

At President Obama's final strategy meeting on Afghanistan, it was obvious how distasteful this decision was for him. While Obama wanted to withdraw, he couldn't just zero out troops in Afghanistan shortly before the next president assumed office, as that would leave his successor with little flexibility for maneuver. Obama cut off any further discussion of a withdrawal, saying simply, "I'm leaving the decision to my successor." As he left office, Obama authorized a force of 8,400 troops to remain in Afghanistan.

Shortly after Trump had assumed office, General John "Mick" Nicholson, the overall commander of the Afghan War, testified before the Senate Armed Services Committee that this troop level was insufficient. "We have a shortfall of a few thousand" advisers to train and assist the Afghan army, Nicholson testified. Nicholson also noted that the war was in a "stalemate" with the Taliban. Those comments irritated White House officials as they thought that they had boxed Trump in even before a decision was made about what to do in Afghanistan, in much the same way President Obama had felt boxed in early in his first term in office when a top-secret Pentagon assessment had leaked that asserted that the Afghan War effort needed significantly more troops.

McMaster had a deep interest in Afghanistan. He had led an anticorruption task force there from 2010 to 2012, handpicked by General Petraeus, who had taken over command in Afghanistan from General McChrystal. Fixing corruption in Afghanistan was like trying to stop hurricanes from landing in Florida, but McMaster—a man of enormous energy who didn't so much enter a room as bound into it—gave it his all and recruited a small group of civilian experts to help him. McMaster and his team targeted the patronage networks that were looting and undermining the Afghan state. When a problem came up in Afghanistan, McMaster told his team, "We're going to crush this."

His time in Afghanistan deeply informed McMaster's views about what to do there once he was in the White House. McMaster had been very frustrated with the Obama administration policy in Afghanistan to publicly announce withdrawal dates from the country. Obama had surged tens of thousands of additional US troops into Afghanistan, but when he gave a speech at West Point on December 1, 2009, announcing the new surge of troops, he also simultaneously announced their withdrawal date. For the Taliban, the Afghan government, and Afghanistan's neighbors such as Pakistan, the headline of Obama's West Point speech was not the surge of new troops but this withdrawal date. In McMaster's view, this had encouraged the Taliban, undermined confidence among Afghans, and affected the hedging strategy of Pakistan's military intelligence service, Inter-Services Intelligence (ISI), which had long supported elements of the Taliban.

It was not only Trump who was skeptical about the Afghan War. Much of the American public had tuned it out as an endless, unwinnable quagmire. On April 13, 2017, Afghanistan was suddenly back in the news because a 22,000-pound Massive Ordnance Air Blast bomb—known colloquially as the "Mother of All Bombs," or MOAB—was dropped near the Afghanistan-Pakistan border, aimed at ISIS militants who were hiding out there in caves and tunnels in the mountains. The MOAB, designed to blow up underground tunnel and cave complexes, was the most lethal nonnuclear bomb in the American arsenal.

ISIS had established a presence in eastern Afghanistan two years earlier, consisting mostly of former members of the Taliban who had rebranded themselves as ISIS. The dropping of the MOAB was ordered by General Nicholson as part of Operation Green Sword, the name that the US military gave to its operations against ISIS. Nicholson had the authority to drop such a bomb, but the deployment of the MOAB, which received a great deal of press coverage as it seemed to presage a more aggressive Trump-led Pentagon, in fact, caught the White House by surprise. Trump's national security staffers had no idea it was going to happen.

The deployment of the MOAB underlined that the Afghan War was not going well. ISIS and al-Qaeda had both established footholds in Afghanistan, while the Taliban controlled around 10 percent of the population, some three million people, and they contested with government forces for control of a much larger proportion, about a third of the population, or around ten million people. Whereas a few years earlier, Kabul, the Afghan capital, had enjoyed a bustling restaurant scene and Westerners could live there and lead relatively normal lives, all that was now gone as a result of the multiple bombings in Kabul by the Taliban, compounded by their targeted kidnapping of Westerners. The resulting exodus of Westerners from the country damaged investment and development efforts in Afghanistan. The war in Afghanistan was now at its lowest point for the Afghans and their American allies since the Taliban were overthrown in the months after 9/11.

The key point of McMaster's book *Dereliction of Duty* was that the Pentagon brass had told President Lyndon Johnson only what he wanted to hear about how the Vietnam War was going. McMaster was not going to make the same mistake with Trump, whose natural inclination was to pull the plug on Afghanistan. It was obvious to McMaster what the United States should do: bulk up its military presence in the country and make no premature promises of withdrawal. Also, because the Taliban had long enjoyed sanctuary in neighboring Pakistan, it was time to turn up the heat on the Pakistanis. Finally, something needed to be done about the endemic corruption marbling the Afghan state.

Faced with the worsening situation in Afghanistan, the Trump administration started a strategic review, led by McMaster, of what to do there. As part of his review, McMaster wanted to visit Afghanistan and neighboring Pakistan to get a sense of what was happening on the ground. This idea angered Mattis, who felt he owned the issue as secretary of defense. It also irritated Tillerson, who felt he owned the issue as secretary of state. Both of them tried unsuccessfully to torpedo McMaster's trip. Yet neither Mattis nor Tillerson presented his own substantive views about what to do in Afghanistan during the review process.

In mid-April 2017, McMaster left for Kabul with a team of officials from the CIA, Pentagon, and State Department. In Kabul, the Afghan interior minister briefed McMaster. After half an hour, McMaster told him: "Thanks. Well, you know, I'm really disappointed. These are the same bullshit talking points that I heard five years ago. You guys have major issues in your organizations to do with corruption."

McMaster asked his team to put together a page of talking points to sell the strategy to increase the troop levels in Afghanistan and also to drive home that there were considerable risks to US counterterrorism operations if there was a precipitous drawdown from the country since much of the infrastructure to locate and kill al-Qaeda and allied groups in the region had been built up in Afghanistan over the past decade and a half.

McMaster's team added to the talking points a packet of photographs of what Afghanistan had looked like under Taliban rule and what it looked like more than a decade and a half later. The CIA provided photographs of the streets around Massoud Circle, a key traffic intersection in Kabul, during the time that the Taliban were in power and had turned the city into a ghost town and also photographs of how it looked now in 2017 jammed with traffic and pedestrians.

McMaster showed Trump some forty photographs of Afghanistan in various phases over the past half century; a third of the photos were before the Soviet invasion in 1979, when the country was a quiet, bucolic place untroubled by the violence to come. Another third of the photos showed Afghanistan under the Taliban regime, and a third were of more recent vintage. The photos were a visual reminder that Afghanistan hadn't always been the hopeless case so many believed it to be.

McMaster felt that for too long US officials working on the Afghanistan account pushed for policies that effectively favored the Taliban.

Also lingering over all this in his mind was the Obama experience of pulling all US troops out of Iraq, which helped pave the way for the collapse of the Iraqi army in the face of ISIS. This was an important counterargument to the common view that the US should just leave Afghanistan on the grounds that "it's always going to be a shithole, and they're killing each other and always going to be killing each other." McMaster pointed out that an American withdrawal might lead to the collapse of the Afghan state, which would pose a risk to the civilized world and provide a psychological victory for the Taliban and other jihadist terrorist organizations.

Trump wanted to "win" in Afghanistan, but the Pentagon wasn't really offering a win against the Taliban, which enjoyed a comfortable safe haven in neighboring Pakistan and some measure of support in rural Pashtun areas. What the Pentagon was offering was a strategy to manage the conflict so that the Taliban didn't take over much of the country and host a number of jihadist groups that they'd long had relations with, including al-Qaeda.

The Pentagon brass knew that a rough rule of thumb to defeat an insurgency was a ratio of twenty troops per thousand of population. Afghanistan had a population of thirty million so that meant six hundred thousand troops were needed to stabilize the country. The roughly four hundred thousand Afghan soldiers and police meant there was still a shortfall of two hundred thousand troops, and filling that gap with American servicemen was a nonstarter, whoever the president was. Insurgencies such as the Taliban could also last many years. It had taken the Colombian government half a century of fighting before it could negotiate a peace deal with the Marxist insurgent group the FARC.

In one of the many meetings about Afghanistan, the chairman of the Joint Chiefs, General Dunford, made the point that a sustained presence in Afghanistan was like buying life insurance. Dunford said, "No one likes writing the check every year for a life insurance policy, but you do it because the downside risk of not doing it just doesn't make sense."

Trump wanted a win. His generals were offering life insurance.

Trump remained convinced that Afghanistan was a futile endeavor, in the name of which the United States had wasted trillions of dollars. He told his advisers, "My New York friends tell me nothing good ever comes out of Afghanistan." Trump bought the "Graveyard of Empires" narrative that the Afghans had defeated first the British and then the Russians and the United States was just the latest great power that was eventually going to fail there.

Also, Trump hated being railroaded. Trump understood himself as the guy who was making the decisions and he did not want to feel that he was being driven to a decision, or that he wasn't making the decisions, somebody else was. On Afghanistan Trump felt he was getting railroaded.

McMaster usually exuded a contagious confidence, but as the months went by it was clear that it was not going to be easy to get his Afghan strategy approved. Bannon, Kellogg, and Trump's homeland security adviser, Tom Bossert, all channeled Trump's extreme skepticism about the Afghan War. Like the president, none of them had ever visited Afghanistan, nor had any of them had any experience fighting jihadist terrorists or any special knowledge about jihadism. Depending on your perspective, this either gave them a fresh pair of eyes to examine "the problem set" or they were simply deeply ignorant about the issue.

McMaster told the skeptics at the White House, "Hey, we're losing the war, but what we have to acknowledge is that we've been operating under a withdrawal strategy for eight years and that *might* have something to do with us losing. The previous approach was, we're not going to fight the Taliban. We're not going to have them as a declared enemy and we're going to tell them we're leaving and we're going to try to negotiate a deal with them while they're in the ascendancy militarily. How the fuck does that work?!"

White House officials briefed reporters that there would be a final decision about what the plan was in Afghanistan sometime in May 2017. That month, Trump attended his first "principals" committee of the

National Security Council to discuss the Afghan War. Surrounded by "his" generals, Trump told them that their plan to stay the course in Afghanistan was bullshit. The generals knew at a deep level about all the blood and treasure that had already been invested in Afghanistan. That was part of their calculus to keep on keeping the faith with the Afghan people and the thousands of Americans who had died there on the battlefield. Trump was a businessman who understood the business concept of "sunk costs." It made no sense to consider the sunk costs already invested in a project when you were making a decision about whether to continue investing in it since those costs could never be recovered. You just cut your losses and moved on.

May came and went without any decision.

Relations between Trump and McMaster were fraying. McMaster didn't go to Mar-a-Lago regularly with the president, which meant that he had less face time with Trump than those who did go. Where other senior officials put a premium on presidential face time, McMaster put a premium on making sure that he had closely vetted the papers that were circulated to other cabinet members and their staffs. McMaster was a grind while those who connected with Trump were schmoozers.

Also, McMaster made a point of saying what he believed, and he could also do it at some length. McMaster tended to communicate with Trump by saying: "Sir, I have five points for you."

Trump hated getting briefed this way and McMaster didn't seem to read the president well. On Air Force One on a foreign trip, Gary Cohn and McMaster were sharing the same room on the flight. Trump walked in and they both stood up. The president wasn't wearing a tie and his shirtsleeves were rolled up. His body language said "I'm not working right now." You could tell he was chilling.

While Cohn made some small talk with Trump about the markets, McMaster immediately launched into "When we land, sir, these are the things that we need to do."

The president replied, "Ah, yeah, it'll be great" and promptly walked out of the room.

Cohn poked some gentle fun at McMaster. "Hey, H. R. How'd that go for you?"

McMaster's inability to click with Trump was puzzling because when he was out of Trump's presence he was charming, funny, and well liked.

One morning during a White House staff meeting, the gruff, deadly serious chief of staff, John Kelly, asked McMaster if he had read a particular piece of sensitive intelligence. McMaster replied, "Sir, I did not. I was in the gym. You don't think a body like this just happens?" The staff cracked up.

McMaster could also quote verbatim chunks of *A Mighty Wind*, a comic mockumentary about folk musicians. When the first draft of the Afghan strategy landed on McMaster's desk that he deemed too wishy-washy, McMaster scrawled on it, "Did we outsource this to the Taliban?"

Trump frequently raised with Mattis and McMaster the issue of the American THAAD missile battery systems that were deployed in South Korea. This was one of their least favorite discussions with the president, as it would always set him off about burden sharing and the South Koreans ripping off the United States.

Trump asked them, "Do you send them a bill? Do they just pay us? How does it work? My generals don't know anything about business. How do you think we fucking pay for this stuff? Find out."

The generals pointed out that the United States owned the THAAD missiles. They had not been "given" to the South Koreans, and they were there to protect the one hundred thousand American citizens living in South Korea. They were also a cheaper option than installing Patriot missiles.

The South Koreans donated the land on which the missiles were stationed. Trump said, "What do you mean they give us the land? They give us some shitty golf courses. Shitty golf courses. No, no, change it. Just change it." He told Mattis, "Jim, call 'em up. We've got to be paid."

When it came to American defense arrangements overseas, Trump always asked, "What are we getting out of it? Why are we paying for everything?" After all, South Korea had one of the largest economies in the world.

The downward trajectory in the relationship between Trump and McMaster began in late April 2017 when McMaster seemed to publicly contradict the president on the deployment of the American missiles in South Korea. Knowing how strongly Trump felt that the South Koreans should pay for the missile systems, McMaster went on TV to say that the US would pay for the billion-dollar system, as the deal for the missiles had already been negotiated.

This pointed to a problem that McMaster faced; he had remained in uniform while he was national security adviser. As a uniformed officer, he was supposed to stay out of politics, but working at the White House for Trump was an inherently political job, in particular because Trump wanted McMaster to defend him on TV.*

This disconnect became obvious in early May 2017 after Trump shared highly classified information with the Russian foreign minister and the Russian ambassador to the United States when they were visiting the White House about ISIS's capabilities to carry out an attack "external" to Syria, intelligence that had come from the Israelis.

Trump told the Russians, "Our interests align in Syria because the civil war is allowing ISIS to still enjoy safe haven there. Isn't this an area where we ought to be working together?" Trump added, "We got this intel and it's telling us there's this threat to passenger jets from laptops filled with explosives made by ISIS."

---

* McMaster really had little choice but to remain in uniform as the process to retire from the military generally took months, especially for those who were wounded as McMaster was and who would require long-term medical treatment. McMaster's armored personnel carrier was blown up in Iraq in 2005 and as a result he had an artificial hip. Trump announced that McMaster was his next national security adviser when he was at Mar-a-Lago on Monday, February 20, 2017. A day later McMaster was working at the White House.

After the story broke in the *Washington Post* on May 15 that Trump had shared this intelligence with the Russians, McMaster gave a very brief statement to the press outside the West Wing of the White House, saying, "What [he] shared was wholly appropriate. . . . I wanted to make clear to everybody that the president in no way compromised any sources or methods." Both of these statements were true; the president could declassify whatever he wanted to whomever he wanted because the president was the ultimate declassification authority. Trump also didn't share sources and methods with the Russians; he didn't even know what the sources and methods were, as that was a level of detail most presidents wouldn't concern themselves with.

The fact that Trump was sharing top-secret information with the Russians and that McMaster was publicly defending the president precipitated a chorus of national security experts to criticize McMaster. Retired lieutenant colonel John Nagl, a leading counterinsurgency theorist, told NPR that McMaster was "diminished in some ways. His integrity has taken a bit of a hit." Pulitzer Prize–winning military journalist Tom Ricks wrote in *Politico* that McMaster should step down.

A massive truck bomb blew up in Kabul's diplomatic quarter on May 31, 2017, killing more than 150 people. The bombing underlined the worsening security situation in Afghanistan. Ordinary Afghans blamed the government for their increasing security problems. McMaster and his team were worried that the fragile Afghan government might fracture under the pressure.

Two weeks later, President Trump delegated the decision about whether to add more troops in Afghanistan to Mattis, but Mattis didn't make any decision about what to do with that authority until it was clear what the president actually planned to do in Afghanistan.

One of the most significant military shifts between Obama and Trump was that Trump changed the rules of engagement in Afghanistan. Under Obama those rules were quite restrictive; American soldiers could engage the Taliban only if they themselves were under attack. Trump allowed commanders leeway to attack the Taliban more or less at will.

As Trump's national security team met to discuss Afghanistan, the subtext of the discussions was, What could be a policy that Trump would agree to? What would fly with him?

Tillerson, who hadn't attended any of the previous meetings on Afghanistan, now intervened in one of the Afghan discussions to say, "I don't know why we're in such a hurry. Well, you may have this figured out, but I just don't have it figured out yet."

During policy deliberations, Tillerson often asked, "What's the rush?" It was the attitude of an oil executive used to investing in long-term projects that might take decades before they could turn a profit.

Tillerson also seemed incapable of focusing on more than one priority at a time. At one point he was focused on Syria, at another he was focused on the Gulf crisis in which a number of Arab states had blockaded Qatar, a US ally. It was almost as if Tillerson thought everything else in the world could wait, or someone else could just take care of it, while he was focused on his small number of priorities in his systematic, deliberate way.

Tillerson was also largely cut off from the rest of the State Department, dealing almost entirely with only a small coterie of close aides. Strangely, Tillerson also didn't do much to defend the State Department from a dramatic 30 percent cut proposed by the Trump administration, a rather unusual position for the leader of a government department. Nor did Tillerson do much to inform Trump about what he was doing. Tillerson's attitude seemed to be, you hired the CEO of an independent company and I'll report in to the board at the end of the year.

The decision-making on Afghanistan started to get even more complicated by late spring 2017 because an alternative plan was in play that was touted by Erik Prince, a former Navy SEAL and the founder of the notorious contracting firm Blackwater, now "rebranded" as Academi.

Prince also happened to be the brother of Betsy DeVos, Trump's education secretary. Both were major donors to Republican causes. In an op-ed in the *Wall Street Journal* on May 31, Prince proposed a plan for Afghanistan that would outsource much of the war to contractors on long-term assignments overseen by an American "viceroy." Prince had two sons who were likely to go into the military, and he did not want them to end up serving in what he thought was a poorly run war.

Prince wrote his *Journal* op-ed "for an audience of one." He knew that President Trump read the *Journal* carefully. Trump circled the op-ed in the paper and asked his advisers to get hold of Prince.

A few days after his *Journal* article came out, Prince received a call from the White House inviting him to discuss his plan. Over lunch with Bannon, McMaster, and Priebus in the chief of staff's office, Prince briefed the plan.

Prince identified a fundamental problem with the Afghan War: the relatively short tours for the US military forces that served there. Army units typically deployed to Afghanistan for a year, while marine units went for even shorter tours. The mordant joke about Afghanistan was that the United States had fought a new war there every year since 9/11.

Prince explained, "You're sending mostly twenty-somethings who have never been out of America before to a very foreign land, where they're going to have to patrol and live on a firebase. And they are bewildered the first three or four months they're there. And then they might be productive for a few months, maybe, but driving around and waiting to get shot at. They're not surprising anybody *ever*, and then they spend the last few months packing up and making sure everybody comes home. And then you lift that entire unit up, send it home, and you repeat it again. If that's not the definition of insanity, I don't know what is."

Prince's solution was to contract veteran, retired special operations soldiers who had deployed multiple times to Afghanistan and other war zones who would embed repeatedly with the same Afghan battalion over long periods of time.

Bannon and Priebus loved the plan. Bannon saw it as a way out of America's longest war.

McMaster agreed with Prince's analysis of the problems in Afghanistan but thought that what he was proposing about using contractors to fight the war wasn't feasible from a legal perspective and that the Afghan government needed to weigh in about the plan, which they were likely to be skeptical of.

Prince followed up his *Journal* piece with a story in *USA Today* claiming that his plan would cost "less than 20% of the $48 billion being spent in Afghanistan." Prince went on CNN, Fox, and NPR to publicize his plan, which he said would save considerable money. Gorka also appeared on CNN to defend the Prince plan, saying, "This is a cost-cutting venture. . . . We open the door here at the White House to outside ideas."

Prince compared the plan to the renovation of Central Park's Wollman ice-skating rink in 1986, when the New York City government, unable to renovate on schedule or on budget, turned to a brash young developer named Donald Trump, who took over the renovation of the rink and completed it in record time.

Two weeks after their White House meeting, Bannon called Prince, saying, "Hey, the Afghan discussion is still getting some legs. You said you could do it for less than a fifth of what's being spent now."

Prince replied, "It's an estimate."

Bannon told Prince, "Prove it. Figure out exactly what you would need. Price it. Come back with a detailed concept of operations."

Prince circulated a detailed account of his plan to senior Trump officials. It called for more than five thousand military contractors to be embedded with each Afghan battalion. The contractors would all be Western special forces veterans hired on contract backed up by a ninety-plane private air force. In Prince's view, this new force would enable the American troop presence to draw down to two thousand in under two years. Prince's plan also emphasized the extraction from Afghanistan of rare earth minerals such as lithium, which would be useful for US high-tech manufacturing.

Stephen Feinberg, a billionaire who owned the giant contracting firm DynCorp International, embraced the Prince plan. The plan seemed a little self-serving as Prince and Feinberg were two of the largest players in the war contracting industry, while trial balloons in the press even put Feinberg forward as the possible "viceroy."

Beyond all that, the Prince plan had some serious legal and political problems. Legally, the Pentagon was not about to contract out its military operations to mercenaries, many of whom wouldn't even be American citizens. It was one thing to have contractors provide base security or train local police forces, it was quite another to have contractors involved in US military operations where they would be killing people.

Prince had an answer for that objection, which was to take these contractors out from under the control of the Pentagon and put them instead under "Title 50," the US authorization for covert action. To those who didn't like Prince's plan, in some ways this was an even worse idea as it meant that a private army of thousands of Americans and other Westerners under the aegis of the CIA would be fighting alongside the Afghan army.

Politically, Afghan leaders didn't want an army of thousands of CIA-sponsored contractors running the war in their country, nor did they yearn for the arrival of an American "viceroy," with all of its implied baggage of the British Empire, which had fought three wars in Afghanistan overseen by the British viceroy in New Delhi.*

Prince did get a sympathetic hearing for his plan at CIA headquarters from its director, Mike Pompeo. Pompeo was first in his class at West Point, so he had credibility with the Pentagon. But top officials at CIA were quite skeptical of the Prince plan and worked to kill it.

Pompeo told Prince, "It will take too long for the agency to spool up to be able to do oversight for the plan."

Prince replied, "The agency would have to only send thirty people. That's it. You send some financial controllers."

In early July, Prince went to see Mattis at his office in the Pentagon,

---

* In his *Journal* op-ed, Prince specifically referenced some of this British imperial history when he pointed to the model of the East India Company that raised local armies in India supported by European professional soldiers who served on a contractual basis for multiyear deployments. Today the East India Company is regarded with little nostalgia in India as it ruthlessly plundered the Indian subcontinent.

spending an hour and a half with him going through the slides of his plan. Mattis observed that the model seemed similar to what the marine corps had done in Nicaragua and the Dominican Republic during the "banana wars" in the 1920s.

Mattis, who had seen firsthand the total destruction caused by war in cities such as Fallujah in Iraq, wondered what would happen if a contractor destroyed an elementary school in Afghanistan. Prince suggested that maybe the contractor could be hauled in front of the Afghan judicial system. Mattis looked at Prince quizzically; the Afghan "justice system" was an almost perfect oxymoron.

It was clear to Prince that Mattis had taken the meeting only because the White House had asked him to do so. Mattis made it clear that the Pentagon wouldn't be considering the contractor option.

National Security Council staffers prepared a memo about the costs of using contractors to wage the war in Afghanistan. They concluded that the promised savings from using mercenaries were likely illusory since a key reason that military veterans took these contractor jobs was the high salaries they paid. The NSC also underlined the legal obstacles to privatizing the war and putting contractors on the front lines. And, not least, America's NATO allies training and advising the Afghan army would pull out of Afghanistan absent a US military presence.

Several members of Trump's cabinet were skeptical about the Prince plan, but other key officials were just as skeptical about McMaster's plan to add more troops. Chief among the latter group was Attorney General Jeff Sessions. Sessions, who had served on the Senate Armed Services Committee for more than a decade, was something of an isolationist, and often asked, "Why are Americans dying in Afghanistan? My sense is the president got elected because he was going to get us out of these *foreign* wars."

In the early months of the Trump administration, before he recused himself from the Russia investigation and angered Trump, Sessions was an influential voice on policy decisions that were beyond the traditional purview of the attorney general. Sessions told other officials, "I love the generals. They're good men, but goddamit I heard this same bullshit; it's always going to get better in eighteen months. McMaster says the same thing: 'Eighteen months it's going to be fine. It all turns around.'" McMaster spent hours trying to persuade Sessions of the wisdom of staying in Afghanistan.

Gary Cohn, Trump's top economic adviser and often an ally of McMaster's, also raised questions about Afghanistan, along the lines of "Aren't we just throwing good money after bad?"

The debate over the Afghan War devolved into a cage match between Bannon and McMaster. Bannon cast the learned general as a globalist who was betraying Trump and his base, while McMaster considered Bannon a rank amateur. Bannon thought McMaster's plan was a slippery slope to "nation building." He also seemed to nurse a grudge that McMaster had eliminated his permanent seat on the National Security Council.

At one meeting on Afghanistan in the Situation Room that was packed with officials from across the government including Mattis and Tillerson, McMaster opened by saying, "The presentation you'll see today is interagency and I want to tell you this is the finest team that has ever come together."

Bannon took strong exception to these opening remarks. He responded by saying, "We've been at this for seventeen years. In this same room has sat people from the widest differences in ideology, from the Bush guys to the Obama guys. Trust me, every one of those people was just as smart as we are. Even the progressives, with whom I disagree totally ideologically, are just as much patriots as we are and thought they were doing what's right for our country and for the country of Afghanistan. And all I have to say as we start this presentation is we're two trillion dollars into this and we're farther away from victory today than we were seventeen years ago, so I don't want to hear how brilliant we are or how brilliant this fucking presentation is."

His eyes bulging out of his bald head, McMaster leaned forward in his seat and stared at Bannon for a full five seconds and said, "Unfortunately, some of us are trying to manipulate the president." The vitriol between the two men was palpable.

In a barroom fight, McMaster, a stocky, bald-headed former rugby player with the coiled energy of a boxer poised to strike, would likely have made short work of Bannon, who hadn't seen the inside of a gym in many years and always dressed like an unmade bed.

But Bannon wasn't going to back down, interjecting, "Let's get on with the presentation, but let's cut the bullshit. I don't want to hear how great we are and how fucked up everyone else is."

Bannon turned to Tom Bossert, Trump's homeland security adviser, and asked him, "The Taliban or al-Qaeda: Right now, can they launch an attack on the homeland?"

Bossert replied that it would be "very difficult, but not a no. But still very difficult."

With the aid of Bossert, Bannon was trying to make the case that the terrorism threat to the United States emanating from Afghanistan was in fact relatively small, while the likelihood that Afghanistan would remain a ward of the United States long into the future was quite large. In this, he was not wrong.

On July 9, CIA director Mike Pompeo made a surprise visit to Afghanistan. Pompeo was there to explore a third option for Trump that wasn't either a complete withdrawal or the addition of thousands more troops. The third option involved the CIA's paramilitary arm, the Special Activities Division, expanding its covert operations in Afghanistan to hunt for Taliban leaders, or some aspect of the Erik Prince plan to use more special forces veterans working under the CIA.

Trump told his advisers he wanted to hear from servicemen who had deployed to Afghanistan, "I want to sit down with some enlisted guys that have been there. I don't want any generals in here. I don't want any officers. I just want enlisted guys," he explained. This was the way Trump ran his hotels and golf clubs; he didn't just talk to the general manager, he also spoke with the doorman and the concierge and the guy doing the greens.

The first group who came to see Trump in early July were Navy

SEALs, most of whom had served multiple tours in Afghanistan. They unloaded on Trump, telling him: "It's unwinnable. NATO's a joke. Nobody knows what they're doing. We don't fight to win. The morale is terrible. It's totally corrupt. The officials in the government are awful people. They lie to you. You don't know who's Taliban or who's not."

Trump loved the discussion so much he said, "I want to do this again." On July 18, Trump met at the White House with four other enlisted servicemen who had served in Afghanistan to get their input about what to do there. Trump told reporters, "I want to find out why we've been there for seventeen years, how it's going, and what we should do in terms of additional ideas. I've heard plenty of ideas from a lot of people, but I want to hear it from the people on the ground."

The servicemen gave the president their version of "ground truth" about Afghanistan, which partly fed into a narrative that Trump already believed: NATO was a waste of time, the NATO guys were just there to punch their tour ticket, the Afghan government and Afghan system were corrupt, and the US didn't have a strategy. But the soldiers also emphasized that the president should continue to support the Afghan mission because Afghanistan remained a place where jihadist terrorists were finding safe haven. One of the soldiers told Trump, "We need to complete our mission there so my grandchildren don't have to go. If we leave, we'll have to go back."

On July 19, a day after his meeting with the Afghan veterans, Trump met with his war cabinet in the Situation Room. Trump's national security team had hoped that this meeting would produce some kind of resolution about what to do in Afghanistan. Instead, it turned into a fiasco.

Trump opened by observing that the servicemen he had spoken to a day earlier "know a lot more than you generals." "We're losing," Trump said. He repeatedly demanded that the Pentagon fire General John "Mick" Nicholson, the well-regarded US commander in Afghanistan who had served in the country for a total of five years. Mattis and Joseph Dunford, chairman of the Joint Chiefs, tried to defend Nicholson's conduct of the war, while also trying to avoid arguing directly with the president.

Mattis felt that it was his responsibility to deal with Trump and insulate the Pentagon from the gale-force political winds emanating from the White House, so Mattis kept key four-star generals like Nicholson away from the president. Nicholson never met with Trump and as a result he was an easy target. Mattis even kept Dunford largely away from Trump. Dunford had been a frequent visitor to the White House when he served as the chairman of the Joint Chiefs for Obama. During the Trump administration, the top US military officer rarely went to the White House.

In the Situation Room, Trump then went into an extended riff comparing the Afghan War review by his war cabinet to the renovation of a Manhattan restaurant in the late 1980s that Trump had dined at frequently over the decades, the 21 Club. Trump asserted that the restaurant had closed for a yearlong renovation and had hired an expensive consultant whose sole suggestion was to expand the kitchen.[*] Fresh off his discussions with the group of Afghan veterans, Trump said that soliciting the advice of the restaurant's waiters would have been smarter than hiring the costly consultant.

It would have been hard to come up with a more insulting analogy to use with the people assembled in the Situation Room. Renovating a chi-chi restaurant in Manhattan was hardly analogous to fighting a complex war on the other side of the world where three key members of Trump's war cabinet had served as general officers. It was also a conflict in which thousands of Americans had died, including a young marine who was particularly well known to some of the senior officials in the "Sit Room."

Three years earlier, General Dunford had been the overall US commander in the theater, and John Kelly, Trump's homeland security chief, had lost a son in Afghanistan, twenty-nine-year-old Marine First Lieutenant Robert Kelly, who was killed by a landmine in 2010. It was Dunford who volunteered to perform the difficult task of delivering the terrible news of the death of his son to his old friend General Kelly.

---

* In fact, in 1987 the 21 Club had closed for two months for a widely lauded renovation.

Four days after his son's death, in a speech in St. Louis, Kelly said that the United States' war against jihadist terrorists would go on for a very long time: "The American military has handed our ruthless enemy defeat after defeat, but it will go on for years, if not decades, before this curse has been eradicated."

Astonishingly, as the decision about the Afghan War was being debated, Trump once said in Kelly's presence that the young American men who had died in Afghanistan had died for a worthless cause. Trump said, "We got our boys who are over there being blown up every day for what? For nothing. Guys are dying for nothing. There's nothing worth dying for in that country." Did Trump not know that Kelly's son had died in Afghanistan? Did he not care?

Dunford, Kelly, and Mattis were close, a closeness forged on the battlefields of Iraq where they had all served together. They also were all marine generals, keenly aware that 349 marines were killed in the southern Afghan province of Helmand in a campaign that began there in 2009 and ended five years later.

The meeting ended inconclusively. Trump was pissed off about his options, which boiled down to staying the course for many years into the future as well as adding thousands more troops, or withdrawing and risking the collapse of the Afghan state and the return of the Taliban to power along with their allies in al-Qaeda and other jihadist groups. There was also something of a third course emerging that Pompeo was considering, which was accelerating the pace of CIA operations in Afghanistan.

Mattis was fuming as he left the meeting with Trump, but he and the other current and former marine generals at the apex of Trump's national security team seemed largely content to let McMaster lead the charge for pushing to augment the number of troops in Afghanistan. McMaster would expend much political capital advocating for an Afghan policy about which there was considerable consensus among Trump's war cabinet yet that was intensely disliked by the president.

An NSC staffer recalled that McMaster "got shot in the face for articulating views that other people also held but were not articulating."

Holding the gun were the America First nationalists in the White House led by Bannon. As Bannon recalled, "On Afghanistan, I lit those fuckers up every day."

Trump's skepticism about the Afghan War was further confirmed when a senior NSC official told him, "We cannot succeed in Afghanistan unless we resolve the Pakistan issue. It doesn't matter if you bring in twenty thousand troops or ten thousand troops. It doesn't matter. We are on a treadmill ad infinitum. This has been the same case from the time Obama and Stan McChrystal went in there." Trump listened but didn't say anything.

Trump was convinced that the United States had long overstayed its welcome and purpose in Afghanistan. In meetings about the Afghan War, Trump was very critical of Bush and Obama, who had allowed the conflict to continue without finding some way to end it. Trump was intent on bringing the war to a close. Mattis, Tillerson, and particularly McMaster worked to convince the president that anything done precipitously in Afghanistan was going to have profoundly negative consequences in South Asia and Central Asia and would undermine the United States' standing as a great power.

When Trump thought that he was being manipulated or managed, he responded negatively, sometimes very harshly. Trump became deeply frustrated with McMaster and thought that he was being driven to certain conclusions on Afghanistan. When Tillerson recognized this, he stepped further away from McMaster, not wanting to be in the blast zone.

As the Afghan War decision dragged on, McMaster fired a number of Bannon's allies at the National Security Council, some of whom were incompetent and others who McMaster believed were ineffective or were trying to undermine him.

The first to go was Rich Higgins, the director for strategic planning at the NSC, who had circulated a bizarre memo rife with conspiracy theories about Trump's purported "deep state" enemies in the US government whom he characterized as Marxists. In Higgins's telling, these Marxists were allied to Islamists in a conspiracy that also included the European Union and the UN. The Higgins memo concluded, "This is a form of population control by certain business cartels in league with cultural Marxists/corporatists/Islamists who will leverage Islamic terrorism threats to justify the creation of a police state." This was not the kind of sober thinking that typically came out of the strategic planning shop at the NSC. McMaster's deputy Ricky Waddell gave Higgins his marching orders on July 21.

Next to go a few days later was the overall lead for the Middle East at the NSC, Derek Harvey. Harvey and McMaster had known each other for years, but McMaster felt compelled to remove him because he didn't play well with others. Harvey went back to the House Intelligence Committee, where he had worked for the chairman of the committee, Representative Devin Nunes, before joining the Trump administration.

Another administration official removed by McMaster who was viewed as a Bannon ally was Ezra Cohen-Watnick who oversaw intelligence at the NSC. Cohen-Watnick had been peripherally (and unwittingly) involved when White House Counsel Michael Ellis briefed Rep. Nunes at a cloak-and-dagger White House meeting that US intelligence agencies had picked up the communications of some members of Trump's transition team suspected of being Russian assets. This briefing was intended to "prove" Trump's claim that Obama had "tapped" his lines at Trump Tower during the transition. In a statement that McMaster made about Cohen-Watnick's departure, he said he was "confident that Ezra would make many further significant contributions to national security in another position in the administration." This is Washington-speak for "Don't let the door hit you on the way out."

Over the summer, Bannon's allies in the far right-wing media began a systematic campaign to discredit McMaster, attacking him personally and also attacking some of the staffers who worked for him. A particular target was Javed Ali, senior director for counterterrorism at the National Security Council, who had served for a decade and a half in the US government in various roles at the Department of Homeland Security, the Defense Intelligence Agency, and most recently at the FBI. Ali was the highest-ranking Muslim American working for the Trump administration, so he was a particularly inviting target for far-right media.

PJMedia.com, a conservative website, claimed that McMaster had yelled at Israeli officials during a meeting at the White House after one of the Israelis had objected to Ali participating in the meeting because of his supposed pro-Hezbollah leanings. The story was totally false.

McMaster and homeland security adviser Tom Bossert went out of their way to defend Ali from these false attacks.

Another proxy target for the attacks on McMaster was Megan Badasch, a longtime Republican operative who worked on the Trump transition team and then worked at the NSC for McMaster. Badasch was identified by the right-wing site the Daily Caller as the purported leaker of transcripts of calls between President Trump and the presidents of Australia and Mexico. Despite the fact that there was absolutely no evidence for this charge, Badasch started receiving death threats on Facebook. Badasch decided to move out of her apartment in Washington, DC, and informed the Secret Service of the threats.

Breitbart News, which Bannon had run before he joined the Trump campaign, ran a slew of stories about McMaster claiming he was projihad and anti-Israel and that he was sabotaging Trump's agenda. These views then started migrating into more mainstream conservative circles. Fox News's Sean Hannity and Laura Ingraham, who both were quite influential with Trump, started tweeting anti-McMaster messages.

The fount of a number of the anti-McMaster stories was Mike Cernovich, a right-wing blogger and conspiracy theorist who was a prominent proponent of the "Pizzagate" story that Hillary Clinton ran a child sex ring out of the basement of a DC pizza joint. Cernovich launched a website, McMasterleaks.com, on which McMaster was portrayed as the puppet of the Jewish financier George Soros. In the telling of his far-right critics, McMaster was supposed to be simultaneously anti-Israel and a puppet of Jewish interests.

The Russians saw an opening to attack McMaster and a wave of

Russian bots amplified the attacks against him on Twitter, so a slew of far-right media stories in the United States aimed at sabotaging an American cabinet official were then amplified by a foreign power.

The attacks on McMaster became so intense that in early August Trump felt compelled to release a statement: "General McMaster and I are working very well together. He is a good man and very pro-Israel. I am grateful for the work he continues to do serving our country."

Stories leaked to the press suggested that McMaster would be promoted to run the war in Afghanistan as a four-star general. For Bannon, this would at least have had the advantage of pushing McMaster out of the White House half a world away to Kabul. In fact, this notion was never seriously considered, but it was another prong of the campaign to undermine McMaster.

Trump's war cabinet met again in the Situation Room on July 26 to discuss Afghanistan, this time without the president. McMaster asked Pence to chair this meeting to try to get to some consensus about what to do about the Afghan War. Generally, Pence wasn't that interested in inserting himself into national security decision-making, but in this case, he was critical to moving the decision on Afghanistan forward.

Pence opened the meeting by asking a favor of Dan Coats, the director of national intelligence and a fellow Indianan, saying, "Could our good friend Dan Coats lead us all in a moment of prayer before we start the meeting?" For some of the senior national security officials gathered in the Situation Room, this was a novel experience. It was the first time that they had said a prayer before beginning their Situation Room deliberations.

Three of the principals in Trump's cabinet then argued for each of the three "courses of action" that had emerged during the Afghan review. Sessions advocated for the withdrawal option. Pompeo argued to increase CIA's counterterrorism operations. And McMaster advocated for the "stay the course" option, which also involved adding thousands more troops.

Two days after this meeting, General John Kelly took over from Reince Priebus as Trump's chief of staff. Kelly, a by-the-book retired four-star marine general with the sober demeanor of a hanging judge, didn't appreciate the freewheeling style of Trump's White House and tried to bring some order to it by limiting who could just wander into the Oval Office.

Early in his tenure at the White House, Kelly addressed hundreds of staffers who gathered in the long, echoing nineteenth-century hallways of the Eisenhower Executive Office Building to give them an overview of how he conceptualized their work. Kelly told the staff: "Your first responsibility is serving the Constitution of the United States. And below that is your responsibility to President Trump. And below him are your own political views on a topic, which are relatively irrelevant." Kelly clearly didn't see his own role as being Trump's consigliere.

Kelly and Mattis were close. Kelly was Mattis's deputy during the invasion of Iraq in 2003. Some White House officials felt that Kelly effectively continued to work as Mattis's deputy when he was the chief of staff.

The White House was consumed by internal feuds that Kelly aimed to quash. Bannon thought "Javanka"—Jared Kushner and his wife, Ivanka Trump—were "globalists" who were absolutely against Trump's policies.

For their part, "Javanka" despised Bannon, blaming him for damaging leaks to the press. This didn't bode well for the chief strategist. In the court of Donald Trump, the only constant was his family; everyone else was just the help.

The feud between Kushner and Bannon was now becoming untenable. The continued sniping against McMaster by Bannon's allies on the far right was also angering White House officials. Kelly and Bannon had a conversation about the timing of Bannon's departure. Bannon hoped to exit the White House around the first anniversary of when he had taken over the Trump campaign in mid-August 2016.

Then came the protests in Charlottesville, Virginia, on August 12, 2017, during which a right-wing domestic terrorist rammed a car into a crowd, killing Heather Heyer, a thirty-two-year-old anti-white-nationalism protester. At a press conference in the lobby of Trump Tower three days later, Trump observed that there were "some very fine people" among the white nationalists gathered in Charlottesville.

Trump said, "Many of those people were there to protest the taking down of the statue of Robert E. Lee. This week, it is Robert E. Lee. And I notice that Stonewall Jackson is coming down. I wonder, is it George Washington next? And is it Thomas Jefferson the week after? You know, you have to ask yourself, where does it stop?"

Off to one side listening to the president's "very fine people" speech was Kelly, who looked like the undertaker at a North Korean state funeral. Kelly bowed his head, folded his arms tightly across his chest, and stared at the floor. Behind Trump was Gary Cohn, stone-faced. Cohn was Jewish, and he knew that hordes of neo-Nazis had gathered in Charlottesville giving "Heil Hitler" salutes and chanting, "Jews will not replace us," all of which was documented extensively on cable news. These were hardly very fine people. In fact they were some of the worst bigots in the country. Cohn contemplated resigning over Trump's seeming sympathy for the white nationalists.

Trump and Cohn had a couple of intense discussions about the possibility that Cohn would resign. Trump asked Cohn, as his leader of tax reform in the White House and the person who he felt could help him get it done, to stay. Cohn agreed to stay. (In Trump and Cohn's lexicon, "tax reform" largely meant lower taxes for corporations and for the very rich.)

During the press conference, Trump was asked about his "confidence" in Bannon. Trump took the opportunity to downplay Bannon's role in his election victory, saying, "I like Mr. Bannon, he is a friend of mine, but Mr. Bannon came on very late. You know that. I went through seventeen senators, governors, and I won all the primaries. Mr. Bannon came on very much later than that. I like him. He is a good man. He is not a racist."

Bannon, a Southerner who grew up in Richmond, Virginia, advised

Trump to hang tight and to repeat what he was saying because there *were* good people on both sides of the debate over the statues of Robert E. Lee. Bannon also talked to Trump about winding up his tenure at the White House. Meanwhile, Trump's billionaire buddies from Manhattan, such as the real estate heavyweight Richard LeFrak, weighed in with the president, telling him that keeping Bannon on was untenable.

Senior serving generals and admirals almost never comment on domestic political matters, so it was a sign of how deeply the Charlottesville attack had agitated Trump's top commanders when the chief of staff of the army, Mark Milley, tweeted, "The Army doesn't tolerate racism, extremism, or hatred in our ranks. It's against our Values and everything we've stood for since 1775." Presenting a united front, the service chiefs of the United States Air Force, Marines, National Guard, and Navy all issued similar public statements condemning extremism and racism.

A week after the Charlottesville terrorist attack, Mattis visited Jordan. In an impromptu speech that was caught on video, Mattis spoke to a group of young servicemen, telling them, "You're a great example for our country right now that's got some problems—you know it and I know it. It's got problems that we don't have in the military, and you just hold the line, my fine young soldiers, sailors, airmen, marines. Just hold the line until our country gets back to understanding and respecting each other and showing it." "Hold the line" was what officers in World War I would tell their troops as the Germans approached their trenches. Mattis in this speech was using the phrase in a metaphorical sense to mean maintaining the values that the military exemplified and that were not on display in Charlottesville.

On August 16, Bannon helped to seal the timing of his departure when he went on the record with the *American Prospect*, a left-leaning journal, to opine: "There's no military solution [to North Korea's nuclear threats], forget it. Until somebody solves the part of the equation that shows me that ten million people in Seoul don't die in the first 30 minutes from conventional weapons, I don't know what you're talking about, there's no military solution here. They got us."

There is an old joke in Washington: "A gaffe is when a politician tells the truth in public." What Bannon told the *Prospect* was, of course, correct; there were no good military solutions to North Korea because the nuclear-armed state had a vast conventional military, much of it positioned just over the border from the South Korean capital, Seoul, which could be unleashed in any military confrontation with the United States.

It was only a week earlier that Trump had told reporters at his golf club in Bedminster, New Jersey, that "North Korea best not make any more threats to the United States. They will be met with fire and fury like the world has never seen." Bannon was now publicly contesting the "fire and fury" narrative, the idea that the president was seriously considering his military options against North Korea.

Bannon departed the White House on Friday, August 18, which meant that he couldn't attend the crucial final meeting about Afghanistan at Camp David, the presidential retreat in the wooded hills of northern Maryland, held the same day. It was at Camp David that Trump would make his decision about what to do about America's longest war. With Bannon gone, there was no one with the juice to argue the case effectively that the Afghan War was an endless drain of resources and an unwinnable conflict.

Trump had spent the previous two weeks at his Bedminster golf club on a working vacation. Mike Pompeo suggested that the CIA use this opportunity to have a meeting with the president, not to make any decisions but just to answer his questions about Afghanistan. Pompeo explained the spirit of the meeting as "Let's talk about what we're doing. How we're doing it. Answer some of the questions he always asks, right? Like, 'What's in it for us? Why do we care? How much does it cost? Could others do more?'"

An idea on the table was that the CIA should assume control of the war and make it a purely counterterrorism mission. But Pompeo and the CIA briefers made it clear to Trump that this approach wouldn't really work. The main effort in Afghanistan was building up the Afghan army, which was a classic "advise and assist" mission. That wasn't a CIA function but very obviously was a US military function. Also the CIA station in Afghanistan was dependent on military protection.

The briefers reminded the president that ISIS and al-Qaeda were both already in Afghanistan and any kind of withdrawal could give these terrorism groups the space they needed to plot attacks on America. At the time, there were an estimated seven hundred ISIS fighters in Afghanistan, and a number of al-Qaeda leaders continued to base there.

And so the decision about what to do in Afghanistan was already largely prebaked by Trump's war cabinet of current and retired senior generals before the Camp David meeting. Kelly, just three weeks into his new job as chief of staff, together with his close friend Jim Mattis, as well as their close colleague the chairman of the Joint Chiefs, General Dunford, and McMaster all agreed on the best way forward.

A one-page "Courses of Action" paper was prepared for the Camp David meeting. In classic military style there were three courses of action proposed, two of which were basically nonstarters: a total withdrawal from Afghanistan, or having the CIA take over the war. The third option was the military's preferred course of action, to make a long-term commitment to Afghanistan and bulk up the number of troops there.*

When it came to the Afghan issue, McMaster was all used up with Trump, so McMaster's deputy Ricky Waddell—a new face and a new voice to the president—summarized the three options for him. Understanding all the downside risks of withdrawing from Afghanistan or turning the mission over entirely to the CIA, the president went with the third option.

Three days after the Camp David meeting, Trump delivered an

---

* In 2009, the Pentagon had presented a similar set of three choices to President Obama, who was also in his first year in office. The first choice was a ten thousand to fifteen thousand troop training mission, the second was adding up to eighty thousand troops, which was well known to be politically impossible, and a third option of adding some forty thousand troops. Obama selected a version of the third option.

unusual prime-time address from Fort Myer in Arlington, Virginia, about his new "South Asia strategy."* The well-delivered, well-written, and well-argued speech largely reflected the consensus views of the generals and of the American national security apparatus about what to do in Afghanistan.

President Trump conceded in the speech, "My original instinct was to pull out—and, historically, I like following my instincts." This was one of the few times in his presidency that Trump publicly admitted that he had changed his mind about an issue.

Sticking it to Obama, Trump said, "A hasty withdrawal would create a vacuum that terrorists, including ISIS and al-Qaeda, would instantly fill, just as happened before September 11th. And, as we know, in 2011, America hastily and mistakenly withdrew from Iraq. As a result, our hard-won gains slipped back into the hands of terrorist enemies."

Trump also made clear that the American commitment to Afghanistan would be conditions-based: "A core pillar of our new strategy is a shift from a time-based approach to one based on conditions. I've said it many times how counterproductive it is for the United States to announce in advance the dates we intend to begin, or end, military options." This was also a criticism of the Obama administration. As we have seen, President Obama had surged tens of thousands of additional US troops into Afghanistan in 2009, but he also simultaneously announced their withdrawal date.

Trump also made it clear that he could easily walk away from the new Afghan policy. "America will work with the Afghan government as long as we see determination and progress. However, our commitment is

---

* The Trump administration referred to its Afghanistan strategy as its "South Asia strategy" in order to distinguish it from the "Af-Pak" strategy of the Obama administration. In reality, this was a distinction without much of a difference since both strategies were largely focused on what to do in Afghanistan. A senior official involved in Afghan policy explained: "They like to call it the South Asia strategy because it sounds more holistic. It is not a South Asia strategy. It is an Afghanistan strategy, with the treatment of Pakistan being almost entirely through the lenses of the Afghanistan strategy."

not unlimited, and our support is not a blank check. . . . Our patience is not unlimited. We will keep our eyes wide open."

Trump came down heavily on Afghanistan's neighbor Pakistan, a longtime sanctuary for the leadership of the Taliban. "No partnership can survive a country's harboring of militants and terrorists who target U.S. servicemembers and officials."

In private, Trump was even more blunt. When the Pakistanis came up, Trump said, "Fuck them. They are getting billions of dollars and they are killing us." Trump told his national security team to zero out any aid to the Pakistanis. And in early January 2018, the Trump administration announced it was suspending all security aid to Pakistan, a total of up to $1.3 billion.

The Trump administration put considerable pressure on the Pakistanis about the fate of American hostages held by the Haqqani network, an element of the Taliban that had longstanding ties to Pakistan's military intelligence agency, Inter-Services Intelligence. Caitlan Coleman from Pennsylvania and her Canadian husband, Josh Boyle, had gone backpacking in Afghanistan in 2012. They were kidnapped by the Taliban and then spirited to Pakistan. Coleman had three children during the five years she was held hostage by the Taliban.

For the Trump national security officials following the case, the young age of Coleman's children was a moral imperative to ramp up the pressure on the Pakistanis, because they knew that the kids would likely become permanently traumatized by their captivity were it to be prolonged.

The Trump administration discovered that the ISI was aiding and abetting the Haqqani cell that was holding Coleman, Boyle, and their children. The Pakistani military agency was caught "red-handed" in the words of a senior Trump administration official. The Trump team told the Pakistanis if they didn't get the hostages out safely, they would send in SEAL Team Six to get the job done. The last time the SEALs had deployed to Pakistan was the raid that killed bin Laden in 2011, which was hugely embarrassing to Pakistan's military because they had no forewarning of the operation and they also weren't able to detect the raid that was happening deep inside Pakistani territory until it was wrapping up.

The Pakistani military launched a rescue operation on October 11, 2017, freeing all five of the hostages unharmed.*

Trump's new Afghan strategy caught the attention of the Taliban leadership. This president looked like he was staying to win in Af-

---

* Far less successful was the case of Kevin King, who, along with his Australian colleague Timothy Weeks, was kidnapped in 2016 from the American University of Afghanistan in Kabul where they both were professors. In captivity, King, who was sixty when he was kidnapped, had significant health problems. The Haqqanis realized that a dead hostage was no good to them. Taliban officials based in Doha, Qatar, contacted senior Qatari officials to tell them they were ready to make a deal for King. Qatari officials relayed this to the National Security Council in March 2018, but a deal didn't materialize and King remained in captivity until November 2019.

On April 26, 2019, Trump tweeted "'. . . Donald J. Trump is the greatest hostage negotiator that I know of in the history of the United States. 20 hostages, many in impossible circumstances, have been released in last two years. No money was paid.' Cheif [sic] Hostage Negotiator, USA!" The Trump administration's record of freeing Americans held hostage by terrorist groups or unjustly detained by despotic regimes such as North Korea was certainly something the president could celebrate. One such success was the release of Coleman and Boyle and their children. So was the release of American citizens Kim Dong Chul, Kim Hak-song, and Kim Sang Duk, who were all held by the North Korean regime on arbitrary charges for more than a year and were released in May 2018 as a result of the negotiations over North Korea's nuclear program between the Trump administration and the North Korean dictator, Kim Jong Un.

The Trump administration did prioritize the return of American hostages. It also benefited from institutions that were created during the Obama administration, which helped to better focus US government efforts to free hostages. The Obama administration was criticized for its feckless response when ISIS was holding four American hostages in Syria in 2014, including the freelance journalist James Foley. A US government official threatened the Foley family with possible prosecution if they tried to raise money for a ransom for their son's release because it was against the law to give money to a terrorist group. European countries routinely negotiated with terrorist groups and paid ransom, as a result of which their citizens were twice as likely to be released than American hostages.

After ISIS murdered James Foley in August 2014, his family lobbied for a better outcome for other families. In part because of the efforts of the Foleys, in 2015 the Obama administration founded the Hostage Recovery Fusion Cell to better coordinate efforts across all the various government agencies, such as the FBI and State Department, that work to free hostages. A presidential envoy on hostages was also appointed at the State Department so that the issue now had a primary advocate there. Those institutions continued to do their work under the Trump administration, and as a result, during the first two years of the Trump administration twenty hostages and unjustly held detainees were released.

ghanistan. US intelligence agencies picked up conversations among Taliban leaders in which they said versions of "Shit! They are really staying!" The Taliban started talking internally about how it would be smart to get serious about peace negotiations with the Americans.

Four days after Trump announced his new South Asia strategy and a week after his mentor Bannon left the White House, Sebastian Gorka was also pushed out. Kelly took an inventory of who was doing what at the White House and concluded that Gorka was only a talking head on TV, a role he could perform just as easily without a White House pass.

The coup de grace for Gorka was when he went on BBC Radio to challenge Secretary of State Rex Tillerson, who had publicly said that a war with North Korea was not imminent. Gorka told the BBC, "You should listen to the president; the idea that Secretary Tillerson is going to discuss military matters is simply nonsensical." As secretary of state, Tillerson was the most senior member of the cabinet after Vice President Pence, while Gorka was a relatively junior White House staffer. It was unprecedented for a staffer to publicly criticize a senior cabinet official in this manner. For Kelly, a stickler for hierarchy, dumping Gorka was not a tough call.

Gorka tried to paint his departure as a resignation and gave a letter claiming as much to the right-wing site the *Federalist*. In the letter, which Gorka addressed to Trump, he wrote that he was resigning, in part, because of the new Afghan policy: "The individuals who most embodied and represented the policies that will 'Make America Great Again,' have been internally countered, systematically removed, or undermined in recent months. This was made patently obvious as I read the text of your speech on Afghanistan this week."

In fact, Gorka didn't resign. The Secret Service issued a "do not admit" directive forbidding Gorka entry to the White House the same day that he was fired. Gorka wasn't even allowed to go back into the White House complex to pick up his belongings, which had to be walked out to his sports car parked nearby. The license plates on Gorka's car read "ART [of] WAR," the title of Sun Tzu's classic treatise on strategy. Gorka was always desperate to be taken seriously as a big-think strategist, to be the George Kennan of the war on terror, but in the end, he was its George Costanza.

The decision to stay the course in Afghanistan and the departure of Bannon and Gorka from the White House was the high-water mark of the influence of the so-called "globalists" in the Trump administration, and the nadir of the influence of the America First nationalists.

But the victories of the globalists would prove short-lived.

Chapter 8

HOUSE OF SAUD, HOUSE OF TRUMP

Saudi Arabia, I get along with all of them. They buy apartments from me. They spend $40 million, $50 million. Am I supposed to dislike them? I like them very much.

—*Trump at a campaign rally in Alabama in 2015*

I have nothing to do with Saudi—just so you understand, I don't make deals with Saudi Arabia. I don't have money from Saudi Arabia. I have nothing to do with Saudi Arabia. I couldn't care less.

—*President Trump on November 20, 2018, following the murder of the journalist Jamal Khashoggi by Saudi agents in Istanbul*

A snowstorm helped to seal the alliance between the House of Saud and the House of Trump. Only seven weeks into the Trump administration, on the morning of March 14, 2017, the Saudi deputy crown prince, Mohammed bin Salman, was scheduled to meet briefly with President Trump at the White House. After that the president was supposed to have lunch with the German chancellor Angela Merkel, but a massive snowstorm was making its way across the northeast of the United States, resulting in more than a thousand flight cancellations at the three Washington, DC, area airports.

Merkel was already on the tarmac in Germany waiting to take off for the United States and aides had told her that her trip might have to be postponed; there was no way her flight could land in Washington given the scale of the storm.

In the Oval Office, as he heard the reports of the snowstorm roaring toward Washington, Trump said, "Oh, I hate to cancel on her. I hate to cancel."

Merkel insisted she wanted to hear from Trump himself if her trip was going to be put off.

So Trump called Merkel, telling her, "I really hate to postpone, but this storm is huge."

The postponement of Merkel's trip meant that the brief meeting between Trump and Mohammed bin Salman was extended to include a formal lunch with the president and key members of his cabinet, which was quite an honor for the thirty-one-year-old prince who wasn't the Saudi head of state, nor even the second in line to the Saudi monarchy, but rather the third in line to the throne. The royal treatment accorded to Mohammed bin Salman—widely referred to by his initials MBS—was indicative of where the Trump team was planning to take its relationship with the young prince who was the country's defense minister. MBS's eighty-two-year-old father, King Salman, was monarch in name, but it was clear that his youngest and favorite son was the emerging center of power in the Saudi kingdom.

Both the scions of wealthy families and only a few years apart in age, MBS and Jared Kushner bonded over a belief that together they could transform the Middle East. They sometimes communicated their plans on WhatsApp, the messaging app that is widely used in the Arab world, including by members of the Saudi royal court.

MBS approached his courtship of Kushner with considerable ardor. Kushner told a senior Trump administration official, "Mohammed bin Salman rushed me in ways that no woman had ever rushed me." For his part, MBS radiated charisma.

The Saudis understood the power of family relationships, and an alliance between the House of Saud and the House of Trump made intuitive sense to them, particularly after their tense relationship with President Obama, who seemed intent on upending the traditional power dynamics of the Middle East with his nuclear agreement with their archrivals, the Iranians. The Saudis also felt that Obama, who had ascended to the presidency on merit, wasn't much of a fan of hereditary autocracies. On Obama's last visit to the kingdom, King Salman didn't even bother to go to the airport to greet Obama when he arrived, as was customary.

The Gulf States' disenchantment with Obama had begun with the Arab Spring in 2011. They couldn't believe that Obama had withdrawn his support from the Egyptian autocrat Hosni Mubarak, a longtime US ally who faced a popular uprising in the streets of Cairo. What did this say about Obama's loyalty to other Arab authoritarian regimes?

The disenchantment only deepened with the Iran nuclear deal. The Gulf States didn't think it hampered Iran's considerable regional ambitions, while it gave Iran access to tens of billions of dollars in Iranian assets that had been frozen in the United States following the 1979 revolution. From the perspective of the Gulf States, Lebanon was now controlled by Iran through its proxy, Hezbollah; Iran controlled Syria through its backing of Bashar al-Assad; Iran controlled much of Iraq because of its influence over many Iraqi political figures; and Iran also lorded over much of Yemen because of its support for the Houthi rebels. The United States under Obama seemed to have given Iran a free hand in the Middle East.

This was also the view of key members of Trump's national security team, who thought that the Obama administration had made a fundamentally flawed assumption that the nuclear agreement and the subsequent lifting of sanctions would enable Iran to be welcomed into the international economy, and the regime would then moderate its behavior. In fact, the tens of billions of dollars in cash that the US gave Iran and the business contracts that were signed by the Iranians generated revenue not for the Iranian people but for the regime and key components such as the Islamic Revolutionary Guard Corps (IRGC), which accelerated its operations across the region in countries such as Lebanon, Iraq, Syria, and Yemen.[*]

On the campaign trail, Trump had repeatedly denounced the Iranian nuclear agreement as "the worst deal ever." The Trump administration and the Gulf States were therefore in lockstep in their deep suspicion of the Iranian regime. What's more, Trump, who had campaigned on a promise of excluding Muslim immigrants from the United States, could use some Arab allies to show that he wasn't anti-Islamic.

Bonding over their common fears about Iran, the Saudi royal family and the Trump family believed they could do business. Trump also respected great wealth, and the Saudi royal family certainly had plenty of that. For his part, Kushner believed that MBS could help deliver a US-brokered solution to the Israeli-Palestinian conflict and that their

---

[*] This was a version of the early twenty-first-century delusion that as the Chinese became better integrated into the world economy and more prosperous, they would open up politically. In fact, the opposite happened.

personal relationship could achieve what decades of professional diplomacy hadn't. The Saudis felt that Kushner spoke for the president and were comfortable with his role as the shadow secretary of state.

Like much of the rest of the world, the Saudis hadn't expected Trump to win the presidential election. When he did, the Saudis and their close allies scrambled to build bridges to the Trump team. The Saudi view of Trump was as transactional as Trump's view of them. A Saudi close to the royal court explained, "Look, he's the emperor of Imperial Rome. We're a satellite state. Whoever is emperor, we come bearing homage. You fucking elected him. You take him out, we'll come to the next guy."

The morning after the election, the Saudis realized with a shock that they hadn't cultivated anybody on the Trump team. Thomas Barrack, a billionaire Lebanese American businessman who had done deals in the Gulf for decades, suddenly became their go-to guy. Barrack was a longtime friend of Trump's and was one of the few people Trump treated like a peer. For the Saudis, Barrack was the way into the president-elect and his team.

The Emiratis, who were closely allied to the Saudis, had done a better job of cultivating the Trump team. Kushner had met with the Emirati ambassador Yousef al-Otaiba in June 2016, a meeting brokered by Barrack. Otaiba was widely regarded as the most well-wired and effective ambassador in Washington, having served there for more than a decade. Suave and handsome, Otaiba spoke effortless American English and knew anyone who was anyone on both sides of the aisle. Otaiba entertained the great and the good with a fleet of servants and Michelin-level dinners at his massive modernist glass-and-concrete compound with its own basketball court, children's playground, and swimming pool that hugged the cliffs above the Potomac River in McLean, Virginia.

Kushner asked Otaiba smart questions, consulting with him on a big foreign policy speech that his father-in-law was delivering during the campaign. Kushner didn't claim to know what he didn't know. This was a welcome change from the Obama team, who didn't ask questions, tending instead to issue instructions.

The fruit of the discussions between Otaiba and Kushner was a meeting during the transition in Manhattan on December 15, 2016, between Mohamed bin Zayed, the crown prince of Abu Dhabi, and Kushner, Steve Bannon, and Mike Flynn. The meeting was at the Four Seasons Hotel rather than at Trump Tower, which was always crawling with reporters. Mohamed bin Zayed, known as MBZ, was the key leader of the seven statelets that made up the United Arab Emirates. In his midfifties, MBZ was something of a mentor to MBS, who saw the wealthy city-states of the Emirates as a model for the business-friendly, more open society that he hoped that Saudi Arabia would one day become.

The meeting was in the penthouse; there were around thirty Emirati officials and security guards milling about. MBZ was dressed in jeans, untied combat boots, and a T-shirt that showed off his buff physique. He looked like a Middle Eastern Sean Connery. Flynn and Kushner talked with MBZ for an hour. Kushner saw the Emiratis and their close allies the Saudis as the key to remaking the Middle East. The Gulf States and Israel could even collaborate on a US-brokered peace between the Palestinians and the Israelis.

The meeting was winding down and MBZ looked over at Bannon. "You haven't said anything."

Bannon said, "Well, the conversation has been great, but I only came to talk about one thing."

MBZ asked, "What's that?"

Bannon said, "The Persian expeditionary force of Hezbollah and their takeover of the Middle East."

MBZ said, "Excuse me. Did you say Persia?"

Bannon replied, "Persia, yes."

"I've been looking for an American like you all my life," MBZ said.

The meeting then went on for another hour, now focused on Iran. MBZ was as perturbed as Bannon that the Iranians had become the most powerful regional player in the Middle East. To counter Iranian plans for hegemony in the Middle East, the group at the Four Seasons discussed how the US had to lead a military alliance with the Gulf States that would also include Israel eventually.

Usually a meeting between the president-elect's team and a key foreign leader such as MBZ would have been flagged to the Obama administration, but this one was not.

MBS's White House lunch helped to tee up Trump's first overseas trip, which was to Saudi Arabia, a trip that Kushner pushed hard for. Traditionally, American presidents make their first overseas trip to close democratic allies such as Canada, but in a coup for the Saudis, the honor went to them. Tillerson and the State Department opposed the idea, saying that much more time was needed to plan such a trip. Mattis was also against the trip on the grounds that the first overseas visit that Trump made should not be to an autocracy. McMaster favored the trip because it would be a chance for the president to move beyond the travel ban controversy and explain that the war against jihadist terrorists was a war of all civilized people against criminals who had perverted their religion. Trump intervened to say he would go if the Saudis promised major weapons purchases and more help on counterterrorism.

On May 19, 2017, three days after Mueller began his work as special counsel, as Air Force One was preparing to take off from Washington for Riyadh, Trump was stewing. The *New York Times* had just run a story that implied that Trump had tried to obstruct the Russia investigation. According to the *Times*, Trump had told senior Russian officials visiting the Oval Office that the reason he had fired Comey was because "I faced great pressure because of Russia. That's taken off." As Air Force One was taking off from Andrews Air Force Base near Washington, DC, around 3:00 pm, everyone's phones were blowing up with the news. Maggie Haberman, the ace *New York Times* reporter who had broken many important stories about the Trump administration, appeared on the TV monitors on the president's plane and started to recap the breaking news on CNN. Haberman said, "I don't know what was in his [Trump's] head, but this is obviously going to be an explosive remark."

Despite Trump's frequent attacks against the *New York Times* and CNN as purported enemies of the people and "fake news," Trump read the *Times* carefully and watched a lot of CNN because those were the two media outlets that had mattered the most when he was coming up as a businessman in New York.

"Trump was in the foulest mood I've ever seen him in my entire life. He was in a fucking foul mood," recalled an official traveling on Air Force One. It was going to be a long twelve-hour flight to Riyadh. Trump barely slept.

Trump was visiting Saudi Arabia at a moment when King Salman had empowered MBS to transform the kingdom from a deeply religious, consensus-based absolute monarchy to a less fundamentalist totalitarian dictatorship with ambitious plans to wean itself from dependence on its vast oil wealth. The Saudi monarchy was now at an inflection point. For the first time in decades, the Saudis could no longer rely on the revenues from oil to maintain their position as the leading Arab state and to buy off any aspirations that their population might have to play a real role in politics. The days of $100-a-barrel oil were now long gone. When oil wealth seemed an endless spigot of gold, the Saudi monarchy had created an almost perfect socialist state: Most Saudis worked for the government, and they all enjoyed subsidies for water, electricity, and gas. No one paid taxes, while health care and education were free. But in 2015, the International Monetary Fund (IMF) warned that, given falling oil prices, the Saudi government could run out of financial reserves in five years if it kept up its present rate of spending. With oil prices dipping down to below $40 a barrel, the Saudi government started cutting government salaries and reducing subsidies.

MBS also tried to diversify the Saudi economy. The Saudi government called it "Vision 2030." The aim was to privatize chunks of the education, health-care, agriculture, mining, and defense sectors and to sell off parts of Saudi Aramco, perhaps the wealthiest company in the world, which was estimated to be worth as much as two trillion dollars. Its annual profits were more than those of Apple and Exxon combined.

At the same time that MBS was trying to implement Vision 2030, he was also moving fast in another direction, trying to curb the power of the religious Wahhabi establishment who together with the Saudi monarchy had turned the kingdom in a more conservative direction following the fall of the American-backed shah of Iran to Shia religious fanatics in 1979. As a counter to the Shia revolutionaries in Iran, Saudi Arabia began to export Sunni Wahhabi ideology around the Muslim world. Curbing the spread of Wahhabism was a goal of US foreign policy since the 9/11 attacks. After all, fifteen of the nineteen 9/11 hijackers were Saudis and their overall commander was another Saudi, Osama bin Laden.

Riyadh sits in the Nejd heartland of Saudi Arabia, where in the mid-eighteenth century the first Saudi king allied with Muhammad bin Abdul-Wahhab, a cleric who promoted a harsh interpretation of Sunni Islam. This alliance was a marriage of convenience that had survived in one form or another for more than two and a half centuries and was the key to the Saudi polity in which the Saudis had retained absolute authority—so much so that their family name was embedded in the name of the country—while the Wahhabi religious establishment sanctioned the rule of the absolute monarchy and largely held sway over the social mores of Saudi society. Compliance with the dictates of Saudi-style Wahhabi Islam was rigorously enforced by members of the feared religious police, known as the Committee for the Promotion of Virtue and the Prevention of Vice, the same name that was used by the Taliban's religious police when the Taliban were in power in Afghanistan.

The religious police patrolled the streets looking for purported malefactors and were given a more or less free hand to do so. In one notorious episode in 2002, in the holy city of Mecca, the religious police prevented girls from fleeing a school that was on fire because they were not properly dressed. Fifteen of them perished in the flames.

Imagine Houston run by an efficient version of the Taliban, and you get an approximation of Riyadh, a sprawling city of more than six million souls built by massive oil revenues, punctuated by soaring skyscrapers, stitched together by smooth freeways, and surrounded by endless sand-colored suburbs that march ever outward to the empty deserts.

In 2016, Riyadh began to change because the wings of the religious police were clipped by MBS. They no longer had the power to arrest suspects. In addition to getting the religious police to back off, MBS also allowed music concerts to be staged. Also important, he allowed women to drive. It was hard to overestimate the symbolic power of this. The issue of women driving was a cultural litmus test in Saudi Arabia, dividing its conservative religious establishment from more liberal Saudi elites, including a good chunk of the vast royal family. As a precautionary prelude before allowing women to drive, MBS had arrested a number of key conservative clerics. MBS also allowed women who were divorced the right to keep their children without having to go to court, a relatively enlightened policy that put Saudi Arabia ahead of a number of other Arab countries.

So far, so good. MBS not only brought new energy to the Saudi royal family, he also had a somewhat plausible plan to prepare the Saudi economy for a post-oil future. MBS also promised a magical moment in the Middle East when the Arab states would deliver a peace deal with the Palestinians, while he was liberating his people from the stultifying yoke of the Wahhabism that had nurtured so many of the 9/11 plotters. For many years, Washington had puzzled over whether Saudi Arabia was more of an arsonist or a firefighter when it came to the propagation of militant Islam. MBS was clearly a firefighter.

The Trump administration also saw great value in the more than $100 billion of putative arms deals that were to be signed during Trump's Riyadh visit. And that was in addition to $55 billion in deals with US companies that would also be announced during Trump's visit.

In return, Trump would receive the perfect platform to give a major speech to the Islamic world. After all, where better to make that speech than in the holy land of Saudi Arabia, home to the sacred cities of Mecca and Medina? And who better to convene the leaders of every Muslim country (minus Iran) to hear Trump speak than the Saudi royal family, who styled themselves as "The Custodians of the Holy Places [Mecca and Medina]"?

When they arrived in Riyadh on May 20, 2017, Trump, Kushner, and key members of Trump's cabinet were treated to a visit designed to appeal to Trump's fetish for being fawned over. King Salman greeted Trump at the steps of Air Force One. A massive honor guard and what seemed to be the largest red carpet in the country ensured it was a royal welcome, a stark contrast to how the Saudis had blown off Obama on his final visit to the kingdom. As Trump's convoy sped through the highways of Riyadh, massive billboards of Trump's face lined the route, a satisfying sight for the man who had made a career out of putting his name on buildings.

The Saudis feted Trump in blinged-out opulent palaces that made Trump Tower look modest. At an old castle, royal guards chanting war songs greeted Trump and his retinue. It was a scene out of *Lawrence of Arabia*. Following a private dinner in the castle with some fifty guests, the ceremonial sword dances began. Trump, Rex Tillerson, and the octogenarian commerce secretary Wilbur Ross all gamely swayed along.

Tillerson, who had spent decades in the Gulf doing deals for Exxon, made what appeared to be his only joke in public during his tenure as secretary of state when he told Chris Wallace of Fox News, "I hadn't been practicing, Chris, but this wasn't my first sword dance."

In Riyadh, Tillerson told reporters that Iran had to end its ballistic missile testing and also had to restore freedom of speech in the country. This was an odd point to make in Saudi Arabia, which was one of the most repressive regimes on the planet, where there was no independent media, no freedom of assembly, and no political parties.

Wilbur Ross seemed similarly oblivious when he told CNBC that on the Saudi trip "there was not a single hint of a protester anywhere there during the whole time we were there. Not one guy with a bad placard."

The trip was something of a high point for Trump's cabinet: Sword dances! Big arms deals in the offing! A bunch of important Arabs giving them love! No protesters! Trump wasn't tweeting crazy stuff!

In Riyadh, Trump delivered his much-anticipated speech to leaders from around the Islamic world. Candidate Trump had previously opined that "Islam hates us" so the speech was billed as a "reset" with the Muslim world, just as President Obama's was eight years earlier when he went to Cairo and declared, "I have come here . . . to seek a new beginning between the United States and Muslims around the world, one based on mutual interest and respect." During the presidential campaign, Trump had panned Obama's Cairo remarks, castigating Obama for a "misguided" speech that didn't condemn "the oppression of women and gays in many Muslim nations, and the systematic violations of human rights."

Of course, it was all a lot more nuanced and complicated when you were the president, and Trump raised none of these issues in his Riyadh speech, instead emphasizing the scourge of terrorism, which was something that pretty much anyone in the Islamic world and the West could agree upon.

Deviating from the printed text of his speech, Trump used the phrase "Islamic terrorism" rather than "Islamist terrorism"—a term that didn't conflate the religion of Islam with terrorism. Old habits can die hard. Since Trump's speech was a largely anodyne account of the need for civilized countries to work together to defeat terrorist groups, the leaders of the fifty-five Muslim-majority countries in the audience paid polite attention to Trump, and no one stirred when the president said "Islamic terrorism" in the land where the Prophet Mohammad had received the verses of the Koran and founded a new religion.

Crucially, during his speech Trump told the leaders of the Gulf States and other Muslim heads of state that he wasn't going to hassle them about human rights, declaring, "We are not here to lecture—we are not here to tell other people how to live, what to do, who to be." Trump's audience found this refreshing. No more lectures about human rights; the United States was backing its traditional allies in the Arab world.

Privately, Trump told the leaders of the Gulf States, "We got to start prioritizing radical Islamic terrorism. It's now blowing back into your societies. We're not going to be allies with you if you're going to be financing this stuff through the back door. These games are going to stop."

While Trump was in Riyadh, Saudi officials described to him what they asserted was their gas-rich neighbor Qatar's support for terrorism. The Saudis had long found Qatar to be an irritant because it hosted the Al Jazeera TV network, which was often critical of other Arab states, and because Qatar was sympathetic to Islamist movements such as the Muslim Brotherhood that the Saudis had officially designated as a terrorist group.

The Saudis and Emiratis were also enraged by the hundreds of millions of dollars of ransom payments that were paid by Qatar in 2017 to Shia militias in Iraq and to jihadist groups in Syria in exchange for the return of members of Qatar's royal family who were taken hostage in Iraq two years earlier when they were on a hunting expedition. It seemed to the Saudis and the Emiratis that Qatar was funding both their Shia and Sunni militant enemies.

The Saudis and Emiratis had contemplated launching a blockade before Trump's visit to Riyadh but didn't want to take the shine off his visit, so they waited until Trump's overseas trip was finished to initiate it.

During one of the meals for the ministers gathered in Riyadh, the Qatari foreign minister was seated off with the staff by the kitchen. He refused to sit there. It was a not-subtle indicator of where things were heading. Tillerson also noticed that the emir of Qatar wasn't being treated respectfully during the meetings in Riyadh. Other White House officials noticed a distinct chilliness aimed at the Qataris from other Gulf leaders.

With the Trump team's acquiescence, a blockade of Qatar began two weeks after Trump's visit to Riyadh. The Saudis led an Arab blockade of Qatar, closing all border crossings and cutting off air and sea travel. The blockade even extended to animals; twelve thousand Qatari camels were expelled from Saudi Arabia.

Blockades are against international law and are acts of war. For that reason, the Saudis and Emiratis framed the issue as a "boycott" rather than a blockade.

The blockade was a long-term goal of the Saudis. They knew that with Obama in the White House a blockade of Qatar wouldn't fly, but Trump was another matter.

Like so many other events in the twenty-first century, the blockade was ushered in with a false news story. Three days after Trump left Riyadh, on May 24, the Qatari government-run Qatar News Agency issued a report that its relations with Israel were "good" and that Iran was an "Islamic power." The news agency attributed these comments to Sheikh Tamim bin Hamad Al-Thani, the emir of Qatar. Qatar quickly issued a denial about those reports, which were improbable on their face, but media outlets in Saudi Arabia and the United Arab Emirates aired them frequently. Malware had been planted in the systems of the Qatar News Agency a month earlier, and IP addresses in the United Arab Emirates were implicated in the cyberattack.

Qatar sat on some of the largest natural gas reserves in the world. As a result, Qatar had among the highest per capita GDP globally and, by Gulf standards, it had a relaxed approach to social mores. It was also home to Al Udeid Air Base, the largest American base in the Middle East. The Qataris paid almost all the costs for the base, the kind of deal that Trump should have found to his liking—an American base almost entirely paid for by another country. Qatar also housed the regional hubs of several leading American universities, including Cornell and Georgetown.

So it was surprising to those who understood Qatar's importance to the United States that President Trump endorsed the blockade and immediately aligned himself with Saudi talking points about Qatar, tweeting, "So good to see the Saudi Arabia visit with the King and 50 countries already paying off. They said they would take a hard line on funding . . . extremism, and all reference was pointing to Qatar. Perhaps this will be the beginning of the end to the horror of terrorism!" Was Trump simply unaware of Qatar's importance to the United States?

When the blockade was announced, Secretary of Defense Jim Mattis and Secretary of State Rex Tillerson were traveling together meeting their counterparts in Australia. They were both completely blindsided. What were the charges against Qatar? The Saudis and the Emiratis claimed that the Qataris were supporting terrorism, but the evidence for this was thin, according to the CIA. It was also brazenly hypocritical for the Saudis to accuse another Arab country of supporting jihadist terrorism when they were long the principal arsonists in this arena. Twenty-five hundred Saudis were estimated to have joined ISIS, while only a handful of Qataris were believed to have joined the terrorist army. The Qataris saw themselves as the "Norway of the Middle East," yet they were being treated like they were a pariah state.

Mattis and Tillerson were the two members of the Trump cabinet who had had the most extensive dealings with the Qataris and they both strenuously objected to the blockade. Mattis understood the key importance of the American base in Qatar for the fight against ISIS. As the former CENTCOM commander, he knew that in many ways the most important American base overseas was the Al Udeid Air Base in Qatar. It was not only the "forward" headquarters of CENTCOM, but it was also where the wars against ISIS and the Taliban were coordinated.

The massive base sprawled for miles in the Qatari desert and was home to around eleven thousand American military servicemen and -women. Trump didn't seem to know about these facts, or if he did know about them he didn't care when he applauded the Saudi-led blockade of Qatar.

Tillerson also had long experience working with the Qataris when he was the CEO of Exxon. It was Tillerson who had helped the Qataris to develop the largest natural gas field in the world, which Qatar shared with its neighbor Iran. As a result, Exxon was the largest investor in Qatar, and Tillerson had known the emir of Qatar since he was a teenager. "Tillerson and Mattis were like *holy fuck*. This can't last. This is literally insane," a senior Trump administration official recalled.

The US ambassador to Qatar, Dana Shell Smith, found out about the blockade from Twitter when she woke up on the morning of June 5. Smith called officials on Mattis's staff. They were not happy.

The Qataris were convinced that they were about to be invaded. Derek Harvey, the overall director of Middle East policy at the White House, called a meeting to discuss the Qatar crisis. Like most Trump administration officials, Harvey was caught totally by surprise by the blockade. During the meeting Sebastian Gorka chimed in to say, "The president is very clear the Qataris have been involved in supporting the Muslim Brotherhood. They are behind Brotherhood groups in Libya. They are behind Palestinian Brotherhood groups. They are funding political opposition parties to the king in Jordan."

Mattis met with Trump in the Oval Office and warned him that the blockade would negatively affect the Pentagon's ability to resupply the critical Al Udeid base. Trump said, "Well, General."

When Trump wasn't happy with something, he would call Mattis "General" as opposed to "Secretary" or "Jim."

Trump said, "General, some of my people are telling me that it's not that bad with Al Udeid, that it's not an issue."

Mattis said, "Well, it could be an issue if we don't get this resolved."

Mattis pushed back on the blockade to no avail, while the Saudis persisted with it, confident that Trump had their back.

Six days after Trump had celebrated the blockade on Twitter, Mattis met with the Qatari defense minister to sign a deal selling thirty-six F-15 fighters to Qatar for $12 billion. While the deal had long been in the works, this was Mattis's way of signaling his displeasure with the blockade. This was an actual arms deal rather than the weapons deals that had been announced in Riyadh, which were mostly agreements only on paper. Mattis hadn't even gone on the Riyadh trip.

Tillerson got on the phone and started calling the leaders of Saudi Arabia and the Emirates, telling them that they could not invade Qatar. Trump hated the idea that his secretary of state was effectively creating policy and acting on his own in ways that the president wasn't convinced were right, because he had bought into the Saudi arguments that the Qataris were dabbling with the Muslim Brotherhood, that Al Jazeera really was a problem, and that the Qataris had relationships with the Iranians.

A month after Trump's visit to Riyadh, in a palace coup MBS forced his cousin Mohammed bin Nayef to step down as crown prince. Nayef was long regarded as a safe pair of hands by the CIA because of his aggressive efforts to stamp out al-Qaeda in the kingdom when he was the minister of the interior. After removing his cousin as crown prince and making himself the heir apparent, MBS also set out to remove all other possible challenges to his total grip on power using a Stalinist playbook, minus the gulags. MBS detained not only critics of the regime but anyone he didn't absolutely control.

In November 2017, some two hundred wealthy businessmen and princes were jailed on charges of corruption in the luxurious confines of the five-star Ritz-Carlton in Riyadh—where six months earlier Trump and Kushner had been royally welcomed. A few days before the arrests, Kushner had made a secretive trip to Riyadh to meet with MBS. What was discussed was murky. The businessmen and princes were only released after more than $35 billion was extracted from them, according to MBS himself in an interview with Bloomberg News. Other Saudi officials put the eventual take at $100 billion. This was surely the most expensive hotel bill in history.

Corruption was also an odd charge in Saudi Arabia, where there was little separation between the ruling family and the resources of the state. For his part, MBS thought nothing of buying expensive trophies for himself, such as a half-billion-dollar yacht he took a fancy to when he saw it docked in the south of France.

Concerned by the erratic actions of MBS, foreign investors began to stay away. Between 2016 and 2017, foreign investment in Saudi Arabia dropped from more than $7 billion to just over $1 billion.

In addition to the prisoners in the Ritz-Carlton, MBS jailed a range of clerics and civil society activists, some of whom faced possible death sentences. Saudi prosecutors sought the death penalty for a twenty-nine-year-old Shia female activist accused of organizing demonstrations for greater Shia rights who was arrested in December 2017. Similarly, the Saudis sought the death penalty for a prominent reformist cleric with more than ten million Twitter followers, Salman al-Awdah, who had called for elections in the Saudi kingdom. Boys were arrested and jailed for many years for taking part in protests. MBS literally crucified some of his opponents. The young crown prince was turning into a millennial Saddam Hussein.

MBS even arrested some of the women activists who had pushed for the right for women to drive on improbable charges that they had conspired with a foreign power. Didn't they get it? Only MBS could bestow rights on his own people; those who demanded their rights were enemies of the kingdom.

In February 2018, MBS fired much of the leadership of the Saudi military and replaced them with his picks. He was even rumored to have put his own mother under house arrest. White House officials ascribed her house arrest to an embarrassing case of dementia. MBS didn't want his mother to be seen in public. MBS even told his father that his mother was receiving treatment for her condition in New York. When King Salman traveled to Manhattan for the annual UN General Assembly, he was excited that he might get to see his wife. Saudi officials told the king that if he saw her, it would upset her treatment.

MBS also upended decades of conservative Saudi foreign policy. In the past, the invariably geriatric Saudi monarch had presided over a foreign policy that was characterized by doing little or nothing overseas. Saudi Arabia was long protected by a US national security umbrella, as it was during the first Gulf War after Saddam Hussein invaded neighboring Kuwait in 1990 and President George H. W. Bush sent half a million soldiers to roll back Saddam's army. The joke at the time was that the Saudi national anthem was "Onward, Christian Soldiers."

A longtime goal of American foreign policy was for the Gulf States to take more ownership of their security. In a case of be careful what you wish for, MBS not only led the blockade of Qatar, in November 2017 he forced the Lebanese prime minister Saad Hariri, who was a dual Lebanese-Saudi citizen, to announce his resignation when he was visiting Saudi Arabia. MBS believed that Hariri was in the pocket of Iran-backed Hezbollah, which was a major political force in Lebanon. Hezbollah assassinated Hariri's father in Beirut in 2005 so this was an odd conclusion to draw. Hariri eventually returned to Lebanon as prime minister and MBS's play backfired badly because Hariri and Hezbollah both emerged stronger after this strange episode.

It was, above all, MBS's conduct of the war in Yemen that damaged his international standing. In 2015, MBS began a campaign in Yemen against the rebel Houthis, who were aligned with Iran, that helped to precipitate what the UN described three years later as the worst humanitarian crisis in the world.

For the Saudis, the war in Yemen was deemed existential; after all, around a tenth of the Saudi population was of Yemeni extraction, and Iran seemed to be encircling them through their support of the Houthis, who had seized the Yemeni capital, Sana'a, in the fall of 2014. The Houthis subsequently fired more than two hundred missiles into Saudi Arabia during the next five years, many of them supplied by Iran. Imagine the reaction in the United States if a Chinese-supported militia had taken over most of Mexico, including Mexico City, and then had fired scores of missiles at major Texan cities and you get an approximation of how the Saudis felt about the Iranian-supported Houthis on their southern border.

The Trump administration largely turned a blind eye to the Saudi conduct of its war in Yemen, despite the fact that the Saudi war effort was dependent at least in part on American intelligence and the US aerial refueling of their jet fighters. In September 2018, Secretary of State Mike Pompeo certified to Congress that the Saudis were trying to reduce civilian casualties in Yemen, a move that was intended to avert any congressional action to stop the American support for the Saudis in Yemen. A month after Pompeo's certification, however, the UN charged the Saudi-led coalition with killing thirteen hundred children in air strikes in Yemen during the previous three years. The UN had earlier charged that air strikes had "hit residential areas, markets, funerals, weddings, detention facilities, civilian boats and even medical facilities." In fairness, the Houthis didn't wear uniforms and launched their missile attacks from civilian areas.

In addition to supporting their war in Yemen, the Trump administration delivered on another key Saudi foreign policy goal when the United States pulled out of the Iran nuclear deal. The agreement that the Obama team had inked with the Iranians in 2015 hadn't constrained Iran from intervening around the Middle East from Syria to Yemen, nor had it stopped their aggressive ballistic missile program. Also "sunset" provisions in the deal meant that Iran could theoretically resume enriching uranium a decade and a half after signing the agreement.

Meanwhile, the Iranian regime had benefited when the United States and the other parties to the nuclear deal—Britain, China, France, Germany, and Russia—had lifted their crippling sanctions.

Certainly, these critiques were all true, but supporters of the deal could point to the fact that the International Atomic Energy Agency repeatedly certified that Iran was sticking to the agreement and wasn't developing nuclear weapons. The United States' European allies broadly supported keeping the Iran deal in place. Indeed, supporters of the deal pointed out that if Trump were ever to strike a deal with North Korea about its nuclear weapons program, he would be lucky to get something that looked like the Iran deal.

Trump hated the Iran agreement. Tillerson and McMaster and to some degree Mattis made the point that if the Trump administration was going to try to rebuild strategic relationships with Saudi Arabia and the Gulf States so that they were prepared to face off against Iran, then it was much better to do that with nuclear weapons off the table. A regionally aggressive Iran without nuclear weapons was a much better outcome than a regionally aggressive Iran armed with nukes. The deal meant that Iran was not able to begin to enrich uranium until 2030 and this gave the administration an open field to run in. But the president never bought into that. Trump believed he had made a campaign promise to kill the deal, and he was listening very closely to what the Israelis and Saudis were telling him about their archrival.

On October 3, 2017, Mattis testified before the Senate Armed Services Committee that Iran was adhering to the agreement. When Senator Angus King of Maine asked Mattis whether he believed the deal was in US national security interests, he replied, "Yes, Senator, I do."

Seven years earlier, when he was CENTCOM commander, Mattis had told President Obama that Iran was his priority one, two, and three. Once he left CENTCOM and was out of uniform, Mattis had time to reflect. In retirement Mattis was living in Washington State and he was also spending time at the Hoover Institution at Stanford University, where he was a fellow. Mattis's views on Iran started to mellow because the Iranians were sticking to the terms of the nuclear deal.

Mattis wanted to stay in the Iran deal not only because it was working but also because it had been negotiated together with close American allies—the British, French, and Germans—and the United States. In Mattis's view, if the United States had made an agreement, you should stick to it. Otherwise, you risked eroding what America's word meant. A sign of Mattis's evaporating *wasta* was how utterly his counsel on the Iran deal was ignored by Trump.

Trump's CENTCOM commander, General Joseph Votel, agreed with Mattis that the United States should not pull out of the deal. For Votel, the deal was performing a function. It addressed one of the threats that Iran posed: the nuclear threat. "So, my issue was, okay, if you are going to take the deal away, then you've got to give me something else. You've got to give me something to offset that," Votel recalled. The number of US aircraft carrier visits to the Middle East was down significantly over the past few years and the US had also pulled some of its Patriot missile batteries out of the region. This meant that the US had less flexibility of maneuver in the Middle East. Pulling out of the Iran deal exposed the US to more risk, not less, in Votel's view.

When it came to Iran, Trump asked, "What are my military options?"

McMaster asked Mattis to produce some options. Mattis simply ignored the president's directive.

Mattis said that the United States was not well positioned "to go up the escalatory ladder in the Middle East" because military assets had been moved from the Middle East to Asia to confront the Chinese threat. Other resources had also been moved to Afghanistan, which for Mattis was the top priority. Of course, it was Mattis himself as secretary of defense who had ordered these moves, which had reduced the American military presence in the Middle East.

Assuming that Hillary Clinton would likely win the 2016 presidential election, the Republican-controlled Congress had passed a measure that the president needed to certify to Congress every ninety days that the Iranians were in compliance with the nuclear agreement. This measure meant that every three months Trump had to sign off on a deal that he hated. This would invariably lead to arguments between the president and key members of his national security team such as Mattis, McMaster, and Tillerson, who thought that exiting the deal didn't make much sense since it might lead to a rift with the European allies who were also parties to the deal, and that the Iranians might also restart their nuclear program. Better to determine if the US could negotiate with its European partners to see if they all collectively might come to an agreement to impose limits on Iran's ballistic missile program, or to extend the sunset clauses on the deal.

The State Department under Tillerson was largely rudderless and many of the key undersecretary and assistant secretary jobs had yet to be filled. There were also no US ambassadors in key countries across the Middle East such as Egypt, Jordan, Qatar, Saudi Arabia, and the United Arab Emirates.

Much of the senior Trump team and Tillerson himself came from the business world, where if the CEO decided something, then it got done. From his office at Exxon—known as the "God Pod"—Tillerson had handed down decisions, which his team of executives would immediately execute. The US government was a much more complicated place to make things happen and required that each department be staffed appropriately at the subcabinet level to ensure that the levers of government actually worked.

Brian Hook, who ran policy planning at State, was one of the only officials on Tillerson's team who got things done, and he was dispatched to Europe to see if he could get the British, French, and Germans to agree to revise the Iran agreement.

Trump told his team, "Don't let the bad existing deal in front of you blind you to the better deal that we can get down the road."

On the campaign trail, Trump had repeatedly called the Iran agreement the worst deal in history. It was also, of course, an Obama deal and Trump took particular satisfaction in killing those. The most reliable guide to what Trump did when he was in office was what he had said when he was campaigning so it was only a matter of time before Trump would kill the deal. McMaster had tried his best, going to Trump twice to present him options on the Iran deal that included keeping it in place. McMaster reasoned that if the US walked away from the deal, the whole conversation would become about the Americans, rather than keeping the focus on Iran's "malign activities" in the Middle East and the inadequacies of the deal, which included not having ballistic missiles covered in the agreement, and its sunset clauses.

Toward the end of his tenure as secretary of state, Tillerson, a deeply religious man, told colleagues that when he had first taken the job he thought he had understood what his role and historical purpose would be, telling them, "I thought I knew what God's plan was for me." Over time, Tillerson realized that his purpose was not so much to do important things but to make sure that disasters did not happen or were mitigated, whether that was the blockade of Qatar, or the undoing of the Iranian nuclear agreement, or Trump irretrievably damaging the NATO alliance.

As Tillerson gained a deeper understanding of Trump's personality, and as he understood the forces that were circling the president such as Stephen Miller, he realized that this was a fairly toxic mix that had to be managed in a skillful way. For his part, Trump thought that Tillerson was trying to control him and limit him and that was beginning to define how Tillerson understood his role. And so Trump decided to fire his secretary of state.

Tillerson ingloriously received the news of his impending defenestration when he was on a trip to Africa, sitting on the toilet suffering from a stomach bug. Kelly called Tillerson when he was in medias res and told him that he was likely to be terminated by tweet at any moment. Tillerson hurried back to Washington, landing at Andrews Air Force Base on March 13 around 4:00 am. He went home and went to sleep.

At 7:44 am, Trump tweeted, "Mike Pompeo, Director of the CIA, will become our new Secretary of State. He will do a fantastic job!"

One of Tillerson's aides called Tillerson at home to wake him up and tell him, "You're fired."

McMaster's departure from the White House was presaged a month before Tillerson was sacked when he spoke at the Munich Security Conference, a meeting of the world's national security leaders that is held annually in Germany. On February 18, McMaster told the Munich audience that the recent indictment in the United States of thirteen Russian officials for meddling in the 2016 presidential election showed it was "now incontrovertible" that Russia had interfered in the American election.

Trump quickly tweeted, "General McMaster forgot to say that the results of the 2016 election were not impacted or changed by the Russians and that the only Collusion was between Russia and Crooked H, the DNC and the Dems. Remember the Dirty Dossier, Uranium, Speeches, Emails and the Podesta Company!"

Once Trump started publicly contradicting his top aides, they were generally toast. It would be only a matter of the time and the method for the inevitable parting of ways.

McMaster had wanted to stay on as national security adviser until August 2018, but it was now clear that this wasn't going to happen.

As a consolation prize, McMaster was offered the choice of a couple of promotions to four-star general. One was to oversee all army soldiers stationed in Asia and the other was to run forces command at Fort Bragg, North Carolina, but McMaster was done and wanted to retire to the Hoover Institution, where he could write books.

On March 22, John Bolton met with Trump at the White House about taking over as national security adviser. Mattis didn't want Bolton in the position and instead pushed for Steve Biegun, who had served on the NSC during the George W. Bush administration. Nonetheless, Trump tapped Bolton.

A week later, Mattis greeted Bolton on the steps leading up to the front entrance of the Pentagon, saying, "I heard you're actually the devil incarnate and I wanted to meet you." They both chuckled at the joke, but the bonhomie wouldn't last.

On the lovely, sunny afternoon of April 6, 2018, McMaster was "clapped out" of the White House by hundreds of cheering staffers. They gathered on both sides of the private road that separated the Eisenhower Executive Office Building and the West Wing of the White House to give McMaster an ovation. McMaster was beloved by National Security Council staffers, some of whom were crying. This was a far from routine send-off for departing senior Trump officials, many of whom had simply slunk away without any celebration of their service.

Three days later, Bolton started in his new job. The mustachioed sixty-nine-year-old had been a movement conservative since he was a teenager. The son of a Baltimore firefighter, Bolton volunteered to work on the Barry Goldwater Republican presidential campaign in 1964 and later interned for President Richard Nixon's vice president, Spiro Agnew. Bolton went to Yale and then to Yale Law School, where he was a contemporary of Bill and Hillary Clinton, though they moved in different circles.

During President Reagan's first term, Bolton was appointed to senior jobs at the US Agency for International Development, and he went on to work in a number of other key positions, culminating in serving as George W. Bush's ambassador to the United Nations.

Bolton was a workaholic who would routinely rise at 3:30 am, and he understood on a deep level how to operate in the DC bureaucracy. Bolton was inclined to bring a gun to any bureaucratic knife fight. As soon as he assumed office as the national security adviser, Bolton immediately fired Tom Bossert, Trump's homeland security adviser, who reported directly to the president and was, at least theoretically, of equal stature to Bolton.

In his memoir, *Surrender Is Not an Option*, Bolton explained that when it came to diplomatic "carrots and sticks," he was "not much of a carrot man." That approach had made him plenty of enemies in Washington. In 2005, Carl Ford, a former assistant secretary of state who had worked with Bolton in the George W. Bush administration, testified before a Senate committee that Bolton was a "kiss-up, kick-down sort of guy."

Bolton was a prominent proponent of the Iraq War, and he never evinced any doubt about the wisdom of that decision, telling the *Washington Examiner* in 2015, "I still think the decision to overthrow Saddam was correct."

Bolton believed that State Department Foreign Service officers were "overwhelmingly Democratic and liberal," and he was deeply skeptical about any kind of constraints on American power. Bolton was an America First guy long before this became a common slogan. The happiest moment Bolton had working at the State Department was "unsigning" the agreement that would have made the United States a party to the International Criminal Court, which he saw as a grave risk for US political and military leaders who might be hauled in front of it. When Bolton pulled the US out of the agreement in 2002, he felt like a kid on Christmas Day.

After Bolton became Trump's national security adviser, he ensured that anyone working for the International Criminal Court who was investigating American soldiers or intelligence officials for possible war crimes in Afghanistan was denied a visa to the United States.

Bolton was also steeped in the arcana of arms-control negotiations and weapons-of-mass-destruction issues. He had served as the top official at the State Department working on arms control in the George W. Bush administration, as a result of which Bolton's skepticism toward Iran was longstanding. In 2015, Bolton wrote in the *New York Times* that the US should bomb Iran because "Iran will not negotiate away its nuclear program," which is exactly what Iran did that same year by negotiating the nuclear agreement with the Obama administration.

It was hardly surprising, then, that with Bolton now in place as national security adviser, Trump announced on May 8, 2018, that he was pulling out of the Iran nuclear agreement. As Bolton stood off to one side behind him, Trump gave a press conference at the White House announcing the pullout, saying, "The fact is that this was a horrible one-sided deal that should never, ever have been made."

The Trump administration imposed tough new sanctions on Iran while the Europeans stuck to the deal, as did the Iranians, at least initially. Trump's Iran strategy didn't seem like much of a real Plan B beyond trying to destroy the Iranian economy in order to foment protests against the regime leading to regime change, long a goal of Bolton's.

The Saudis were elated at the actions taken against their archrival. The Saudi Foreign Ministry announced that it welcomed the Trump administration's pulling out of the Iran deal and the reimposition of draconian sanctions.

The Saudi celebration would prove short-lived because a week later Trump fulfilled another of his campaign promises. This one was not at all to their liking. Trump had appointed his bankruptcy lawyer, David Friedman, to serve as US ambassador in Israel. After his nomination was announced, Friedman said he looked forward to moving the US embassy from Tel Aviv to "Israel's eternal capital, Jerusalem." Palestinians also regarded Jerusalem as their capital, while Muslims in general look upon it as a sacred city as it was the place from which the Prophet Muhammad was supposed to have ascended into heaven from the Al Aqsa mosque in east Jerusalem, the third holiest site in the Muslim world. It was for this reason that the United States embassy was always in Tel Aviv rather than in Jerusalem.

Friedman was an ultra-Zionist who had called supporters of the progressive Jewish group J Street "far worse than kapos" for supporting a two-state solution. Kapos were the Jews in Nazi concentration camps that guarded other prisoners. Friedman also said that he did not believe Israeli settlement activity was illegal and that the Trump administration could support Israel if it annexed parts of the West Bank.

On May 15, 2018, Friedman, together with Kushner and his wife, Ivanka, opened the new US embassy in Jerusalem alongside the buoyant Israeli prime minister Benjamin Netanyahu, who was so close to the Kushner family that he had once slept in Jared Kushner's childhood bedroom in New Jersey.

Kushner declared, "Peace is within reach." While the Kushners were celebrating peace, only fifty miles away Israeli forces in Gaza were simultaneously killing scores of Palestinians who were protesting the move of the US embassy to Jerusalem.

Trump was becoming increasingly sure of his moves on the world stage. His critics had predicted that if he moved the embassy to Jerusalem, it would inflame the whole Middle East. They said that pulling out of the Iran deal would deeply anger European allies and set Iran down the path to nuclear enrichment again. They said that slapping tariffs on steel and aluminum would damage the American economy, and pulling out of the Paris climate agreement would accelerate global warming. When these bad things didn't immediately come to pass, the phrase around the White House was "Well, that was a nothing burger." What that didn't take into account was that Trump was gradually eroding the US-led global order that had generally worked in America's favor.

Four months before the US embassy was moved to Jerusalem, Kushner had his interim top-secret security clearance downgraded to secret, which meant he joined the more than three and a half million other Americans with secret clearances. That was nearly the population of the city of Los Angeles. Kushner's inability to secure a top-secret clearance was in part tied to the various foreign powers that were attempting to manipulate him through his multiple businesses, including China, Israel, Mexico, Qatar, and the United Arab Emirates.*

---

* A number of these countries were aware that Kushner had made a terrible real estate deal when he had paid a record $1.8 billion for the Manhattan office building 666 Fifth Avenue at the height of the real estate boom in 2007. Shortly after Trump's election, Kushner entered into discussions with companies and investors close to the Chinese and Qatari governments to secure additional financing for the building, which had never turned a profit. When Kushner entered the White House, he divested himself of his personal interest in 666 Fifth Avenue. Eventually, in August 2018, Brookfield Properties, in which the government of Qatar had a major interest, purchased a ninety-nine-year lease for the troubled office building.

When the news broke in late February 2018 that Kushner's clearance was downgraded, Kushner's lawyer, Abbe Lowell, claimed that it would "not affect Mr. Kushner's ability to continue to do the very important work he has been assigned by the President." This was baloney, served with generous helpings of bunkum and balderdash. To operate effectively with adversaries such as the Chinese and even allies such as the Saudis, Kushner required, at a minimum, a top-secret clearance. Meetings of the National Security Council operated at the top-secret level as a baseline and pretty much anybody doing any work of any significance in national security would not discuss what he or she knew with someone holding clearances only at the secret level. Without a top-secret clearance, Kushner was no more well informed than a careful newspaper reader since materials at the secret level were typically smart diplomatic analyses, not real intelligence of the kind that top national security officials needed for decision-making.

Kushner also was now barred from receiving the President's Daily Brief, the crown jewel of the intelligence community, which was delivered to the president and a dozen other top officials every day.

Trump publicly said he would let his chief of staff, John Kelly, make the call about the level of Kushner's clearance. In late February, Kelly downgraded Kushner's clearance, but in May the president secretly reversed that decision, ordering that Kushner receive a top-secret clearance, ignoring the concerns of both Kelly and the White House counsel, Don McGahn.

This decision was of a piece with the administration's somewhat cavalier approach to national security, underlined by the granting of clearances to twenty-four other Trump administration officials—including Ivanka Trump—despite the objections of the intelligence community because of a variety of possible concerns that included foreign influence, conflicts of interest, personal conduct, financial problems, drug use, and criminal conduct. Intelligence officials concerned about what they felt were "illegitimate clearances" worked hard to conceal "sources and methods" when they circulated intelligence to Trump officials.

The sloppy approach to national security extended to Kushner's use of the commercial platform WhatsApp to communicate with MBS, President Trump's regular use of an iPhone, and the casual atmosphere at Mar-a-Lago, where the business of state was sometimes conducted by Trump in full view of the club guests.

Moving the American embassy to Jerusalem was long a goal of the Israeli government, but previous US administrations had punted on this to avoid losing influence with the Palestinians. Trump had ordered the embassy move while extracting no concessions from the Israeli government, such as ceasing or even slowing its settlement-building in Palestinian territory. It was the Art of the Giveaway.

After the embassy move, Palestinian Authority president Mahmoud Abbas declared that Kushner and his team could no longer be considered honest brokers. Palestinian officials stopped meeting with Kushner. What was the point?

The Trump administration kept driving a stake into the heart of any US-brokered peace plan with punitive measures against the Palestinians, such as withdrawing American support for the United Nations Relief and Works Agency (UNRWA), which educated hundreds of thousands of displaced Palestinian kids living as refugees in countries around the Middle East.

The US ambassador to the United Nations, Nikki Haley, was angered by the vote at the UN in December 2017 in which 128 countries had condemned the United States for its plan to move the American embassy to Jerusalem and only 8 countries had voted with the United States to support the move. UNRWA was a convenient target for Haley.

Kushner felt that UNRWA was part of the old paradigm that was preventing peace from emerging in the Middle East. The only way forward was "BREAKING!" organizations such as UNRWA, Kushner wrote in an email that he sent to senior Trump administration officials in January 2018.

Neither Haley nor Kushner suggested a Plan B for what would happen if UNRWA failed. The State Department, Pentagon, and intelligence community had a consensus view that UNRWA was contributing to stability in the region since it was providing a secular education to half a million Palestinian kids around the Middle East. If UNRWA failed, who would teach the kids: Hamas? No one? Also, historically the US government had not used humanitarian aid as a political tool. The States had continued to provide aid to Syrians, for instance, even as it was trying to force Assad out of power.

Tillerson, who despised Haley because she operated as if he didn't exist, went to Trump and told him that it was important to continue funding UNRWA. Trump didn't know or care about UNRWA and told his secretary of state that it was fine to keep funding the organization.

Haley found out and she went to Trump and got the decision reversed.

Tillerson went back to Trump and argued for half the money for UNRWA. After all, the funds for UNRWA were State Department monies that he controlled, not Haley. After this meeting, Tillerson released $60 million to UNRWA before anyone could stop him.

King Salman, the Saudi monarch, repeatedly condemned the US embassy move to Jerusalem. In 1986, the Saudi monarchy had awarded itself the title "Custodian of the Holy Places." It was a title that the Saudis took seriously and there was no way they were going to play along with Kushner's peace plan if the Trump administration seemed intent on ceding the holy city of Jerusalem to the Israelis. Kushner's much-vaunted plan remained a work in progress, but one thing was clear: the fantasy that the Saudis could bribe or strong-arm the Palestinians to accept a Kushner-constructed peace agreement was now dead on arrival. The Art of the Non-deal.

A further confirmation that Kushner's peace plan had blown up on the launchpad came after an election in Israel on April 9, 2019, following which Netanyahu was unable to form a coalition government and had to call for new elections to be held in September 2019. It was inconceivable that Kushner or Trump would put forward any peace plan that required even the most minimal of concessions from the Israelis during an election season when their key foreign policy goal was the maintenance in power of the right-wing government of Netanyahu, which had not the slightest interest in moving forward on any plan that gave the Palestinians anything even approximating their own state. Trump's Middle East envoy, Jason Greenblatt, said that the Trump administration would likely push back the announcement of the overall peace plan until November 2019.

Kushner's plan to bring peace to Palestine was to secure $50 billion of investment for Palestinian projects as a prelude to a political settlement. But no country, including the United States, actually put a dime of that money on the table. Talk about a leveraged real estate investment. This was like Kushner's father-in-law's real estate play where investors paid him to put the Trump name on a building while he put no money up himself. Unsurprisingly, the Palestinians boycotted the much-ballyhooed "Palestinian investment conference" that Kushner hosted in Bahrain in late June 2019 to discuss the $50 billion plan. At the conference, Treasury Secretary Steve Mnuchin, a reliable Trump family retainer, declared that the West Bank and Gaza were "going to be a hot I.P.O."

As far as could be discerned from reports about what else might be in the tightly held Kushner plan, there was no provision for an actual Palestinian state nor for the return of any Palestinian lands annexed by the Israelis. In fact, quite the reverse, the plan would likely try to codify Israel's annexations of Palestinian territory. It was as if the British in 1947 had told Jewish leaders in Palestine (now modern-day Israel): "We have a really great deal for you: we will offer you a lot of nonexistent investment, and we will also prevent you from gaining your own state." It was not an obvious recipe for success.

Chapter 9

THE MURDER OF JAMAL KHASHOGGI

Will no one rid me of this meddlesome priest?

—*Henry II in 1170 discussing Thomas Becket,
the archbishop of Canterbury. Henry's knights
subsequently murdered Becket.*

There's not a smoking gun, there's a smoking saw.

—*Senator Lindsey Graham, Republican of South Carolina*

On October 2, 2018, Jamal Khashoggi, a prominent Saudi writer, entered the Saudi consulate in Istanbul to obtain paperwork so that he could marry his Turkish fiancée, Hatice Cengiz, who was waiting for him outside the building. A contributor to the *Washington Post*, Khashoggi, age fifty-nine, was a critic of the Saudi regime and was living in self-imposed exile in the United States. Khashoggi felt comfortable in Turkey; after all, he was friendly with the powerful Turkish president Recep Tayyip Erdogan, and although he was certainly a critic of MBS, he was not a typical dissident as he had served as an adviser to a key member of the royal family, Prince Turki al-Faisal, when the prince was the Saudi ambassador first to the United Kingdom and then to the United States.

It was Khashoggi's second visit to the Istanbul consulate to obtain the papers for his forthcoming marriage. On the first visit, consular officials had told him to come back to pick up the paperwork. In the meantime, a fifteen-man team of Saudi intelligence agents, military officers, and members of the royal guard who protected MBS had arrived in Istanbul from Riyadh on private jets. Their plan was to remove Khashoggi by force to Riyadh or murder him if he put up resistance. Recording devices deployed in or near the consulate by the Turkish government picked up their plans.

"First we will tell him 'We are taking you to Riyadh.' If he doesn't come, we will kill him here and get rid of the body," said one of the members of the team.

A key team member was Salah Mohammed Tubaigy, a leading Saudi forensic pathologist who specialized in autopsies, who had brought an electric autopsy saw to the consulate. Tubaigy told the team, "I have never worked on a warm body until now, but I can handle that easily. Normally while working on a cadaver, I put on my headphones and listen to music. And I drink my coffee and smoke my cigarette."

Greeting Khashoggi when he entered the consulate was Saudi colonel Maher Abdulaziz Mutreb, who was part of MBS's security detail and had known Khashoggi when they both had worked at the Saudi embassy in London.

Mutreb told Khashoggi, "We came to take you to Riyadh."

"I won't go," Khashoggi replied.

Saudi agents then set upon Khashoggi, pulling a plastic bag over his head to asphyxiate him. Khashoggi exclaimed, "Don't cover my mouth. I have asthma! Don't, you will strangle me!"

Ten minutes after he had entered the consulate, Khashoggi was dead. The sound of the buzzing of Tubaigy's autopsy saw could be heard on the audio recovered from the consulate. Chunks of Khashoggi's body were then put in small suitcases and members of the team rolled them out of the building. Khashoggi's remains were never found, which was a particularly grave sin in Islam, a religion that puts a great premium on the swift burial of the body.

The Saudi hit team gathered up Khashoggi's clothes. One of the team, who was around the same height and build as Khashoggi, put Khashoggi's clothes on and exited the consulate through a back door, making sure that he was recorded by surveillance cameras around Istanbul in a clumsy effort to pretend that Khashoggi had abandoned his fiancée, who was still waiting for him outside the front of the consulate.

A member of the hit squad called a superior and said "tell your boss" that the operation was completed. The call was intercepted by Turkish intelligence, which shared it with the CIA. The "boss" was believed by the Turks to be MBS.

A day after Khashoggi's murder, MBS told Bloomberg News that Khashoggi had left the consulate unmolested. The Saudi ambassador to the United States, Prince Khalid bin Salman, who is MBS's brother, said claims that Khashoggi had been killed in Istanbul were "absolutely false, and baseless."

This was the first of a series of lies, cover stories, and rationalizations that the Saudi government told about Khashoggi's murder. It was a textbook case of how to keep a damaging story alive by not admitting enough of the facts as soon as feasible. Instead, the Saudis prevaricated for weeks as more and more details about the murder were dribbled out to the media by the Turkish government, which reveled in the chance to embarrass the Saudis, their regional rival.

The Saudis floated a story that the murder was the result of "rogue killers" who had had an argument with Khashoggi that got out of hand and had degenerated into a fistfight in which he was accidentally killed. This story was undercut by the fact that the hit team included a forensic pathologist with an autopsy saw, which suggested a high degree of premeditation. And it defied common sense that MBS, who ran the kingdom as a dictatorship, wasn't generally aware of the operation to silence Khashoggi in which members of his own security detail played a key role. However, there was no definitive proof linking MBS to the murder.

Another line of attack pursued by the Saudis was to blame the victim. Days after the murder, MBS told Kushner and Trump's national security adviser John Bolton in a phone call that Khashoggi was a dangerous Islamist and a longtime member of the Muslim Brotherhood, an Islamist movement that the Saudi government labeled a terrorist group. Trump administration officials had also long contemplated designating the Brotherhood as a terrorist organization. In fact, the Brotherhood is a political movement with considerable popularity and legitimacy in the Middle East.

Trump's allies also adopted the line that there was something shady about Khashoggi. Corey Stewart, the Republican nominee for a Senate seat in Virginia in 2018, appeared on CNN and told Anderson Cooper that Khashoggi was "a mystery guy. He's a mystery figure. There are a lot of things that say he was a bad guy . . . there's a lot of reports out there that he was connected to the Muslim Brotherhood, reports that he was connected to Osama bin Laden."

It was true that as young men, Khashoggi and bin Laden had known each other because Khashoggi was the first journalist from a major Arab news organization to profile bin Laden when he was fighting the Soviets in Afghanistan in the late 1980s. Both men were idealistic and religious and were opposed to the communist invasion of a Muslim country and the brutal tactics of the Soviet military, and both were members of the Muslim Brotherhood. On May 4, 1988, Khashoggi wrote a story for *Arab News* that quoted bin Laden as saying, "It was God alone who protected us from the Russians during their offensive last year. Reliance upon God is the main source of our strength." Seven years later, when bin Laden was based in Sudan, Khashoggi visited him there. Bin Laden told his old friend that he was thinking of returning to Saudi Arabia and renouncing his war against the Saudi regime. That, of course, didn't happen—and in 1996 bin Laden moved to Afghanistan, where he launched his war against the United States.

While bin Laden became the world's most wanted terrorist, Khashoggi went on to have a distinguished career as a writer and editor and the adviser to Prince Turki. Khashoggi also steadily moved away from his earlier Islamism and instead embraced a more liberal political vision. Long before Khashoggi's views were a matter of controversy, in 2005 he told a journalist, "Right now I don't believe that we must create an Islamic state. I think an Islamic state would be a burden, maybe would fail, and people will have a big disappointment. Maybe it would shake our belief in the faith if we insist on establishing an Islamic state. What if the Islamic state failed? Like in Iran. Then we are going to doubt the religion itself. The Quran stresses that it is prohibited to force the religion on others. 'There is no compulsion in religion.' It's a matter of choice."

S audi officials and their close allies the Emiratis told their White House counterparts that Khashoggi's murder was variously a Turkish plot or that Qatar had arranged it. With each evolving, implausible explanation, White House officials would tell them, "No, that's bullshit. Go back again. Come back with something else."

After Khashoggi's murder, Trump was on the phone regularly with Saudi king Salman, who genuinely seemed to know absolutely nothing about the plot. Contrary to reports that Salman, who was in his eighties, was out of it, the soft-spoken monarch was quite lucid and focused on the Khashoggi issue. The king's attitude was, this can't possibly be true. We would not have done this. No one in my family or my regime would have done this.

The conversations between Trump and King Salman and MBS were kept very secret. Typically, there would be several senior officials listening in to a call with an important foreign leader and then a transcript of the call would be circulated to those officials. To prevent leaks, no transcript was made of Trump's calls with King Salman or with MBS, and only Pompeo or Bolton would be in the room for them.

In public Trump was defending the Saudis, but when he spoke to King Salman he was blunt, saying, "This is a huge problem. Where's the body? We've got to resolve this. We've got to get his body back to his family. Wouldn't you want that? Did you know anything about it? Did your son know anything about it?" Salman always denied any knowledge of the murder plot.

Trump also spoke to MBS separately, asking him, "Did you know anything about this? Did you have any role? Mohammed, I need to know. Was there a bone saw? Because if there was a bone saw, that changes everything. I mean, I've been in some pretty tough negotiations. I've never had to take a bone saw with me."

MBS told the president, "I don't know. We're trying to find out. Where the body is, we don't know. We know it was given to a Syrian."

Trump asked the crown prince quizzically, "Just a random Syrian walking around in Turkey?"

MBS replied, "Well, we don't know. We're trying to find out. It was given to a Syrian living in Turkey, and we don't know where he took the body."

Trump said, "Okay. Well, keep us updated. We got to know. We got to know."

Trump added, "You know, we're sticking by you. This is an important relationship, but you guys have to get to the bottom of this."

White House officials believed that the amateur nature of the murder plot meant that it was likely not undertaken as an official matter by the Saudi intelligence services. An officially sanctioned assassination by a professional intelligence service would have not been so messy; Khashoggi would have died in a mysterious car crash or taken a nasty accidental fall from a building and it would all be plausibly deniable. The Khashoggi murder was certainly none of that.

White House officials blamed Saud al-Qahtani for the murder plot. Qahtani was MBS's closest adviser and he also played a key role in deploying sophisticated technologies to monitor any whiff of dissent in the kingdom. Qahtani also tracked any threats against MBS from other members of the royal family. MBS believed it was Qahtani who kept him safe. Trump administration officials tagged Qahtani, whom they referred to as "Rasputin," with playing a key role in all of MBS's flawed decisions, such as targeting civilians in the ham-handed conduct of the war in Yemen and the decision to kidnap the Lebanese prime minister, as well as overseeing the interrogations of the businessmen and royals who were held at the Ritz.

"You name some dumb shit they've done, and Saud Qahtani is there. It's like your drunk fraternity buddy," said a Trump administration official.

Trump officials knew that MBS could be in power for the next fifty years, so they wanted smart advisers around him. Their advice was to get rid of Qahtani, and he subsequently dropped out of sight, but like so many things in the opaque kingdom, it wasn't clear if Qahtani was still advising MBS or was even charged with any role in Khashoggi's murder.

Six weeks after Khashoggi's murder, the Treasury Department sanctioned Qahtani and sixteen other Saudi officials believed to have had a role in the assassination.

On CBS's *60 Minutes* on October 13, 2018, Trump promised "severe punishment" for the Saudis if it was proven that they had murdered Khashoggi. Khashoggi, after all, was both a legal resident of the United States and a journalist who was contributing regularly to a major American media institution. He also had two children with US passports. Trump, however, also told *60 Minutes* "we would be punishing ourselves" to jeopardize American arms sales to Saudi Arabia, deals that he frequently trumpeted as amounting to more than $100 billion. This was an excellent example of falling into the trap of believing your own propaganda: as of when Trump talked to *60 Minutes*, only $4 billion of new arms sales to the Saudis had been approved by the State Department following Trump's Riyadh visit.

A month later, Trump repeated his claim about huge arms sales to the Saudis when he told reporters, "I'm not going to destroy our economy by being foolish with Saudi Arabia. . . . It's 'America First' for me. It's all about 'America First.' We're not going to give up hundreds of billions of dollars in orders, and let Russia, China, and everybody else have them."

Trump also told Fox News, "Will anybody really know?" if MBS had ordered the Khashoggi hit. Trump said that the crown prince had told him "maybe five times at different points" and "as recently as a few days ago" that he had nothing to do with the murder.

The Turks provided the audio of Khashoggi's murder to the CIA director Gina Haspel, which she listened to. Trump said he would skip hearing the audio of the murder because "it's a suffering tape, it's a terrible tape."

Trump's defense of MBS was of a piece with his repeated defenses of Vladimir Putin's efforts to swing the 2016 American presidential election against Hillary Clinton and his praise for the North Korean dictator Kim Jong Un, whom Trump said that he had "fallen in love with." The CIA concluded with a "medium to high" degree of confidence that the Khashoggi hit was ordered by MBS.

Up until Khashoggi's murder, it was possible to emphasize the positive case for MBS, that he was genuinely reforming Saudi Arabia's society and economy. In March 2018, MBS had even visited Hollywood and Silicon Valley, where he ditched his Arab robes in favor of a suit and where he was feted as a reformer by film stars and tech industry heavyweights. But after the murder of Khashoggi, the positive case was largely glossed over in the West where MBS was increasingly viewed as an impetuous autocrat.

Even reliable Trump allies in Congress were outraged by the Khashoggi murder. Senator Lindsey Graham told Fox News that MBS was "toxic" and "has got to go." As Stalin once observed, "One death is a tragedy; one million is a statistic." Tens of thousands of civilians had died during the Saudi-led war in Yemen, but it was Khashoggi's murder and dismemberment by Saudi agents that proved to be a tipping point for Congress.

In Congress, members who were concerned by the Saudi conduct of the war in Yemen started calling to end American intelligence support to the Saudis, and to end US refueling for Saudi aircraft involved in the conflict. Mattis preempted some of these calls by announcing on November 11, 2018, that American aircraft would no longer refuel Saudi planes. The skepticism about the Saudis was now bipartisan; a group of Republican senators asked Trump to suspend negotiations over a US-Saudi civil nuclear agreement because of concerns about the conduct of the war in Yemen and the murder of Khashoggi.

Trump was really big on getting the Saudis to "buy American" for their civilian nuclear program. The American civil nuclear industry was in poor shape and a big Saudi buy could help revive it. The Chinese were also angling to sell the Saudis their civilian nuclear technology and Trump was keen to block that, but he also understood that, for the moment, Congress would nix the Saudi purchase of nuclear technology because of concerns about how that technology could be weaponized.

Trump called King Salman and told him, "Look, Saudi nuclear. Commercial nuclear technology, we support it, but it's not the right time for it. We just know Congress won't allow it, and you guys will get in a lot of trouble internationally. You just shouldn't be pursuing this right now."

After Turkish president Recep Tayyip Erdogan officially confirmed that the Saudis had murdered Khashoggi, the Trump administration signaled that its long acquiescence in the conduct of the Saudi-led war in Yemen had finally evaporated. Mattis called for a cease-fire in Yemen, as did Secretary of State Mike Pompeo.

The Saudis consistently denied that MBS had any role in Khashoggi's murder and instead ascribed it to a rogue operation by overzealous retainers. They charged eleven of them, five of whom faced a possible death penalty, although who exactly was charged and why wasn't clear given the opaque nature of the Saudi legal system.

What was clear was that MBS was going to remain the real power in Saudi Arabia, and the Trump administration was intent on maintaining close ties with the crown prince. In March 2018, the Senate voted to end any American support for the war in Yemen, and the House approved a similar resolution a month later. To no one's great surprise, Trump vetoed the resolution on April 16, 2019. A month later, against considerable congressional opposition, Trump pushed through $3 billion of arms sales to the Saudis, citing purported national security concerns. The alliance between the House of Trump and the House of Saud would hold.

Chapter 10

FROM "FIRE AND FURY" TO "LOVE"

To really understand how Trump sees the world,
you have to layer multiple lenses on top of each other.
Trump believes he alone, often through sheer force of will,
can solve certain problems. That's one lens. Layered on top of that
is his belief that all of life is a negotiation, and that every negotiation is
a zero-sum game. There's no such thing as a "win-win;" someone will win
and someone will lose. Layered on top of that is his belief that personal
relationships are paramount, taking precedence in all negotiations,
even over mutual interests. And layered on top of that is his
belief that creating chaos gives him an advantage, because
he's more comfortable in the mayhem than anyone else.

—*Cliff Sims, former special assistant to President Trump*

Chapter 18

FROM "FIRE AND
FURY" TO "LOVE"

I n mid-April 2017, Trump and his top national security officials gathered in the Oval Office for a briefing on North Korea. Trump sat behind his massive Resolute desk as officials crowded in around him, including Steve Bannon, Jared Kushner, and H. R. McMaster. The briefing consisted largely of highly classified images of North Korea's nuclear facilities and military sites.

The briefers knew that Trump was more of a visual learner than a briefing book kind of guy, so the National Geospatial-Intelligence Agency (NGA) had made a three-dimensional model of a secret North Korean facility that they brought in to the Oval Office. Virtually unknown outside of Washington, NGA played a critical role in assessing intelligence derived from satellites and other sources. NGA had built a similar model of bin Laden's compound in Pakistan that Obama's war cabinet had found useful as they planned the raid that would end up killing al-Qaeda's leader. The briefers placed the model of the North Korean building in front of Trump. Trump was fascinated by the model, which was about the size of a coffee table. The president asked just how strong the defenses were around the secret North Korean facility.

During the transition, when Trump had met with Obama at the White House, Obama had told the president-elect that North Korea would be his biggest foreign policy headache. Trump took the problem seriously and made it a priority that he was going to try to solve using a combination of "maximum pressure" involving tightening tough sanctions on North Korea and, maybe, by trying to do a deal with the regime to disarm, a deal that had eluded previous presidents for decades.

North Korea launched two long-range missiles during the first half of April 2017. The missile launches threatened American allies like Japan, and ultimately they seemed poised to hit American targets such as Guam and Hawaii. Satellite imagery showed that North Korea was now expanding its underground nuclear testing facilities. During his first months in office, Trump frequently wondered out loud, "How is it possible that presidents from Eisenhower on have allowed a country to reach a point where it could destroy an American city and have not responded?"

As the briefing on North Korea progressed in the Oval Office, Trump suddenly turned on McMaster, telling him, "You need to fucking fire the press people at the Pentagon!"

Trump had been stewing for days because he had publicly warned that an American "armada" was steaming toward North Korea, but it turned out that the armada led by the USS *Carl Vinson* aircraft carrier was in fact somewhere off the coast of Australia heading in completely the opposite direction, information that was confirmed to the media by low-level spokesmen at the Department of Defense.

No one in the Oval Office said anything about Trump's desire to fire the officials in the Pentagon press shop. They were simply doing one of the key parts of their jobs, which was to correct inaccurate information.

During the Oval Office briefing, Trump was shown a well-known satellite image of North Korea at night. On North Korea's northern border was China awash in pinpricks of light, while to the south was South Korea also all lit up at night. Between China and South Korea was an almost entirely dark North Korea with only a tiny, faint light emanating from its capital, Pyongyang. The image eloquently told the story of the almost total failure of the North Korean economy.

At first, Trump was disoriented by the North Korean portion of the photo, asking: "Is that the ocean?"

Gradually Trump began to focus on the photo, looking closely at South Korea and its capital, Seoul. The distance from the North Korean border to Seoul was only twenty-three miles.

Trump remarked: "Why is Seoul so close to the North Korean border?"

Trump was regularly briefed that North Korea possessed vast numbers of artillery batteries that could potentially kill millions in Seoul in the event of a war.

Referring to the inhabitants of Seoul, Trump said, "They have to move."

The officials in the Oval Office weren't sure if Trump was joking.

Trump repeated, "They have to move!"

The metropolitan area of Seoul was one of the largest cities in the world with a population of twenty-five million, more than the population of Australia. Was the president seriously suggesting that twenty-five million people needed to leave their homes in Seoul and move elsewhere? No one knew what to say.

During 2017, North Korea launched twenty missile tests that increasingly threatened American targets. On July 4, North Korea launched an intercontinental ballistic missile capable of reaching the continental United States. With a guffaw Kim Jong Un told a North Korean news agency: "The American bastards must be quite unhappy after closely watching our strategic decision. I guess they are not too happy with the gift package we sent them for the occasion of their Independence Day."

The intensifying North Korean missile launches pushed China, long a close ally of the North Koreans, to adopt a more skeptical posture to the Kim Jong Un regime. Trump skillfully switched the security conversation with the Chinese, which was all about the South China Sea and potential conflict between China and the United States, and turned it into one of cooperation over North Korea. Trump presented this in a way that guaranteed Chinese interests, which was the maintenance of a buffer North Korean state between China and South Korea. Trump insisted that the United States wasn't interested in regime change in North Korea or the unification of the Korean Peninsula and that the United States was quite happy to have North Korea survive as long as it didn't have the capability to strike the American homeland. This reassurance helped to get the Chinese to play a role in the enforcement of United Nations sanctions against North Korea.

The US ambassador to the United Nations, Nikki Haley, adeptly steered significant sanctions against the North Koreans that the Chinese also supported through the UN Security Council. The sanctions included cuts to oil imports to North Korea as well as making it illegal for the North Koreans to export coal, iron ore, and seafood. The sanctions also obligated countries around the world to seize North Korean ships that were engaged in sanctions-busting. The new sanctions started undercutting Kim's key goal of improving the terrible North Korean economy.

Meanwhile, Mattis was slow rolling any kind of potential military response against North Korea. When Vice President Pence and McMaster planned for a war game at Camp David in the fall of 2017 so they could better understand the military options that the United States had in North Korea, Mattis simply ignored their requests for support for the war game. Mattis never sent any military planners for the war game and so the session never happened. McMaster also wanted the US Navy to provide options about intercepting North Korean ships that might be sanctions-busting. Mattis refused to provide those options because he worried that such interceptions might spiral out of control and spark a wider conflict.

During the fall of 2017, Trump started ramping up his rhetoric against Kim, trolling the stocky North Korean dictator on Twitter and also ridiculing him at his raucous rallies, calling him "Little Rocket Man."

At the same time, Trump poured considerable cold water on outreach by the State Department to the North Koreans, tweeting, "I told Rex Tillerson, our wonderful Secretary of State, that he is wasting his time trying to negotiate with Little Rocket Man. Save your energy Rex, we'll do what has to be done!"

Standing next to his top generals, who were gathered for an annual formal dinner at the White House in early October 2017, Trump cryptically told reporters that they might be witnessing "the calm before the storm." What did this mean? It wasn't clear, but it added to the jitters about a possible war with North Korea.

Before the dinner, in front of a group of White House reporters in the Cabinet Room, Trump had demanded that his generals "provide me with a broad range of military options, when needed, at a much faster pace." Clearly, the commander in chief was beginning to realize that Mattis's Pentagon was slow rolling the military options that he expected to have available to him, and Trump was willing to call out his top generals publicly about it.

The same month that Trump met with the generals, the air force held an elaborate three-day exercise in the Ozark Mountains of Missouri, which bear some resemblance to the topography of North Korea, and dropped the largest nonnuclear bomb in the US arsenal, the bunker-busting 22,000-pound Massive Ordnance Air Blast bomb that had been deployed in Afghanistan in April 2017.

On January 2, 2018, Trump tweeted, "North Korean Leader Kim Jong Un just stated that the 'Nuclear Button is on his desk at all times.' Will someone from his depleted and food starved regime please inform him that I too have a Nuclear Button, but it is a much bigger & more powerful one than his, and my Button works!"

Three weeks later, Trump was watching Fox News. On-screen was General Jack Keane, the retired four-star general whom Trump had wanted to be his secretary of defense, who was advocating measures the Trump administration could take to increase pressure on the North Koreans. Keane, who acted almost as a shadow national security adviser for Trump, advised that a signal that the North Koreans would certainly understand that the United States was serious about a possible military operation against them would be to "stop sending the military families to South Korea. That doesn't make any sense to me whatsoever. It should be what we call an unaccompanied tour. Troops only."

Trump told his national security team, "I want an evacuation of American civilians from South Korea."

A senior White House official tried to object, saying, "Well, sir, if you're trying to signal that you're ready to strike and start a war; if you're trying to crash the South Korean stock market; if you're trying to alienate an ally of seventy years: This is the way to do it."

Trump ordered, "Go do it!"

Pentagon officials were panicked by Trump's order. Chief of staff

John Kelly talked to Trump and said, "Look, this is really complicated. This has a lot of moving parts. I'd like to request that you give us the time to work this through and we'll have options to present to you."

Pentagon officials were quite reluctant to make South Korea an unaccompanied tour as they thought that it would be provocative to the North Koreans, who would likely view it as an act of war. Over time, Trump simply dropped the idea.

The Trump administration and North Korea seemed perilously close to going to war. And then the unexpected happened. Trump watched South Korean president Moon Jae-in do something groundbreaking, which was to invite the North Koreans to the Winter Olympics in South Korea held during February 2018. By having the North Koreans attend the Olympics, and even have them march together in the Olympic parade with their South Korean counterparts, Moon created an opening for Trump. Trump saw an opportunity to break a dynamic that was leading the United States into conflict with North Korea and instead to focus on a meeting between himself and Kim Jong Un. With the South Koreans operating as a back channel, on March 8 Trump accepted Kim's invitation to meet.

It was five days later that Trump fired Rex Tillerson as secretary of state. Part of Trump's calculus had been that if he was going to be in a long-term process of negotiations with the North Koreans, he did not want Tillerson at the table. Trump had already turned over the North Korean portfolio to CIA director Mike Pompeo, now elevated to be secretary of state.

In April 2018, Kim declared that he was suspending nuclear weapons and missile tests. However, Trump's newly minted national security adviser, John Bolton, seemed intent on sabotaging any accommodation with the North Koreans. A month before he had started to work at the White House, Bolton had written a piece for the *Wall Street Journal* in which he laid out the purported legal arguments for a preemptive war against North Korea. This would be a redo of the invasion of Iraq in 2003.

Within weeks of taking up his position as national security adviser, Bolton said publicly that the administration was contemplating the

"Libya model" for North Korea. This referred to the Libyan dictator Muammar el-Qaddafi, who had agreed to abandon his weapons-of-mass-destruction program in the early 2000s in exchange for lifting the onerous sanctions that were then in place on his regime. A few years later, in 2011, US-backed rebels toppled Qaddafi's regime. The rebels then hunted Qaddafi down and killed him in a ditch. For Kim, the "Libya model" was code for regime change; Kim had no intention of ending up dead in a ditch. Keeping his nukes was key to Kim's plan to remain in power indefinitely.

The North Korean first deputy prime minister, Kim Kye-gwan, said of Bolton, "We do not hide our feeling of repugnance towards him."

Sarah Sanders, the White House press secretary, quickly distanced the administration from the "Libya model," saying, "I'm not aware that that's a model that we're using."

Trump met in Singapore with Kim on June 12, 2018. The symbolism of the two leaders meeting was undeniably important since it seemed that a war between their countries was a real possibility just a few months earlier, but the pageantry of the summit couldn't disguise the fact that the two leaders didn't agree on much of anything of substance. Both sides agreed on the need for "denuclearization," but that term meant radically different things to Trump and to Kim. It was a longstanding goal of American foreign policy to achieve the "complete, verifiable, irreversible dismantlement" of the North Korean nuclear program. For the North Koreans, denuclearization meant getting the United States to withdraw any American nuclear weapons in the region surrounding North Korea and also to formally end the Korean War, which would entail a peace agreement and the withdrawal of the twenty-eight thousand American soldiers stationed in South Korea.

At the end of the Singapore meeting, Trump announced that he would be stopping joint US–South Korean military exercises. This announcement hadn't been coordinated with the Pentagon or with the South Koreans and it surprised Mattis. Trump also adopted the language that the North Koreans used for these joint exercises, describing them as "war games."

Trump took to Twitter to declare, "There is no longer a Nuclear Threat from North Korea." There was absolutely no evidence for this, but Trump basked in the notion that he should be awarded the Nobel Peace Prize. A nuclear deal with the North Koreans had eluded three previous presidents, but Trump believed he could pull it off. From a negotiating standpoint, Trump had claimed victory before anything had really changed and now he had a strong incentive to ensure that some kind of deal—any kind of deal—was struck with Kim.

Four months after the Singapore summit, Trump spoke at a Make America Great Again rally in West Virginia, where he declared his love for the North Korean dictator, saying of Kim, "I was really being tough, and so was he. And we would go back and forth. And then we fell in love, okay? No, really. He wrote me beautiful letters, and they're great letters. We fell in love."

Despite the letters, which were surprisingly affectionate—almost like a son talking to a father—the love fest didn't pay off. Dan Coats, the top US intelligence official, on January 29, 2019, testified before the Senate Intelligence Committee that the consensus of the intelligence community was that North Korea was "unlikely to completely give up its nuclear weapons and production capabilities because its leaders ultimately view nuclear weapons as critical to regime survival." Trump, who had a history of warring with his own intelligence agencies, was enraged by the coverage of Coats's testimony, which he believed undercut his efforts with Kim.

A month after Coats's testimony, Trump and Kim met again, this time in Hanoi, the capital of Vietnam. Trump wanted to go big and persuade the North Koreans to give up their nuclear weapons material and production facilities in exchange for the lifting of all sanctions. As Coats had predicted, Kim rejected this proposal. Instead, the North Koreans put on the table ceasing the production of plutonium at their Yongbyon nuclear facility, which was a well-known source of material for North Korea's nuclear weapons, in exchange for the removal of all the United Nations sanctions enacted since 2016. Trump decided to walk away from the negotiating table since the North Korean offer left other uranium enrichment facilities functioning in North Korea, while dropping the UN sanctions would have ended any leverage he had over the North Koreans.

Three months after the failed talks in Hanoi, the North Koreans launched some short-range ballistic missiles. At a press conference in Japan in late May 2019, Trump contradicted Bolton, who had just told reporters that those launches contravened UN Security Council resolutions. Trump said he wasn't bothered by the launches and he observed that Kim was a "smart man."

During his Japan trip, Trump also tweeted that he agreed with a recent statement by Kim that his Democratic rival, Joe Biden, was a "fool of low IQ." It was unprecedented for a president to deploy the talking points of a longtime enemy of the United States to attack a domestic political opponent.

A month later, Trump was in Japan again for a meeting of the world's largest economies, known as the G20. On June 29, Trump tweeted from his hotel room a seemingly spontaneous invitation to Kim to meet at the Korean Demilitarized Zone. "If Chairman Kim of North Korea sees this, I would meet him at the Border/DMZ just to shake his hand and say Hello(?)!" Trump tweeted.

At the Demilitarized Zone, Trump took a few steps into North Korean territory and so became the first sitting American president to visit North Korea. Trump and Kim shook hands for the cameras. Both men put a great premium on iconography, and they both got the photo op they wanted. The tin-pot dictator, whose country's entire economy was smaller than that of the state of Vermont, was meeting the leader of the world's superpower as a peer, while Trump could claim that he had averted a war with the North Koreans.

Trump continued to view his rapprochement with Kim as his best road to Oslo to pick up a Nobel Peace Prize. And he would have certainly deserved the prize if he had been able to come to some sort of accommodation with Kim where the North Koreans significantly cut back their nuclear program in exchange for real sanctions relief and there was a true normalization of relations between North Korea, South Korea, and the United States.

Trump engineered an unprecedented opening with North Korea and significantly lowered tensions with the eccentric, brutal nuclear-armed state, but his efforts to dismantle its nuclear weapons program ultimately led nowhere, as others had in the past. The love fest between Trump and Kim continued, but so did Kim's nuclear weapons production.

Chapter 11

PISSING OFF ALLIES, EMBRACING PUTIN

There is only one thing worse than fighting with allies,
and that is fighting without them.

—*Sir Winston Churchill*

We've had a president who dislikes our friends and
bows to our enemies, something that we've never
seen before in the history of our country.

—*Candidate Donald Trump, April 27, 2016*

Canadian master corporal Byron Greff, age twenty-eight, died in a suicide bombing in Kabul on October 29, 2011. Seventeen months later, British lance corporal Jamie Webb of Manchester, age twenty-four, died from the blast of a roadside bomb in southern Afghanistan on March 26, 2013. They were just two of the many hundreds of soldiers from countries allied to the United States who fought and died in Afghanistan to defend it. The Afghan War was the first and only war waged under NATO's Article 5 collective defense obligation that an attack on one member country was an attack on all its members. That war was triggered, of course, by the attack on President Trump's hometown on September 11, 2001.

During the course of the NATO combat mission, the total number of dead soldiers in Afghanistan from the United Kingdom was 455, from Canada, 158, from France, 86, and from Germany, 54. Yet Trump was constantly berating NATO allies for not paying more for their own defense, as if their blood spilled on the battlefield had no value.

When Trump visited the NATO headquarters building in Brussels on May 25, 2017, he stood beside the 9/11 memorial at the building, a massive steel beam from one of the World Trade Center's towers. Trump didn't mention the hundreds of European soldiers who had died in Afghanistan defending the United States, choosing instead to focus on the twenty-three NATO countries that were "still not paying what they should be paying and what they're supposed to be paying for their defense. This is not fair to the people and taxpayers of the United States."

Obama had also pressed NATO countries to pay 2 percent of their GDP for their defense, which few did. Obama pressed behind the scenes, while Trump did it in public, and he often framed the issue as if NATO allies were ripping off the United States. In fact, the 2 percent of GDP was an agreed-upon target for every NATO country to reach by the year 2024. This target had absolutely no effect on US defense spending.[*]

Trump found it particularly irksome that while the Germans had the second largest economy in the NATO alliance, they ponied up only around 1 percent of their GDP on defense while the United States spent around 4 percent. Trump's refrain was "Guys, you got to be allies." In Trump's view, you were an ally when you started writing checks.

On March 17, 2017, German chancellor Angela Merkel arrived in Washington on her first official visit to President Trump. Merkel and Trump did not enjoy the warm relationship that she had enjoyed with Obama, to put it mildly. A year and a half earlier, Trump had attacked Merkel on the campaign trail because she had accepted some million Syrian refugees, saying, "What she's done in Germany is insane. It is insane. They're having all sorts of attacks."

Trump interpreted the Germans' underspending on defense as if he were a landlord collecting on overdue rent, which drove the Germans nuts. Trump's staff produced a chart showing that Germany was purportedly $600 billion in arrears. Trump waved the "invoice" at Merkel, who told Trump, "Don't you understand this is not real?"

The contrast of NATO allies' support for the United States in Afghanistan and the behavior of the Russians was striking. In March 2018, the top US commander in Afghanistan, General John "Mick" Nicholson, told the BBC that Russian weapons were smuggled to the

---

[*] Any direct spending that members of the alliance provided to the NATO budget was dependent on the size of a country's GDP, so the US provided $685 million, around a fifth of the total, while Germany, France, and the UK were the next largest contributors.

Taliban and that they "provide some degree of support to the Taliban." Yet Trump always treated Russian president Vladimir Putin like a peer rather than a pariah who controlled a gangster state that ordered the assassinations of enemies in countries that were close American allies, such as the United Kingdom.

On July 8, 2018, a British woman, Dawn Sturgess, died from exposure to Novichok, a nerve agent produced by Russia. Sturgess had inadvertently come into contact with the agent as a result of the Russian plot to murder a former Russian spy who was living in England.

The episode produced considerable consternation at the CIA. Agency officials were keenly aware that the Russians had been an adversary of the United States for many decades. The CIA officials noticed that some partner intelligence agencies at other governments did not want to share their intelligence with the agency because—whatever the exact truth of the nature of Putin's relationship with Trump—these partner agencies simply had to assume the worst: that Trump was somehow in the pocket of Putin who was, after all, a former KGB officer.

Now the Russians had conducted an attack with a nerve agent on the territory of arguably the closest ally of the United States. A CIA official remarked, "Imagine if Iran had conducted that incident: Would it even exist as a country?" The fact that Trump didn't call out the attack for what it was, a state-sponsored terrorist attack, gave some CIA officials heartburn.

Two days after Sturgess died, Trump told reporters as he was departing for a NATO summit in Brussels and then on to the United Kingdom, "I have NATO. I have the UK, which is in, somewhat, turmoil. And I have Putin. Frankly, Putin may be the easiest of them all. Who would think?"

Who indeed? It was just so much easier to deal with Putin, who invaded neighboring countries, attempted to swing American elections as a matter of routine, and had his political opponents jailed and even killed.

A month earlier, Trump had attended a Group of Seven (G7) summit in Canada of the world's largest economies. Trump demanded the reinstatement of Russia, which had been pushed out of the group after Putin had seized parts of Ukraine in 2014. This demand was rejected.

At the same time he was bromancing Putin, Trump was dumping on America's closest allies. As he left the G7 summit on Air Force One, Trump blasted his host, Prime Minister Justin Trudeau, taking to Twitter to accuse him of making "false statements" about United States–Canada tariff negotiations. Canada was the largest market for American exports, around $360 billion a year. Russia imported only a relatively piffling $12 billion of American exports.

During a breakfast meeting at the opening of the NATO summit on July 11, 2018, Trump made the absurd claim to top NATO officials that "Germany is totally controlled by Russia." As Trump attacked the Germans, John Kelly, Trump's chief of staff, sat nearby looking like he would have preferred to be anywhere else on the planet. Kelly looked down and away from Trump while pursing his lips and shifting his body stiffly.

When she was later asked by reporters about Kelly's evident discomfort, the White House press secretary Sarah Sanders made what was surely one of the funniest observations ever uttered about the stoic four-star marine general who had helped lead the invasion of Iraq in 2003, saying that Kelly "was displeased because he was expecting a full breakfast and there were only pastries and cheese."

There was, of course, a time when it was true that the Russians really did control tens of millions of Germans when communist East Germany was a fiefdom of the Soviet Union. It was precisely because of the NATO alliance that stood up to the Soviets that East and West Germany became a unified liberal democracy.

German chancellor Angela Merkel, who was raised in East Germany, jabbed back at Trump, saying, "I have witnessed this myself, that a part of Germany was controlled by the Soviet Union. And I am very happy that we are today unified in freedom as the Federal Republic of Germany."

On a visit to the United Kingdom a day after the NATO summit, Trump turned his guns on another close ally, British prime minister Theresa May, telling a reporter that she was botching Brexit, while praising her main Conservative Party political opponent, Boris Johnson.

Trump also dumped on the Muslim mayor of London for his handling of terrorism.

Trump's berating of American allies while making nice with America's enemies might have made sense if there were some kind of grand strategic plan behind it, but it was hard to discern one. On May 31, 2018, Trump slapped tariffs on European imports such as steel and aluminum, and the Europeans increased their own retaliatory tariffs on American products such as motorcycles and orange juice. Was a trade war with the European Union, the world's largest trading bloc, really a smart idea? And playing footsie with Putin achieved what, precisely? The Russian economy was roughly the size of Italy's. Putin also worked against American interests by interfering in US elections, propped up American enemies such as the Syrian dictator Bashar al-Assad, and undercut key American alliances like NATO.

Five days after publicly attacking the Germans for purportedly being controlled by the Russians, Trump met in Finland with Putin for a two-hour meeting that included no other officials. At a press conference in the Finnish capital, Helsinki, standing next to Putin, instead of endorsing the unanimous finding of US intelligence agencies that Russia had interfered in the 2016 presidential election, Trump observed that Putin was "extremely strong and powerful in his denial. . . . He just said it's not Russia. . . . I don't see any reason why it would be." Well, that's settled then!

For good measure, Trump dumped on his own country, saying, "I think that the United States has been foolish. . . . We've all been foolish. . . . We're all to blame." In fact, as Special Counsel Robert Mueller's investigation painstakingly revealed, the ones to blame were a small coterie of officers in Russia's military intelligence agency GRU, acting under the orders of Putin.

Within hours of Trump's bizarre press conference, the director of national intelligence, Dan Coats, who oversaw the seventeen American intelligence agencies, released a statement pushing back on Trump, saying, "The role of the Intelligence Community is to provide the best information and fact-based assessments possible for the President and

policymakers. We have been clear in our assessments of Russian meddling in the 2016 election and their ongoing, pervasive efforts to undermine our democracy." It was an unusually direct public rebuke from
Coats, a longtime conservative Republican. Intelligence officials were
delighted that Coats quickly and unequivocally defended their work.

Trump's attacks on the intelligence community during the transition
had sabotaged morale at the CIA during Trump's first year in office, but
agency officials were pleasantly surprised that CIA director Mike
Pompeo—who personally could be "a dick" when he dealt with them—
had never tried to downplay or politicize the intelligence about Russia,
despite the proclivities of Trump, who never seemed to accept the fact
that the Russians had interfered in the 2016 presidential election to
help him.

By Trump's second year in office, CIA officials were "numb to the
circus" and just kept doing their jobs, according to an agency veteran.
But the official also said that Trump had done lasting damage to institutions such as the CIA and the FBI because "more and more American
people distrust us because of his campaign of vilification and lies. He
has vilified us as exploitative and greedy partisans who do not care about
America or Americans, just making a quick and easy buck off the taxpayers or pushing our hidden partisan agendas from within like moles.
No one trusts us to make selfless, disinterested decisions for the better-
ment of America and—most significantly—in service of the Constitution that we dedicate our lives to upholding and defending."

Trump's performance in Helsinki was a sobering reminder to the
CIA rank and file that Trump was prepared to take the word of a former
KGB officer over the careful work of his own intelligence agencies.

When Trump returned from Finland, he encountered intense push-
back from both Democrats and Republicans about what he had said in
Helsinki. Trump's favorite national security analyst, Fox News's retired
general Jack Keane, went on television to blast Trump's press conference
with Putin as "stunning and disappointing."

At a hastily arranged press conference at the White House, Trump
said that he had mangled his syntax when he had said he saw no reason

why Russia would have tried to interfere in the 2016 election, claiming, "The sentence should have been, 'I don't see any reason why it *wouldn't* be Russia.' Sort of a double negative. . . . You can put that in. And I think that probably clarifies things pretty good by itself."

Three days later, NBC's Andrea Mitchell interviewed Coats at the Aspen Security Forum. In the middle of the interview, a producer handed a note to Mitchell that flagged some breaking news. Mitchell told Coats that Trump had just invited Putin to the White House in the fall. Coats looked so surprised that it appeared like he might have been just pulling Mitchell's leg. Of course, the director of national intelligence knew that Putin was going to be visiting the White House!

The Aspen audience began to realize that Coats wasn't joking when he said, "Say that again."

Coats then added with a soupçon of sarcasm, "Okay. That's going to be special."

Trump's national security team did not share the president's enthusiasm for Putin. During his confirmation hearings to become defense secretary, Mattis described the Russians as the number one threat to the United States and said that he thought that Putin was seeking to break up the NATO alliance.

In December 2017, the Trump administration rolled out its national security strategy, a key planning document that every president since Ronald Reagan had published to warn about threats to American national security and how best to respond to them. What was most newsworthy about the strategy document, which was overseen by McMaster, was the extent to which it portrayed Russia and China, America's traditional major state antagonists, as threatening. The document asserted that Russia and China "want to shape a world antithetical to U.S. values and interests," which seemed quite at odds with the president's own embrace of Russia. The document also described Russian aggression against its neighbors: "With its invasions of Georgia and Ukraine, Russia demonstrated its willingness to violate the sovereignty of states in the region."

Russia was "using information tools in an attempt to undermine the legitimacy of democracies. . . . The American public and private sectors must recognize this and work together to defend our way of life," according to the strategy document. The document went on to link Russia's "information operations" to a broader campaign to influence public opinion across the globe, noting that its influence campaigns blended covert intelligence operations and false online personas with state-funded media, third-party intermediaries, and paid social media users, or "trolls." This, of course, was similar to the US intelligence community's conclusions that Russia had meddled in the 2016 election.

Similarly, before he became Trump's third national security adviser, John Bolton had called Putin a "liar" and Russia's election-meddling in 2016 an "act of war." Working for Trump, Bolton had moderated his tone on Putin, but clearly he was naturally a skeptic of Putin and his works.

The Trump administration seemed to have two sets of policies about Russia. There was the policy of the administration, which took a fairly hard line on Russia, for instance, expelling sixty Russian diplomats in March 2018 after the Russian government's attempt to assassinate the former Russian spy in the United Kingdom using the nerve agent. Three months earlier, the Trump administration had also approved some $40 million of arms sales to the Ukrainian government, which was fighting Russian-backed rebels in Eastern Ukraine.

During his last public speech as national security adviser at the Atlantic Council in Washington on April 3, 2018, H. R. McMaster blasted Putin, saying, "He may believe that his aggressive actions— . . . in cyberspace, in the air, and on the high seas—can undermine our confidence, our institutions, and our values. Perhaps he believes that our free nations are weak and will not respond to his provocations. He is wrong." McMaster added that "we have failed to impose sufficient costs" on Russia for subverting American democracy.

If the Trump administration generally took a tough line on Russia, the president went out of his way to mollycoddle Putin. Two weeks after McMaster's speech, Trump was watching UN ambassador Nikki Haley on TV when she announced new sanctions on Russia for its support of the Syrian regime, which had once again used chemical weapons against its own people. Trump became incensed and dispatched a White House official to tell reporters that Haley had suffered from "momentary confusion." Haley shot back on Fox News that she didn't get confused. The White House official then told the *New York Times*, "The policy was changed and she wasn't told about it, so she was in a box."

When Trump met with Putin at the G20 meeting in late June 2019 in Japan, both leaders had a good laugh about the purported "fake news" outlets in each other's countries. Russia was one of the most difficult and dangerous countries in the world to operate in for journalists. Trump also jokingly told the former KGB officer not to meddle in the American elections again.

Trump wasn't the first American leader who thought he could do business with Putin. In 2001, George W. Bush said he found Putin "to be very straightforward and trustworthy. We had a very good dialogue. I was able to get a sense of his soul." Secretary of State Hillary Clinton pushed for a "reset" with Russia during Obama's first term. Of course, neither Bush nor Clinton was the possible beneficiary of Putin's efforts to sabotage one of the United States' core interests: its ability to hold elections free of foreign influence. And Putin remained what he always was, an unreconstructed KGB officer committed to maintaining his authoritarian rule and expanding Russian influence wherever he could, in particular if that would also undermine American interests.

Chapter 12

REVOLT OF THE GENERALS

Through your actions, you have embarrassed us in the eyes of our children, humiliated us on the world stage and, worst of all, divided us as a nation.

—*Admiral William H. McRaven in the* Washington Post, *August 16, 2018*

On the New Year's morning of 2019—not traditionally a time for recrimination—a presidential tweet denigrated retired general Stanley McChrystal, the commander of the Afghan War who had resigned because of the disparaging remarks that officers on his staff had made to a reporter about senior Obama administration officials.

Trump tweeted, "'General' McChrystal got fired like a dog by Obama. Last assignment a total bust. Known for big, dumb mouth. Hillary lover!"

This tweet followed an interview that McChrystal gave to ABC News in which he had described Trump as immoral and dishonest. Trump was known for being a counterpuncher, so on one level it wasn't surprising he reacted this way to McChrystal's withering criticism, but when you stepped back, the degree to which Trump was now battling America's generals was startling, considering how he had begun his presidency.

Trump came into office besotted by military brass, appointing Generals Flynn, Kelly, Mattis, and McMaster to key roles. A year and a half later, Trump was at war with the four-star officers he had once embraced. That war was sparked by former CIA director John Brennan, who tweeted after Trump's Helsinki summit with Putin that "Donald Trump's press conference performance in Helsinki rises to & exceeds the threshold of 'high crimes & misdemeanors.' It was nothing short of treasonous. Not only were Trump's comments imbecilic, he is wholly in the pocket of Putin." A public charge by a former CIA director that Trump was committing treason was a serious matter.

Trump, of course, fired back. Former CIA directors traditionally kept their security clearances, which allowed them to continue to give advice in classified settings to current intelligence officials. A month after the Helsinki summit, White House press secretary Sarah Sanders announced that Brennan's clearances were going to be yanked because he had made "a series of unfounded and outrageous allegations."

Admiral Bill McRaven, the architect of the SEAL raid that killed Osama bin Laden in 2011, was on vacation in a remote part of Colorado with scant access to cell phone or internet coverage when he heard the news that Brennan's clearances had been revoked. McRaven rarely made public statements of a political nature, but it stuck in his craw that Trump was bullying Brennan who had, among other services to the United States, played a key role in the decision to green-light the bin Laden operation.

When he found a spot where he could make a call, McRaven phoned Karen Tumulty, a columnist at the *Washington Post* whom he had known since high school. McRaven dictated a short but withering open letter to Trump that soon appeared in the *Post* that read, "Dear Mr. President: Former CIA director John Brennan, whose security clearance you revoked on Wednesday, is one of the finest public servants I have ever known. Few Americans have done more to protect this country than John. He is a man of unparalleled integrity, whose honesty and character have never been in question, except by those who don't know him. Therefore, I would consider it an honor if you would revoke my security clearance as well, so I can add my name to the list of men and women who have spoken up against your presidency."

McRaven piled on: "Like most Americans, I had hoped that when you became president, you would rise to the occasion and become the leader this great nation needs. A good leader tries to embody the best qualities of his or her organization. A good leader sets the example for others to follow. A good leader always puts the welfare of others before himself or herself. Your leadership, however, has shown little of these qualities. Through your actions, you have embarrassed us in the eyes of our children, humiliated us on the world stage and, worst of all, divided us as a nation."

There was arguably no American military officer more revered than McRaven because of his key role in avenging the 9/11 attacks, so when McRaven's letter appeared, Trump managed only an uncharacteristically tepid response, saying, "I don't know McRaven," as if the fact that he didn't know the retired admiral therefore invalidated McRaven's criticisms.

Three months after McRaven published his letter in the *Post*, Chris Wallace of Fox News asked Trump to respond to comments that McRaven had made that Trump's attacks on the news media "may be the greatest threat to democracy in my lifetime." Trump responded that McRaven was a "Hillary Clinton backer and an Obama backer." In fact, McRaven had taken no position on the 2016 presidential election. After Trump's interview, McRaven told CNN, "I did not back Hillary Clinton or anyone else. I am a fan of President Obama and President George W. Bush, both of whom I worked for."

Few who worked at senior levels in the administration of President Trump left with their reputations unsullied. Even fewer left on their own terms. Jim Mattis was one of the latter. The break between Mattis and Trump represented the most consequential split between those in the Trump administration who valued the United States' international alliances and commitments and those, like Trump, who did not. Others had gone before Mattis; McMaster also valued American allies, having served alongside them in Afghanistan and Iraq. But Mattis was the longest-serving senior cabinet official to leave the administration, and he resigned on principle, in particular regarding how Trump treated America's international alliances.

Trump's split with Mattis was a long time coming. For much of his tenure as secretary of defense, Mattis had performed the neat trick of keeping some independence from Trump but also not pissing him off. Mattis avoided the spotlight, giving almost no interviews or press conferences. When the *New York Times Magazine* ran a major profile of Mattis in March 2018, he wouldn't sit for an interview or even a photograph. The Trump administration had only one star and that was Trump.

Yet Mattis also didn't perform North Korean–level flattery of the Great Leader. When Trump convened his first full cabinet meeting on June 12, 2017, cabinet officials outdid one another to flatter the president as the TV cameras rolled. Chief of Staff Reince Priebus told Trump, "On behalf of the entire senior staff around you, Mr. President, we thank you for the opportunity and the blessing that you've given us to serve your agenda and the American people."* Mattis took a different tack, thanking the "men and women of the Department of Defense" rather than thanking Trump.

Mattis and Trump had fundamental policy differences that began to add up over time. The blockade of Qatar was one of the first. Anyone who understood the Middle East even superficially understood that the United States had a variety of frenemies in the region who sometimes worked to help American interests by, for instance, maintaining a predictable and reasonably priced supply of oil and gas, but that the same countries also supported jihadists in some manner. Singling out Qatar, which was home to arguably the most important US military base outside the United States, made no sense when it was the Saudis who had kicked out large numbers of American soldiers from their country after 9/11 and who also had done so much to export jihadist ideology around the world.

After the blockade of Qatar, the Saudis told White House officials that they would be willing to host a base similar to Qatar's Al Udeid Air Base on their soil.

American officials laughed at the notion, saying, "No, we already did that, and you kicked us out. We're not doing that again."

In 2003, the George W. Bush administration had pulled almost all US troops out of Saudi Arabia and turned over to Saudi control the

---

* The following month, Trump dumped Priebus as his chief of staff.

massive Prince Sultan Air Base, which had once housed tens of thousands of American servicemen. The long-term presence of those American soldiers on the "holy land" of Saudi Arabia was the central reason that Osama bin Laden and his followers had turned against the United States. That's why the key American base in the Middle East was now in Qatar.

A month after the beginning of the Qatar blockade, the Pentagon was blindsided by a Trump tweet ordering the banning of transgender individuals serving in uniform. This tweet came less than a month after Mattis had announced a six-month review of the matter.

For their part, White House officials became increasingly frustrated with what they believed to be Mattis's efforts not to provide a range of military options to the president, in particular for any kind of potential showdown with Iran. They learned that Mattis had instructed his generals not to provide such options. Mattis was focused on the wars against ISIS and in Afghanistan as well as the challenge posed by China, and the message he sent to his team was that there should be no more commitments in the Middle East that might draw the United States into a larger war, especially with Iran. Mattis refused to acknowledge a cabinet memo about the situation in Iraq's Kurdistan region, which was a legitimate order from the president. Mattis refused to even do information operations in Iraq on the basis that it might provoke the Iranians to attack American bases in Iraq.

Mattis's caution was underlined by his reaction to the Assad regime's continued use of chemical weapons against its own people. In late February 2018, the regime used chemical weapons in a rebel-held suburb of Damascus. McMaster, Tillerson, and Trump all wanted to take action against Assad, but Mattis slow rolled the military options.

A little over a month later, on April 7 the regime unleashed a chemical weapons attack in a rebel-controlled area of Damascus, killing dozens of civilians. This attack was going to be hard to ignore. The video of the victims foaming at the mouth as they died was disturbing and affected Trump in much the same visceral way that the similar attack in Syria had affected him a year before.

Just four days earlier, Trump had met with his top generals and national security officials and had railed against the continuing US military presence in Syria and how much it was costing. They pushed back, including the chairman of the Joint Chiefs, Joseph Dunford, who said it would be premature to withdraw, as it would leave Syria to the Iranians and Russians.

Mattis felt that the US needed to be in Syria long after the defeat of ISIS in order to stabilize the country.

Trump regularly told his war cabinet that the US needed to "get out" of Syria. An argument against that position that seemed to resonate with Trump was not to replicate the mistake that Obama had made when he pulled out all American forces from Iraq at the end of 2011, which had made the country vulnerable to the rise of ISIS.

Three days after the chemical weapons attack, the emir of Qatar, Tamim bin Hamad Al-Thani, visited the White House. Trump's views about the Qatar blockade were shifting. The intelligence community had produced an assessment that said the last time that Qatar had had any role in financing terrorism was in 2014. Trump realized that the Saudi claims about the perfidy of the Qataris were massively overblown.

The emir urged Trump to take real action against Assad as opposed to the largely symbolic cruise missile attacks that the president had authorized a year earlier that had damaged a Syrian airfield that the Syrians had quickly repaired. The emir told Trump, "If the action is like last year, it will be useless. Assad only understands force. If you do something only symbolic, it will make him even stronger."

Trump didn't disagree with the Qatari emir. He also felt that any military operation against the Assad regime shouldn't be merely symbolic. Trump tweeted that American missiles "will be coming, nice and new and 'smart!'"

The initial assessment of the April 7 chemical weapons attack in Damascus was that the Assad regime had used the nerve agent sarin together with less lethal chlorine gas. As the assessment went on, American analysts came to doubt that sarin was used, determining instead that chlorine was used in high concentrations in a closed space that produced symptoms in the victims that were similar to those caused by sarin.

In response, Bolton wanted to strike not only targets in Syria that were producing chemical weapons, but also targets associated with Assad as well as his "enablers," the Russian and Iranian forces in Syria that were helping to prop up the Assad regime. Mattis and Dunford were horrified. Mattis made it very clear that any American operation in Syria had to be done in such a way that it did not kill Russians because he was convinced that if that happened, the United States would be at war with Russia. For Mattis, a military operation that spiraled out of control in Syria could spark a wider conflict.

White House officials considered whether there should be a sustained campaign against Assad's regime as well as attacks directed against targets associated with Assad himself. Some officials wanted to destroy Assad's air force and render all of his airfields unusable so that he couldn't launch chemical weapons attacks from the air. But Mattis did not provide the military options necessary for those kinds of operations and instead offered a plan to attack sites where the regime was manufacturing or storing chemical weapons.

Unlike McMaster, Bolton had, at least initially, a good relationship with Trump. Bolton, only a week into his new job as national security adviser, told Dunford that the relatively limited military option the Pentagon was offering was not the robust response that the president wanted.

Pentagon officials pushed back on the White House, saying there wasn't time to "develop" other targets. This was disingenuous. There were well-known targets, such as the headquarters of Assad's elite Fourth Armored Division, which was responsible for protecting the regime, but the Pentagon wanted to avoid any Iranian casualties, and Iranian advisers might be embedded with such a unit. Mattis also wanted to avoid the possibility of killing any of the Russian forces that were helping to prop up Assad. Mattis was additionally concerned that a really big strike against Assad's regime might force the Russians to move to protect Assad.

A senior Trump administration official recalled that Mattis and Dunford "did one of the best rope-a-dopes I have ever seen as they used the whole military planning process to just drag this thing out and really socialize the idea that if we're not careful, we're going to be at war, and that war could become a world war."

Mattis made the point that as awful as deploying chemical weapons was, it was used at a tactical level by a local commander in response to a situation that the commander felt had gotten out of hand, and the casualty numbers were actually relatively small. It wasn't as if a strategic interest of the United States had been fundamentally threatened.

In the end, Mattis carried the day and the plan for the military operation consisted of a little more than one hundred missiles aimed at Assad's chemical weapons production and storage facilities.

The exact timing of the strike was highly classified. There was a deception operation to suggest that the strikes would happen three days later than they actually did.

When the operation was carried out, nobody was killed. After the strikes, Mattis gave a press briefing in which he emphasized, "We used a little over double the number of weapons this year than we used last year. It was done on targets that we believed were selected to hurt the chemical weapons program. We confined it to the chemical weapons-type targets. We were not out to expand this. We were very precise and proportionate." Mattis was not going to do anything that might precipitate a wider war in the Middle East.

The second US military operation against Syria in April 2018 was the beginning of Mattis's undoing with President Trump because by the end of the process the president understood that Mattis was "managing" him, which Trump deeply resented. For his part, Mattis believed that at any moment the president could do something irrational, so he had to be the force for reason.

Mattis often said, "We have to make sure reason trumps impulse."

White House officials realized that Mattis believed Trump was a loose cannon and that Mattis didn't want to enable any bad decisions by providing military options that Trump could then seize upon. White House officials started to refer to "Mad Dog" Mattis as "Little Baby Kitten" Mattis.

In fact, the premise behind Mattis's view of Trump was questionable. When it came to the actual use of force, Commander in Chief Trump wasn't impulsive, but generally cautious about American military operations despite his often hyperventilating public rhetoric. Trump ramped up the US troop presence in Afghanistan in 2017 only with the greatest reluctance, and in 2019 he authorized a significant drawdown of those troops. The US strikes against Syrian regime targets in 2017 and 2018 were well calibrated not to lead to a wider conflict. As soon as ISIS's geographical "caliphate" was largely eliminated, Trump routinely told his advisers that he wanted to pull American forces out of Syria, and he withdrew the bulk of those forces in early 2019. Beginning in the spring of 2018, Trump went out of his way to embrace Kim Jong Un and to avoid any moves that might lead to war with the North Koreans.

Trump's America First foreign policy gathered steam during the spring and summer of 2018, and it created further tensions between the president and his secretary of defense. Trump told his senior advisers that he was thinking of pulling the United States out of NATO. Trump also feuded publicly with allies at a NATO summit in Brussels in July, calling them "delinquent" in their defense spending and making the false claim that "many countries owe us a tremendous amount of money for many years back." That's not the way NATO worked. As mentioned above, each country in the alliance had agreed to spend 2 percent of their GDP on defense by 2024. None of that spending was "owed" to any other country.

This all contrasted with Mattis's deep support of NATO. At his confirmation hearing, Mattis described it as "the most successful military alliance probably in modern world history and maybe ever." On his first day in office, Mattis made it a point to call the NATO secretary-general, the British defense secretary, and the Canadian defense minister to emphasize the continuing American commitment to the alliance.

Trump had kowtowed to Putin at the Helsinki summit in July 2018. Several months later, Mattis said publicly at the Reagan Defense Forum in California, "We simply cannot trust" Putin.

In June 2018, Trump attended a much-ballyhooed summit in Singapore with Kim and later declared, "We fell in love." This love affair had scant impact on the dictator's nuclear ambitions. The North Koreans accelerated their ballistic missile program at more than a dozen secret bases, yet Trump had canceled joint US–South Korea military exercises, a staple of the alliance for decades. The move blindsided Mattis and was a gift to the North Koreans.

Mattis was also frustrated with the management style of the new national security adviser, John Bolton. Where McMaster had convened relatively frequent meetings of the National Security Council, Bolton dealt with few officials on the NSC and kept his own counsel. Instead of conducting "principals" meetings in person, Bolton convened "paper committees" where he would send around papers with which the principals could "concur" or "non-concur" with a particular course of action by a certain date. Some of this was because Bolton—despite his fearsome reputation—was a classic shy introvert.

Mattis complained to Bolton about the collapse of a formal national security review process because of the lack of NSC meetings chaired by Bolton. Bolton ignored Mattis.

When mortar attacks landed in the US embassy compound in Baghdad on September 6, 2018, likely launched by a Shia militia with ties to Iran, Bolton asked for a range of military options against the Iranians. Mattis was alarmed by the request. Bolton then tried to go directly to CENTCOM to ask for options that he believed were completely legitimate for him to be able to provide to Trump. Mattis blocked Bolton.

Another point of tension was the deployment of active-duty soldiers to the United States–Mexico border in late October 2018 just before the midterm elections. Trump made "the crisis at the border" a central theme of that election. Trump ordered more than five thousand troops to the border to deal with the purported "invasion" of asylum seekers that were then approaching.

Mattis knew that soldiers weren't trained to act as Border Patrol agents, and he remembered the tragic incident when President Bill Clinton had ordered marines to the border to hunt for drug smugglers in 1997. The marines had accidentally killed an eighteen-year-old American kid who was grazing his family's goats near the border. The marines simply hadn't trained to do domestic law enforcement.

The border deployment of troops also looked like the military was being used for a political stunt. Even on Fox there was some skepticism about Trump's claim of an invasion. Fox News anchor Shepard Smith noted, "Tomorrow is one week before the midterm election, which is what all of this is about. There is no invasion. No one's coming to get you. There's nothing at all to worry about."

A sign of the fraying relationship between Trump and Mattis came when Trump told Lesley Stahl on CBS's *60 Minutes* in an interview that aired on October 14, 2018, that Mattis was "sort of a Democrat." This was not intended to be a compliment. It was also wildly off the mark, as Mattis was not affiliated with any party.

Trump, who had a schoolboy penchant for nicknames, also began to refer to his secretary of defense not as "Mad Dog" Mattis, but as "Moderate Dog."

What especially irked Mattis was Trump's decision in the first week of December to ignore his recommendation that the air force chief of staff, General David Goldfein, become the next chairman of the Joint Chiefs. Mattis's view was that he got to choose his own chairman, who was both the top officer in the US military and his principal military adviser. Trump instead chose General Mark Milley, who was the army chief of staff. Milley presented a gruff, tough-guy persona of the type that appealed to Trump, but he was also a Princeton grad who thought carefully about strategy. Mattis felt that Trump was blithely ignoring his advice on an issue that Mattis thought was of critical importance.

Days after the decision to appoint Milley as chairman was announced by Trump—by tweet—President Recep Tayyip Erdogan of Turkey started threatening to launch attacks against Kurdish forces in Syria that were advised by some two thousand American troops. By then the US-backed Kurdish forces known as the Syrian Democratic Forces had largely defeated ISIS on the ground in Syria. Trump's advisers wanted him to tell Erdogan that American forces in Syria would fire on the Turkish military if they attacked the Kurdish forces. Trump told his advisers, "I'm not gonna do this: start a war with a NATO ally which has the biggest army in Europe."

Trump also was annoyed that the Saudis had reneged on what he believed was an agreement that they would secure $4 billion to pay the costs of US military operations in Syria, operations that after all benefited the Saudis against two of their archenemies, Iran and ISIS.

Trump's attitude was "Why are my people dying so that we can then turn the country over to Iran and Russia when Assad doesn't leave? It's not our neighborhood. This isn't our fight. If you want us there, you pay for it."

Trump told King Salman, "It doesn't all have to come from you; it could come from other Arab states, but we're counting on you guys on bringing this home for us if you want us to stay in Syria because it's going to cover our operational costs in Syria."

King Salman made some polite *"Inshallah"* ("God willing") responses to Trump about the $4 billion. *Inshallah* can mean a wide range of things in the Middle East, from "Hmmm, interesting idea. Let me think about it" to "Likely this won't happen in our lifetimes," but Trump thought he had secured a deal with the Saudis.

Trump spoke with Erdogan in a phone call on December 14 during which the Turkish leader reminded Trump that he had repeatedly said that the US troops were in Syria only to defeat ISIS and now that that had happened, wasn't it time for them to leave? Turkey could handle any residual ISIS problem. Trump surprised Erdogan and Bolton, who was also on the call, when he suddenly pledged to withdraw all American troops from Syria. Trump told Erdogan, "It's all yours. We are done."

The CENTCOM commander, General Votel, knew that the Turks,

in fact, didn't have a realistic plan to defeat ISIS. "We had spent quite a bit of time looking at the various options that the Turks had proposed, and it was hard to see one that was feasible that would be better than what we had with the Syrian Democratic Forces," recalled Votel.

Bolton, Mattis, and Pompeo met Trump at the White House to try to persuade him not to pull out the troops in Syria. Such a move risked the return of ISIS and also handed a victory to the Iranian forces in Syria who were backing Assad.

Two days after Trump's call with Erdogan, Brett McGurk, who managed the global coalition to defeat ISIS, publicly warned against a withdrawal from Syria at the Doha Forum in Qatar, an annual gathering of national security officials from around the world. While McGurk described ISIS as a "significantly degraded organization," he warned that "no one who does this day to day is naive enough to know you can just declare victory and walk away. We have to maintain pressure on these networks really, for a period of years."

McGurk was traveling to Iraq when he received a call from Secretary of State Mike Pompeo telling him that Trump was indeed declaring victory and walking away from Syria. Against the advice of his national security advisers and with no consultation with key allies such as the Saudis, Trump made the troop withdrawal announcement via a tweet on December 19. Trump wrote, "We have defeated ISIS in Syria, my only reason for being there during the Trump Presidency." In a video also posted on Twitter, Trump declared, "Our boys, our young women, our men—they're all coming back, and they're coming back now."

There was no way McGurk, who coordinated the efforts of the many dozens of countries that made up the coalition against ISIS, could sell the new Syria policy to American allies who had long been assured that the United States would remain in Syria to ensure that ISIS didn't stage a comeback. McGurk told colleagues, "Listen, my legs got chopped out from under me. I can't stick around and do this." McGurk resigned.

General Dunford, the chairman of the Joint Chiefs, called Votel to inform him that the United States was pulling out of Syria. Votel then had the difficult job of informing the Syrian Democratic Forces about what was happening. Within a couple of hours, Votel had the commander of the SDF, General Mazloum Kobani Abdi, up on a secure videoconference.

Votel told Mazloum: "The President has directed us to withdraw all our forces from Syria. We just received the orders so have not had a chance to fully assess how it would be done, but I wanted to ensure you heard about it from me and not through the media."

Votel had visited Mazloum in Syria repeatedly and had gotten to know him pretty well. Votel found that Middle Eastern commanders such as Mazloum tended to take bad news better than their American counterparts, but still this was tough as they both knew that now the SDF could be exposed to the much larger forces of the Turkish military that were seeking to destroy them. Votel emphasized to Mazloum that the Americans would be as deliberate as possible with their withdrawal. Votel saw no strategic rationale for the withdrawal and would have recommended against it if he had been consulted, which he hadn't been.

What was particularly odd about Trump's policy shift was it did exactly what Trump repeatedly had warned against during his campaign. It gave America's enemies an early heads-up about US military plans. During the campaign, Trump also had critiqued the total American troop withdrawal from Iraq under Obama as helping pave the way for the rise of ISIS. Why risk any kind of repeat of this in Syria?

The announcement of the precipitous pullout of the American soldiers from Syria was an early Christmas present to Assad and his allies Putin and Iran, as well as to ISIS and al-Qaeda's affiliate in Syria. It also left the US-backed Kurdish forces that did almost all the fighting against ISIS vulnerable to attack by the powerful Turkish military. In effect, Trump's decision risked abandoning an American ally on the battlefield.

At 7:30 am on December 20, the day after Trump had tweeted about pulling out of Syria, Mattis decided to go to see the president. Mattis was livid about abandoning the Kurdish forces to their fate. At 3:00 pm Mattis met with Trump in the Oval Office and tried to persuade the president to reverse his decision. Trump wouldn't budge, so Mattis pulled out a two-page resignation letter.

Mattis's letter called out Trump on the need for "showing respect" to longtime allies. Mattis reminded Trump that twenty-nine NATO countries had fought "alongside" the US since 9/11. Mattis also took Trump to task for his mollycoddling of Russia and its "authoritarian model." In a final dig, Mattis reminded the president that he based his critique of Trump's policies on "over four decades of immersion in these issues." That was a not-so-subtle reminder that Trump was a national security neophyte and the first president who had neither served in the military nor ever held political office.

After Mattis announced his resignation, he said that he would stay in the job until the end of February to allow for an orderly transition.

Trump canceled his Christmas trip to Mar-a-Lago due to the government shutdown he had precipitated because Congress, in his view, hadn't funded his border wall sufficiently. So Trump was stuck at the White House watching a ton of cable news. Trump gave CNN the Stalinist appellation "the enemy of the people," but he watched hours of the network. Trump seethed over the laudatory coverage of Mattis's resignation on principle. Some of the coverage focused on the fact that Mattis was the last of the "axis of adults" to leave the administration, a group that also included Cohn, Kelly, McMaster, and Tillerson, all of whom had tried to moderate Trump's often-petulant policy choices.

Trump called Secretary of State Mike Pompeo and asked him to tell Mattis he was being pushed out two months early. (Trump never did his own dirty work.) Mattis was out of his job at the end of December.

Trump turned again to one of his most trusted military advisers, Fox News analyst and retired general Jack Keane, and asked him if he would take the secretary of defense job. For the second time in two plus years, Keane turned down Trump's offer. After the decade-and-a-half-long illness of his wife and her subsequent death, Keane was now remarrying at the end of 2019, and he preferred to be an informal outside adviser rather than taking on the top job at the Pentagon.

Mattis was replaced by Patrick Shanahan, a longtime Boeing executive who had no previous military or government experience before he was appointed to be Mattis's deputy in 2017. Trump nominated Shanahan to be the next secretary of defense. As the confirmation process moved forward, reporters found out that almost a decade earlier Shanahan had had a domestic violence dispute with his wife and in a separate incident his seventeen-year-old son had attacked his wife with a baseball bat, causing her serious injuries, an action Shanahan had defended at the time. Six months after assuming the position of acting secretary of defense, Shanahan dropped out of consideration for the top Pentagon job to "devote more time to his family," according to Trump. This was one of the oldest euphemisms in Washington, DC. There was scant chance Shanahan was going to survive what would surely have been a brutal confirmation hearing.

What was mystifying was that Shanahan had spent six months as the secretary of defense—in many ways the most important cabinet post—despite his limited qualifications for the job and also a history of violence in his family that might have disqualified most officials from obtaining the most sensitive of security clearances.

After Mattis resigned, Trump tweeted, "When President Obama ingloriously fired Jim Mattis, I gave him a second chance. Some thought I shouldn't, I thought I should." It was true that Mattis's term as commander of Central Command was wound up early by the Obama administration, but far from giving Mattis a "second chance," Trump was quite eager to install Mattis as his secretary of defense. Trump had publicly compared Mattis to one of his heroes, General George Patton, shortly after he tapped Mattis for the Pentagon job.

Following his resignation, Mattis initially maintained an eloquent silence about his time in Trumpworld. Mattis took seriously what the French term the *devoir de réserve*—the duty of reserve—meaning that public officials should keep silent about their time in office.

Mattis went back to his quiet retirement in Washington State and renewed his fellowship at the Hoover Institution at Stanford. Mattis's office was not far from that of H. R. McMaster, who also was a fellow at Hoover. They occasionally bumped into each other in the hallways, but other than exchanging the briefest of greetings, the two veterans of Trump's war cabinet didn't spend any time together.

Just as Trump's relationship with Mattis had soured, so too did it with Mattis's friend John Kelly. For Mattis, Kelly had been a great source of information, guidance, and atmospherics about what was happening at the White House. In late July 2017, Trump had tweeted, "I am pleased to inform you that I have just named General/Secretary John F Kelly as White House Chief of Staff. He is a Great American." Over time the bromance fizzled—as it so often did with Trump—and Kelly left the White House at the end of December 2018.

Kelly saw his tenure in the White House best measured by what he had prevented President Trump from doing—for instance, from pulling out of Afghanistan, as was the president's first instinct, or withdrawing from NATO, or pulling American forces out of South Korea.

Trump, who had become famous for a TV show in which his trademark line was "You're fired," set records for the level of turnover at the White House and in his cabinet. Kelly was one of the four top generals that Trump had brought in to run his administration. Flynn was fired within a month of Trump assuming office. McMaster resigned under pressure after just over a year as national security adviser. Mattis resigned after two years as secretary of defense. Trump then claimed, incorrectly, that he had fired Mattis. Kelly resigned when he was no longer on speaking terms with the president, which made his job as chief of staff untenable.

The differences between Trump and US military leaders were more than merely stylistic, although Trump's lack of decorum and rudeness were certainly at odds with the military's honor-based values. Military leaders tended to want to sustain overseas military commitments, which they saw as vital to securing world order, whether that was to defeat ISIS, or to contain a nuclear-armed North Korea, or to prevent Afghanistan from reverting to control by the Taliban. Trump believed he was elected to end foreign entanglements and that alliances like NATO were ripping off the United States. The generals knew that NATO allies had fought shoulder to shoulder with them since the 9/11 attacks.

Two weeks after Trump had said that the withdrawal of US troops from Syria would happen immediately, the Pentagon and the president came to an agreement to pull them out over a period of four months.

John Bolton was dispatched to the Middle East to provide some kind of ex post facto cleanup for Trump's hasty decision on Syria, which wasn't coordinated with American allies. On January 6, 2019, Bolton muddied the waters further, saying on a visit to Israel that the US would only withdraw from Syria if ISIS was completely defeated and if the safety of America's Kurdish allies fighting ISIS was guaranteed, a process that could take years.

This produced a furious response from Erdogan, who thought he had made a deal with Trump. Erdogan said on TV, "Bolton's remarks in Israel are not acceptable. It is not possible for me to swallow this. Bolton made a serious mistake."

Trump weighed in, tweeting about Syria: "We will be leaving at a proper pace while at the same time continuing to fight ISIS and doing all else that is prudent and necessary!"

It was hard to keep track of all the zigzagging on Syria. Leaving immediately! Leaving in four months! Leaving in, maybe, years!

Keane visited Trump at the White House on February 12, 2019. Keane thought that a total US pullout from Syria was a serious strategic error. He also believed that if you gave Trump the same old arguments, he would quickly tune you out, but if you came to him with new information, the president would give you a fair hearing.

Unfurling a map of Syria in the Oval Office, Keane showed Trump where the Iranian presence in the country was the strongest, where al-Qaeda still maintained a fighting force, and where the US coalition had destroyed the ISIS safe haven. Keane pointed out that the oil fields, most of which were in the east of the country, toward the Syrian border with Iraq, were under the control of the US coalition forces.

Keane told Trump, "If we just walk away and pull the troops out, the Russians and the Syrian regime will own the airspace, the Iranians will own the ground, and the Iranians will take control of the oil fields. The money they make out of this will then fund their proxies in Syria and Yemen as well as reduce the impact of US sanctions on Iran."

Trump said, "That's very interesting. That's a big deal."

In the end, the real "deep state"—retired senior generals such as Keane and officials at the Pentagon and State Department—managed to keep many hundreds of American soldiers in Syria indefinitely to ensure that ISIS didn't return in force and also to maintain some kind of American leverage over events in Syria.

But like so much else in Trump's consistently inconsistent foreign policy, he then changed his mind again. Trump green-lighted the invasion of Syria by the Turks on October 9, 2019, exposing America's Kurdish allies to the wrath of the second largest military in NATO. This came after a call between Trump and President Erdogan in which Trump said he would be pulling American forces out of northeastern Syria, where their presence was effectively preventing a Turkish invasion. Trump also tweeted "it is time for us to get out of these ridiculous Endless Wars, many of them tribal, and bring our soldiers home."

Then Trump shifted gears again, threatening on Twitter to "obliterate" the Turkish economy if the Turks did "anything that I, in my great and unmatched wisdom, consider to be off limits." The United States hadn't ever threatened a longtime NATO ally in this manner. Could anyone make sense of President Trump's Syria policy, other than Donald Trump?

Chapter 13

WITHDRAWAL

There is no instance of a country having
benefited from prolonged warfare.

—*Sun Tzu*

The worst thing you can possibly do in a deal
is to seem desperate to make it. That makes
the other guy smell blood, and then you're dead.

—*Donald Trump,* The Art of the Deal

The underlying theme in President Trump's State of the Union address on February 5, 2019 was withdrawal. Trump pointed to the nearly seven thousand American servicemen killed in the United States' long post-9/11 wars and the more than fifty thousand who were wounded. He also asserted that the US had "spent more than $7 trillion in fighting wars in the Middle East."

The president said that the two thousand US soldiers in Syria were being withdrawn now that ISIS was largely evicted from the territory it had held there. Trump also confirmed that his administration was holding "constructive talks" with the Taliban. Progress in those negotiations, Trump said, would enable a drawdown of the estimated fourteen thousand US troops in Afghanistan, leaving some kind of residual force to focus on "counterterrorism."

All of this was consistent with what Trump had said during the presidential campaign, when he repeatedly complained about the trillions of dollars that the US had spent on its post-9/11 wars in the greater Middle East.

Trump's State of the Union address acknowledged the obvious: he seemed to be reversing course on Afghanistan. After many months of debate in the National Security Council, on August 21, 2017, Trump had announced his new "South Asia strategy," which was to remain in Afghanistan for an unspecified length of time without announcing any withdrawal dates until "conditions" had improved.

In early 2018, as ISIS was on the run in Iraq and Syria, the Pentagon increasingly treated Afghanistan as "the main effort" and started moving significant resources to the country including Intelligence, Surveillance and Reconnaissance (ISR) assets.

Now that stay-the-course strategy in Afghanistan was dead, and it was to be replaced by direct American negotiations with the Taliban and a withdrawal of US troops.

In early December 2018, the Pentagon received an unexpected order to draw down the number of US soldiers in Afghanistan to zero. Just as Mattis resigned, that order was revised. Trump ordered the Pentagon to pull out seven thousand US troops from Afghanistan, about half the American servicemen in the country. As with the abrupt announcement of the pullout of US troops from Syria, this did again what Trump repeatedly had criticized Obama for during his campaign: gave America's enemies a heads-up about US military plans.

The hastily announced drawdown was not a politically useful message to send to the struggling Afghan government, or to Afghanistan's problematic neighbors, or to the Taliban, which had recently started negotiating directly with the United States. The principal Taliban demand was the withdrawal of American forces from Afghanistan. Trump styled himself as a great dealmaker, but he was giving the enemy what they wanted without exacting any concessions. The Art of the Giveaway, again.

Zalmay Khalilzad, an Afghan American who was Trump's special representative for Afghanistan, was leading the talks with the Taliban on the American side. Those talks were directly between the United States and the Taliban, long a key demand of the Taliban, which reviled the Afghan government as a puppet of the United States. Following a marathon six days of discussions between American diplomats and the Taliban in the Qatari capital, Doha, in late January 2019 Khalilzad tweeted, "Meetings here were more productive than they have been in the past. We made significant progress on vital issues." This tweet precipitated a flurry of news stories about a potential peace deal.

Khalilzad also tweeted that he had briefed Afghan president Ashraf Ghani "on the progress we have made." The Afghan government was excluded from the Taliban talks despite the fact that their outcome would likely deeply affect the Afghan people that it represented. Afghans were asking: Were the United States–Taliban talks a prelude to peace, or a betrayal of a US ally in which the terms of their surrender to the Taliban were being discussed without them?

The veteran American diplomat Ryan Crocker certainly thought it was the latter. Under the self-explanatory headline "I Was Ambassador to Afghanistan. This Deal Is a Surrender," Crocker, writing in the *Washington Post* on January 29, 2019, compared the negotiations with the Taliban "to the Paris peace talks during the Vietnam War. Then, as now, it was clear that by going to the table we were surrendering; we were just negotiating the terms of our surrender." The Paris peace deal was followed by the eventual collapse of the South Vietnamese government, which was America's ally, and the unification of the country under North Vietnam's communist leader, Ho Chi Minh.

Taliban officials told reporters in late January 2019 that the United States had agreed to a draft peace agreement that American troops would withdraw from Afghanistan within a year and a half. This would mean US troops would leave Afghanistan a few months before the American presidential election in early November 2020. President Trump could make good on one of his signature campaign promises, which was ending America's foreign wars.

I n early 2019, as the negotiations between the United States and the Taliban gathered pace, Kabul was a city on edge. The Taliban were at their strongest since their regime fell in the months after the 9/11 attacks. Twenty-foot-high concrete blast walls surrounded the "Green Zone" that sheltered the US embassy and key Afghan government buildings. It was the largest US embassy in the world, yet the US officials working there rarely left the Green Zone, and if they did, it was by helicopter.

Discussion of the withdrawal of US troops created a crisis of confidence among the many Afghans who had benefited from the post-Taliban era. The beneficiaries of that era included women and ethnic minorities such as the Hazaras as well as the new millennial generation of urban Afghans who were children when the Taliban were in power and had no nostalgia for an era when the country was taken back to the Middle Ages. A senior Afghan female official described the United States–Taliban talks simply as a "betrayal."

President Ghani and Khalilzad had a five-decade relationship that stretched back to when they were young Afghan students who both attended the American University of Beirut. They had quite different styles, crystallized in the books they each had written. Ghani cowrote *Fixing Failed States* with development expert Clare Lockhart, a technocratic account of how to fix countries such as Afghanistan, while Khalilzad wrote *The Envoy*, a memoir of his many years as a diplomat. If Ghani was the workaholic technocrat, Khalilzad was the wheeler-dealer looking to work out an arrangement.

Khalilzad hadn't spoken to President Trump directly about his negotiations with the Taliban, but Secretary of State Mike Pompeo and Khalilzad seemed to be trying to fulfill a campaign promise by Trump that the United States should extricate itself from its expensive foreign wars. "Trump sincerely wants to get the fuck out of Afghanistan," a Trump administration official explained. Khalilzad was given wide latitude to make that happen.

Khalilzad joked with his Taliban counterparts, asking them, "When was the last time you were in Kabul?" All concerned knew full well that it had been at least eighteen years since any of the Taliban leadership had set foot in the capital city.

Khalilzad told the Taliban negotiators, "You know there has been quite a lot of change since you were last there. It was a dead city before 9/11. Now it's an alive city. Women are driving. Women are in the cafés and restaurants. There are millions of people."

Khalilzad's point to the Taliban was that they needed to accommodate themselves to all these new realities.

The "framework" for a possible peace agreement that Khalilzad negotiated was that the Taliban agreed that they would not allow Afghanistan to be used as a launching pad for attacks by international terrorist groups such as al-Qaeda. This was a demand that the United States has made for the past two decades, since al-Qaeda had bombed two US embassies in Africa in August 1998, killing more than two hundred people, attacks that the group had carried out when it was based in Taliban-controlled Afghanistan. The Taliban continued to shelter bin Laden after those bombings, even as he was planning the far more lethal 9/11 attacks. After 9/11, the Taliban then refused to hand bin Laden over to the United States and the long Afghan War began.

In return for the Taliban pledge that they would no longer provide a safe haven to international terrorist groups, US forces would withdraw from Afghanistan, ending America's longest war. Also, there were discussions between the Taliban and US officials about a cease-fire, as well as of direct negotiations between the Afghan government and the Taliban.

Khalilzad told the Taliban, "We'll talk to you directly in Doha about our core interests on counterterrorism and your core interests on our troop withdrawal timeline, but you have to guarantee that you'll talk to the other Afghans, including the Afghan government, and also other key stakeholders to resolve your own inter-Afghan conflicts, so that once we do leave, there's some stability in governance, institutions, and a political roadmap for the country to move forward, so you don't just revert back into civil war."

The Taliban agreed to that, sort of, but then they said, "We want agreement with you first on the first two issues, counterterrorism and troop withdrawal, before we'll move into the negotiations with the other Afghans, but trust us. We'll move into negotiations with the other Afghans."

Khalilzad told the Taliban, "We can come up with the contours of what our troop withdrawal timeline might look like and what counterterrorism guarantees you'll give us, but that's all going to be conditioned on making progress on the two other issues, a cease-fire and progress on inter-Afghan discussions." Khalilzad had a mantra: "Nothing is agreed until everything is agreed."

But the Taliban were seemingly in no mood for any kind of real compromise. A senior Taliban negotiator, Sher Mohammad Abbas Stanekzai, said in an interview with a Pashtu language website in February 2019 that the Taliban would not negotiate with the Afghan government until the full withdrawal of foreign forces, including all troops, advisers, and contractors. Stanekzai also said that the Taliban planned to abolish the Afghan army and that the Afghan constitution would be amended and based on their version of sharia law. In other words, following the withdrawal of all US forces, the Taliban wanted the Afghan government to unilaterally disarm and they would then write a new constitution they regarded as sufficiently Islamic.

The Afghan constitution ratified in 2004 guaranteed the rights of women to work and girls to be educated. Given the Taliban's dismal track record about the rights of women and girls, it was hard to believe that these rights wouldn't be curtailed or even abolished in a future Taliban utopia.

Adding to the anxiety of many Afghans was the meeting in Moscow on February 5, 2019, between the Taliban and leading Afghan politicians such as former Afghan president Hamid Karzai. Again, the Afghan government played no role in those discussions. One of the Afghan delegates at the Moscow meeting said the mood of the Taliban there was "victorious." Nothing, of course, would have given the former KGB officer, Russian president Vladimir Putin, greater satisfaction than handing the United States a bloody nose in Afghanistan just as the US-backed Afghan guerillas did to the Soviets in Afghanistan during the 1980s.

The Afghan government was increasingly embittered by the fact that they had been cut out of the negotiations with the Taliban. Hamdullah Mohib, the thirty-six-year-old Afghan national security adviser and a protégé of Ghani's, told journalists in Washington, DC, in mid-March 2019 that Khalilzad was "stonewalling" the Afghan government about the Taliban negotiations. "There isn't proper access to information. The last people to find out are us," Mohib told the reporters.

Mohib then launched a supremely undiplomatic attack on the American negotiator, saying, "Knowing Ambassador Khalilzad's own history, personal history, he has ambitions in Afghanistan. . . . The perception in

Afghanistan and the people in the government think, perhaps, perhaps all this talk is to create a caretaker government of which he will then become the viceroy."

Accusing a senior American diplomat of cooking up a deal with the Taliban so he could become the viceroy of Afghanistan was a strong charge. State Department officials freaked out and summoned Mohib for a dressing down.

After that, whenever Mohib appeared at any meetings with US officials, they all walked out. Relations between the US government and the Taliban now appeared to be warmer than the Trump administration's relations with the democratically elected Afghan government.

Meanwhile, the cofounder of the Taliban, Mullah Baradar, was living in Qatar, from where he was leading the negotiations with the Americans. The good cleric certainly seemed to be enjoying the diversions of Doha a whole lot more than living in the harsh, mountainous deserts of southern Afghanistan.

In February 2019, when retired general Jack Keane had met with Trump in the Oval Office to discuss the US presence in Syria, he also took the opportunity to give the president his thoughts about the war against jihadist terrorists in Afghanistan and elsewhere, telling him, "The Afghans are doing the fighting, we are advising them, and we have a small counterterrorism force that is going after the high-value targets."

Keane went on, "Ever since 9/11, we have said it makes sense to fight specifically only those radicals who could do danger to the American people. So we're not involved in the entire global radical Islamic movement, far from it, we're interested in those who may be a danger to the security of the American people. And that's in four or five places, like against Al-Qaeda in the Arabian Peninsula in Yemen. Let's assume there's a miracle and we get a peace treaty in Afghanistan. We should keep a small contingent of American forces there to make certain that al-Qaeda and ISIS do not build a safe haven again and we should keep those forces there indefinitely."

"Indefinitely?!" Trump asked.

Keane replied, "Indefinitely! We're doing that right now in Yemen,

Libya, and East Africa. There's no pressure to get out of there. We have established a condition: as long as a particular terrorist organization is a threat to the American people, then we should be involved."

These arguments seemed to have made some impression on Trump. Five months later in an interview with Fox News anchor Tucker Carlson—long a skeptic of America's wars overseas—the president said of Afghanistan, "I call it the Harvard of terrorists. . . . I'll give you a tough one. If you were in my position and . . . a great central casting general walks up to your office . . . and you have some really talented military people saying, 'I'd rather attack them over there than have them hit us over here and fight them on our land.' It's something you always have to think about. Now, I would leave and will leave—we will be leaving very strong intelligence, far more than you would normally think because it's very important."

In an Oval Office meeting with the Pakistani prime minister Imran Khan on July 22, 2019, Trump improbably claimed to reporters, "If we wanted to fight a war in Afghanistan and win it, I could win that war in a week. I just don't want to kill 10 million people. I have plans on Afghanistan that if I wanted to win that war, Afghanistan would be wiped off the face of the Earth." Had Trump contemplated dropping nuclear weapons on Afghanistan? It wasn't clear. After Khan's visit to the White House, a number of stories appeared in the media reporting that a peace agreement between the United States and the Taliban was imminent. Retired General David Petraeus, who generally avoided making any kind of public statement criticizing American government policy, took to the op-ed pages of the *Wall Street Journal*, declaring that "the kind of U.S. withdrawal that was inadvisable in Iraq eight years ago would be indefensible for Afghanistan today." This was a strong statement coming from the general who had commanded both the wars in Afghanistan and Iraq.

The Trump administration seemed to be trying to thread an impossible needle, which was to cut a peace deal with the Taliban, who were demanding a total American withdrawal from Afghanistan, while at the same time ensuring that the country would not revert into becoming a "Harvard for terrorists," which a complete US withdrawal would surely help to enable. Meanwhile, the Trump administration was treating the Taliban as if they were a government in waiting while it was excluding the legitimate, elected Afghan government from any role in its negotiations with the Taliban.

Meanwhile, the Taliban also had their own disagreements. The "Quetta Shura," the overall command of the Taliban, wanted all the American forces to leave Afghanistan within six months, while the chief Taliban negotiator Mullah Baradar had agreed with Khalilzad to a timeline of under two years.

On August 17, 2019, Khalilzad traveled to brief Trump about the negotiations at the president's Bedminster, New Jersey, golf club where he was spending a working vacation. Trump had only met Khalilzad briefly once before.

Attending the briefing was Secretary of State Mike Pompeo; National Security Adviser John Bolton; the chairman of the Joint Chiefs, General Joseph Dunford, who had been overall commander of the Afghan War; and the CIA director, Gina Haspel. After the meeting Trump tweeted, "Just completed a very good meeting on Afghanistan. Many on the opposite side of this 19 year war, and us, are looking to make a deal—if possible."

This bland tweet didn't represent the real disagreements about the Afghan War that were then roiling Trump's national security team. Khalilzad was pressing to give the Taliban a date certain for getting American troops to zero in Afghanistan. The reliably hawkish Republican senator Lindsey Graham, who had Trump's ear, had visited Bedminster earlier in the month and warned the president not to go to zero in Afghanistan. The CIA and the Pentagon were adamantly opposed to going to zero and wanted to keep four or five bases to continue counterterrorism operations in Afghanistan and across the border in neighboring Pakistan. Even if these bases were staffed by CIA officers, they would still need military units to guard them and to carry out raids.

In their negotiation with Khalilzad, the Taliban had agreed not to let terrorists use any of the areas that they controlled in Afghanistan and, more important, they had also agreed to break publicly with al-Qaeda.

In return the United States would commit to a partial drawdown of some five thousand troops with the eventual goal of a possible complete withdrawal, which was conditioned on the Taliban keeping their side of the bargain. The United States also gave itself an important out: When a new Afghan government was installed, the new government could ask for American troops to be posted to Afghanistan and the United States could then potentially agree to such a request.

The next stage, if everything went to plan, was for the Afghan government and the Taliban to sit down together and begin negotiating what role the Taliban might play in Afghan politics going forward. Afghanistan had been at war for four decades since the Soviets had invaded the country in 1979. Might this be the beginning of a lasting peace? No one knew.

But then Trump suddenly developed some serious buyer's remorse. On September 7, 2019, Trump surprised even his close advisers with a tweet that "the major Taliban leaders and, separately, the President of Afghanistan, were going to secretly meet with me at Camp David on Sunday." Trump wrote that he had "cancelled the meeting and called off peace negotiations," because the Taliban had "admitted to an attack in Kabul that killed one of our great soldiers."

It seemed that Trump was now focused on the fact that a withdrawal agreement with the Taliban might saddle him with a bad deal in Afghanistan that could become a real headache in his second term, should he secure one. However you dressed it up, Khalilzad was negotiating a withdrawal agreement with the Taliban. And simply because the US withdrew its troops from a conflict didn't mean the war was over, as Obama had discovered when he had pulled all American troops out of Iraq in 2011. It also wasn't possible to pick a worse moment to be cozying up to the Taliban, considering that photos of the Taliban leadership meeting with Trump at Camp David would have landed on front pages just as the United States started commemorating the eighteenth anniversary of the 9/11 attacks. Trump pronounced that the talks with the Taliban were now "dead."

Chapter 14

THE "INVASION"

The central image is that of a vast and sinister conspiracy,
a gigantic and yet subtle machinery of influence set in motion to undermine
and destroy a way of life. . . . The paranoid spokesman sees the fate of
this conspiracy in apocalyptic terms—he traffics in the birth and death of
whole worlds, whole political orders, whole systems of human values.
He is always manning the barricades of civilization. He constantly
lives at a turning point: it is now or never in organizing resistance
to the conspiracy. Time is forever just running out.

—*"The Paranoid Style in American Politics,"*
from The Paranoid Style in American Politics
and Other Essays, *Richard Hofstadter, 1965*

This attack is a response to the Hispanic invasion of Texas.

—*Patrick Cursius, a right-wing terrorist*
who killed twenty-two people at a Walmart
in El Paso, Texas, on August 3, 2019

J ust ahead of the midterm elections, in the fall of 2018, a caravan of more than seven thousand migrants, mostly from Central America, was wending its way north through Mexico toward the southern border. This was a political gift to President Trump who had, of course, run on a "get-tough on immigration and terrorism" platform during his presidential campaign.

Trump tweeted that "unknown Middle Easterners are mixed in" with the thousands of migrants. The intent of this tweet was surely to play on American fears about the possibility of mysterious Middle Easterners attacking the country, as they had on 9/11. Of course, the notion of a Middle Eastern terrorist joining a caravan of migrants who were covered by TV reporters almost continuously for many weeks was implausible on its face.

There was another problem with this notion: all the lethal terrorist attacks in the United States since 9/11 were carried out by US citizens or legal residents. In addition, of the more than four hundred jihadist terrorism cases prosecuted in the United States since 9/11, not one of the terrorists had infiltrated the country across the southern border. And the State Department's Bureau of Counterterrorism observed in 2017 that there was "no credible information that any member of a terrorist group has traveled through Mexico to gain access to the United States."

The Trump administration framed the necessity of a southern border wall, in part, as a response to a purported national security emergency involving terrorists. This was hogwash. The year 2018 saw one of the lowest annual numbers of jihadist terrorism cases in the United States—nineteen—since the rise of ISIS. The largest number of such cases was in 2015 when there were eighty. While the number of terrorism cases wasn't an exact proxy for levels of threat, it certainly said something about the scale of the threat. The United States had seen a steep decline in the number of jihadist terrorism cases by 2018.

In the days before the 2018 elections, Fox News anchors and Trump started whipping up hysteria about the approaching caravan. *Fox & Friends* cohost Pete Hegseth claimed that the caravan of asylum seekers "looks a lot more like an invasion than anything else." Trump tweeted, "This is an invasion of our Country and our Military is waiting for you!"

The paranoia surrounding the migrants' caravan had lethal consequences. Ten days before the midterm elections, on October 27, Robert Bowers murdered eleven worshippers at a Pittsburgh synagogue. Before he carried out the massacre at the synagogue, Bowers posted frequently about the migrants making their way through Mexico. Adopting Trump's language, Bowers repeatedly called them "invaders." Bowers also posted multiple anti-Semitic rants on the Gab social media network. Bowers blamed the Jewish philanthropist George Soros for financing the migrant caravan, which was a common conspiracy theory among a virulent minority of Trump's supporters.

I n early January 2019, Chris Wallace of Fox News interviewed Sarah Sanders, the then–White House press secretary, and challenged her on the supposed terrorist threat at the southern border. Sanders asserted, "We know that 4,000 known or suspected terrorists come into our country illegally and we know that the most vulnerable point of entry is at our southern border."

This was a misleading statistic since these four thousand individuals were not terrorists but had shown up as a "hit" on a watch list of more than a million and a half individuals who were deemed to have some possible link to terrorism. The four thousand people turned away from entering the US were those who may have had some kind of putative connection to terrorism. They were not proven terrorists, otherwise they would have been arrested and charged. And there wasn't a case since 9/11 of a terrorist being arrested at the border.

Since 9/11, three foreign terrorist organizations had mounted serious plots to attack the United States, and all the plotters flew into the country from South Asia and the Middle East. None of them crossed over the United States–Mexico border. Najibullah Zazi was trained by al-Qaeda to blow up bombs in the Manhattan subway in 2009. He arrived in the United States from Pakistan by plane. So too did Faisal Shahzad, whom the Pakistani Taliban trained to blow up a bomb in Manhattan a year later. Neither plot succeeded.

"Underwear Bomber" Umar Farouk Abdulmutallab flew into the country on Christmas Day 2009 on the plane that he tried unsuccessfully to blow up over Detroit. Al-Qaeda in Yemen had trained him.

The only cross-border infiltration by a terrorist was two years before 9/11 when Ahmed Ressam, an Algerian, was arrested on a ferry arriving in Washington State from Canada on December 14, 1999. As Ressam's car rolled out of the ferry, a US customs inspector pulled him over. Agents found more than one hundred pounds of explosives in Ressam's car. Ressam planned to bomb Los Angeles International Airport. Despite the Ressam case, fomenting fears of terrorists crossing the border from Canada hadn't gained much political traction in the United States.

Trump kept pushing the conspiracy theory that mysterious Middle Easterners were crossing the southern border, tweeting on January 18, 2019, "Border rancher: 'We've found prayer rugs out here. It's unreal.' . . . People coming across the Southern Border from many countries, some of which would be a big surprise." Trump linked to a story in the conservative *Washington Examiner* that cited an anonymous rancher in New Mexico who had supposedly found the prayer rugs. Oddly, there were no photos of the rugs.

John Kelly, having been commander of SOUTHCOM under Obama and then head of the Department of Homeland Security for Trump, understood the issues about the southern border well. Kelly often said privately that "the wall" was a misnomer and that it would not run from "sea to shining sea" as Trump often claimed. In fact, there was no need for a physical wall in many sections of the border where there were inhospitable deserts or American Indian reservations.

Kelly told Trump that the wall "wasn't the Maginot Line," the defensive line of fortresses and concrete fortifications the French had built after World War I on their eastern border to try to prevent the Germans from invading France. "The wall" wasn't really a wall; it was better border infrastructure. Of course, "Build better border infrastructure" wasn't quite as catchy a slogan as "Build the wall!"

In the end, only around sixty miles of wall—or to be more precise, steel bollard fence—were built during the first two and a half years of Trump's presidency. Despite all of Trump's rhetoric about combating the invading immigrants from the south, the number of migrants trying to cross the southern border was at a thirteen-year high in 2019.

The real issue wasn't the lack of a southern border wall from the Atlantic to the Pacific but the appalling conditions in the Central American countries of El Salvador, Guatemala, and Honduras, which had some of the world's highest homicide rates and were riven by drug violence and gangs. The migrants from Central America were fleeing the desperate conditions in their countries and were willing to make the long and often dangerous trek to the United States to take their chances there. Building better border infrastructure wasn't going to do much of anything to stem the flow of Central American asylum seekers.

The Trump administration's counterterrorism strategy correctly observed that the United States had "long faced a persistent security threat from domestic terrorists who are not motivated by a radical Islamist ideology but are instead motivated by other forms of violent extremism." The most lethal terrorist attack against Hispanics in American history was a bleak reminder of this. Patrick Cursius, a twenty-one-year-old white man shot and killed twenty-two people at a Walmart in Texas on August 3, 2019. Minutes before the attack, the shooter had posted a manifesto on 8chan, an online message board often featuring racist postings, about his support for the terrorist who had killed fifty-one worshippers at two mosques in Christchurch, New Zealand, five months earlier. Just as school shooters learn from other school shooters, terrorists also learn from other terrorists. The terrorist who carried out the Christchurch attack had posted his own manifesto to 8chan just before he carried out the attacks at the mosques.

The online manifesto by the El Paso shooter referred to a purported Hispanic invasion of Texas as the rationale for his terrorist attack. As mentioned above, Trump had also described immigrants coming across the southern border as an "invasion." However, in the manifesto, the shooter said that his views about immigrants had predated Trump becoming president.

With the 22 fatalities in the El Paso attack, terrorists motivated by far-right ideology had killed 109 people in the United States since the 9/11 attacks, while jihadist militants had killed 104. Trump needed to recognize that the threat posed by far-right terrorists was of a similar scope to that posed by jihadist terrorists and that he should use the bully pulpit of his presidency to attack the ideological underpinnings of right-wing violence—rather than stoking its flames.

To his credit, two days after the El Paso attack Trump made formal remarks at the White House in which he condemned "racism, bigotry and white supremacy." This was the teleprompter Trump. Would he return to being the president who trafficked in white identity politics when he was back on Twitter or addressing one of his raucous rallies? By the end of the summer of 2019 the answer was obvious.

Chapter 15

THE PLANES WERE LEAVING

Everybody has a plan until they get punched in the mouth.

—*Heavyweight boxer Mike Tyson*

During the evening of June 20, 2019, President Trump pulled back air strikes on three Iranian targets that could have killed as many as 150 people. Trump tweeted that the operation was called off because it wasn't a "proportionate" response to Iranian forces bringing down an unmanned US surveillance drone several days earlier.

"The planes were leaving" when the president called off the mission, according to a senior Trump administration official.

Trump tweeted "10 minutes before the strike I stopped it." Trump pulled back from the brink of a much larger confrontation with Iran that was advocated by Bolton, who, like a number of hawks in recent American history, hadn't served in any wars and had avoided service in Vietnam by taking a deferment while he was attending Yale. Yet Bolton hadn't met a war he didn't love.

It wasn't quite John F. Kennedy adeptly managing the Cuban Missile Crisis, but it was one of the better moments of Trump's presidency since it stopped an escalatory set of responses that could have embroiled the United States in a shooting war with Iran.

Such a potentially lethal strike also surely would have needed, at an absolute minimum, congressional buy-in, and more properly it would have needed an actual congressional resolution for the use of force. US presidents had sometimes disputed Congress's authority over military strikes, but congressional approval was how things should work, according to the War Powers Act of 1973. And Trump had neither congressional buy-in nor an authorization for the use of force for a conflict with Iran.

An escalatory strike of this scale could also have posed serious risks to Americans in the Middle East. Unlike the Syrian regime against which Trump launched air strikes in 2017 and 2018, Iran had the capacity to launch significant retaliatory operations across the Middle East. Iran and its proxies had major presences in Lebanon, Iraq, Syria, and Yemen. Iran also had thousands of missiles with ranges of up to 1,500 miles that could hit targets around the region, including Israel, and could reach as far as southeastern Europe. The more hard-line elements in Iran could easily unleash their forces or proxies against American troops in both Iraq and Syria or against American commercial targets around the Middle East.

Iran also wasn't Syria, where Trump had launched the strikes in 2017 and 2018 after the Syrian regime used chemical weapons against its own people. Those strikes enforced a significant international norm against the use of chemical weapons and had considerable support around the world. Indeed, the British and the French both participated in the 2018 strikes.

There also would have been scant support for strikes against Iran by America's European allies, who supported the Iran nuclear deal, because the Iranians had been sticking to the terms of the agreement. The International Atomic Energy Agency had repeatedly certified that Iran had stuck to the terms of the nuclear deal. Yet, less than a month after Bolton became national security adviser, the US pulled out of the Iran deal.

Trump had largely created the crisis with Iran by pulling out of the deal in the spring of 2018 and imposing tough new sanctions on the Iranians with no real Plan B for what would come next, once the Iranians started pushing back against the sanctions that were crippling their economy.

In June 2019, Iran responded to the new US sanctions by threatening that it would start pulling out of parts of the nuclear deal. Around the same time, US officials briefed reporters about intelligence suggesting Iran or its proxies were planning to attack American forces in Iraq and Syria or at sea.

Bolton ordered up military options that were briefed to top Trump national security officials that called for as many as tens of thousands of American troops to deploy to the Middle East if Iran attacked American targets in the region or resumed work on its nuclear weapons program.

In recent weeks, Bolton had also pushed for a coup in Venezuela against the socialist strongman president Nicolás Maduro. The US-backed coup attempt fizzled. Trump blamed Bolton for the botched coup. Trump said that he actually moderated the bellicose Bolton: "I'm the one who tempers him, which is OK. I have John Bolton and I have people who are a little more dovish than him." When Trump met with Kim Jong Un for the third time at the DMZ to discuss North Korea's nuclear program, along tagged Jared and Ivanka Kushner, and Tucker Carlson. Meanwhile, Bolton, who had spent much of his professional career focused on arms control issues, went on a previously scheduled trip to . . . Mongolia.

Given the amount of turnover in his cabinet, Trump couldn't get rid of Bolton immediately, but he started thinking about other candidates to be his national security adviser. Trump was intrigued by Fox News talking head Colonel Douglas Macgregor, who had been H. R. McMaster's superior officer during the legendary Battle of 73 Easting during the first Gulf War and like McMaster had also obtained a doctorate. Unlike McMaster, Macgregor was an extreme skeptic about American military interventions in the greater Middle East, appearing on Fox to rail against the "globalist elite" on Capitol Hill and at the Pentagon and State Department who were purportedly pushing for the continuation of the Afghan War. Macgregor also appeared on Fox strongly opposing any kind of conflict with Iran. In the end Trump chose Robert O'Brien, who had worked as the Trump administration's chief hostage negotiator at the State Department, and had ingratiated himself with the president with his work on freeing hostages.

The enemy always gets a vote in any conflict. The Iranian deep state—the Islamic Revolutionary Guard Corps and its elite Quds Force—as well as Iranian proxies around the Middle East started fighting back to signal their anger with the Trump-imposed sanctions. In May 2019, two Saudi oil tankers and two other ships were attacked in the Strait of Hormuz in the Persian Gulf. US intelligence assessed that Iran was behind the attacks. Oil facilities in Saudi Arabia were also attacked by armed drones. Houthi rebels in Yemen—armed with Iranian missiles—launched attacks at an airport in Saudi Arabia, wounding twenty-six and sending a clear message that Iran could turn the heat up on the Trump administration's close ally, Saudi crown prince Mohammed bin Salman.

The Iranian regime also understood that Trump was quite sensitive to the price of oil, which tended to spike whenever tensions rose in the Middle East. Oil prices jumped to over sixty-four dollars a barrel after the Iranians shot down the US drone.

As a result of the increasing tensions with Iran, Bolton announced that the United States was deploying a carrier strike group and a bomber task force to the Middle East, and the Pentagon deployed a total of 2,500 more troops to the Middle East. But the story got more complicated because Trump then sent mixed messages regarding his true intentions. He said he wanted to talk to the Iranians, and he also tweeted that a war with Iran would be "the official end of Iran." After the US drone was shot down, he tweeted, "Iran made a very big mistake!" Trump approved the strikes against Iranian missile batteries and radars and then he abruptly called off the operation.

The new round of US sanctions more than halved Iran's oil exports, its key revenue source. As a result, Iran had to reduce its support for key regional proxies such as Lebanese Hezbollah, forcing the organization to cut the salaries it paid to its fighters and to withdraw some of its troops from Syria, as well as to reduce spending on Al-Manar, its TV station in Lebanon. A key goal of Trump's "maximum pressure" campaign against Iran—forcing Iran to reduce its support for its proxy forces in the Middle East—had started to work.

The sanctions were also putting considerable pressure on Iranian officials to suggest renewed discussions about their nuclear program. Iran's foreign minister Mohammad Zarif told reporters in New York on July 18, 2019, that in exchange for the lifting of the sanctions, Iran would allow international inspectors greater latitude to inspect its nuclear program.

Zarif didn't have a huge amount of juice with the mullahs who actually ran the show in Iran, but Iran's hard-line former president, Mahmoud Ahmadinejad, certainly did. Around the same time that Zarif made his offer, Ahmadinejad told the *New York Times*, "Mr. Trump is a man of action. He is a businessman and therefore he is capable of calculating cost-benefits and making a decision. We say to him, let's calculate the long-term cost-benefit of our two nations and not be shortsighted." This came a month after Trump had said he would speak to the Iranians with "no preconditions."

Of course, there were plenty of reasons to be concerned that the confrontation with Iran could easily end in a deeper conflict instead of at the negotiating table. Iran announced in July 2019 that it was breaching the terms of the nuclear deal by enriching uranium beyond the 3.67 percent purity allowed by the agreement, enriching it above 4.5 percent. This was still a very long way from the 90 percent purity that would be needed for a nuclear weapon, but it was a small step down the road to reactivating Iran's nuclear weapons program, the program that Trump had repeatedly said he would never allow.

The same day that Zarif was telling reporters in New York that he was ready to parley, Trump announced that the US had brought down an Iranian drone that was flying too close to the USS *Boxer* in the Strait of Hormuz. The Iranians denied it was one of their drones. The following day, the Iranians seized a British oil tanker that was cruising in the Strait of Hormuz.

The brinkmanship between Iran and the United States and its closest allies seemed likely to produce some kind of incident that could lead to escalatory responses on both sides. At the same time, could Trump be pulling off what he had always wanted, which was a new set of negotiations for a new deal with Iran? If so, this would truly be a "Nixon goes to China" moment for the Trump administration, which was already talking to both the North Koreans and the Taliban. Perhaps the Iranians and the Americans would follow Churchill's admonition "To jaw-jaw is always better than to war-war"?

Chapter 16

COMMANDER IN CHIEF

It's not titles that honor men, but men that honor titles.

—*Machiavelli*

L'état c'est moi.

—*Louis XIV*

Patriotism is the last refuge of a scoundrel.

—*Samuel Johnson in 1775*

Trump turned the traditional celebration of Independence Day in Washington, DC, into a spectacle starring himself. On the steps of the Lincoln Memorial on the evening of July 4, 2019—where more than half a century earlier Dr. Martin Luther King Jr. had delivered one of the most influential speeches in American history—Trump gave a speech recounting the heroism of the five branches of the American military from the Revolutionary era to the post-9/11 wars. It was a roll call of America's greatest military hits: George Washington's Continental Army, American "flyboys" during World War I, the Battle of Midway, the marines raising the flag at Iwo Jima, and the SEALs who killed bin Laden.

Confounding his critics, who feared that Trump would turn his July 4 speech into a MAGA rally, the president didn't attack the news media, Democrats, the Mueller "witch hunt," or any other of his familiar targets. Nor did Trump trumpet his own achievements. Instead, Trump played the role of the nonpartisan, patriotic commander in chief advancing what was for him a rare message of national unity when he declared, "As we gather this evening in the joy of freedom, we remember that we all share a truly extraordinary heritage. Together, we are part of one of the greatest stories ever told—the story of America."

Trump had a schoolboy fascination with military hardware, and he reveled in the ceremonial aspects of being the commander in chief. Trump was deeply impressed by the French display of military might that he had seen at the Bastille Day celebration in Paris two years earlier when he was visiting the French president Emmanuel Macron. Macron had made Trump the guest of honor at the celebration that commemorated the beginning of the French Revolution. Trump watched as dozens of French tanks rolled by and Mirage fighter jets roared overhead. Trump loved the display, telling aides afterward that it was "awesome" and that they should mount a similar parade back in Washington. Trump said such a parade could "show off our military and help to educate Americans about it." Trump told his advisers, "We can't be outshone by the French."

Initially, Trump planned a major military parade for Veterans Day, November 11, 2018, in Washington, DC, but the Pentagon quietly killed the plan, partly because of concerns about costs, which were estimated to be up to $50 million.

Months later Trump ordered the Pentagon to put on a spectacular show for his July 4 speech, and this time the generals came through. As a light rain fell on Independence Day, Trump, standing behind a bulletproof screen on the Lincoln Memorial, narrated a flyby of some of the most advanced aircraft in the air force, saying, "You will soon see beautiful brand new F-22 Raptors" and "one magnificent B-2 stealth bomber." Trump ended his speech by introducing a show by the navy's "famous, incredible, talented" Blue Angels flight team.

Beyond his love of the showmanship of his role as commander in chief, how has Trump performed substantively in his duties, as the commander of the US military, to keep Americans safe? One of the few institutions that Trump didn't attack as president was the military. Instead, Trump presided over substantial increases in defense spending, targeting $750 billion for fiscal 2020, while Obama's defense budgets were in the $600 billion range. Trump may have soured on the generals who worked for him, but his romance with the military writ large was one of the constants of his presidency.

Once you got past their rhetorically quite different styles, there was an important commonality between Presidents Obama and Trump as commanders in chief. Both presidents saw themselves as elected to get the United States out of the seemingly endless, expensive post-9/11 wars.

The Trump administration continued the Obama doctrine of avoiding big, conventional wars and kept in place much of the "small footprint" counterterrorism architecture that Obama had developed, including his overall approach to the war against ISIS in Iraq and Syria and his reliance on special operations forces and drones to hunt and kill jihadist terrorists. In Pakistan, Somalia, and Yemen, Trump continued the drone campaigns that were a signature of Obama's administration.

Trump, like Obama, did not send any additional prisoners to Guantanamo, instead relying on federal courts to try alleged terrorists, nor did he push for the coercive interrogations of suspected terrorists to resume despite comments he had made on the campaign trail that he was in favor of torture for terrorists.

Trump could change his mind about any given issue, which made it hard for the United States to have a coherent America First strategy, as demonstrated by his abrupt decisions to pull US forces out of both Afghanistan and Syria. Trump then changed his mind again on Syria, opting to leave the residual force there, and he also reversed himself on Afghanistan when he scrapped the talks with the Taliban. Trump whipsawed between offering talks with the Iranian regime and authorizing a military strike against Iranian military targets, which he then called off. Trump went from threatening North Korea with "fire and fury" to declaring his "love" for Kim within the space of a little over a year.

Trump avoided making major unforced foreign policy errors, such as George W. Bush's decision to go to war in Iraq, a war of choice that helped create Al-Qaeda in Iraq, which later evolved into ISIS and which also helped to spread sectarianism around the Middle East. Trump also avoided getting sucked into a larger war in Syria and avoided a military confrontation with North Korea.

When it came to the actual use of force, Commander in Chief Trump was rather cautious about sending more US troops to Afghanistan in 2017, doing so only with great hesitancy. Trump also surprised his advisers by announcing a total pullout from Syria at the end of 2018 after much of ISIS was defeated. The following year, Trump canceled a military operation against the Iranians, and he also avoided making any moves that might provoke a conflict with the regime of Kim Jong Un.

It's also true that Trump didn't score any major foreign policy triumphs, such as expelling Saddam from Kuwait (George H. W. Bush); engineering a peaceful end to the Cold War (Reagan and George H. W. Bush); or authorizing the raid that killed bin Laden (Obama).

That said, Trump did have some foreign policy wins. During 2017, Trump oversaw an effective campaign against ISIS; he made a long-term military commitment to Afghanistan, where the Taliban had been steadily seizing territory; he drew a clear "red line" when he responded robustly to Assad's use of nerve agents in Syria by launching cruise missile attacks against Syrian military targets; and he made his first overseas trip as president to Saudi Arabia, where he spoke to the leaders of more than fifty Muslim countries, a trip that was generally seen as a success because of his effective outreach to Arab states.

In 2018, Trump could point to fewer foreign policy wins. Trump once again responded robustly to the Assad regime's repeated use of chemical weapons, but by moving the US embassy in Israel from Tel Aviv to Jerusalem, Trump torpedoed any possibility of the United States brokering a peace deal between the Israelis and Palestinians. Trump feuded publicly with major Western allies at summits in Brussels and Quebec while kowtowing to Russian president Vladimir Putin at a subsequent summit in Helsinki. Trump then defended the Saudi crown prince Mohammed bin Salman after his minions had murdered Jamal Khashoggi, a murder that underlined both the crown prince's impetuousness and the Trump administration's wishful thinking about him.

And in 2019, there were even fewer foreign policy wins. By the end of 2018, the "axis of adults"—Cohn, Kelly, Mattis, McMaster, and Tillerson—had all departed, so the world got to see Trump increasingly unplugged. Meetings between Trump and Kim Jong Un in Hanoi and at the Demilitarized Zone between North and South Korea yielded no tangible results. Meanwhile, the newly imposed sanctions on the Iranians certainly began to bite, but Iran also restarted a modest uranium enrichment program.

Also, in February 2020, the Trump administration signed an agreement with the Taliban to withdraw all US troops from Afghanistan, in exchange for which the Taliban would break ties with al-Qaeda and negotiate a peace settlement with the Afghan government. The Taliban failed to observe those conditions, yet Trump tweeted that all US troops would leave Afghanistan by Christmas 2020. That benchmark came and went, and Trump left 2,500 troops in the country. It was left to Trump's successor, President Joe Biden, to end America's longest war.

Trump's shadow secretary of state, Jared Kushner, had a sole diplomatic achievement, grandiosely termed the "Abraham Accords," which were signed at the White House on September 15, 2020, and normalized relations between Israel and two Arab monarchies, Bahrain and the United Arab Emirates. The fantasy of the accords was that the Palestinians would forget about their legitimate grievances with Israel because of large-scale investments that Kushner would help secure for them, while the Arab states would put pressure on the Palestinians to make peace with the Israelis. The Arab nations would then have more leverage on Israel to moderate its stance on the Palestinian issue. In the end, none of this happened, which was underlined by the May 2021 conflict in Gaza where 12 Israelis died and more than 240 Palestinians were killed.

Trump's warm embrace of Kim, MBS, and Putin underlined how Trump favored dictators over longtime democratic allies such as Canada, France, Germany, Mexico, and the United Kingdom, all of whose leaders he dissed at one point or another. It also emphasized how he tended to undermine the NATO alliance, the most successful alliance the United States had entered into since World War II as it helped to contribute to the peaceful implosion of the Soviet Union. And despite all of Trump's badgering and bluster, when he came into office only six of the twenty-nine NATO countries were spending the 2 percent of their GDP on defense that they had all agreed to spend by 2024. By the fall of 2019, only one more country had reached that target, Latvia.

Historians are likely to find that Trump got one really big foreign policy issue at least in part right, which was China. While the US was distracted by its post-9/11 wars, China made great advances economically and militarily. China did so, in part, by stealing American secrets through cyber espionage, such as the theft of the plans for the most advanced US fighter jet, the F-35, which was almost identical to China's J-31 stealth fighter. China also engaged in large-scale intellectual property theft through "forced transfer," in which American companies doing business in China had to partner with Chinese companies—which were really extensions of the Chinese government—and then had to transfer their intellectual property and processes to those Chinese companies. Intellectual property theft by the Chinese was estimated to cost the US economy between $200 billion to $600 billion annually.*

A few days after taking office, Trump made a rash decision to pull the United States out of the Trans-Pacific Partnership, which was a trade deal between a dozen Pacific countries, including the United States, that was, in part, designed to contain the rise of China. During the campaign, Trump had misunderstood what the TPP actually did, claiming, "It's a deal that was designed for China to come in, as they always do, through the back door and totally take advantage of everyone." In fact, China was not part of the deal and, if anything, the deal disadvantaged the Chinese. Peremptorily pulling out of the TPP seemed more like an effort to kill a deal that was negotiated by Obama rather than because any serious consideration was given to what the partnership aimed to accomplish in terms of containing the Chinese.

It was striking, then, that both the national security strategy review overseen by National Security Adviser H. R. McMaster and the defense strategy review overseen by Secretary of Defense Jim Mattis prioritized "great power" competition with China and Russia over the long-running wars with jihadist militants. And clearly, given the relatively small size

---

* Intellectual property theft, unfair trade practices, and cyber espionage were far from the only reason that the United States had a $400 billion trade deficit with China. China was a nation of savers and the United States was a nation of buyers and so some kind of significant trade deficit was going to be baked into the relationship. Also, trade deficits by themselves were not necessarily bad things since what was important was the overall health of the US economy rather than trade imbalances with particular countries that could pay much lower wages to their workers than was the case in the United States.

of the Russian economy, it was China—the world's second largest economy—rather than Russia that posed the greatest potential threat to American interests.

The national security strategy called out China in a number of areas, accusing the Chinese of stealing US intellectual property every year valued at "hundreds of billions of dollars," and it pointed out that China was "building the most capable and well-funded military in the world, after our own," including a "diversifying" nuclear arsenal.

Some in the Trump administration even saw the emerging contest with China in stark "Clash of Civilizations" terms. Speaking at a conference in Washington in 2018, Kiron Skinner, the head of policy planning at the State Department, said that the conflict was "a fight with a different civilization and a different ideology." Skinner added that this was "the first time that we will have a great power competitor that is not Caucasian."

As a trade war between the United States and China intensified in September 2018, Trump slapped tariffs on $200 billion of Chinese goods. Trump told advisers that he was imposing these costs on the Chinese economy because the Chinese military budget was around $200 billion. For Trump, the military aspirations of the Chinese could be combated with higher tariffs, which he seemed to believe were somehow paid by the Chinese government rather than by American companies and consumers.

A year later Trump imposed additional tariffs on $300 billion of Chinese exports to the United States. This move spooked the markets, and it wasn't clear if the Chinese would respond by significantly opening up to American imports, in particular agricultural products, as Trump was demanding. Trump's brinkmanship with the Chinese also ran the real risk of precipitating a global economic slowdown or even a recession. The Trump administration then announced that the new tariffs would only be applied just before Christmas 2019, a tacit admission that the tariffs penalized Americans, who ended up paying higher prices for Chinese goods such as cell phones, computers, games, and toys.

Trump seemed to have skipped his Trade 101 class when he attended the Wharton School at the University of Pennsylvania, as he had a mercantilist conception of trade where there could only be "winners" and "losers," which was contrary to the views of almost every modern economist, who believed that free trade tended to lift all economic boats in the long term. This was why the Republicans were overwhelmingly the party of free trade until Trump came along.

This mercantilism meshed with Trump's overall conception of life, which he cast in bleak nineteenth-century social Darwinian terms as a zero sum competition of winners and losers and the survival of the fittest. In fact, as our understanding of evolution has deepened, we know that society functions not because of some Darwinian struggle but because of "reciprocal altruism"—I'll scratch your back, if you scratch mine—a concept that Trump didn't seem to understand.

Identifying China as a strategic rival of the United States was an important conceptual shift for the United States, because previous administrations had emphasized engagement with the Chinese, believing that as they started to play by the rules of the international system and liberalized their economy they would prosper and then they would liberalize their authoritarian form of governance. That, of course, didn't happen. The Trump administration demanded fair and reciprocal trade and economic practices from the Chinese, but as of the fall of 2019 that effort seemed to have stalled.

Trump presided over a far larger number of "freedom of navigation" exercises in the South China Sea, which was critical to global trade because at least $3 trillion of goods transited it every year. China was trying to turn the vast South China Sea into a Chinese lake by building a string of artificial, militarized islands across it, which was part of China's "winning without fighting" strategy that avoided direct conflict with the United States yet allowed the Chinese to keep expanding their spheres of influence. During Obama's two terms in office, there were only four freedom of navigation exercises in the South China Sea. By the summer of 2019, Trump had presided over eleven such exercises.

Trump also pressed for the creation of a new Space Force that would take charge of US military operations in space in part because China was moving aggressively to militarize its operations in space, such as developing missiles capable of taking out American satellites critical to so many of the Pentagon's communications and operations.

If Trump got the measure of China largely right, historians will not treat Trump kindly on the other great issue of the twenty-first century: climate change. For years, the Pentagon had considered climate change an important national security issue that would influence the kind of conflicts that the United States might fight and also the disposition of American bases and forces around the world. Yet, on June 1, 2017, Trump pulled the United States out of the Paris climate agreement that was ratified by 185 countries and aimed to reduce the carbon emissions that contributed to climate change. Trump justified leaving the agreement by saying, "I was elected by voters of Pittsburgh, not Paris. I promised I would exit or renegotiate any deal which fails to serve US interests."

Trump seemed to have doubts that climate change was even happening. It was one thing to reject the overwhelming scientific consensus that climate change was caused by human activity, but it took a particular kind of determined Know Nothingism for Trump to ignore the fact that the earth was warming significantly. Trump had denied this basic truth in 2012, describing climate change as an "expensive hoax" perpetrated by the Chinese, tweeting that "the concept of global warming was created by and for the Chinese in order to make U.S. manufacturing noncompetitive." Six years later when he was president, Trump told *60 Minutes* confusingly, "I'm not denying climate change. But it could very well go back. You know, we're talking about over . . . millions of years."

A year later, Trump seemed to conflate routine shifts in the weather with systematic climate change when he tweeted, "Large parts of the Country are suffering from tremendous amounts of snow and near record setting cold. Amazing how big this system is. Wouldn't be bad to have a little of that good old fashioned Global Warming right now!" In July 2019, Trump mystifyingly opined in an interview, "I believe that there is a change in weather and I think it changes both ways."

Trump's fuzziness about whether climate change was even happening had policy repercussions that went beyond leaving the Paris climate agreement. Rising sea levels caused by climate change meant that two places close to Trump's heart, Manhattan and the Atlantic coast of southern Florida, would face serious problems by 2060. By then, a third of Lower Manhattan would be at risk from storm surges, while sea levels around Palm Beach would rise by two feet. Trump could have taken the position that while he didn't believe the science that climate change was caused by human activity, he did believe climate change was a real problem and as a result he was going to instigate major infrastructure projects to mitigate its consequences in places such as Manhattan and southern Florida. That didn't happen. Instead, Trump fiddled while the world burned.

Trump spent much of his presidency undermining the institutions that undergird and defend American democracy. It used to be leftists who tended to decry the CIA, the FBI, and Department of Justice. Now it was Trump and his supporters. A key element of the United States' unwritten constitution has been that the president wouldn't attack key organs of his own government. That notion now seems quaint. A veteran CIA official lamented, "Of all the institutions that have been attacked, it has been the jugulars of the CIA and the FBI that Trump has slashed at the most and the most frequently. The two organizations that are charged with speaking truth to power and identifying and punishing the 'liars,' no matter where the truth comes from or its consequences."

Trump's attacks on the intelligence community intensified in August 2019 when he accepted the resignation of Dan Coats, the director of national intelligence. Coats's departure was utterly predictable because he had performed his job, which was to tell the truth. Unfortunately, his boss didn't like the truths he was telling. On some of the key national security issues of the Trump administration—Iran, North Korea, and Russia—the director of national intelligence and the president fundamentally disagreed about the facts.

Trump's animus against Coats began in earnest when he testified about the findings of the *Worldwide Threat Assessment of the US Intelligence Community* to the Senate Intelligence Committee on January 29, 2019. The assessment generally attracted scant political controversy because it was an annual account of the threats that the United States faced. The 2019 Worldwide Threat Assessment would be different. Coats testified that North Korea was unlikely "to completely give up its nuclear weapons." Experts on North Korea almost universally shared the view that it was quite doubtful that Kim Jong Un would give up all his nukes, yet Trump was angered by the coverage of Coats's testimony, which undercut his claims that North Korea no longer posed a nuclear threat.

Coats also testified that the 2015 Iran nuclear agreement was working: "We continue to assess that Iran is not currently undertaking the key nuclear weapons-development activities we judge necessary to produce a nuclear device." If that was the case, why was Trump constantly claiming that Iran was a big threat and the Iran nuclear agreement was a terrible deal?

The morning after Coats's testimony, Trump let loose a tweet storm, writing, "The Intelligence people seem to be extremely passive and naive when it comes to the dangers of Iran. They are wrong!" The president also tweeted, "Perhaps Intelligence should go back to school!"

All this came around six months after Coats had publicly rebuked Trump when the president had met with Putin in Helsinki and sided with the Russian president over his own intelligence agencies' findings about Russia's interference in the 2016 election.

Trump nominated an obscure Texas Republican to replace Coats, Representative John Ratcliffe, whose principal qualification for the job appeared to be his unquestioning fealty to Trump. Ratcliffe, a three-term

House member and former US attorney, was previously the mayor of Heath, Texas, population just under nine thousand. By contrast, Coats had served in the Senate and House for two and a half decades and also was US ambassador to Germany for four years.

When he put forward Ratcliffe, Trump claimed, "I think we need somebody like that in there. We need somebody strong that can rein it in. Because, as I think you've all learned, the intelligence agencies have run amok. They have run amok."

Ratcliffe had publicly made inflated claims about his role in prosecuting terrorism cases. That, together with his scant qualifications to oversee the intelligence community, ensured that his nomination was quickly withdrawn.

When Coats was a senator, he served with another senator who famously observed that "everyone is entitled to his own opinion, but not to his own facts." Trump seemed to want to reverse Senator Daniel Patrick Moynihan's well-known dictum so it would now be "I'm entitled to my own facts, which will match my opinions."

Trump's desire to adjust the facts so they would fit his opinions could also be seen in his treatment of the press, which he routinely referred to as fake news and enemies of the people, except for those on Fox News who were his slavish supporters or close advisers. It was almost as if the greenroom at Fox News had taken over the West Wing. Three of Trump's most influential advisers—Sean Hannity, Tucker Carlson, and Lou Dobbs—were anchors on Fox. A key Trump military adviser, retired general Jack Keane, was a Fox analyst. Trump's national security adviser, John Bolton; deputy national security adviser, K. T. McFarland; communications directors, Bill Shine and Mercedes Schlapp; deputy to the chief strategist, Sebastian Gorka; and State Department spokespersons, Heather Nauert and Morgan Ortagus were all former Fox News executives, anchors, or talking heads.

There was simply no precedent in American history for this large-scale integration of a media institution and a presidential administration. It was often hard to discern if it was Fox News that was driving the national security agenda of the White House, or if it was the White

House that was driving the agenda of Fox News. Often it was both. Tucker Carlson helped to talk Trump out of the Iran strike that was slated for the evening of June 20, 2019. The following week, Carlson went on Trump's trip to the Demilitarized Zone between North Korea and South Korea and publicly defended the president's embrace of the despotic Kim by saying, "You've got to be honest about what it means to lead a country. It means killing people. Not on the scale the North Koreans do, but a lot of countries commit atrocities, including a number that we are closely allied with."

Jack Keane talked Trump out of pulling all US troops from Syria in early 2019, and he also defended Trump's diplomacy with Kim on Fox News following the president's trip to the DMZ.

Trump was a bully who treated even the most senior members of his cabinet with contempt. Trump publicly said that departed secretary of state Rex Tillerson was "as dumb as a rock." After Mattis resigned, Trump said, "What's he done for me? How has he done in Afghanistan? Not too good. As you know, President Obama fired him, and essentially so did I." And Trump so berated Homeland Security Secretary Kirstjen Nielsen in front of his cabinet in May 2018 about the flow of migrants crossing the southern border that she considered resigning—and ultimately she did a year later.

Trump also played on America's racial divisions, promoted baseless conspiracy theories, lied or made false claims thousands of times when he was president, and made most matters of state about himself. A classic example of this was when Trump floated the idea in August 2019 that he was interested in buying the massive and strategic island of Greenland, which is an autonomous region of Denmark. When the Danish prime minister called the offer "absurd," Trump promptly canceled a long-planned trip to Denmark. This was the action of a five-year-old boy who didn't get a toy he wanted.

Was Trump an outlier or a harbinger? One way to answer that

question is to do the thought experiment about what the world would have looked like if Hillary Clinton had won the American presidential election. The United States would be abiding by the Iran nuclear deal along with its key European allies. America's NATO partners would not feel insulted when they dealt with the president, and Vladimir Putin would not be embraced. Trump certainly brought his own special brand of America First policies that wouldn't necessarily be the policies of another president.

That said, roughly half of American voters voted for Trump, and his America Firstism appealed to many of those hurt by the 2008 financial crash who felt that "the elites," whether Democrats or Republicans, didn't operate in their interests. Many Trump voters also felt that recent immigrants were "jumping the queue" and were "line cutters" grabbing an unfair share of the economic pie. This was a common view across much of the West, and as a result ultranationalist, nativist parties moved from the margins to become central political players in much of Europe. Some politicians in Western countries, including the United States, would continue to try to unmoor themselves from "the international order," whether through Brexit-like maneuvers or through anti-immigrant nativism. Polls also routinely showed that a solid bipartisan majority of Americans wanted the United States to play a smaller role in the world. Their views were unlikely to change after Trump had left office.

Trump ended his July 4 speech with a message of national unity, saying, "We all share the same heroes, the same home, the same heart, and we are all made by the same Almighty God."

Dr. King had declared in exactly the same spot where Trump gave his Independence Day speech, "And so let freedom ring from the prodigious hilltops of New Hampshire. Let freedom ring from the mighty mountains of New York. Let freedom ring from the heightening Alleghenies of Pennsylvania."

Trump mimicked King, saying, "And from the banks of the Chesapeake to the cliffs of California, from the humming shores of the Great Lakes to the sand dunes of the Carolinas, from the fields of the heartland to the everglades of Florida, the spirit of American independence will never fade, never fail, but will reign forever and ever and ever."

It was, of course, always a perennial question if Trump could really ever summon the better angels of his nature and act as a commander in chief who was a uniter rather than a divider. On July 4, 2019, he showed a glimpse of that possibility.

Ten days later, no such glimpse was in evidence when Trump tweeted of four progressive Democratic congresswomen of color known as "the Squad," "Why don't they go back and help fix the totally broken and crime infested places from which they came."

Three of the four representatives were born in the United States, so it was hard to figure out which countries they could "go back" to. The tweet was widely condemned as racist, yet only four Republicans supported a House vote abjuring it. The party of Lincoln was now the party of Trump. The 2020 election would be fought by a president who continued to use the white identity politics that had launched his political career. This was a commander in chief who would not represent all Americans, only those who supported him.

During his presidential campaign, Trump had advanced two seemingly contradictory big ideas about the kind of commander in chief he would be. He had called for a greatly expanded military and an unconstrained war against terrorists. At the same time, he had also railed against America's seemingly endless wars in the Middle East. Two and a half years into his term, Trump had largely achieved his goals: the Pentagon was considerably better resourced while ISIS was largely defeated. At the same time, Trump was also drawing down from the wars in Afghanistan, Iraq, and Syria.

Now the generals who had guided his national security policies were all long gone from his administration. They were troubled by the cavalier way in which Trump treated institutions such as NATO that were sacred to them, as well as by his routine denigrations of US allies and his fellow Americans. What remained was Trump himself, a veteran only of the New York Military Academy, a military-style boarding school, who thrilled to the ceremonial aspects of being commander in chief but was generally reluctant to send American forces into harm's way. What wasn't clear was how the mercurial president might react to a genuine crisis. That test came on September 14, 2019, when a barrage of missiles and drones targeted two of the world's most important oil facilities in Saudi Arabia, knocking out about half of the country's oil capacity and immediately spiking oil prices almost 15 percent. The Trump administration blamed Iran for the attacks, as did the Saudis, which raised the specter of a war between them.

Three months earlier Trump had ordered up the military strikes against Iran and then called them off at the last minute. Trump then said that he would sit down with the Iranian leadership without preconditions. Trump's posturing back and forth between aggression and conciliation might have worked for a Manhattan real estate deal, but the stakes are much higher when you are dealing with the complex calculations of a regional power such as Iran, which has long regarded the US as a foe.

A day after the attacks in Saudi Arabia, President Trump tweeted that the United States was "locked and loaded depending on verification" of who was behind the attacks. The Trump administration blamed Iran for the attacks, which posed a quandary for Trump: Despite his close alliance with MBS, he didn't want to get embroiled in another war in the Middle East. In the end, Trump chose restraint.

Following the killing of a US contractor in Iraq in December 2019, likely by an Iran-backed Shia militia, Trump showed no such restraint. He authorized the killing of Qasem Soleimani, who ran Iran's military operations in the Middle East. Soleimani was killed by missiles hitting his vehicle near Baghdad's airport on January 3, 2020. The teenager who had reveled in his time at a military-style boarding school in New York was now finally his own general.

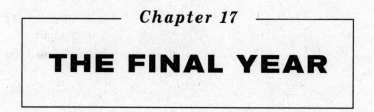

Chapter 17

THE FINAL YEAR

The Vatican of the American foreign policy establishment is the Council on Foreign Relations, the members-only organization established in 1921, three years after the end of World War I, to try to help prevent another global cataclysm. The Council has long been at the heart of the internationalist project that the United States led after World War II, symbolized by NATO. So it wasn't surprising that Jim Mattis launched his memoir, *Call Sign Chaos: Learning to Lead*, at the Council's headquarters, a limestone-face mansion built in 1919 on Manhattan's Upper East Side.

Every Vatican has its pope and the Council's was currently Richard Haass, a pillar of the national security establishment who served under George W. Bush as director of policy planning at the State Department. Haass moderated Mattis's book talk in early September 2019 before an audience of *le tout* New York, including Tina Brown, the former editor of the *New Yorker* and *Vanity Fair* and her husband, Sir Harold Evans; former New York police commissioner Ray Kelly; and Obama's secretary of Homeland Security, Jeh Johnson.

In the course of the event, Haass observed that the 2020 presidential election would be "a truly consequential election, arguably the most in our lifetime." It seemed quite unlikely that Haass would be voting for Trump in this truly consequential election. Indeed, there didn't seem to be any Trump supporters in the audience beyond Trump's former deputy national security adviser, K. T. McFarland.

As he would throughout his book tour, Mattis avoided direct criticism of President Trump. "I'm old fashioned: I don't write about sitting presidents." But no one was confused as to why he pushed the importance of America's traditional allies as a key theme at the Council. Mattis explained that he "had the privilege to fight many, many times for this country. Not once did I fight in an all-American formation. When this town was attacked on 9/11, I went into Afghanistan. . . . Alongside us were Canadian troops and German troops. . . . Their town wasn't attacked. They were there because we were attacked."

Mattis concluded his remarks with a warning about the perilous state of the American body politic, invoking as he did so the esoteric concept of "usufruct." As Mattis described it, usufruct means that in an agrarian society, "A son or daughter, they can take over the land of their parents. You can do whatever you want, plant crops, but you must turn the land over in as good a shape or better than you found it. I think that is what has to guide us right now: as good a shape or better. I'm not convinced what we're turning over to the younger generation is in as good a shape or better than it was given to us, and that does worry me." Left unsaid was President Trump's role in all this, but the implication was clear; Mattis believed that Trump had corroded American institutions and alliances.

If Haass was the pope of the foreign policy establishment, his Washington, DC, analogue was David Bradley. Republican and Democratic administrations came and went, but the permanent Washington establishment endured, at the apex of which was Bradley. He had made a sizable fortune from the Advisory Board, a consulting firm that he had founded in 1979 and sold for a reported $300 million two decades later. Bradley used some of the proceeds to purchase the venerable *Atlantic* magazine at a moment when it was hemorrhaging red ink. Bradley moved the magazine to Washington from Boston, hired top-tier journalists such as its editor, Jeffrey Goldberg, and made it into a profitable enterprise that consistently won top journalism awards. In 2017 Laurene Powell Jobs, Steve Jobs's widow, bought a majority stake in *The Atlantic* for $100 million.

In a vast neo-Georgian house a stone's throw from the British embassy, the courtly Bradley and his elegant wife, Katherine, presided over dinners and parties for the great and the good. Heads of state, foreign ministers, four-star generals, senators, leading TV news anchors, and the occasional CIA director all enjoyed the Bradleys' generous hospitality, including delicious butler-served meals under the warm light of candle-lit chandeliers.

It was at the Bradleys' that Mattis had his book party. In the crowd were Mattis's close friend, General John Kelly, who Trump had forced out as his chief of staff; General John "Mick" Nicholson, Trump's commander in Afghanistan, who Trump had wanted to fire; Eliot Cohen, the senior George W. Bush administration official who was one of the leaders of the "Never Trump" movement; and Michèle Flournoy, a top Obama official at the Pentagon, who Mattis had wanted to install as his number two, but who had balked because of her misgivings about Trump. There was also a heavy contingent of the "Fake News," including Bob Woodward and David Ignatius of the *Washington Post*, Andrea Mitchell of NBC News, Dana Bash of CNN, Margaret Brennan of CBS, and Susan Glasser of the *New Yorker*. This was no MAGA rally.

A party guest asked Mattis who some of his heroes were, and he immediately named three Marines with whom he had served, all of whom had been immigrants to the United States, from the Caribbean, Mexico, and Canada. Mattis observed that recent immigrants served in disproportionately high numbers in the US military. No one missed the implied critique of Trump's policies on immigration.

Mary Louise Kelly, the coanchor of NPR's *All Things Considered* asked Mattis what it would take for him to criticize President Trump publicly. Could there ever come a time when he felt he had to speak out if he felt that the country was truly imperiled? Mattis became animated saying he would never do that, observing that, "Mike Flynn and John Allen—I could not disagree more strongly with what they did." Retired lieutenant general Mike Flynn, of course, had campaigned for Trump and had led chants of "Lock Her Up!" at the 2016 Republican convention, while Allen, a retired four-star Marine general like Mattis, had spoken at the Democratic convention the same year and had made his own spirited speech in favor of Hillary Clinton.

Yet Mattis's own book told a more nuanced story. While Mattis said little about Trump, his critiques of Obama and Joe Biden were unvarnished. Mattis was especially critical of Obama and Biden's decision to withdraw all US troops from Iraq at the end of 2011. Mattis believed it was necessary to leave a "residual force" of troops in Iraq, but Biden, who was in charge of Iraq policy for the Obama administration, "wanted our forces out of Iraq. Whatever path led there fastest, he favored," according to Mattis. Mattis had argued that the vacuum left by a total US withdrawal would be "filled by Sunni terrorists."

Of course, Mattis turned out to be right, but he was now in uncharted territory as one of the most revered military leaders of the post-9/11 era who was publicly taking to task both the previous president and the current leading Democratic candidate, and yet he was avoiding any direct criticisms of Trump.

This underlined some difficult questions about the proper role of military leaders and their civilian bosses that H. R. McMaster had laid out so well in *Dereliction of Duty*, his account of the Vietnam War and the generals who served under President Lyndon Johnson. The generals owed the president their best military advice irrespective of politics, but in any case the president was free simply to do whatever he wanted as commander in chief. The generals either could go along for the ride or resign, as Mattis had.

And what if the commander in chief started making rash decisions, such as making a deal with the North Koreans that enabled them to continue their nuclear program? Or what if he provoked a trade war with China that severely damaged the global economy? At this point in the Trump presidency these seemed like live possibilities.

By now the "axis of adults" had all long moved on, either because they were forced out or because they had resigned on principle, and Trump had surrounded himself with yes-men and was running his cabinet like he had run his real estate company. His key foreign policy adviser was his son-in-law, Jared Kushner. His key economic advisers, Larry Kudlow and Peter Navarro, not Gary Cohn, were egging on the president to ramp up his trade war with China. Trump largely ignored his national security adviser, John Bolton and eventually forced him out of office in September 2019, while his new secretary of defense, Mark Esper, was competent but hardly had the stature of Mattis. "Acting" White House Chief of Staff Mick Mulvaney was a Trump factotum and certainly no John Kelly. Secretary of State Mike Pompeo was "a heat-seeking missile for Trump's ass" in the memorable words of a former US ambassador quoted in a *New Yorker* profile of Pompeo. CIA Director Gina Haspel was a CIA lifer who just kept her head down.

The danger of having Trump surrounded by a team of acolytes was underscored by what became potentially the greatest threat to his presidency, which was a call that he made on July 25, 2019, to Ukrainian president Volodymyr Zelensky. Trump asked the Ukrainians to investigate his key political opponent Joe Biden, as well as his son Hunter Biden, who had done business in Ukraine while his father was vice president. Bolton had advised against making this call, thinking Trump would use it to air his personal grievances, but the call went ahead anyway with Pompeo listening in, as well as Vice President Pence's national security adviser, the dozy Trump loyalist, retired lieutenant general Keith Kellogg.

The United States had an interest in supporting Ukraine's sovereignty in particular because Putin had seized Crimea from Ukraine in 2014, and he continued to support rebels in the eastern half of the country. US support for Ukraine came in the form of some $400 million of military assistance, which Trump had put on hold just before his call with the Ukrainian president. There appeared to be an implied quid pro quo: investigate my political opponent and I will release the military aid you desperately need. The Democrats saw this as an easy-to-understand example of Trump's abusing his official position for personal, political gain sufficient to rise to the "high crimes and misdemeanors" necessary for impeachment. Ukrainian investigators had concluded that the Bidens hadn't broken any laws, yet here was Trump trying to gather dirt on his political opponent, telling the Ukrainian president: "I would like you to do us a favor, though."

Trump's call with the Ukrainian president was also perplexing because he referred elliptically to the hack against the Clinton campaign in 2016, suggesting that in fact it had originated in Ukraine rather than in Russia as his own intelligence services had concluded. This was a common conspiracy theory on the loony right, but here was the president of the United States urging the Ukrainians to investigate an absurd falsehood. Making matters worse, Trump had dispatched his personal lawyer, Rudy Giuliani, to Ukraine to investigate this conspiracy theory and also to gather dirt on the Bidens. Any sane person wouldn't have the erratic and bombastic Giuliani defend them even for a parking ticket. It was perhaps fitting that Trump, whose political career had been launched with one conspiracy theory—Obama was a non-American Muslim—might have his presidency derailed in the pursuit of another conspiracy theory: that it was Ukraine that had intervened in the 2016 election rather than Putin.

On October 3, 2019, Trump doubled down on his theory about the Bidens during one of his periodic "chopper talks" on the White House South Lawn with reporters. Trump encouraged the Ukrainians to investigate the Bidens, and he said he was also contemplating asking the Chinese to look into Hunter Biden's business deals in China. He said this shortly before a Chinese delegation was to arrive in Washington to restart its contentious, stalled trade talks with the Trump administration. Now the president was encouraging a key rival of the United States to investigate his political opponent. It was these kinds of statements and actions that had moved House Speaker Nancy Pelosi away from her initial skepticism about impeachment; the sitting president appeared to be abusing his office for his own gain.

Pelosi instigated an impeachment process that, in December 2019, charged Trump with abuse of power for pressuring the Ukrainian government to investigate Biden, and obstruction of Congress's investigation of this issue. But the Republican-controlled Senate eventually acquitted the president on February 5, 2020.

In some ways, even more damaging to Trump's reputation than the impeachment was his reaction to the nationwide protests following the murder of George Floyd by a police officer in Minneapolis on May 25, 2020. Trump threatened to send the federal military to quell the unrest that was roiling American cities, but the military is barred from domestic law enforcement by the Posse Comitatus Act of 1878. Under some rare circumstances, federal troops have been deployed in the US. The last time they were called up for such duty was during the 1992 Los Angeles riots, which followed the acquittal of police officers who brutally beat Rodney King. More than fifty people were killed in those riots. The federal troops were called in at the invitation of California's governor, rather than unilaterally deployed as President Trump threatened to do.

On a call about the protests with the nation's governors on June 1, Trump praised Joint Chiefs chairman General Mark Milley as "a warrior" and asserted that Milley "hates to see the way it's being handled in the various states. And I've just put him in charge." Putting Milley "in charge" was a strange formulation since the United States' top military officer was not responsible for domestic law enforcement. That was the role of the police and, in some cases, the National Guard under the control of state governors. On the call with the governors, Defense Secretary Mark Esper blathered about dominating "the battle space," as if the protests and riots in American cities were taking place in Baghdad in 2003. Trump told the governors, "If you don't dominate, you're wasting your time. They're going to run all over you, you'll look like a bunch of jerks."

That evening, protesters gathered outside the White House and were met with violence. Not since one of Trump's heroes, General Douglas MacArthur, had led a mounted charge to disperse an encampment of homeless veterans just outside the White House in 1932 had the country seen such an application of violence against unarmed protesters outside "the People's House."

Police, with National Guard troops in reserve, attacked the peaceful protesters with flash grenades and tear gas. It was the kind of scene associated with banana republics, not Western democracies. Even worse was the purpose of this travesty—which was to allow Trump a photo op outside St. John's Church, the "church of the presidents" just outside the White House grounds. There, Trump held up a Bible for the cameras, which became an iconic image of his presidency as the coronavirus ravaged the United States and riots raged in its cities.

The next day, former Joint Chiefs chairman Admiral Mike Mullen wrote in *The Atlantic*, "It sickened me yesterday to see security personnel—including members of the National Guard—forcibly and violently clear a path through Lafayette Square to accommodate the president's visit outside St. John's Church. I have to date been reticent to speak out on issues surrounding President Trump's leadership, but we are at an inflection point, and the events of the past few weeks have made it impossible to remain silent."

Former defense secretary Jim Mattis evidently felt similarly and finally broke his long silence about Trump, issuing a blistering statement: "Donald Trump is the first president in my lifetime who does not try to unite the American people—does not even pretend to try. Instead, he tries to divide us. We are witnessing the consequences of three years of this deliberate effort." Predictably, only hours after Mattis released his statement, Trump struck back on Twitter, calling him "the world's most overrated general."

Mattis was part of a growing anti-Trump chorus made up of revered retired senior military officers. General Martin Dempsey, former chairman of the Joint Chiefs, told NPR that Trump's threat to use military force against protesters was "very troubling" and "dangerous." Trump's former chief of staff, General John Kelly, also weighed in, saying, "I think we need to look harder at who we elect. I think we should look at people that are running for office and put them through the filter: What is their character like? What are their ethics?" General Vincent Brooks, who had commanded all US troops in South Korea during Trump's first two years in office, released a statement expressing his "dismay and disappointment" at "the manipulation of the image of the military by our president," while General Colin Powell, the chairman of the Joint Chiefs under President George H. W. Bush, told CNN that Trump had "drifted away" from the Constitution.

Even Mark Esper, Trump's defense secretary and a former US Army officer, started distancing himself from Trump, saying in the Pentagon briefing room on June 3 that he did not support Trump's calls to invoke the Insurrection Act and use active-duty troops to quell the protests. Trump was furious at Esper and shouted at him at the White House later that same day. It was only a matter of time before Esper would be fired, as he had committed the cardinal sin of publicly refusing to pay blind obeisance to Trump. On November 9, just days after his defeat in the presidential election, Trump tweeted that Esper had been "terminated."

Trump had long had a boyish fascination with the military, idolizing World War II generals Patton and MacArthur, and his administration had also presided over a major expansion of US military budgets, but when President Trump took his short walk from the White House to St. John's Church, his path violently cleared of peaceful protesters, he lost the support of key elements of the US military that he so revered. During Trump's presidency, current and former senior military leaders issued more than three hundred public statements, which were overwhelmingly critical of Trump for his leadership of the nation, for his stance on civil rights issues, and for his foreign policy choices. As military leaders, both those in uniform and in retirement, generally stay out of politics, the outpouring was unprecedented.

Among those who separated themselves from Trump was his top military adviser General Milley, who said it was a "mistake" for him to have appeared in uniform alongside Trump as the president walked from the White House toward St. John's Church. Milley issued the apology in a video commencement address to graduates of the National Defense University, saying, "I should not have been there. My presence in that moment and in that environment created a perception of the military involved in domestic politics."

During his last year in office, Trump lost not only the support of military leaders, but also the support of much of the public because of his continued mishandling of the most significant public health crisis in the United States in a century.

Occasionally Trump seemed to grasp the true dimension of that crisis. At a White House press briefing on March 29, 2020, Trump sounded like he had just been mugged by reality, talking soberly about the more than two million Americans who could die if the US government did nothing to stop the spread of the coronavirus. Trump seemed to be citing an influential study by Imperial College London that projected up to 2.2 million Americans might die if no efforts were made to mitigate the spread of the coronavirus. The work of scientists and the advice of experts seemed to have brought a welcome change in Trump's thinking when he announced at the briefing that all of the social distancing guidelines that his administration had instituted on March 16, 2020, were now being extended until the end of April. At the briefing, Trump also commended the nation's top infectious disease official, Dr. Anthony Fauci, for his handling of the crisis response.

The March 29 briefing stood out because, for once, Trump behaved like a normal president who was keeping Americans safe by making sensible policy decisions on their behalf. But Trump went on to cling to quackery, saying, for instance, at a White House roundtable event on May 18, 2020, of the anti-malaria drug hydroxychloroquine, "Couple of weeks ago, I started taking it. Cause I think it's good, I've heard a lot of good stories." Trump's own Food and Drug Administration had warned only the previous month of the dangers of taking hydroxychloroquine outside of a hospital or a clinical study setting "due to risk of heart rhythm problems." Even Fox News anchor Neil Cavuto warned his viewers not to follow Trump's example, saying, "If you are in a risky population here, and you are taking this as a preventative treatment to ward off the virus or in a worst-case scenario, you are dealing with the virus, and you are in this vulnerable population, it will kill you."

The president was not the only Trump to play fast and loose with the reality of the contagion. A day before his father's bizarre hydroxychloroquine admission, Eric Trump told Fox News that Democrats were milking the pandemic for political gain and were trying to prevent his father from holding campaign rallies. And he predicted that after the presidential election on November 3, 2020, the "coronavirus will magically all of a sudden go away and disappear and everybody will be able to reopen."

Meanwhile, Jared Kushner positioned himself as the overall czar of the coronavirus relief effort. Just like his dismal peacemaking efforts in the Middle East, Kushner added another layer of confusion to the muddled White House coronavirus response by, for example, promoting the speedy development of thousands of drive-through nationwide testing sites. In the end, only seventy-eight testing sites ever materialized. At the end of April 2020, Kushner touted to Fox News the "great success" of the Trump administration in fighting the coronavirus. Kushner told the network that he hoped the US would be "really rocking again" by July. At the time, the official death toll for Americans was already the worst in the world, and the US economy had shrunk by around 5 percent.

Kushner's blithe predictions that the United States would soon be rocking were publicly contradicted by the bleak and accurate assessments of the Trump administration's leading public health officials. The director of the Centers for Disease Control, Robert Redfield, angered Trump when he told the *Washington Post* on April 21, 2020, that a second wave of the coronavirus could possibly "be even more difficult than the one we just went through." Redfield was summoned to the White House the following day to clear up his "misquote" in front of President Trump and the assembled White House press corps. Redfield instead doubled down and said that the second wave "was going to be more difficult and potentially complicated." Vice President Pence, who was leading the nation's coronavirus task force, pushed back in the *Wall Street Journal* in a June 2020 op-ed entitled "There Isn't a Coronavirus 'Second Wave.'"

The Trump White House also started employing the oldest political trick in the book, which was to shoot the messenger who brought unwelcome news—in this case the seventy-nine-year-old Dr. Anthony Fauci, whom 67 percent of the public trusted to give them accurate information about the virus, as opposed to only 28 percent for Trump, according to a *New York Times* poll released in June 2020. A month after that poll was released, Trump's top trade adviser, Peter Navarro, attacked Fauci in

USA Today, writing that Fauci "has been wrong about everything I have interacted with him on." Navarro, who had no medical expertise, was critiquing Fauci, who had served six US presidents as their top infectious disease expert. Around the same time that Navarro's piece in *USA Today* was published, Trump told Fox News' Sean Hannity that Fauci was "a nice man, but he's made a lot of mistakes."

A Trump administration initiative that did save lives was Operation Warp Speed, which debuted on May 15, 2020, and was a great achievement of public health policy. The fastest vaccine ever previously developed was for mumps, which had taken four years to produce during the 1960s. Within a year of the coronavirus first appearing in the country, the United States had produced safe, effective vaccines. This wasn't fast enough for Trump, who had wanted them to be available by Election Day, but it certainly was a testament to American science and manufacturing and to the Department of Defense as it helped with the logistics of vaccine distribution. And it was also a credit to Trump and his administration that they backed the vaccine race and reduced any red tape impeding the pharmaceutical companies.

Operation Warp Speed invested $2.5 billion in Moderna, which produced a testable vaccine on humans in only two months using novel mRNA technology. Pfizer didn't take US government money, but the government placed a $5 billion order for 100 million doses with the company, and in doing so guaranteed demand for Pfizer's vaccine. After clinical trials, both Pfizer and Moderna produced vaccines that were more than 90 percent effective. These were astonishing results given that the Food and Drug Administration had put its threshold for approval for any vaccine at 50 percent effective or above.

As the November presidential election approached, Trump, understandably, wanted to change the narrative from fighting the virus to opening up the economy, but biology wasn't so easily corralled. This was underlined when Trump himself contracted COVID during the fall of 2020. Aged seventy-four and overweight, Trump was susceptible to a severe form of the disease. On October 2 at the White House, Trump's blood oxygen levels were dangerously low and he had trouble breathing. He was given oxygen twice. Trump took the short helicopter ride to Walter Reed National Military Medical Center. There he received some of the best medical treatment in the world, including a monoclonal antibody cocktail made by Regeneron that wasn't widely available and a steroid, dexamethasone, which was only used for severe cases of COVID-19, as well as remdesivir, an antiviral drug.

Trump's chief of staff Mark Meadows told reporters, "The president's vitals over the last 24 hours were very concerning and the next 48 hours will be critical in terms of his care." Trump was furious that his chief of staff had leveled with the media about his real condition, which the White House physician, Dr. Sean Conley, was publicly portraying as merely a case of fatigue, a cough, and a stuffy nose. On his third day in the hospital, Trump staged a quick drive-by in his motorcade to wave at supporters and reporters gathered outside Walter Reed.

When Trump arrived back at the White House after four days in the hospital, he walked up the staircase of the south entrance, removed his mask, and saluted the helicopter that had brought him home. He then tweeted a video in which he told Americans that COVID wasn't something to fear: "One thing that's for certain: don't let it dominate you. Don't be afraid of it. You're going to beat it. We have the best medical equipment, we have the best medicines, all developed recently." What Trump didn't say is that he had been quite ill and had only recovered thanks to some of the best doctors on the planet.

Despite Trump's brush with serious illness, his coronavirus response coordinator, Dr. Deborah Birx, told a congressional committee that Trump was "distracted" by the presidential election during the fall of 2020 and "had gotten somewhat complacent through the campaign season." She also said that "if we had fully implemented the mask mandates, the reduction in indoor dining, the getting friends and family to understand the risk of gathering in private homes, and we had increased testing, that we probably could have decreased fatalities into the 30-percent-less to 40-percent-less range," saving more than 130,000 lives.

Six weeks after Trump lost the 2020 presidential election to Joe Biden, retired lieutenant general Mike Flynn, Trump's first national security advisor, told the conservative Newsmax channel on December 17 that Trump "could take military capabilities, and he could place them in those states and basically rerun an election in each of those states." Flynn added for good measure, "I mean, it's not unprecedented. These people are out there talking about martial law like it's something that we've never done. Martial law has been instituted 64 times." Flynn seemed to be calling for a coup. In response, General James McConville, the army chief of staff, issued an unusual statement that said, "There is no role for the U.S. military determining the outcome of an American election."

A day after Flynn had told Newsmax that Trump could "rerun" the election while deploying the military, Flynn and his lawyer Sidney Powell met with Trump at the White House, where they discussed how they might reverse the purportedly "rigged" presidential election, which Biden had won by large margins both in the electoral college vote and in the popular vote. In one of the battiest meetings that had ever occurred in the Oval Office, Powell spun a byzantine tale about how Dominion Voting Systems had rigged their ballot machines to switch votes from Trump to Biden, a plot that somehow involved the socialist government in Venezuela. Powell urged that Trump should grant emergency powers to her and other Trump acolytes to seize the Dominion voting machines.

All this trumpery climaxed on January 6, 2021. To a crowd of thousands of his supporters outside the White House, some wearing body armor and many wearing quasi-military outfits, Trump spouted a geyser of baseless conspiracy theories about his loss in the presidential election. Trump then urged the mob to go to the Capitol: "You'll never take back our country with weakness. You have to show strength, and you have to be strong. . . . We fight like hell. And if you don't fight like hell, you're not going to have a country anymore." The mob took the president at his word. Trump's personal lawyer, Rudy Giuliani, who had lost the moral standing he had once had as mayor of New York during the 9/11 attacks, also incited the pro-Trump mob, telling them they needed to contest the election results with "trial by combat."

The mob then assaulted the Capitol, breaking through windows and doors. "It looked like a medieval battle scene," said Washington, DC, police officer Michael Fanone, who was beaten by the rioters. The mob also interrupted the election certification of President-Elect Biden, which was presided over by Vice President Pence in the Senate. Earlier in the day, Trump had told Pence he was a "pussy" if he didn't overthrow the election. As the mob rampaged, Trump tweeted that Pence lacked "the courage" to overturn the election results. The rioters started chanting, "Hang Mike Pence! Hang Mike Pence!" The vice president was hustled by the Secret Service out of the Senate chamber to a secure location.

That evening, Trump was unrepentant about the mayhem he had helped to foment, tweeting: "These are the things and events that happen when a sacred landslide election victory is so unceremoniously & viciously stripped away from great patriots who have been badly & unfairly treated for so long. Go home with love & in peace. Remember this day forever!" This tweet was later deleted.

A number of senior Trump administration officials resigned in protest within a day of the Trump-inspired insurrection on Capitol Hill, including: Matthew Pottinger, the deputy national security adviser; Elaine Chao, the transportation secretary; Betsy DeVos, the education secretary; Tyler Goodspeed, the acting chairman of the White House Council of Economic Advisers; Mick Mulvaney, Trump's former acting chief of staff, who resigned as special envoy to Northern Ireland; and Stephanie Grisham, First Lady Melania Trump's chief of staff. Even Senator Mitch McConnell, the Republican leader of the Senate who was usually a reliable cheerleader for Trump, said publicly, "The mob was fed lies. They were provoked by the president."

The service chiefs of all the branches of the military, led by the chairman of the Joint Chiefs, General Milley, took the extraordinary measure of sending a joint letter to the two million members of the active-duty and reserve units of the US military and National Guard, decrying the insurrection as a "direct assault on the U.S. Congress, Capitol building and our Constitutional process" and confirming that "President-elect Biden will be inaugurated and will become our 46th Commander in Chief." The message was clear: the US military would not be assisting Trump in any of his efforts to mount a coup against the Constitution they had sworn an oath to serve. For good measure, Trump's former secretary of defense, General Jim Mattis, issued a statement that called out his former boss by name: "An effort to subjugate American democracy by mob rule was fomented by Mr. Trump."

Two days after the Capitol Hill riot, General Milley made a phone call to reassure his Chinese counterpart that the United States was stable and was not considering a military strike against China, telling General Li, "We are 100 percent steady. Everything's fine."

The assault on the Capitol triggered Trump's second impeachment trial. Again, he was acquitted by the Senate, but he now had the distinction of being the only American president to be impeached twice. Trump also had the distinction of being the only president in American history who publicly and consistently refused to accept his electoral loss and continued to foment the lie that the election was stolen from him, with the result that two-thirds of Republicans believed that the presidential election was illegitimate.

On January 20, 2021, Trump departed the White House for the final time on a helicopter that took him to Joint Base Andrews, where he delivered the last remarks of his presidency to some of his supporters.

Before boarding Air Force One for the flight to Mar-a-Lago, his gilded palace in Florida, Trump promised them, "We will be back in some form."

——— ACKNOWLEDGMENTS ———

Thanks to those who agreed to be interviewed for this book and also to those who helped make those interviews happen.

David Sterman and Melissa Salyk-Virk are stellar colleagues who worked on all phases of the book, performing and organizing research and overseeing the fact checking. Catherine York, Daiva Scovil, John Luebke, Wesley Jefferies, Ian Wallace, Sumaita Mulk, Robin Bradley, Alyssa Sims, Albert Ford, and Chris Mellon all also helped.

All these very smart people work or have worked at New America, which has been my home for almost two decades. I am lucky to work there with Anne-Marie Slaughter, Awista Ayub, Paul Butler, Kevin Carey, Cecilia Muñoz, Yuliya Panfil, Peter Singer, Heather Hurlburt, Doug Ollivant, Shaena Korby, Barry Howard, Cathy Bryan, Dana Ju, Ariam Mohamed, Joanne Zalatoris, Alison Yost, Tanya Manning, Jewel Stafford, Angela Spidalette, Jason Stewart, all of whom make New America such a congenial place to work. Thanks also to the former president of New America, Steve Coll.

Thanks to Michael Crow, the president of Arizona State University (ASU), who hired me as a professor, and to Jim O'Brien, ASU senior vice president and chief of staff. It has been a pleasure to launch under their guidance the Center on the Future of War, which is now in its sixth year. Thanks also at ASU to Magda Hinojosa, Pat Kenney, Candace Rondeaux, Nick Rasmussen, Elizabeth Wentz, Stefanie Lindquist, Jonathan Kinkel, and Jeffrey Kubiak.

A great deal of thanks is owed to my partner in the Future of War project, Daniel Rothenberg, who is simply the ideal colleague, very smart, well organized, and thoughtful. Daniel read the manuscript of this book carefully and his observations have improved it. Richard Galant, managing editor at CNN.com, is one of the best editors in the business; he unfailingly identifies the weaknesses in a story, and he does so in a manner that doesn't make you feel like a fool. A number of themes and stories in this book were first developed under Rich's guidance. Rich generously read and commented on the manuscript while on vacation. (A busman's holiday!) Ken Ballen has provided valuable feedback on several of my books, including this one.

I have worked at CNN in one capacity or another for three decades, and am grateful to continue to work there today with so many of its excellent anchors, reporters, executives, and producers. In particular: Wolf Blitzer, Amy Entelis, Fareed Zakaria, Brian Todd, Dugald McConnell, Jay Shaylor, Jim Sciutto, Charlie Moore, Anderson Cooper, Kerry Rubin, Kari Pricher, Susan Chun, Poppy Harlow, Rebecca Kutler, Michael Smerconish, Rick Davis, Pat Wiedenkeller, Yaffa Frederick, Jamie Crawford, Adam Levine, Debbie Berger, Sam Feist, Courtney Sexton, Jon Adler, Jennifer Dargan, John King, Jessica Metzger, and Brianna Keilar. Jeff Zucker has turned CNN into the powerhouse it is today; Anderson rightly observed that he is "the first CNN president to actually watch CNN."

Thanks also to the advisory council for New America's International Security Program, particularly Tom Freston and Bob Niehaus. And thanks to Kati Marton and David and Katherine Bradley. Thanks also to the foundations and program officers who have supported our work, especially Marin Strmecki of the Smith Richardson Foundation, Lisa Magarrell at the Open Society Foundation, and Hillary Wiesner at Carnegie.

Thanks to Greg Barker for the work we have done together making several films about America's long post-9/11 wars. And thanks to Vinnie Malhotra at Showtime, Banks Tarver of Left/Right, Russ Smith, and John Battsek. Thanks to Matt Jones and Rainey Foster of Leading Authorities and to Clark Forcey for your help over the years. Thanks also to Jennie Malloy, Igor Aronov, and Aleksander Ferguson. Thanks to Bruce Hoffman for involving me in the scholarly journal *Studies in Conflict and Terrorism*. Thanks for your friendship to Karen Greenberg, Meena and Liaquat Ahamed, Chris and Holly Fussell, Joel Rayburn and Clare Lockhart, Henry and Sandra Schuster, Tom Carver and Katty Kay, Gavin and Odile Wilson, Kate Boo and Sunil Khilnani, Gianni Koskinas, Rachel Klayman, Josh Geltzer and Katherine Boone, Elizabeth Campbell and Nabil Mohamad,

Mark Isaksen and Daniel Walth, Sid and Jackie Blumenthal, Jim Sciutto and Gloria Riviera, and Thomas and Holly Espy.

Thanks to my fellow board members at the James Foley Foundation and Diane Foley and to my fellow board members at the Global Special Operations Foundation and to Stu Bradin and Meaghan Keeler-Pettigrew. The work of these foundations intersects with many of the themes of this book.

Tina Bennett of WME is widely and justly regarded as the best nonfiction agent in the business, and I consider myself very lucky to have been one of her authors for the past two decades. Also at WME, many thanks to Henry Reisch for his wise counsel and support, and thanks also to Bradley Singer and Eric Simonoff.

At Penguin this book was very ably shepherded by assistant editor, Mia Council, and well publicized by Liz Calamari. Thanks to Yuki Hirose for the legal review and also to Susan VanHecke for the very helpful copyedit. Thanks to Darren Haggar for the striking book cover and Lucia Bernard for the handsome interior design of the book. I had the good fortune to have Scott Moyers as the editor of this book who was simply a joy to work with. Scott had a multitude of smart ideas about the overall structure and direction of the book.

Above all, thanks to my wife, Tresha Mabile. Books can take a toll on families; the missed vacations and weekends start to add up, and I hope that we can make up some of that time. Tresha is the most wonderful wife, mother, and work partner, and it is to her and to our son, Pierre, and our daughter, Grace, that this book is dedicated. Thanks also to our families. Pierre, age seven, took a strong interest in the progress of this book. "What page are you on?" he asked me every morning. Pierre thought the cover of the book should show President Trump holding an AK-47 surrounded by soldiers with RPGs. We didn't go that route in the end, but when Pierre and Grace are old enough to read this book, I hope they will realize that the reason Daddy spent so much time at his desk was because he was writing about a consequential American president and the generals and officials who served under him, and the world they made.

BIBLIOGRAPHY

Abutaleb, Yasmeen and Damian Paletta. *Nightmare Scenario: Inside the Trump Administration's Response to the Pandemic That Changed History.* New York: Harper, 2021.

Acosta, Jim. *The Enemy of the People: A Dangerous Time to Tell the Truth in America.* New York: Harper, 2019.

Alberta, Tim. *American Carnage: On the Front Lines of the Republican Civil War and the Rise of President Trump.* New York: Harper, 2019.

Bergen, Peter L. *The Longest War: The Enduring Conflict between America and Al-Qaeda.* New York: Free Press, 2011.

———. *Manhunt: The Ten-Year Search for bin Laden from 9/11 to Abbottabad.* New York: Crown, 2012.

Bolton, John. *The Room Where It Happened: A White House Memoir.* New York: Simon and Schuster, 2020.

Bolton, John. *Surrender Is Not an Option: Defending America at the United Nations and Abroad.* New York: Threshold Editions, 2007.

Cha, Victor. *The Impossible State: North Korea, Past and Future.* New York: HarperCollins, 2012.

Christie, Chris. *Let Me Finish: Trump, the Kushners, Bannon, New Jersey, and the Power of In-Your-Face Politics.* New York: Hachette Books, 2019.

Clapper, James R., and Trey Brown. *Facts and Fears: Hard Truths from a Life in Intelligence.* New York: Viking, 2018.

Coll, Steve. *Private Empire: ExxonMobil and American Power.* New York: Penguin, 2012.

Comey, James. *A Higher Loyalty: Truth, Lies, and Leadership.* New York: Flatiron Books, 2018.

D'Antonio, Michael. *The Truth About Trump.* New York: St. Martin's, 2016.

D'Antonio, Michael, and Peter Eisner. *The Shadow President: The Truth About Mike Pence.* New York: Thomas Dunne Books, 2018.

Farrow, Ronan. *War on Peace: The End of Diplomacy and the Decline of American Influence.* New York: W. W. Norton, 2018.

Flynn, Michael T., and Michael Ledeen. *The Field of Fight: How We Can Win the Global War Against Radical Islam and Its Allies.* New York: St. Martin's, 2016.

Garrett, Major. *Mr. Trump's Wild Ride: The Thrills, Chills, Screams, and Occasional Blackouts of an Extraordinary Presidency.* New York: All Points Books, 2018.

Ghani, Ashraf, and Clare Lockhart. *Fixing Failed States: A Framework for Rebuilding a Fractured World.* New York: Oxford University Press, 2008.

Gorka, Sebastian. *Defeating Jihad: The Winnable War.* Washington, DC: Regnery, 2016.

———. *Why We Fight: Defeating America's Enemies—With No Apologies.* Washington, DC: Regnery, 2018.

Green, Joshua. *Devil's Bargain: Steve Bannon, Donald Trump, and the Storming of the Presidency.* New York: Penguin, 2017.

Groen, Michael S. *With the 1st Marine Division in Iraq, 2003: No Greater Friend, No Worse Enemy.* Quantico, VA: History Division, Marine Corps University, 2006. https://catalog.hathitrust.org/Record/005634802.

Hanson, Victor Davis. *The Case for Trump.* New York: Basic Books, 2019.

Hayden, Michael V. *The Assault on Intelligence: American National Security in an Age of Lies.* New York: Penguin, 2018.

Isikoff, Michael, and David Corn. *Russian Roulette: The Inside Story of Putin's War on America and the Election of Donald Trump.* New York: Twelve, 2018.

Johnston, David Cay. *It's Even Worse Than You Think: What the Trump Administration Is Doing to America.* Rev. ed. New York: Simon and Schuster, 2019.

Kessler, Ronald. *The Trump White House: Changing the Rules of the Game.* New York: Crown Forum, 2018.

Khalilzad, Zalmay. *The Envoy: From Kabul to the White House, My Journey Through a Turbulent World.* New York: St. Martin's, 2016.

Kitfield, James. *Twilight Warriors: The Soldiers, Spies, and Special Agents Who Are Revolutionizing the American Way of War.* New York: Basic Books, 2016.

Koffler, Keith. *Bannon: Always the Rebel.* Washington, DC: Regnery, 2017.

Kranish, Michael, and Marc Fisher. *Trump Revealed: The Definitive Biography of the 45th President.* New York: Scribner, 2016.

Kurtz, Howard. *Media Madness: Donald Trump, the Press, and the War Over the Truth.* New York: Regnery, 2018.

Landler, Mark. *Alter Egos: Hillary Clinton, Barack Obama, and the Twilight Struggle Over American Power.* New York: Random House, 2016.

Lasch, Christopher. *The Culture of Narcissism: American Life in an Age of Diminishing Expectations.* New York: W. W. Norton, 1979.

Lewandowski, Corey R., and David N. Bossie. *Let Trump Be Trump: The Inside Story of His Rise to the Presidency.* New York: Center Street, 2017.

———. *Trump's Enemies: How the Deep State Is Undermining the Presidency.* New York: Center Street, 2018.

Lewis, Michael. *The Fifth Risk.* New York: W. W. Norton, 2018.

Liang, Qiao, and Wang Xiangsui. *Unrestricted Warfare: China's Master Plan to Destroy America.* Brattleboro, VT: Echo Point Books and Media, 2015.

Macgregor, Douglas. *Warrior's Rage: The Great Tank Battle of 73 Easting.* Annapolis, MD: Naval Institute Press, 2012.

Mattis, Jim, and Kori N. Schake, eds. *Warriors and Citizens: American Views of Our Military.* Stanford, CA: Hoover Institution Press, 2016.

Mattis, Jim, and Bing West. *Call Sign Chaos:* Learning to Lead. New York: Random House, 2019.

McCabe, Andrew G. *The Threat: How the FBI Protects America in the Age of Terror and Trump.* New York: St. Martin's, 2019.

McChrystal, Stanley. *My Share of the Task: A Memoir.* New York: Portfolio/Penguin, 2013.

McMaster, H. R. *Dereliction of Duty: Lyndon Johnson, Robert McNamara, the Joint Chiefs of Staff, and the Lies That Led to Vietnam.* New York: HarperCollins, 1997.

Miller, Greg. *The Apprentice: Trump, Russia and the Subversion of American Democracy.* New York: Custom House, 2018.

Nazaryan, Alexander. *The Best People: Trump's Cabinet and the Siege on Washington.* New York: Hachette Books, 2019.

O'Brien, Timothy L. *TrumpNation: The Art of Being the Donald.* New York: Warner Business Books, 2005.

Partlow, Joshua. *A Kingdom of Their Own: The Family Karzai and the Afghan Disaster.* New York: Knopf, 2016.

Perry, Mark. *The Pentagon's Wars: The Military's Undeclared War Against America's Presidents.* New York: Basic Books, 2017.

Pillsbury, Michael. *The Hundred-Year Marathon: China's Secret Strategy to Replace America as the Global Superpower.* Reprint. New York: St. Martin's, 2016.

Postman, Neil. *Amusing Ourselves to Death: Public Discourse in the Age of Show Business.* New York: Penguin Books, 2005.

Prince, Erik. *Civilian Warriors: The Inside Story of Blackwater and the Unsung Heroes of the War on Terror.* New York: Portfolio/Penguin, 2013.

Proser, Jim. *No Better Friend, No Worse Enemy: The Life of General James Mattis.* New York: Broadside Books, 2018.

Raspail, Jean. *The Camp of the Saints.* Translated by Norman Shapiro. Alexandria, VA: Institute for Western Values, 1975.

Rayburn, Joel. *Iraq After America: Strongmen, Sectarians, Resistance.* Stanford, CA: Hoover Institution Press, 2014.

Rayburn, Joel D., and Frank K. Sobchak, eds. *The U.S. Army in the Iraq War, Volume 2: Surge and Withdrawal 2007–2011.* Carlisle, PA: Strategic Studies Institute and US Army War College Press, 2019.

Rhodes, Ben. *The World as It Is: A Memoir of the Obama White House.* New York: Random House, 2018.

Rodman, Peter W. *Presidential Command: Power, Leadership, and the Making of Foreign Policy from Richard Nixon to George W. Bush.* 1st ed. New York: Vintage, 2010.

Salkin, Allen, and Aaron Short. *The Method to the Madness: Donald Trump's Ascent as Told by Those Who Were Hired, Fired, Inspired—and Inaugurated.* New York: All Points Books, 2019.

Schadlow, Nadia. *War and the Art of Governance: Consolidating Combat Success into Political Victory.* Washington, DC: Georgetown University Press, 2017.

Sciutto, Jim. *The Shadow War: Inside Russia's and China's Secret Operations to Defeat America.* New York: HarperCollins, 2019.

Sekulow, Jay. *Unholy Alliance: The Agenda Iran, Russia, and Jihadists Share for Conquering the World.* New York: Howard Books, 2016.

Sherman, Jake, and Anna Palmer. *The Hill to Die On: The Battle for Congress and the Future of Trump's America.* New York: Crown, 2019.

Sims, Cliff. *Team of Vipers: My 500 Extraordinary Days in the Trump White House.* New York: Thomas Dunne Books, 2019.

Spicer, Sean. *The Briefing: Politics, the Press, and the President.* Washington, DC: Regnery, 2018.

Stone, Roger. *The Making of the President 2016: How Donald Trump Orchestrated a Revolution.* New York: Skyhorse, 2017.

Strauss, William, and Neil Howe. *The Fourth Turning: What the Cycles of History Tell Us About America's Next Rendezvous with Destiny.* New York: Broadway, 1997.

Trump, Donald. *Great Again: How to Fix Our Crippled America.* New York: Threshold Editions, 2016.

Trump, Donald, and Tony Schwartz. *Trump: The Art of the Deal.* Reprint. New York: Ballantine Books, 2015.

Trump, Donald, and Dave Shiflett. *The America We Deserve.* 1st ed. Los Angeles: Renaissance Books, 2000.

United States Government and United States Army. *The U.S. Army in the Iraq War, Volume 1: Invasion, Insurgency, Civil War 2003–2006.* Carlisle, PA: Strategic Studies Institute and US Army War College Press, 2019.

Ward, Vicky. *Kushner, Inc.: Greed. Ambition. Corruption. The Extraordinary Story of Jared Kushner and Ivanka Trump.* New York: St. Martin's, 2019.

West, Bing, and Ray L. Smith. *The March Up: Taking Baghdad with the United States Marines.* New York: Bantam Dell, 2004.

Whipple, Chris. *The Gatekeepers: How the White House Chiefs of Staff Define Every Presidency.* New York: Broadway Books, 2018.

Wolff, Michael. *Fire and Fury: Inside the Trump White House.* New York: Henry Holt, 2018.

———. *Siege: Trump Under Fire.* New York: Henry Holt, 2019.

Woodward, Bob. *Fear: Trump in the White House.* New York: Simon and Schuster, 2018.

———. *Rage.* New York: Simon and Schuster, 2020.

———. *Peril.* New York: Simon and Schuster, 2021.

—— NOTES ——

EPIGRAPHS

ix   **"Our politics, religion, news"**: Neil Postman, *Amusing Ourselves to Death: Public Discourse in the Age of Show Business* (New York: Penguin Books, 1985).

ix   **"From this day forward"**: Donald J. Trump, "Remarks of President Donald J. Trump—as Prepared for Delivery" (Inaugural Address, January 20, 2017), https://www.white house.gov/briefings-statements/the-inaugural-address/.

ix   **"If you asked Babe Ruth"**: Eric Dash, "The Midas Touch, with Spin on It," *New York Times*, September 8, 2004, https://www.nytimes.com/2004/09/08/business/the-midas -touch-with-spin-on-it.html.

ix   **"We are all enrolled"**: Tom Toles, "We Are All Enrolled in Trump University Now," *Washington Post*, November 11, 2016, https://www.washingtonpost.com/news/opinions /wp/2016/11/11/we-are-all-enrolled-in-trump-university-now/.

ix   **"A certain grasp"**: Carl von Clausewitz, Michael Eliot Howard, and Peter Paret, *On War* (Princeton: Princeton University Press, 2008), 608, http://search.ebscohost.com /login.aspx?direct=true&scope=site&db=nlebk&db=nlabk&AN=390520.

PROLOGUE

xv   **Donald Trump returned**: "Former President Trump Visits New York City Police and Fire Departments," C-SPAN, September 11, 2021, https://www.c-span.org/video/?514591-1 /president-trump-visits-york-city-police-fire-departments.

xv   **skipped the official memorial ceremonies**: Katie Rogers, "Where's Trump on 9/11? Not at Ground Zero," *New York Times*, September 11, 2021, https://www.nytimes .com/2021/09/11/us/where-was-trump-9-11-anniversary.html.

xv   **This was a lie:** "Fact Check: Courts Have Dismissed Multiple Lawsuits of Alleged Electoral Fraud Presented by Trump Campaign," Reuters, February 15, 2021, https://www .reuters.com/article/uk-factcheck-courts-election/fact-check-courts-have-dismissed -multiple-lawsuits-of-alleged-electoral-fraud-presented-by-trump-campaign-idUSK BN2AF1G1; Alyza Sebenius, "Election Was Most Secure in American History, U.S. Officials Say," *Bloomberg*, November 12, 2020, https://www.bloomberg.com/news/arti cles/2020-11-13/election-was-most-secure-in-american-history-u-s-officials-say.

xv   **The same day:** George W. Bush, "Remarks by President George W. Bush at the Flight 93 National Memorial in Shanksville, Pennsylvania," George W. Bush Presidential Center, September 11, 2021, https://www.bushcenter.org/about-the-center/newsroom /press-releases/2021/09/remarks-president-bush-shanksville-9-11.html.

xv   **"There is little cultural":** Bush, "Remarks by President George W. Bush."

xvi **forest of headlines:** Amy B. Wang and Caroline Anders, "George W. Bush Compares 'Violent Extremists at Home' to 9/11 Terrorists in 20th Anniversary Speech," *Washington Post*, September 11, 2021, https://www.washingtonpost.com/politics/2021/09/11 /george-w-bush-compares-violent-extremists-home-911-terrorists-20th-anniversary -speech/; Zeke Miller, "Bush Warns of Domestic Extremism, Appeals to 'Nation I Know,'" Associated Press, September 11, 2021, https://apnews.com/article/donald -trump-george-w-bush-fe5493786f03bc30a5e88d9958e12a8d; John Wagner and Amy B. Wang, "Trump Takes Aim at George W. Bush, Saying He Shouldn't 'Lecture' about Threat of Domestic Terrorism," *Washington Post*, September 13, 2021, https://www .washingtonpost.com/politics/trump-takes-aim-at-george-w-bush-saying-he-shouldnt -lecture-about-threat-of-domestic-terrorism/2021/09/13/ad66d9e6-14b0-11ec-b976 -f4a43b740aeb_story.html.

xvi **slammed the Biden administration:** "Former President Trump Visits New York City Police and Fire Departments."

xvi **the Taliban raised:** "The Latest: Taliban Flag Flies at Afghan Presidential Palace," Associated Press, September 11, 2021, https://www.yahoo.com/now/latest-brother-for mer-afghan-vp-093007896.html.

xvi **"surrender agreement":** Michael Crowley, "Some Former Trump Allies Say His Taliban Deal Laid the Groundwork for Chaos," *New York Times*, August 20, 2021, https:// www.nytimes.com/2021/08/20/world/some-former-trump-allies-say-his-taliban-deal -laid-the-groundwork-for-chaos.html.

xvi **dropped to their deaths:** Gerry Shih, Niha Masih, and Dan Lamothe, "The Story of an Afghan Man Who Fell from the Sky," *Washington Post*, August 26, 2021, https://www .washingtonpost.com/world/2021/08/26/story-an-afghan-man-who-fell-sky/.

xvi **Thirteen US service members:** Shawn Boburg et al., "The 13 U.S. Service Members Killed in the Kabul Airport Attack," *Washington Post*, August 29, 2021, https://www .washingtonpost.com/national-security/2021/08/27/us-service-members-killed -kabul-airport-names/.

xvi **In 2018, Trump authorized:** Mujib Mashal and Eric Schmitt, "White House Orders Direct Taliban Talks to Jump-Start Afghan Negotiations," *New York Times*, July 15, 2018, https://www.nytimes.com/2018/07/15/world/asia/afghanistan-taliban-direct-neg otiations.html.

xvi **agreement with the Taliban:** "Agreement for Bringing Peace to Afghanistan between the Islamic Emirate of Afghanistan Which Is Not Recognized by the United States as a State and Is Known as the Taliban and the United States of America," US Department of State, February 29, 2020, https://www.state.gov/wp-content/uploads/2020/02/Agreement-For-Bringing-Peace-to-Afghanistan-02.29.20.pdf.

xvi **Despite these agreements:** "Twelfth Report of the Analytical Support and Sanctions Monitoring Team Submitted Pursuant to Resolution 2557 (2020) Concerning the Taliban and Other Associated Individuals and Entities Constituting a Threat to the Peace Stability and Security of Afghanistan," United Nations Security Council, June 1, 2021, https://www.undocs.org/pdf?symbol=en/S/2021/486.

xvi **five thousand Taliban prisoners:** Alan Cullison and Saeed Shah, "Taliban Commander Who Led Attack on Afghan City Was Released from Prison Last Year, Officials Say," *Wall Street Journal*, August 3, 2021, https://www.wsj.com/articles/taliban-commander-who-led-attack-on-afghan-city-was-released-from-prison-last-year-officials-say-11628010527.

xvii **thousands of allied NATO forces:** Kathy Gannon, "Formal Start of Final Phase of Afghan Pullout by US, NATO," Associated Press, May 1, 2021, https://apnews.com/article/joe-biden-kabul-afghanistan-b06334b7f884e5392a92136ee03f610a.

xvii **more than fifteen thousand contractors:** Idrees Ali and Phil Stewart, "Pentagon Chief Says Removal of All Contractors from Afghanistan Under Way," Reuters, May 6, 2021, https://www.reuters.com/world/asia-pacific/removal-all-contractors-afghanistan-underway-pentagon-chief-2021-05-06/.

xvii **member of al-Qaeda's leadership:** "Twelfth Report of the Analytical Support and Sanctions Monitoring Team Submitted Pursuant to Resolution 2557 (2020) Concerning the Taliban and Other Associated Individuals and Entities Constituting a Threat to the Peace Stability and Security of Afghanistan," 10fn11.

xvii **acting interior minister:** Sudarsan Raghavan, "The U.S. Branded the Haqqanis Terrorists and Issued $5 Million Bounties. Now They're in Power in the Taliban Government," *Washington Post*, September 11, 2021, https://www.washingtonpost.com/world/asia_pacific/haqqanis-afghanistan-taliban/2021/09/10/71f82620-123b-11ec-baca-86b144fc8a2d_story.html; Peter Bergen, "He's on the FBI's Most-Wanted List and Is Now a Key Member of the Taliban's New Government," CNN, September 9, 2021, https://www.cnn.com/2021/09/09/opinions/haqqani-taliban-government-afghanistan-bergen/index.html.

xvii **Trump met with Kim:** James Doubek, "Trump Meets North Korea's Kim Jong Un and Says Nuclear Negotiations Will Resume," NPR, June 30, 2019, https://www.npr.org/2019/06/30/737365074/trump-to-meet-kim-jong-un-at-dmz.

xvii **the state of Vermont:** Art Woolf, "Vermont Has Second Smallest GDP in Nation. Here's What That Means for Your Taxes," *Burlington Free Press*, May 17, 2018, https://www.burlingtonfreepress.com/story/money/2018/05/17/vermont-has-second-smallest-gdp-nation-what-means-taxes/614678002/.

xviii **"saved the United States":** This section draws on Peter Bergen, "Bolton Book Oozes with Contempt for His Old Boss," CNN, June 23, 2020, https://www.cnn.com/2020/06/22/opinions/bolton-book-oozes-with-contempt-trump-bergen/index.html, and John Bolton, *The Room Where It Happened: A White House Memoir* (New York: Simon and Schuster, 2020), 110.

xviii **an easy mark:** Bolton, *The Room Where It Happened*, 331.

xviii **twenty-seven letters:** Bob Woodward, *Rage* (New York: Simon and Schuster, 2020), 106.

xviii **continued producing fissile material:** Josh Smith, "North Korea Fires More Missiles Than Ever amid Coronavirus Outbreak," Reuters, March 28, 2020, https://www.reuters .com/article/us-northkorea-missiles/north-korea-fires-more-missiles-than-ever -amid-coronavirus-outbreak-idUSKBN21F0Y2.

xviii **"worst deal in history":** John Bolton, "The Iran Deal Was Betrayed by Its Own Abysmal Record," White House, May 10, 2018, https://trumpwhitehouse.archives.gov/artic les/iran-deal-betrayed-abysmal-record/.

xviii **Trump's own intelligence agencies:** Daniel R. Coats, "Worldwide Threat Assessment of the US Intelligence Community," Office of the Director of National Intelligence, January 29, 2019, https://www.dni.gov/files/ODNI/documents/2019-ATA-SFR---SSCI .pdf; "CIA Director: Iran 'Technically' in Compliance with Nuclear Deal," C-SPAN, January 29, 2019, https://www.c-span.org/video/?c4777163/cia-director-iran-technically -compliance-nuclear-deal.

xviii **which he did in 2018:** Mark Landler, "Trump Abandons Iran Nuclear Deal He Long Scorned," *New York Times*, May 8, 2018, https://www.nytimes.com/2018/05/08/world /middleeast/trump-iran-nuclear-deal.html.

xviii **20 percent purity:** "Iran Nuclear Crisis: Tehran to Enrich Uranium to 20%, IAEA Says," BBC, January 1, 2021, https://www.bbc.com/news/world-middle-east-55509048.

xviii **accumulated enough fissile material:** Laurence Norman, "Iran Has Started Producing Uranium Metal, in Violation of 2015 Accords, IAEA Says," *Wall Street Journal*, February 10, 2021, https://www.wsj.com/articles/iran-has-started-producing-uranium-metal -in-violation-of-2015-accords-iaea-says-11612981889.

xix **pull out of NATO:** Bolton, *The Room Where It Happened*, 137.

xix **most successful . . . largely despised:** "Trump Defence Chief Mattis Hails Nato as 'Bedrock' of Co-Operation," BBC, February 15, 2017, https://www.bbc.com/news /world-europe-38979190; Richard Wike et al., "America's Image Abroad Rebounds with Transition from Trump to Biden," Pew Research Center, June 10, 2021, https:// www.pewresearch.org/global/2021/06/10/americas-image-abroad-rebounds-with -transition-from-trump-to-biden/.

xix **the 2020 election was rigged:** Caitlin Dickson, "Poll: Two-Thirds of Republicans Still Think the 2020 Election Was Rigged," Yahoo News, August 4, 2021, https://news.ya hoo.com/poll-two-thirds-of-republicans-still-think-the-2020-election-was-rigged -165934695.html.

xix **Paris climate agreement:** Matt McGrath, "Climate Change: US Formally Withdraws from Paris Agreement," BBC, November 4, 2020, https://www.bbc.com/news/science -environment-54797743; Michael D. Shear, "Trump Will Withdraw U.S. from Paris Climate Agreement," *New York Times*, June 1, 2017, https://www.nytimes.com/2017/06 /01/climate/trump-paris-climate-agreement.html.

xx **the hottest year:** Oliver Milman, "2020 Was Hottest Year on Record by Narrow Margin, Nasa Says," *Guardian*, January 14, 2021, https://www.theguardian.com/environ ment/2021/jan/14/2020-hottest-year-on-record-nasa.

xx   **"within a couple of days"**: Daniel Wolfe and Daniel Dale, "'It's Going to Disappear': A Timeline of Trump's Claims That Covid-19 Will Vanish," CNN, October 31, 2020, https://www.cnn.com/interactive/2020/10/politics/covid-disappearing-trump -comment-tracker/.

xx   **no more dangerous**: Tommy Beer, "All The Times Trump Compared Covid-19 To The Flu, Even After He Knew Covid-19 Was Far More Deadly," *Forbes*, September 10, 2020, https://www.forbes.com/sites/tommybeer/2020/09/10/all-the-times-trump-compared -covid-19-to-the-flu-even-after-he-knew-covid-19-was-far-more-deadly/?sh=4a4b8a 28f9d2.

xx   **"anybody that wants a test"**: Yasmeen Abutaleb and Damian Paletta, *Nightmare Scenario: Inside the Trump Administration's Response to the Pandemic That Changed History* (New York: HarperCollins, 2021), 114.

xx   **"a beautiful time"**: Annie Karni and Donald G. McNeil Jr., "Trump Wants U.S. 'Opened Up' by Easter, Despite Health Officials' Warnings," *New York Times*, March 24, 2020, https://www.nytimes.com/2020/03/24/us/politics/trump-coronavirus-easter .html.

xx   **COVID-19 testing strategy**: Abutaleb and Paletta, *Nightmare Scenario*, 83.

xx   **Trump pressed for states**: "The U.S. Sets Another Daily Record for New Cases, Surpassing 59,000," *New York Times*, July 8, 2020, https://www.nytimes.com/2020/07/08 /world/coronavirus-updates.html.

xx   **spike of cases there**: Maggie Astor and Noah Weiland, "Coronavirus Surge in Tulsa 'More Than Likely' Linked to Trump Rally," *New York Times*, July 8, 2020, https:// www.nytimes.com/2020/07/08/us/politics/coronavirus-tulsa-trump-rally.html. This section draws on Peter Bergen, "A Colossal Failure of Trump's Leadership," CNN, July 28, 2020, https://edition.cnn.com/2020/07/29/opinions/colossal-failure-of-trump-leadership -bergen/index.html.

xx   **Republican governor Kevin Stitt**: Barbara Hoberock, "Watch Now: Kevin Stitt 'Pretty Shocked' to Be First Governor to Test Positive for COVID-19," *Tulsa World*, July 16, 2020, https://tulsaworld.com/news/local/watch-now-kevin-stitt-pretty-shocked-to-be first-governor-to-test-positive-for-covid/article_781a1f60-e4d1-5158-85e8-b89b1a6fb 510.html.

xx   **suggested that injecting bleach**: Meridith McGraw and Sam Stein, "It's Been Exactly One Year since Trump Suggested Injecting Bleach. We've Never Been the Same," *Politico*, April 23, 2021, https://www.politico.com/news/2021/04/23/trump-bleach-one-year -484399.

xx   **the drug hydroxychloroquine**: Berkeley Lovelace Jr. and Kevin Breuninger, "Trump Says He Takes Hydroxychloroquine to Prevent Coronavirus Infection Even Though It's an Unproven Treatment," CNBC, May 18, 2020, https://www.cnbc.com/2020/05/18 /trump-says-he-takes-hydroxychloroquine-to-prevent-coronavirus-infection.html.

xx   **revoked "emergency use"**: "FDA Cautions Against Use of Hydroxychloroquine or Chloroquine for COVID-19 Outside of the Hospital Setting or a Clinical Trial Due to Risk of Heart Rhythm Problems," US Food and Drug Administration, accessed October 26, 2021, https://www.fda.gov/drugs/drug-safety-and-availability/fda-cautions-against-use -hydroxychloroquine-or-chloroquine-covid-19-outside-hospital-setting-or.

xx **because there was more testing:** Jane C. Timm, "Fact Check: Trump Blames Testing for Spike in COVID-19 Cases. Experts Fault Reopening of States.," NBC News, June 10, 2020, https://www.nbcnews.com/politics/donald-trump/fact-check-trump-blames -testing-spike-covid-19-cases-experts-n1228671.

xxi **Fauci, as an "alarmist":** Kristen Holmes and Devan Cole, "Trump Calls Fauci 'a Little Bit of an Alarmist' as Coronavirus Cases Rise," CNN, July 19, 2020, https://www.cnn .com/2020/07/19/politics/trump-fauci-alarmist-coronavirus/index.html.

xxi **low of 32 percent:** Julie Pace and Hannah Fingerhut, "AP-NORC Poll: US Course at Record Low, Trump Sinks on Virus," Associated Press, July 26, 2020, https://apnews .com/article/virus-outbreak-election-2020-ap-top-news-elections-joe-biden-43a09 6bc2bcf376de04b696c5143ee99.

xxi **barred non-US citizens:** Erica Werner et al., "Trump Administration Announces Mandatory Quarantines in Response to Coronavirus," *Washington Post*, January 31, 2020, https://www.washingtonpost.com/us-policy/2020/01/31/trump-weighs-tighter-china -travel-restrictions-response-coronavirus/.

xxi **nomination of Amy Coney Barrett:** Kevin Liptak, "Inside One Celebration That Helped Spread the Virus across the US Government," CNN, October 7, 2020, https:// www.cnn.com/2020/10/03/politics/trump-covid-amy-coney-barrett-event/index.html.

xxi **By August 2020:** Christina Maxouris and Eliott C. McLaughlin, "US Tops 5 Million Covid-19 Cases, with Five States Making Up More Than 40% of Tally," CNN, August 9, 2020, https://www.cnn.com/2020/08/09/health/us-coronavirus-sunday/index.html; "U.S. Coronavirus Cases Soar as 18 States Set Single-Day Records This Week," *New York Times*, August 6, 2020, https://www.nytimes.com/2020/07/25/world/coronavirus -covid-19.html.

xxi **made up 37 percent:** Sarah Evanega et al., "Coronavirus Misinformation: Quantifying Sources and Themes in the COVID-19 'Infodemic,'" Cornell CALS/Alliance for Science, September 2020, https://allianceforscience.cornell.edu/wp-content/uploads/2020 /09/Evanega-et-al-Coronavirus-misinformationFINAL.pdf.

xxii **vaccinated in secret:** Maggie Haberman, "Trump and His Wife Received Coronavirus Vaccine before Leaving the White House," *New York Times*, March 1, 2021, https:// www.nytimes.com/2021/03/01/us/politics/donald-trump-melania-coronavirus-vacc ine.html.

xxii **four hundred thousand Americans died:** Dylan Scott, "America's Covid-19 Death Toll Has Surpassed 400,000," *Vox*, January 19, 2021, https://www.vox.com/2021/1/19 /22238568/us-covid-19-deaths-how-many-400000.

xxii **40 percent higher:** Steffie Woolhandler et al., "Public Policy and Health in the Trump Era," *The Lancet* 397, no. 10275 (February 2021): 705–53, https://doi.org/10.1016/S01 40-6736(20)32545-9.

CHAPTER 1: THE WAR ROOM

3 **"Mr. President: Are you sending":** "Trump Says 'We'll See' about Increasing Troop Levels in Afghanistan," CBS News, July 20, 2017, https://www.cbsnews.com/news /trump-says-well-see-about-increasing-troop-levels-in-afghanistan/.

3   **one of his favorite lines:** "Trump Says 'We'll See' about Increasing Troop Levels in Afghanistan," *CBS News*.

4   **Bannon, a voluble ringmaster:** "The Turbulent Story of Steve Bannon—Video Profile," *Guardian*, August 18, 2017, https://www.theguardian.com/us-news/video/2016/nov/15/stephen-bannon-and-the-alt-right-in-the-white-house-video-explainer.

5   **"By reading, you learn":** Geoffrey Ingersoll, "General James 'Mad Dog' Mattis Email about Being 'Too Busy to Read' Is a Must-Read," *Business Insider*, May 9, 2013, https://www.businessinsider.com/viral-james-mattis-email-reading-marines-2013-5.

5   **Bannon kept a dog-eared:** Qiao Liang and Wang Xiangsui, *Unrestricted Warfare* (Beijing: PLA Literature and Arts, 1999), http://www.c4i.org/unrestricted.pdf.

5   **Bannon gave a copy:** Alan Rappeport, "A China Hawk Gains Prominence as Trump Confronts Xi on Trade," *New York Times*, November 30, 2018, https://www.nytimes.com/2018/11/30/us/politics/trump-china-trade-xi-michael-pillsbury.html.

6   *vision du monde:* "Watch Steve Bannon Explain How He Sees the World," excerpt from *Frontline*, "Bannon's War" episode, aired May 23, 2017, https://youtu.be/P8zPZRxAC_Y.

7   **fight to seize Baghdad:** Paul Szoldra, "Trump's Cabinet Is Starting to Look Like the Staff of One of the Most Storied Units of the Iraq War," *Business Insider*, December 7, 2016, https://www.businessinsider.com/trumps-marine-general-picks-iraq-war-2016-12.

10   **In 1987, Trump:** For more on this point, see Jacob M. Schlesinger, "Trump Forged His Ideas on Trade in the 1980s—and Never Deviated," *Wall Street Journal*, November 15, 2018, https://www.wsj.com/articles/trump-forged-his-ideas-on-trade-in-the-1980sand-never-deviated-1542304508.

10   **"ripping us off":** Jim Tankersley and Mark Landler, "Trump's Love for Tariffs Began in Japan's '80s Boom," *New York Times*, May 15, 2019, https://www.nytimes.com/2019/05/15/us/politics/china-trade-donald-trump.html.

11   **quarter of global output:** Robbie Gramer, "Infographic: Here's How the Global GDP Is Divvied Up," *Foreign Policy*, February 24, 2017, https://foreignpolicy.com/2017/02/24/infographic-heres-how-the-global-gdp-is-divvied-up/.

11   **2 percent of their GDP:** Christina Wilkie, "Trump Is Pushing NATO Allies to Spend More on Defense. But So Did Obama and Bush," *CNBC*, July 11, 2018, https://www.cnbc.com/2018/07/11/obama-and-bush-also-pressed-nato-allies-to-spend-more-on-defense.html.

11   **Of the twenty-nine countries:** "The US Spent $686 Billion on Defense Last Year—Here's How the Other NATO Countries Stack Up," *CNBC*, July 6, 2018, https://www.cnbc.com/2018/07/03/nato-spending-2017.html.

11   **spent around $250 billion:** Michael E. O'Hanlon, "Permit (Part of) Trump's Defense Buildup Without Blowing Up the Deficit," *Brookings* (blog), January 31, 2018, https://www.brookings.edu/blog/order-from-chaos/2018/01/31/permit-trumps-defense-buildup-without-blowing-up-the-deficit/.

11   **spent around $700 billion:** Robert Burns, "A Pentagon Budget Like None Before: $700 Billion," *Military Times*, February 11, 2018, https://www.militarytimes.com/news/pentagon-congress/2018/02/11/a-pentagon-budget-like-none-before-700-billion/.

13 **Tillerson considered Trump:** "Rex Tillerson Reflects on Firing, Working for 'Undisciplined' Trump," CBS News, December 7, 2018, https://www.cbsnews.com/news/rex-tillerson-bob-schieffer-interview-houston-firing-trump-tweet-tillerson-insult-2018-12-07/.

14 **190,000 American soldiers:** Gen. Mark A. Milley, "2017 Posture Statement of the U.S. Army," February 2016, https://www.army.mil/article/163561/2017_posture_statement_of_the_us_army.

15 **"Steve, that was spectacular":** Cliff Sims, *Team of Vipers: My 500 Extraordinary Days in the Trump White House* (New York: Thomas Dunne Books, 2019), 154.

CHAPTER 2: IN THE BEGINNING

17 **"Well, I don't have":** Author interview with Barack Obama, April 28, 2016.

17 **"He doesn't have":** Andrew Kaczynski and Nathaniel Meyersohn, "Trump in Crazy 2011 Interview: 'I'm Very Proud' to Be a Birther," *BuzzFeed News*, September 21, 2016, https://www.buzzfeednews.com/article/andrewkaczynski/trump-in-crazy-2011-interview-im-very-proud-to-be-a-birther.

17 **"I wouldn't believe Donald Trump":** "It's Leona's Turn in Playboy—Donald Is a 'Skunk,'" Associated Press, September 21, 1990, https://www.latimes.com/archives/la-xpm-1990-09-21-ca-959-story.html.

19 **Muslim Americans polled:** "American Attitudes: Immigration, Civil Rights, Surveillance, Profiling, and Hate Crimes," Zogby Analytics, 2017, https://d3n8a8pro7vhmx.cloudfront.net/aai/pages/12479/attachments/original/1501521073/Poll__7-2017.pdf?1501521073.

19 **Another poll, from 2015:** Peter Schroeder, "Poll: 43 Percent of Republicans Believe Obama Is a Muslim," *The Hill*, September 13, 2015, https://thehill.com/blogs/blog-briefing-room/news/253515-poll-43-percent-of-republicans-believe-obama-is-a-muslim.

20 **no evidence for this:** "Trump 'Wrong' in Claiming US Arabs Cheered 9/11 Attacks," BBC News, November 23, 2015, https://www.bbc.com/news/world-us-canada-34902748.

20 **Clinton proposed a robust:** For an account of this episode, see Mark Landler, *Alter Egos: Hillary Clinton, Barack Obama, and the Twilight Struggle Over American Power* (New York: Penguin Random House, 2016), 208–12.

21 ***Wall Street Journal*-NBC News:** Lucy McCalmont, "Poll: Beheading News Makes Impact," *Politico*, September 9, 2014, https://www.politico.com/story/2014/09/poll-james-foley-isil-110783.

21 **campaign rally in Iowa:** "Trump: I'd Bomb the S-*t Out of ISIS," https://www.facebook.com/cnn/videos/10154213275786509.

22 **"total and complete shutdown":** Ed Pilkington, "Donald Trump: Ban All Muslims Entering US," *Guardian*, December 7, 2015, https://www.theguardian.com/us-news/2015/dec/07/donald-trump-ban-all-muslims-entering-us-san-bernardino-shooting.

22 **"putting our troops"**: Ed Pilkington, "Donald Trump: Ban All Muslims Entering US," *Guardian*, December 7, 2015, https://www.theguardian.com/us-news/2015/dec/07 /donald-trump-ban-all-muslims-entering-us-san-bernardino-shooting.

22 **"We wanted none"**: Corey Lewandowski and David N. Bossie, *Let Trump Be Trump: The Inside Story of His Rise to the Presidency* (New York: Center Street, 2017), 97.

22 **Polling in early 2016:** Murtaza Hussain, "Majority of Americans Now Support Trump's Proposed Muslim Travel Ban, Poll Shows," *The Intercept*, March 30, 2016, https:// theintercept.com/2016/03/30/majority-of-americans-now-support-trumps-proposed -muslim-ban-poll-shows/.

22 **"We must be smart!"**: Donald J. Trump (@realDonaldTrump), "Appreciate the congrats for being right on radical Islamic terrorism. . . . ," Twitter, June 12, 2016, 12:43 pm, https://twitter.com/realdonaldtrump/status/742034549232766976.

23 **sixty-five thousand Syrian refugees:** Rebecca Kaplan, "Hillary Clinton: U.S. Should Take 65,000 Syrian Refugees," *Face the Nation*, CBS, September 2015, https://www .cbsnews.com/news/hillary-clinton-u-s-should-take-65000-syrian-refugees/.

23 **"ISIS will hand her":** Ivan Levingston, "Trump: ISIS Will Give Clinton MVP Award, 'Her Only Competition Is Barack Obama,'" CNBC, August 11, 2016, https://www .cnbc.com/2016/08/11/trump-isis-will-give-clinton-mvp-award-her-only-competition -is-barack-obama.html.

23 **During the presidential campaign:** Peter Eavis, "There's a Disconnect in Americans' Worry About Terrorism," *New York Times*, June 15, 2016, https://www.nytimes.com /2016/06/16/upshot/theres-a-disconnect-in-americans-worry-about-terrorism.html.

24 **"Never Trump" movement:** Scott Detrow, "'Never Trump' Campaign Launches Last-Ditch Effort to Stop Nomination," *All Things Considered*, NPR, July 13, 2016, https:// www.npr.org/2016/07/13/485895835/opposition-forces-prepare-last-ditch-effort -to-thwart-donald-trump.

24 **Signatories to the letter:** "Open Letter on Donald Trump from GOP National Security Leaders," *War on the Rocks*, March 2, 2016, https://warontherocks.com/2016/03/open -letter-on-donald-trump-from-gop-national-security-leaders/.

24 **Kellogg had commanded:** Alan Yuhas, "Keith Kellogg: Who Is Trump's Acting National Security Adviser?," *Guardian*, February 14, 2017, https://www.theguardian.com /us-news/2017/feb/14/keith-kellogg-who-is-trumps-acting-national-security-adviser-.

25 **Papadopoulos had highlighted:** Missy Ryan and Steven Mufson, "One of Trump's Foreign Policy Advisers Is a 2009 College Grad Who Lists Model UN as a Credential," *Washington Post*, March 22, 2016, https://www.washingtonpost.com/news/checkpoint /wp/2016/03/21/meet-the-men-shaping-donald-trumps-foreign-policy-views/.

25 **one of nine children:** Associated Press, "Michael Flynn Returns to Beach Town Where He Grew Up Surfing," CBS News, July 17, 2017, https://www.cbsnews.com/news /michael-flynn-returns-to-beach-town-where-he-grew-up-surfing/.

26 **Flynn used to joke:** Author interview with Michael Flynn, 2014.

26 **out-of-the-box thinker:** Michael T. Flynn and Michael Ledeen, *The Field of Fight: How We Can Win the Global War against Radical Islam and Its Allies* (New York: St. Martin's, 2016), 16–17.

26   **Al-Qaeda in Iraq:** This paragraph draws on Stanley McChrystal, *My Share of the Task: A Memoir* (New York: Portfolio/Penguin, 2013).

27   *Rolling Stone* **reporter:** Michael Hastings, "The Runaway General: The Profile That Brought Down McChrystal," *Rolling Stone*, June 22, 2010, https://www.rollingstone.com/politics/politics-news/the-runaway-general-the-profile-that-brought-down-mcchrystal-192609/.

27   **The Flynn brothers were watching:** James Kitfield, *Twilight Warriors: The Soldiers, Spies, and Special Agents Who Are Revolutionizing the American Way of War* (New York: Basic Books, 2016), 234–35.

27   **accepted McChrystal's resignation:** David Gura, "Obama Accepts McChrystal's Resignation, Appoints Petraeus as His Replacement," NPR, June 23, 2010, https://www.npr.org/sections/thetwo-way/2010/06/23/128048080/president-obama-makes-statement-about-mcchrystal-meeting.

27   **rare night off in Paris:** McChrystal, *My Share of the Task*, 384.

27   **Flynn was a registered Democrat:** Krishnadev Calamur, "Donald Trump's Choice for National Security Adviser Has One Priority: Combatting 'Radical Islamic Terrorism,'" *The Atlantic*, November 18, 2016, https://www.theatlantic.com/news/archive/2016/11/michael-flynn-trum-national-security-adviser/508115/.

28   **seventeen thousand employees:** P. W. Singer and Emerson T. Brooking, *LikeWar: The Weaponization of Social Media* (Boston: Eamon Dolan/Houghton Mifflin Harcourt, 2018).

28   **orchestrated by Iran:** Peter Bergen, "The Mystery of Mike Flynn," CNN, December 18, 2018, https://www.cnn.com/2018/12/05/opinions/mystery-of-michael-flynns-fall-from-grace-bergen/index.html.

28   **coin the term "Flynn facts":** Bergen, "The Mystery of Mike Flynn."

29   **releasing those documents:** Flynn and Ledeen, *The Field of Fight*, 5.

29   **a "jayvee" team:** David Remnick, "Going the Distance: On and off the Road with Barack Obama," *New Yorker*, January 19, 2014, https://www.newyorker.com/magazine/2014/01/27/going-the-distance-david-remnick.

29   **on February 11, 2014:** "Clapper, Flynn Testify Al-Qaeda Not on 'Path to Defeat,'" video excerpt from US Armed Services Committee Meeting SD-G50, "Current and Future Worldwide Threats," February 11, 2014, https://www.inhofe.senate.gov/news/video-and-audio/view/clapper-flynn-testify-al-qaeda-not-on-path-to-defeat.

29   **CNN's Evan Perez asked Flynn:** Lieutenant General Michael Flynn, "The Global Threat Picture as the Defense Intelligence Agency Sees It," interview by Evan Perez, Aspen Institute Homeland Security Program 2014, July 26, 2014, https://www.aspeninstitute.org/videos/general-michael-flynn-on-global-threat-picture-defense-intelligence-agency-sees.

30   **morale at the agency:** James R. Clapper and Trey Brown, *Facts and Fears: Hard Truths from a Life in Intelligence* (New York: Viking, 2018), 330.

30   **terror was largely over:** Flynn and Ledeen, *The Field of Fight*, 4.

30   **country was heading:** Dana Priest, "Trump Adviser Michael T. Flynn on His Dinner with Putin and Why Russia Today Is Just Like CNN," *Washington Post*, August 15,

2016, https://www.washingtonpost.com/news/checkpoint/wp/2016/08/15/trump-adviser
-michael-t-flynn-on-his-dinner-with-putin-and-why-russia-today-is-just-like-cnn/.

31 **he wasn't paid by the Russians:** Zack Beauchamp, "It Sure Seems Like Michael Flynn
Lied to Federal Investigators about His Russia Ties," *Vox*, May 22, 2017, https://www
.vox.com/world/2017/5/22/15678186/michael-flynn-investigators-cummings.

31 **paid Flynn $33,750:** Ken Dilanian, "Russians Paid Mike Flynn $45K for Moscow Speech,
Documents Show," NBC News, March 16, 2017, https://www.nbcnews.com/news
/us-news/russians-paid-mike-flynn-45k-moscow-speech-documents-show-n734506.

31 **RT was similar to CNN:** Priest, "Trump Adviser Michael T. Flynn."

32 **"threat they pose against us":** Jason Russell, "Excerpts from Monday Night's Speeches,"
Washington Examiner, July 18, 2016, https://www.washingtonexaminer.com/excerpts
-from-monday-nights-speeches-including-willie-robertson-sheriff-clarke-and-joni-ernst.

32 **"Get fired up!":** "Michael Flynn Leads 'Lock Her Up' Chant at 2016 RNC," 2016 Republican National Convention, accessed July 30, 2019, https://www.youtube.com
/watch?v=tx94428MYcc.

32 **"Lock her up, that's right!":** "Michael Flynn Leads 'Lock Her Up' Chant at 2016 RNC."

32 *The Field of Fight*: Flynn and Ledeen, *The Field of Fight*, 2–4, 8, 159, 164.

33 **gripped by conspiracy theories:** Bergen, "The Mystery of Mike Flynn."

33 **"I have personally seen":** Andrew Kaczynski, "Michael Flynn Once Claimed Arabic
Signs on Southern Border Guide 'Radicalized Muslims' into US," CNN, December 9,
2016, https://www.cnn.com/2016/12/08/politics/kfile-michael-flynn-arabic-signs-on
-border/index.html.

34 **Comet Ping Pong pizzeria:** "Incoming National Security Adviser's Son Spreads Fake
News about D.C. Pizza Shop," *Politico*, December 4, 2016, https://www.politico.com
/story/2016/12/incoming-national-security-advisers-son-spreads-fake-news-about-dc
-pizza-shop-232181.

34 **"intel on this wasn't 100 percent":** Matthew Haag and Maya Salam, "Gunman in 'Pizzagate' Shooting Is Sentenced to 4 Years in Prison," *New York Times*, January 22, 2017,
https://www.nytimes.com/2017/06/22/us/pizzagate-attack-sentence.html.

34 **"Until #Pizzagate proven":** Michael Flynn Jr. (@mflynnJR), "Until #Pizzagate Proven
to Be False, It'll Remain a Story. The Left Seems to Forget #PodestaEmails and the
Many 'Coincidences' Tied to It," Twitter via Internet Archive Wayback Machine,
December 4, 2016, https://web.archive.org/web/20161205032236/https://twitter.com
/mflynnJR/status/805611056009768960.

34 **This proved too much:** Matthew Rosenberg, Maggie Haberman, and Eric Schmitt,
"Trump Fires Adviser's Son from Transition for Spreading Fake News," *New York
Times*, December 6, 2016, https://www.nytimes.com/2016/12/06/us/politics/michael
-flynn-son-trump.html.

35 **glorified clip job:** Andrew Reynolds, "Stop Calling Him 'Dr.': The Academic Fraud
of Sebastian Gorka, Trump's Terrorism 'Expert,'" *Haaretz*, April 27, 2017, https://
www.haaretz.com/opinion/the-academic-fraud-of-trumps-terrorism-expert
-1.5465216.

35   *Understanding Terror Networks*: Marc Sageman, *Understanding Terror Networks* (Philadelphia: University of Pennsylvania Press, 2004).

35   **Marine Corps University:** "Sebastian Gorka Ph.D.—Nationally Syndicated Radio Show Host of AMERICA First on the SALEM Radio Network" LinkedIn, n.d., https://www.linkedin.com/in/sebastian-gorka-ph-d-0a86a35.

35   **a major Republican donor:** Greg Jaffe, "For a Trump Adviser, an Odyssey from the Fringes of Washington to the Center of Power," *Washington Post*, February 20, 2017, https://www.washingtonpost.com/world/national-security/for-a-trump-adviser-an-ody ssey-from-the-fringes-of-washington-to-the-center-of-power/2017/02/20/0a326260 -f2cb-11e6-b9c9-e83fce42fb61_story.html.

35   **It later emerged that Saunders:** Jaffe, "Odyssey."

35   **soon to be radicalized:** Spencer Ackerman, "FBI Fired Sebastian Gorka for Anti-Muslim Diatribes," *Daily Beast*, July 10, 2017, https://www.thedailybeast.com/fbi-fired-sebastian -gorka-for-anti-muslim-diatribes.

35   **he was paid $8,000:** Jacey Fortin, "Who Is Sebastian Gorka? A Trump Adviser Comes Out of the Shadows," *New York Times*, February 17, 2017, https://www.nytimes.com /2017/02/17/us/politics/dr-sebastian-gorka.html.

36   **Gorka's book, *Defeating Jihad*:** Sebastian Gorka, *Defeating Jihad: The Winnable War* (Washington, DC: Regnery Publishing, 2016).

36   **"a direct existential threat":** Gorka, *Defeating Jihad*, 41, 120.

36   **fighting an "ideological war":** Bill Gertz, "For White House Counterterror Adviser, Media Attacks Are Latest Theater of Battle," *Washington Free Beacon*, February 27, 2017, https://freebeacon.com/national-security/white-house-counterterror-adviser-media -attacks-latest-theater-battle/.

36   **frequent appearances on TV:** Jack Miles, "With His Power Unchecked, Michael Flynn Could Lead Trump Into War with Iran," *HuffPost*, February 1, 2017, https://www .huffpost.com/entry/flynn-trump-iran_b_5890fbcee4b0522c7d3dba76; Fortin, "Who Is Sebastian Gorka?"; Pamela Engel, "Sebastian Gorka, Trump's Combative New National Security Aide, Is Widely Disdained within His Own Field," *Business Insider*, February 22, 2017, https://www.businessinsider.com/sebastian-gorka-trump-bio-profile-2017-2.

36   **Obama responded to this:** "Obama on ISIS," Wilson Center, August 5, 2016, https:// www.wilsoncenter.org/article/obama-isis.

36   **forty-five thousand ISIS fighters:** Kristina Wong, "General: 45,000 ISIS Fighters Killed in Two Years," *The Hill*, August 11, 2016, https://thehill.com/policy/defense /291179-general-isis-fighters-becoming-easier-to-kill.

36   **Also, Obama asserted:** Maya Rhodan, "President Obama: Stigmatizing Muslims 'Feeds the Terrorist Narrative,'" *Time*, December 6, 2016, https://time.com/4592640 /president-obama-national-security-speech-muslims/.

37   **His father, Khizr Khan, made:** "Khizr Khan's powerful DNC speech," CNN, July 29, 2016, https://www.cnn.com/videos/politics/2016/07/29/dnc-convention-khizr-khan -father-of-us-muslim-soldier-entire-speech-sot.cnn.

37 joked with Howard Stern: Andrew Kaczynski, "Trump, Comparing Sex to Vietnam, Said in 1998 He Should Receive the Congressional Medal of Honor," CNN Business, October 14, 2016, https://money.cnn.com/2016/10/14/media/trump-stern-vietnam-stds/index.html.

37 "look at his wife": Steve Turnham, "Donald Trump to Father of Fallen Soldier: 'I've Made a Lot of Sacrifices,'" ABC News, July 30, 2016, https://abcnews.go.com/Politics/donald-trump-father-fallen-soldier-ive-made-lot/story?id=41015051.

37 TV screen at the convention: Turnham, "Donald Trump to Father."

38 "thousands of jobs": Turnham, "Donald Trump to Father."

39 fifty leading Republicans: Carol Morello, "Former GOP National Security Officials: Trump Would Be 'Most Reckless' American President in History," Washington Post, August 8, 2016, https://www.washingtonpost.com/world/national-security/group-of-50-former-gop-national-security-officials-trump-would-be-most-reckless-president-in-american-history/2016/08/08/6715042c-5d9f-11e6-af8e-54aa2e849447_story.html.

39 Americans cast their votes: Chris Alcantara, Kevin Uhrmacher, and Emily Guskin, "Clinton and Trump's Demographic Tug of War," Washington Post, October 16, 2016, https://www.washingtonpost.com/graphics/politics/2016-election/the-demographic-groups-fueling-the-election/.

40 possible commander in chief: Alan Yuhas, "Benjamin Netanyahu to Meet with Clinton and Trump on Sunday," Guardian, September 23, 2016, https://www.theguardian.com/us-news/2016/sep/23/benjamin-netanyahu-israel-trump-clinton-meeting.

41 top four issues: "Top Voting Issues in 2016 Election," Pew Research Center, July 7, 2016, https://www.people-press.org/2016/07/07/4-top-voting-issues-in-2016-election/.

41 article he wrote: Lt. Gen. Michael T. Flynn, "Our Ally Turkey Is in Crisis and Needs Our Support," The Hill, https://thehill.com/blogs/pundits-blog/foreign-policy/305021-our-ally-turkey-is-in-crisis-and-needs-our-support.

41 half a million dollars: Adam K. Raymond, "Mike Flynn's Firm Was Paid to Make a Pro-Erdogan Propaganda Film While He Advised Trump," New York, May 31, 2017, http://nymag.com/intelligencer/2017/05/mike-flynns-firm-made-a-pro-erdogan-propaganda-film.html.

41 Syria to fight ISIS: Margaret Hartmann, "Every Shady, Possibly Illegal Thing Michael Flynn Has Been Accused Of," New York, December 7, 2017, http://nymag.com/intelligencer/2017/12/every-shady-thing-michael-flynn-has-been-accused-of.html.

CHAPTER 3: ALL THE BEST PEOPLE

43 "I'm going to surround": Robert Costa, "Trump Ends Relationship with Longtime Political Adviser Roger Stone," Washington Post, August 8, 2015, https://www.washingtonpost.com/news/post-politics/wp/2015/08/08/trump-ends-relationship-with-longtime-political-adviser-roger-stone/.

43 "Well, I watch the shows": Donald J. Trump, interview by Chuck Todd, Meet the Press, NBC, August 19, 2015, https://www.nbcnews.com/meet-the-press/meet-press-transcript-august-16-2015-n412636.

45   **won the presidency:** Corey Lewandowski and David N. Bossie, *Let Trump Be Trump: The Inside Story of His Rise to the Presidency* (New York: Center Street, 2017), 97.

46   **planning to proceed:** Chris Christie, *Let Me Finish: Trump, the Kushners, Bannon, New Jersey, and the Power of In-Your-Face Politics* (New York: Hachette Books, 2019), 307.

46   **senior role in Trump's cabinet:** Christie, *Let Me Finish*, 258, 388.

46   **governor Scott Walker:** Christie, *Let Me Finish*, 339.

46   **no plaudits in Trumpworld:** Alexander Nazaryan, *The Best People: Trump's Cabinet and the Siege on Washington* (New York: Hachette Books, 2019), 20.

46   **he was being vaporized:** Christie, *Let Me Finish*, 1–2.

47   **convicted of witness tampering:** Daniel Victor, "Chris Christie Says Jared Kushner's Father Committed a 'Loathsome' Crime," *New York Times*, January 30, 2019, https://www.nytimes.com/2019/01/30/us/politics/chris-christie-charles-kushner.html.

47   **consigned to the garbage:** Christie, *Let Me Finish*, 76.

47   **'Let's start from scratch':** Major Garrett, *Mr. Trump's Wild Ride: The Thrills, Chills, Screams, and Occasional Blackouts of an Extraordinary Presidency* (New York: All Points Books, 2018), 70.

48   **during the campaign:** Eric Bradner and Catherine Treyz, "Romney Implores: Bring Down Trump," CNN Politics, March 3, 2016, https://www.cnn.com/2016/03/03/politics/mitt-romney-presidential-race-speech/index.html.

51   **"he is the real deal":** David Greene, "Trump's Transition Team Works Over The Weekend On Cabinet Selections," *Morning Edition*, NPR, November 21, 2016, https://www.npr.org/2016/11/21/502841560/trumps-transition-team-works-over-the-weekend-on-cabinet-selections.

51   **"I come in peace":** Thomas Ricks, "Fiasco," *Armed Forces Journal* (blog), August 1, 2006, http://armedforcesjournal.com/fiasco/.

51   **"Number one Iran":** Greg Jaffe and Adam Entous, "As a General, Mattis Urged Action against Iran. As a Defense Secretary, He May Be a Voice of Caution.," *Washington Post*, January 8, 2017, https://www.washingtonpost.com/world/national-security/as-a-general-mattis-urged-action-against-iran-as-a-defense-secretary-he-may-be-a-voice-of-caution/2017/01/08/5a196ade-d391-11e6-a783-cd3fa950f2fd_story.html.

52   **hostility to Iran:** Mark Perry, "James Mattis' 33-Year Grudge gainst Iran," *Politico*, December 4, 2016, https://www.politico.com/magazine/story/2016/12/james-mattis-iran-secretary-of-defense-214500.

52   **commander of Southern Command:** Jerry Markon, "Trump Considering Retired General Who Clashed with Obama, Ex-Bush Official for Homeland Security," *Washington Post*, November 21, 2016, https://www.washingtonpost.com/news/powerpost/wp/2016/11/21/trump-considering-retired-general-who-clashed-with-obama-ex-bush-official-for-homeland-security/.

52   **"going into the administration":** Peter Bergen, "The General Now in Command at the White House Faces Ultimate Test," CNN, July 30, 2017, https://www.cnn.com/2017/07/30/opinions/john-kelly-general-in-command-at-white-house-bergen/index.html.

53   **made up of 240,000 employees:** Andrew Glass, "Homeland Security Department Begins Operations, Jan. 24, 2003," *Politico*, January 24, 2019, https://www.politico.com/story/2019/01/24/homeland-security-department-begins-2003-1116070.

53   **gone to the White House:** Peter L. Bergen, *The Longest War: The Enduring Conflict between America and Al-Qaeda* (New York: Free Press, 2011), 280–81.

56   **messy confirmation process:** Josh Dawsey and Shane Goldmacher, "Giuliani Pulls Name from Contention for Secretary of State," *Politico*, December 9, 2016, https://www.politico.com/story/2016/12/giuliani-pulls-name-from-contention-for-secretary-of-state-232439.

57   **"Just met with General Petraeus":** Donald J. Trump (@realDonaldTrump), "Just met with General Petraeus—was very impressed!," Twitter, November 28, 2016, 1:01 pm, https://twitter.com/realdonaldtrump/status/803343150907617284.

57   **Trump Tower to advise Bannon:** Matthew Nussbaum, "Robert Gates Huddling with Trump Friday," *Politico*, December 2, 2016, https://www.politico.com/blogs/donald-trump-administration/2016/12/robert-gates-meeting-with-trump-friday-232118.

58   **$250 billion a year:** Trefis Team, "How Have Exxon Mobil's Revenues And EBITDA Changed in Recent Years?," *Forbes*, May 29, 2018, https://www.forbes.com/sites/great speculations/2018/05/29/how-have-exxon-mobils-revenues-and-ebitda-changed-in-recent-years/.

58   **on par with Pakistan:** Hufsa Chaudhry, "Budget 2020: Govt Predicts 2.4pc Growth, Rs7 Trillion in Expenditures," *Dawn*, June 11, 2019, https://www.dawn.com/news/1484102.

58   **lived in Yemen:** Philip Bump, "Who Is Rex Tillerson, the ExxonMobil Chairman Who May Become Secretary of State?" *Washington Post*, January 11, 2017, https://www.washingtonpost.com/news/the-fix/wp/2016/12/10/who-is-rex-tillerson-the-exxonmobil-chairman-who-may-become-secretary-of-state/.

59   **almost two decades:** Josh Rogin, "Inside Rex Tillerson's Long Romance with Russia," *Washington Post*, December 13, 2016, https://www.washingtonpost.com/news/josh-rogin/wp/2016/12/13/inside-rex-tillersons-long-romance-with-russia/.

59   **Order of Friendship award:** David Filipov, "What Is the Russian Order of Friendship, and Why Does Rex Tillerson Have One?," *Washington Post*, December 13, 2016, https://www.washingtonpost.com/news/worldviews/wp/2016/12/13/what-is-the-russian-order-of-friendship-and-why-does-trumps-pick-for-secretary-of-state-have-one/.

59   **"God's not through with you":** Cheryl K. Chumley, "Rex Tillerson: The Man with a Mission from God," *Washington Times*, March 22, 2017, https://www.washingtontimes.com/news/2017/mar/22/rex-tillersons-wife-see-gods-not-through-you/.

59   **Trump transition team:** Harper Neidig, "Mike Rogers Leaves Trump Transition Team," *The Hill*, November 15, 2016, https://thehill.com/blogs/blog-briefing-room/news/306026-report-former-gop-rep-leaves-trump-transition-team.

62   **retired career diplomat:** Eliana Johnson, "White House Pushing Back against Mattis Appointment," *Politico*, March 2, 2017, https://www.politico.com/story/2017/03/jim-mattis-appointment-white-house-pushback-anne-patterson-235633.

62   **Trump officials and supporters:** Johnson, "White House Pushing Back."

62   **clinched the Republican nomination:** Elliott Abrams, "When You Can't Stand Your Candidate," *Weekly Standard*, May 6, 2016, https://www.washingtonexaminer.com /weekly-standard/when-you-cant-stand-your-candidate.

63   **"home in New Jersey":** "Donald Trump on Russia, Advice from Barack Obama and How He Will Lead," *Time*, December 7, 2016, https://time.com/4591183/time-person -of-the-year-2016-donald-trump-interview/.

64   **thirty-five Russian diplomats:** Lauren Gambino, Sabrina Siddiqui, and Shaun Walker, "Obama Expels 35 Russian Diplomats in Retaliation for US Election Hacking," *Guardian*, December 30, 2016, https://www.theguardian.com/us-news/2016/dec/29/barack -obama-sanctions-russia-election-hack.

65   **"give him the info":** Donald J. Trump (@realDonaldTrump), "Julian Assange said 'a 14 year old could have hacked Podesta'—why was DNC so careless? Also said Russians did not give him the info!," Twitter, January 4, 2017, 4:22 am, https://twitter.com /realdonaldtrump/status/816620855958601730.

65   **"political witch hunt":** Michael D. Shear and David E. Sanger, "Putin Led a Complex Cyberattack Scheme to Aid Trump, Report Finds," *New York Times*, January 6, 2017, https://www.nytimes.com/2017/01/06/us/politics/donald-trump-wall-hack-russia .html.

66   **secret hacking campaign:** Mark Hensch, "US Caught Russian Officials Cheering Trump Win: Report," *The Hill*, January 5, 2017, https://thehill.com/policy/international /russia/312961-us-caught-russian-officials-cheering-trump-win-report.

66   **"90 days of taking office":** Jacob Pramuk, "Trump Won't Say Whether Russia Hacked Democrats but Says Election Outcome Wasn't Affected," CNBC, January 6, 2017, https://www.cnbc.com/2017/01/06/trump-wont-say-whether-russia-hacked-democrats -but-says-election-outcome-wasnt-affected.html.

66   **information about Trump:** Evan Perez, Jim Sciutto, Jake Tapper, and Carl Bernstein, "Intel Chiefs Presented Trump with Claims of Russian Efforts to Compromise Him," CNN, January 12, 2017, https://www.cnn.com/2017/01/10/politics/donald-trump -intelligence-report-russia/index.html.

67   **Miller had rebelled:** Lisa Mascaro, "How a Liberal Santa Monica High School Produced a Top Trump Adviser and Speechwriter," *Los Angeles Times*, January 17, 2017, https://www.latimes.com/politics/la-na-pol-trump-speechwriter-santamonica-20170117 -story.html.

67   **Bannon was producing conservative:** Joshua Green, *Devil's Bargain: Steve Bannon, Donald Trump, and the Storming of the Presidency* (New York: Penguin Press, 2017), 65.

68   **"I pick you, general":** Steve Benen, "Why Trump Is So Preoccupied with 'Central Casting,'" *TheMaddowBlog*, MSNBC, February 28, 2017, http://www.msnbc.com/rachel -maddow-show/why-trump-so-preoccupied-central-casting.

69   **"CIA's Memorial Wall":** Ryan Browne, "Ex-CIA Chief Brennan Bashes Trump over Speech during CIA Visit," CNN, January 22, 2017, https://www.cnn.com/2017/01/21 /politics/trump-to-cia-i-am-so-behind-you/index.html.

69   **Andrew Jackson in his office:** Susan B. Glasser, "The Man Who Put Andrew Jackson in Trump's Oval Office," *Politico*, January 22, 2018, http://politi.co/2mZOuHp.

70   **seat on the NSC:** Mallory Shelbourne, "Ex-Defense Secretary: Trump's Changes to Security Council a 'Big Mistake,'" *The Hill*, January 29, 2017, https://thehill.com /business-a-lobbying/316775-gates-big-mistake-to-remove-dni-and-chairman-of -joint-chiefs-from-nsc.

72   **Special Initiatives Group:** Julie Smith and Derek Chollet, "Bannon's 'Strategic Initia- tives' Cabal Inside the NSC Is Dangerous Hypocrisy," *Foreign Policy*, February 1, 2017, https://foreignpolicy.com/2017/02/01/bannons-strategic-initiatives-cabal-inside-the -nsc-is-dangerous-hypocrisy/.

72   **"real import to the president":** Sebastian Gorka, interview by Jake Tapper, *The Lead with Jake Tapper*, CNN, February 1, 2017, http://edition.cnn.com/TRANSCRIPTS /1702/01/cg.02.html.

72   **"new sheriff in town":** Greg Jaffe, "For a Trump Adviser, an Odyssey from the Fringes of Washington to the Center of Power," *Washington Post*, February 20, 2017, https://www .washingtonpost.com/world/national-security/for-a-trump-adviser-an-odyssey-from -the-fringes-of-washington-to-the-center-of-power/2017/02/20/0a326260-f2cb-11e6 -b9c9-e83fce42fb61_story.html?noredirect=on.

72   **"the alpha males are back":** "Gorka: The Alpha Males Are Back on January 20th," Fox News, December 16, 2016, https://www.youtube.com/watch?v=mUMQ7hWpX6g.

72   **captain in Afghanistan:** Mark Landler and Jane Perlez, "A Veteran and China Hand Advises Trump for Xi's Visit," *New York Times*, April 4, 2017, https://www.nytimes.com /2017/04/04/world/asia/matthew-pottinger-trump-china.html.

73   **publication in 2010:** Matt Pottinger, Michael T. Flynn, and Paul D. Batchelor, "Fixing Intel: A Blueprint for Making Intelligence Relevant in Afghanistan" Center for a New American Security, January 4, 2010, https://www.cnas.org/publications/reports/fixing -intel-a-blueprint-for-making-intelligence-relevant.

73   **punched him in the face:** Matt Pottinger, "Mightier Than the Pen," *Wall Street Journal*, December 15, 2005, https://www.wsj.com/articles/SB113461636659623128.

75   **botched rescue attempt:** Barbara Starr, Jim Sciutto, and Ray Sanchez, "U.S.: Al Qaeda Kills Hostages during SEALS Raid in Yemen," CNN, December 7, 2014, https://www .cnn.com/2014/12/06/world/meast/yemen-u-s-hostage-killed/index.html.

76   **six women were also killed:** Iona Craig, "Death in Al Ghayil: Women and Children in Yemeni Village Recall Horror of Trump's 'Highly Successful' SEAL Raid," *The Inter- cept*, March 9, 2017, https://theintercept.com/2017/03/09/women-and-children-in-yemeni -village-recall-horror-of-trumps-highly-successful-seal-raid/.

77   **"successful operation by all standards":** "Press Briefing by Press Secretary Sean Spicer," White House, February 2, 2017, https://www.whitehouse.gov/briefings-statements/press -briefing-press-secretary-sean-spicer-020217/.

77   **video was about a decade old:** Nicole Gaouette and Ryan Browne, "Military Botches Release of Video Seized in Yemen Raid," CNN, February 3, 2017, https://www.cnn.com /2017/02/03/politics/yemen-raid-videos/index.html.

77   **refused to meet the president:** Martin Pengelly, "Father of Navy Seal Killed in Yemen Calls for Investigation into 'Stupid Mission,'" *Guardian*, February 26, 2017, https://www.theguardian.com/us-news/2017/feb/26/father-navy-seal-yemen-trump-investigation-stupid-mission.

78   **"And they lost Ryan":** Phillip Carter, "Trump Just Blamed the Military for the Botched Yemen Raid. That's a Disgrace." *Vox*, February 28, 2017, https://www.vox.com/policy-and-politics/2017/2/28/14766918/trump-blame-military-yemen-seal-botched-raid-pentagon-fox.

78   **"more victories in the future":** Maggie Penman, "In Emotional Moment of Speech, Trump Addresses Navy SEAL's Widow," NPR, February 28, 2017, https://www.npr.org/sections/thetwo-way/2017/02/28/517849426/in-emotional-moment-of-speech-trump-addresses-navy-seals-widow.

78   **"in that moment, period":** Jason Kurtz, "Van Jones on Trump: 'He Became President of the United States in That Moment, Period,'" CNN, March 1, 2017, https://www.cnn.com/2017/03/01/politics/van-jones-trump-congress-speech-became-the-president-in-that-moment-cnntv/index.html.

CHAPTER 4: ENTER McMASTER

79   *"Above all President Johnson":* H. R. McMaster, *Dereliction of Duty: Lyndon Johnson, Robert McNamara, the Joint Chiefs of Staff, and the Lies That Led to Vietnam* (New York: Harper Perennial, 1998), 61.

81   **twenty-four days on the job:** Greg Miller and Philip Rucker, "Michael Flynn Resigns as National Security Adviser," *Washington Post*, February 14, 2017, https://www.washingtonpost.com/world/national-security/michael-flynn-resigns-as-national-security-adviser/2017/02/13/0007c0a8-f26e-11e6-8d72-263470bf0401_story.html.

81   **Mattis's top deputy:** Julie Hirschfeld Davis, "Ex-Admiral and Member of Navy SEALs Is Top Choice to Replace Flynn," *New York Times*, February 14, 2017, https://www.nytimes.com/2017/02/14/us/politics/robert-harward-national-security-adviser.html.

82   **Broadwell suddenly popped up:** Eli Watkins, "Paula Broadwell: Petraeus Has Paid His Price, Slams 'Double Standard,'" CNN, February 15, 2014, https://www.cnn.com/2017/02/14/politics/paula-broadwell-david-petraeus/index.html.

82   **Trump appointed retired lieutenant general:** "Vice President Mike Pence Announces Lieutenant General (Ret) Keith Kellogg as National Security Adviser," White House, April 23, 2018, https://www.whitehouse.gov/briefings-statements/vice-president-mike-pence-announces-lieutenant-general-ret-keith-kellogg-national-security-adviser/.

84   **proclivity to call for:** John R. Bolton, "To Stop Iran's Bomb, Bomb Iran," *New York Times*, March 26, 2015, https://www.nytimes.com/2015/03/26/opinion/to-stop-irans-bomb-bomb-iran.html; John Bolton, "The Legal Case for Striking North Korea First," *Wall Street Journal*, February 28, 2018, https://www.wsj.com/articles/the-legal-case-for-striking-north-korea-first-1519862374.

85   **Battle of 73 Easting:** H. R. McMaster, "Eagle Troop at the Battle of 73 Easting," *The Strategy Bridge*, February 26, 2016, https://thestrategybridge.org/the-bridge/2016/2/26/eagle-troop-at-the-battle-of-73-easting.

86   **"lived in abject fear":** Interview with Tresha Mabile, producer, *American War Generals* (National Geographic, 2014).

86   **Rice in congressional testimony said:** *Iraq in U.S. Foreign Policy: Hearing before the Committee on Foreign Relations, United States Senate,* 109th Cong. (2005) (statement of Secretary of State Condoleezza Rice), https://www.govinfo.gov/content/pkg/CHRG -109shrg27403/html/CHRG-109shrg27403.htm.

86   **his 1997 book:** McMaster, *Dereliction of Duty.*

88   **instant bestseller:** Sarah Begley, "Lt. Gen. H. R. McMaster's Book Dereliction of Duty Rockets to Top of Best Seller List," *Time,* February 22, 2017, https://time.com/4678741 /hr-mcmaster-national-security-adviser-book-dereliction-duty-best-seller/.

88   **Another NSC official McMaster sidelined:** Adam Entous, "The Agonizingly Slow Downfall of K. T. McFarland," *New Yorker,* January 29, 2018, https://www.newyorker .com/news/news-desk/the-agonizingly-slow-downfall-of-k-t-mcfarland.

88   **withdrew her nomination:** Shane Harris, "K. T. McFarland Withdraws Nomination to Be Trump's Ambassador to Singapore," *Washington Post,* February 2, 2018, https:// www.washingtonpost.com/world/national-security/kt-mcfalrand-withdraws-nomi nation-to-be-trumps-ambassador-to-singapore/2018/02/02/8da67a02-0862-11e8-ae28 -e370b74ea9a7_story.html.

89   **only national security adviser:** Stephen J. Hadley, "The Role and Importance of the National Security Advisor," Bush School of Government & Public Service, 2017, https://bush.tamu.edu/scowcroft/papers/hadley/.

89   **"Geographical Pivot of History":** H. J. Mackinder, "The Geographical Pivot of History," *Geographical Journal* 23, no. 4 (April 1904): 421, https://doi.org/10.2307 /1775498.

90   **Trump gave his speech:** Nahal Toosi, "Breaking with Bush and Obama, Trump Talks About 'Radical Islamic Terrorism,'" *Politico,* February 28, 2017, https://www.politico .com/story/2017/02/donald-trump-congress-speech-radical-islamic-terrorism-235531.

90   **Gorka tweeted triumphantly:** Sebastian Gorka (@SebGorka), "After 8 years of obfuscation and disastrous Counterterrorism policies those 3 words are key to Victory against Global Jihadism.," Twitter, March 1, 2017, 3:58 am, https://twitter.com/sebgorka/status /836908458045759488?lang=en.

90   **Egyptian-born Dina Powell:** Michael R. Gordon, "Dina Powell, Donald Trump Aide, Named to National Security Post," *New York Times,* March 15, 2017, https://www .nytimes.com/2017/03/15/us/politics/dina-powell-donald-trump-aide-named-to -national-security-post.html.

90   *War and the Art of Governance*: Nadia Schadlow, *War and the Art of Governance: Consolidating Combat Success into Political Victory* (Washington, DC: Georgetown University Press, 2017).

CHAPTER 5: THE TRAVEL BAN

93   **"For every complex problem":** "H. L. Mencken Quotes," BrainyQuote, n.d., https:// www.brainyquote.com/quotes/h_l_mencken_129796.

93 **"It's not a Muslim ban"**: "Trump Says New Order on Refugees Is Not a Muslim Ban," *Reuters*, January 28, 2017, https://www.reuters.com/article/us-usa-trump-immigration-ban-idUSKBN15C0UY.

95 **"love, deeply, our people"**: Michael D. Shear and Helene Cooper, "Trump Bars Refugees and Citizens of 7 Muslim Countries," *New York Times*, January 27, 2017, https://www.nytimes.com/2017/01/27/us/politics/trump-syrian-refugees.html.

96 **Abdul Razak Ali Artan**: Pete Williams et al., "Suspect Identified in Ohio State Attack as Abdul Razak Ali Artan," NBC News, November 28, 2016, https://www.nbcnews.com/news/us-news/suspect-dead-after-ohio-state-university-car-knife-attack-n689076.

96 **"yet one more tragic reminder"**: Julie Hirschfeld Davis, "Donald Trump Calls Ohio State Attack a 'Tragic Reminder' on Immigration," *New York Times*, December 8, 2016, https://www.nytimes.com/2016/12/08/us/politics/donald-trump-ohio-state-attack-refugee.html.

96 **"You know my plans"**: Mark Landler, "Trump Suggests Berlin Attack Affirms His Plan to Bar Muslims," *New York Times*, December 21, 2016, https://www.nytimes.com/2016/12/21/us/politics/donald-trump-syria-policy.html.

96 **fifteen thousand Syrian refugees**: Deborah Amos, "The U.S. Has Accepted Only 11 Syrian Refugees This Year," NPR, April 12, 2018, https://www.npr.org/sections/parallels/2018/04/12/602022877/the-u-s-has-welcomed-only-11-syrian-refugees-this-year.

96 **nearly five million people**: Danielle Paquette, "Trump's Travel Ban on 'Bad Dudes' Actually Keeps out Women and Children," *Washington Post*, January 30, 2017, https://www.washingtonpost.com/news/wonk/wp/2017/01/30/president-trump-wanted-to-ban-bad-dudes-he-could-block-more-women-and-children/.

96 **Any ISIS terrorist**: Peter Bergen, "Syrian Refugees Are Not a Threat to U.S.," CNN, November 21, 2015, https://www.cnn.com/2015/11/21/opinions/bergen-syrian-refugees-not-a-threat-to-us/index.html.

97 **"refugees get the most scrutiny"**: Peter Bergen, "Syrian Refugees Are Not a Threat to U.S.," CNN.com, November 21, 2015, https://www.cnn.com/2015/11/21/opinions/bergen-syrian-refugees-not-a-threat-to-us/index.html.

97 **None of the terrorists**: Peter Bergen and David Sterman, "Trump's Travel Ban Wouldn't Have Stopped These Deadly Terrorists," CNN, January 30, 2017, https://www.cnn.com/2017/01/30/opinions/travel-ban-wouldnt-have-stopped-these-deadly-terrorists-bergen-sterman/index.html.

98 **Steve Bannon and Stephen Miller**: Ashley Parker, Philip Rucker, and Robert Costa, "From Order to Disorder: How Trump's Immigration Directive Exposed GOP Rifts," *Washington Post*, January 30, 2017, https://www.washingtonpost.com/politics/from-order-to-disorder-how-trumps-immigration-directive-exposed-gop-rifts/2017/01/30/b4e42044-e70f-11e6-b82f-687d6e6a3e7c_story.html; Shane Harris, "Conservative Pundit Sebastian Gorka Brings 'Global Jihadist Movement' Theory into White House," *Wall Street Journal*, February 21, 2017, https://www.wsj.com/articles/conservative-pundit-sebastian-gorka-brings-global-jihadist-movement-theory-into-white-house-1487650120.

98 **The executive order completely blindsided:** "Executive Order Protecting the Nation from Foreign Terrorist Entry into the United States," White House, January 27, 2017, https://www.whitehouse.gov/presidential-actions/executive-order-protecting-nation -foreign-terrorist-entry-united-states/.

98 **no time to review:** "DHS Implementation of Executive Order #13769 'Protecting the Nation from Foreign Terrorist Entry into the United States' (January 27, 2017)," DHS Office of the Inspector General, January 18, 2018, https://www.oig.dhs.gov/sites/default /files/assets/2018-01/OIG-18-37-Jan18.pdf.

99 **"The president is signing":** Michael D. Shear and Ron Nixon, "How Trump's Rush to Enact an Immigration Ban Unleashed Global Chaos," *New York Times*, January 29, 2017, https://www.nytimes.com/2017/01/29/us/politics/donald-trump-rush-immigration -order-chaos.html.

99 **whether green card holders:** "DHS Implementation of Executive Order #13769."

99 **planes were already:** Joanna Walters, Edward Helmore, and Saeed Kamali Deghan, "US Airports on Frontline as Donald Trump's Travel Ban Causes Chaos and Protests," *Guardian*, January 28, 2017, https://www.theguardian.com/us-news/2017/jan/28/air ports-us-immigration-ban-muslim-countries-trump.

99 **"you see it all over":** "Trump Says New Order on Refugees Is Not a Muslim Ban."

99 **"dissent channel" cable:** Felicia Schwartz, "State Department Dissent, Believed Largest Ever, Formally Lodged," *Wall Street Journal*, February 1, 2017, https://www.wsj.com /articles/state-department-dissent-believed-largest-ever-formally-lodged-1485908373.

100 **not to defend the ban:** Ryan Lizza, "Why Sally Yates Stood Up to Trump," *New Yorker*, May 29, 2017, https://www.newyorker.com/magazine/2017/05/29/why-sally-yates-stood -up-to-trump.

100 **Trump immediately fired:** Michael D. Shear et al., "Trump Fires Acting Attorney General Who Defied Him," *New York Times*, January 30, 2017, https://www.nytimes .com/2017/01/30/us/politics/trump-immigration-ban-memo.html; Matt Zapotosky, Lori Aratani, and Justin Jouvenal, "Federal Judge Temporarily Blocks Trump's Entry Order Nationwide," *Washington Post*, February 4, 2017, https://www.washingtonpost .com/world/national-security/federal-judge-temporarily-blocks-trumps-immigration -order-nationwide/2017/02/03/9b734e1c-ea54-11e6-bf6f-301b6b443624_story.html.

100 **"will be overturned":** Donald J. Trump (@realDonaldTrump), "The opinion of this so-called judge, which essentially takes law-enforcement away from our country, is ri- diculous and will be overturned!," Twitter, February 4, 2017, 5:12 am, https://twitter .com/realDonaldTrump/status/827867311054974976.

100 **"A terrible decision":** Donald J. Trump (@realDonaldTrump), "Because the ban was lifted by a judge, many very bad and dangerous people may be pouring into our country. A terrible decision," Twitter, February 4, 2017, 1:44 pm, https://twitter.com/realdonald trump/status/827996357252243456.

100 **"touched American soil":** Cliff Sims, *Team of Vipers: My 500 Extraordinary Days in the Trump White House* (New York: Thomas Dunne Books, 2019), 191.

100 **review of the issue:** Julie Hirschfeld Davis and Somini Sengupta, "Trump Administra- tion Rejects Study Showing Positive Impact of Refugees," *New York Times*, September

18, 2017, https://www.nytimes.com/2017/09/18/us/politics/refugees-revenue-cost-report -trump.html.

101 **Homeland Security internal report:** Matt Zapotosky, "DHS Report Casts Doubt on Need for Trump Travel Ban," *Washington Post*, February 24, 2017, https://www .washingtonpost.com/world/national-security/dhs-report-casts-doubt-on-need-for -trump-travel-ban/2017/02/24/2a9992e4-fadc-11e6-9845-576c69081518_story.html; Vivian Salama, "AP Exclusive: DHS Report Disputes Threat from Banned Nations," Associated Press, February 24, 2017, https://www.apnews.com/39f1f8e4ceed4a30a4570 f693291c866.

101 **"Bowling Green massacre":** Samantha Schmidt and Lindsey Beyer, "Kellyanne Conway Cites 'Bowling Green Massacre' That Never Happened to Defend Travel Ban," *Washington Post*, February 3, 2017, https://www.washingtonpost.com/news/morning -mix/wp/2017/02/03/kellyanne-conway-cites-bowling-green-massacre-that-never -happened-to-defend-travel-ban/.

102 **To "prove" that the media:** Peter Bergen, "Trump's Terrorism Claim Is Baloney," CNN, February 7, 2017, https://www.cnn.com/2017/02/07/opinions/trump-claim-on -under-covering-terrorism-is-baloney-bergen/index.html.

105 **"vast majority of individuals":** "Remarks by President Trump in Joint Address to Congress," White House, February 28, 2017, https://www.whitehouse.gov/briefings -statements/remarks-president-trump-joint-address-congress/.

106 **On March 6:** "Executive Order Protecting the Nation from Foreign Terrorist Entry into the United States," White House, March 6, 2017, https://trumpwhitehouse.archives.gov /presidential-actions/executive-order-protecting-nation-foreign-terrorist-entry-united -states-2.

106 **Hawaii filed a motion:** Oliver Laughland, "Hawaii Becomes First State to Sue over Trump's Revised Travel Ban," *Guardian*, March 9, 2017, https://www.theguardian.com /us-news/2017/mar/08/revised-travel-ban-hawaii-legal-challenge-trump.

106 **"extra level of safety":** Donald J. Trump (@realDonaldTrump), "We need to be smart, vigilant and tough. We need the courts to give us back our rights. We need the Travel Ban as an extra level of safety!," Twitter, June 3, 2017, 4:17 pm, https://twitter.com/realdonald trump/status/871143765473406976.

106 **Trump issued a third version:** "Presidential Proclamation Enhancing Vetting Capabilities and Processes for Detecting Attempted Entry into the United States by Terrorists or Other Public-Safety Threats," White House, September 24, 2017, https://www .whitehouse.gov/presidential-actions/presidential-proclamation-enhancing-vetting -capabilities-processes-detecting-attempted-entry-united-states-terrorists-public-safety -threats/.

106 **version would not have prevented:** David Sterman and Peter Bergen, "Trump's New Travel Ban Still Doesn't Fly," CNN, September 25, 2017, https://www.cnn.com/2017 /09/25/opinions/trump-travel-ban-still-doesnt-fly-opinion-bergen-sterman/index.html.

106 **Sayfullo Saipov plowed:** Holly Yan and Dakin Andone, "Who Is New York Terror Suspect Sayfullo Saipov?," CNN, November 2, 2017, https://www.cnn.com/2017/11/01 /us/sayfullo-saipov-new-york-attack/index.html.

107 **"Would love to"**: Donald J. Trump (@realDonaldTrump), "Would love to send the NYC terrorist to Guantanamo but statistically that process takes much longer than going through the Federal system . . . ," Twitter, November 2, 2017, 4:50 am, https://twitter .com/realdonaldtrump/status/926053970535243777.

107 **had yet to begin**: Joanna Walters, "Will Accused 9/11 Architect Khalid Sheikh Mohammed Ever Come to Trial?," *Guardian*, September 11, 2017, https://www.theguardian .com/us-news/2017/sep/11/will-khalid-sheikh-mohammed-come-to-trial-9-11-attacks.

107 **Mary Anne MacLeod**: Mary Pilon, "Donald Trump's Immigrant Mother," *New Yorker*, June 24, 2016, https://www.newyorker.com/news/news-desk/donald-trumps-immigrant -mother.

CHAPTER 6: ASSAD AND ISIS

109 **"Fear, honor, and interest"**: "An Introduction to the Work of Thucydides," The Great Thinkers, accessed August 2, 2019, https://thegreatthinkers.org/thucydides /introduction/.

109 **"I know more"**: John T. Bennett, "On Afghanistan, Trump Bets on Generals He Once Criticized," *Roll Call*, August 21, 2017, https://www.rollcall.com/news/politics/trump -will-keep-thousands-u-s-troops-afghanistan.

111 **Assad's air force**: Rick Gladstone, "U.N. Panel Points Finger at Syria in Sarin Attack on Village," *New York Times*, October 26, 2017, https://www.nytimes.com/2017/10/26 /world/middleeast/syria-chemical-khan-shekhoun.html.

111 **"I'm having to enforce"**: Cliff Sims, *Team of Vipers: My 500 Extraordinary Days in the Trump White House* (New York: Thomas Dunne Books, 2019), 189.

113 **Trump selected the strike option**: "Statement by Secretary of Defense Jim Mattis on the U.S. Military Response to the Syrian Government's Use of Chemical Weapons," US Department of Defense, April 10, 2017, https://www.defense.gov/Newsroom/Releases /Release/Article/1146758/statement-by-secretary-of-defense-jim-mattis-on-the-us -military-response-to-the/source/GovDelivery/.

114 **one of his best speeches**: "Transcript and Video: Trump Speaks about Strikes in Syria," *New York Times*, April 6, 2017, https://www.nytimes.com/2017/04/06/world/middleeast /transcript-video-trump-airstrikes-syria.html.

115 **gave him a rousing endorsement**: Jessica Chasmar, "CNN's Fareed Zakaria: 'Donald Trump Became President' Last Night," *Washington Times*, April 7, 2017, https://www .washingtontimes.com/news/2017/apr/7/fareed-zakaria-donald-trump-became-presi dent-last-/.

115 **Assad emptied his prisons**: Maria Abi-Habib, "Assad Policies Aided Rise of Islamic State Militant Group," *Wall Street Journal*, August 22, 2014, https://www.wsj.com /articles/assad-policies-aided-rise-of-islamic-state-militant-group-1408739733.

115 **within thirty days**: Candace Smith, "Donald Trump Wants Plan within 30 Days to Defeat ISIS If Elected," ABC News, September 7, 2016, https://abcnews.go.com /Politics/donald-trump-plan-defeat-isis-30-days-elected/story?id=41905399.

116 **General Joseph Votel:** Peter Bergen, "A Conversation with the General Running the War against ISIS," CNN, October 30, 2016, https://www.cnn.com/2016/10/30/world /man-whos-running-war-vs-isis-bergen/index.html.

116 **There was a debate:** Helene Cooper, Mark Landler, and Alissa J. Rubin, "Obama Allows Limited Airstrikes on ISIS," *New York Times*, August 7, 2014, https://www .nytimes.com/2014/08/08/world/middleeast/obama-weighs-military-strikes-to-aid -trapped-iraqis-officials-say.html.

117 **Abdul-Wahab al Saadi:** Peter Bergen, "Bergen: It Wasn't Trump but This General's Elite Soldiers Who Defeated ISIS," CNN, December 16, 2017, https://www.cnn.com /2017/12/15/opinions/it-wasnt-trump-but-this-generals-elite-soldiers-who-defeated -isis-bergen/index.html.

118 **"The importance of Raqqa":** Bergen, "A Conversation with the General Running the War against ISIS."

120 **Trump visited CENTCOM:** Jim Garamone, "Trump: America Will Stand with Those Who Stand for Freedom," *DOD News*, February 6, 2017, https://www.centcom.mil /MEDIA/NEWS-ARTICLES/News-Article-View/Article/1073221/trump-america -will-stand-with-those-who-stand-for-freedom/.

120 **pointed to the Strait of Hormuz:** "Strait of Hormuz: The World's Most Important Oil Artery," Reuters, July 5, 2018, https://www.reuters.com/article/us-iran-oil-factbox-id USKBN1JV24O.

121 **Obama directed that the plans:** Adam Entous, Greg Jaffe, and Missy Ryan, "Obama's White House Worked for Months on a Plan to Seize Raqqa. Trump's Team Took a Brief Look and Decided Not to Pull the Trigger.," *Washington Post*, February 2, 2017, https:// www.washingtonpost.com/world/national-security/obamas-white-house-worked-for -months-on-a-plan-to-seize-raqqa-trumps-team-deemed-it-hopelessly-inadequate/2017 /02/02/116310fa-e71a-11e6-80c2-30e57e57e05d_story.html.

121 **Bush had done something similar:** Peter L. Bergen, *The Longest War: The Enduring Conflict between America and Al-Qaeda* (New York: Free Press, 2011), 194–95.

122 **Trump approved a plan:** Dion Nissenbaum, Gordon Lubold, and Julian E. Barnes, "Trump Set to Arm Kurds in ISIS Fight, Angering Turkey," *Wall Street Journal*, May 9, 2017, https://www.wsj.com/articles/trump-approves-direct-arming-of-kurds-in-fight -against-isis-1494353541.

122 **two thousand troops:** John Ismay, "U.S. Says 2,000 Troops Are in Syria, a Fourfold Increase," *New York Times*, December 6, 2017, https://www.nytimes.com/2017/12/06 /world/middleeast/us-troops-syria.html.

122 **larger than a cell phone:** Ron Nixon, Adam Goldman, and Eric Schmitt, "Devices Banned on Flights from 10 Countries over ISIS Fears," *New York Times*, March 21, 2017, https://www.nytimes.com/2017/03/21/us/politics/tsa-ban-electronics-laptops-cabin .html.

122 **Raqqa was liberated:** "Syrian Democratic Forces Liberate Raqqa," US Department of Defense, October 20, 2017, https://dod.defense.gov/News/Article/Article/1349213 /syrian-democratic-forces-liberate-raqqa/.

122 **Trump took a victory lap:** Zachary Cohen and Dan Merica, "Trump Takes Credit for ISIS 'Giving Up,'" CNN, October 17, 2017, https://www.cnn.com/2017/10/17/politics /trump-isis-raqqa/index.html.

123 **forty-five thousand ISIS fighters:** "Department of Defense Press Briefing by Lieutenant General Sean MacFarland, Commander, Combined Joint Task Force-Operation Inherent Resolve via Teleconference from Baghdad, Iraq," US Department of Defense, August 10, 2016, https://dod.defense.gov/News/Transcripts/Transcript-View/Article /911009/department-of-defense-press-briefing-by-lieutenant-general-sean-macfarland -comm/.

123 **seventy thousand ISIS fighters:** Robin Wright, "ISIS Jihadis Have Returned Home by the Thousands," *New Yorker*, October 23, 2017, https://www.newyorker.com/news /news-desk/isis-jihadis-have-returned-home-by-the-thousands.

123 **began in October 2016:** "How the Battle for Mosul Unfolded," BBC News, July 10, 2017, https://www.bbc.com/news/world-middle-east-37702442.

123 **"There was no difference":** Bergen, "It Wasn't Trump but This General's Elite Soldiers Who Defeated ISIS."

124 **eleven thousand soldiers:** "Statement to Public Opinion," SDF Press, March 23, 2019, https://sdf-press.com/en/2019/03/statement-to-public-opinion-14/.

124 **seventeen American servicemen:** "Casualty Status as of 10 a.m. EDT Aug. 13, 2019," US Department of Defense, August 13, 2019, https://www.defense.gov/Newsroom /Casualty-Status/.

124 **number close to zero:** "Terrorism Situation and Trend Report 2019," Europol, n.d., https://www.europol.europa.eu/activities-services/main-reports/terrorism-situation -and-trend-report-2019-te-sat.

124 **"ISIS still commands":** Daniel R. Coats, "Statement for the Record: Worldwide Threat Assessment of the US Intelligence Community," Senate Select Committee on Intelligence, January 29, 2019, https://www.dni.gov/files/ODNI/documents/2019-ATA -SFR---SSCI.pdf.

CHAPTER 7: THE LONGEST WAR

125 **"Let's get out":** Donald J. Trump (@realDonaldTrump), "Let's get out of Afghanistan. Our troops are being killed by the Afghanis we train and we waste billions there. Nonsense! Rebuild the USA," Twitter, January 11, 2013, 1:55 pm, https://twitter.com/real donaldtrump/status/289807790178959360.

125 **"The first, the supreme":** Carl von Clausewitz, Michael Eliot Howard, and Peter Paret, *On War* (Princeton: Princeton University Press, 2008), 88.

127 **"six trillion dollars":** Allison Kaplan Sommer, "What Did Clinton and Trump Say about the Middle East in the First Presidential Debate?," *Haaretz*, September 27, 2016, https://www.haaretz.com/world-news/.premium-what-did-clinton-trump-say-about -middle-east-in-first-debate-1.5443170.

127 **rich in copper, gold:** James Risen, "U.S. Identifies Vast Mineral Riches in Afghanistan," *New York Times*, June 13, 2010, https://www.nytimes.com/2010/06/14/world

/asia/14minerals.html?mtrref=undefined&gwh=19CB4075E09A9C8409869182058
EE6FF&gwt=pay&assetType=PAYWALL.

128 **China had made an expensive:** Laura Zhou, "Is There Still Hope for China, Afghanistan's Long-Stalled US$3 Billion Copper Mining Deal?," *South China Morning Post*, May 12, 2017, https://www.scmp.com/news/china/diplomacy-defence/article/2093852 /talks-aim-jump-start-china-miners-stalled-afghanistan.

128 **Mattis had advocated:** Jim Mattis and Bing West, *Call Sign Chaos: Learning to Lead* (New York: Random House, 2019), 206.

129 **Obama had seriously considered:** Author interviews with Obama administration officials.

130 **testified before the Senate:** Michael R. Gordon, "U.S. General Seeks 'a Few Thousand' More Troops in Afghanistan," *New York Times*, February 9, 2017, https://www.nytimes .com/2017/02/09/us/politics/us-afghanistan-troops.html.

130 **comments irritated White House officials:** Carol E. Lee and Courtney Kube, "Trump Says U.S. 'Losing' Afghan War in Tense Meeting with Generals," NBC News, August 2, 2017, https://www.nbcnews.com/news/us-news/trump-says-u-s-losing-afghan-war -tense-meeting-generals-n789006.

131 **"We're going to crush this":** Joshua Partlow, *A Kingdom of Their Own: The Family Karzai and the Afghan Disaster* (New York: Knopf, 2016), 157.

131 **speech at West Point:** "Remarks by the President in Address to the Nation on the Way Forward in Afghanistan and Pakistan," White House, December 1, 2009, https:// obamawhitehouse.archives.gov/the-press-office/remarks-president-address-nation -way-forward-afghanistan-and-pakistan.

131 **Massive Ordnance Air Blast bomb:** Helene Cooper and Mujib Mashal, "U.S. Drops 'Mother of All Bombs' on ISIS Caves in Afghanistan," *New York Times*, April 13, 2017, https:// www.nytimes.com/2017/04/13/world/asia/moab-mother-of-all-bombs-afghanistan.html.

132 **deployment of the MOAB:** Peter Bergen, "Why the 'Mother of All Bombs' and Why Now?," CNN, April 14, 2017, https://www.cnn.com/2017/04/13/opinions/why-mother -of-all-bombs-and-why-now-bergen/index.html.

133 **McMaster left for Kabul:** "Top U.S. Security Official Visits Kabul After Massive Bomb," *Radio Free Europe/Radio Liberty*, April 16, 2017, https://www.rferl.org/a/afghanistan -us-mcmaster-visit/28433445.html.

134 **rough rule of thumb:** Steven M. Goode, "A Historical Basis for Force Requirements in Counterinsurgency," US Army, March 26, 2010, https://www.army.mil/article/36324 /a_historical_basis_for_force_requirements_in_counterinsurgency.

138 **McMaster seemed to publicly contradict:** "McMaster Says US Will Pay for THAAD Anti-Missile System in South Korea," Fox News, April 30, 2017, https://www.foxnews .com/politics/mcmaster-says-us-will-pay-for-thaad-anti-missile-system-in-south-korea.

138 **shared highly classified information:** Adam Goldman, Eric Schmitt, and Peter Baker, "Israel Said to Be Source of Secret Intelligence Trump Gave to Russians," *New York Times*, May 16, 2017, https://www.nytimes.com/2017/05/16/world/middleeast/israel -trump-classified-intelligence-russia.html.

139 **A massive truck bomb:** Josh Smith, "Kabul Truck-Bomb Toll Rises to More Than 150 Killed: Afghan President," Reuters, June 6, 2017, https://www.reuters.com/article/us -afghanistan-blast-idUSKBN18X0FU.

139 **Trump delegated the decision:** Nicole Gaouette, "Trump Delegates Troop Decisions, to Praise and Concern," CNN, June 16, 2017, https://www.cnn.com/2017/06/16 /politics/trump-military-troops-afghanistan-mattis/index.html.

141 **Prince proposed a plan:** Erik Prince, "The MacArthur Model for Afghanistan," *Wall Street Journal*, May 31, 2017, https://www.wsj.com/articles/the-macarthur-model-for -afghanistan-1496269058.

142 **a story in *USA Today*:** Erik Prince, "Erik Prince: 'Restructure' the Afghanistan War," *USA Today*, August 7, 2017, https://www.usatoday.com/story/opinion/2017/08/07/erik -prince-restructure-afghanistan-war-editorials-debates/104389448/.

142 **Prince went on CNN:** Sophie Tatum, "Blackwater Founder Questions US Afghanistan Strategy," CNN, August 7, 2017, https://www.cnn.com/2017/08/07/politics/erik-prince -afghanistan-cnntv/index.html; "Blackwater Founder Backs Outsourcing Afghan War -Fighting to Contractors," NPR, July 24, 2017, https://www.npr.org/2017/07/24/5389 70956/blackwater-founder-backs-outsourcing-afghan-war-fighting-to-contractors.

142 **Gorka also appeared:** Jamie McIntyre, "Jim Mattis: New Afghanistan Strategy Isn't Finished Yet," *Washington Examiner*, July 14, 2017, https://www.washingtonexaminer .com/jim-mattis-new-afghanistan-strategy-isnt-finished-yet.

142 **embraced the Prince plan:** Rosie Gray, "Erik Prince's Plan to Privatize the War in Afghanistan," *The Atlantic*, August 18, 2017, https://www.theatlantic.com/politics/archive /2017/08/afghanistan-camp-david/537324/.

146 **Pompeo made a surprise visit:** David Brunnstrom, "Pompeo, in Surprise Visit to Afghanistan, Urges Taliban Peace Talks," Reuters, July 9, 2018, https://www.reuters.com /article/us-afghanistan-usa-pompeo/pompeo-in-surprise-visit-to-afghanistan-urges -taliban-peace-talks-idUSKBN1JZ1N9.

147 **Trump told reporters:** "Remarks by President Trump at Luncheon with Servicemembers," White House, July 18, 2017, https://www.whitehouse.gov/briefings-statements /remarks-president-trump-luncheon-servicemembers/.

148 **Dunford had been:** "Visitor Access Records," The White House President Barack Obama, accessed August 15, 2019, https://obamawhitehouse.archives.gov/briefing-room /disclosures/visitor-records.

148 **During the Trump administration:** Andrew Restuccia et al., "All the President's Guests The UNAUTHORIZED White House Visitor Logs," *Politico*, accessed August 15, 2019, https://www.politico.com/interactives/databases/trump-white-house-visitor-logs -and-records/index.html.

148 **lost a son in Afghanistan:** Luis Martinez, "Son of Marine General Killed in Afghanistan," ABC News, November 11, 2010, https://abcnews.go.com/News/star-marine-generals -son-killed-afghanistan/story?id=12122030.

149 **"The American military":** Lt. Gen. John Kelly, "Four Days Later," Center for a New American Security, November 3, 2010, https://www.cnas.org/publications/blog/four -days-later.

149 **349 marines were killed:** Thomas Gibbons-Neff, "'It's like Everyone Forgot': On a Familiar Battlefield, Marines Prepare for Their Next Chapter in the Forever War," *Washington Post*, August 22, 2017, https://www.washingtonpost.com/news/checkpoint /wp/2017/08/22/its-like-everyone-forgot-on-a-familiar-battlefield-marines-prepare -for-their-next-chapter-in-the-forever-war/.

150 **The first to go:** Rosie Gray, "An NSC Staffer Is Forced Out Over a Controversial Memo," *The Atlantic*, August 2, 2017, https://www.theatlantic.com/politics/archive /2017/08/a-national-security-council-staffer-is-forced-out-over-a-controversial-memo /535725/.

151 **The Higgins memo:** Jana Winter and Elias Groll, "Here's the Memo That Blew Up the NSC," *Foreign Policy*, August 10, 2017, https://foreignpolicy.com/2017/08/10/heres-the -memo-that-blew-up-the-nsc/.

151 **gave Higgins his marching orders:** Gray, "An NSC Staffer Is Forced Out Over a Controversial Memo."

151 **Another administrative official removed:** Kevin Liptak, "NSC Official Ezra Cohen-Watnick Removed," CNN, August 2, 2017, https://www.cnn.com/2017/08/02/politics /nsc-ezra-cohen-watnick/index.html.

151 **particular target was Javed Ali:** Michael Warren, "White House Watch: The Fake News War on McMaster," *Weekly Standard*, September 19, 2017, https://www.washington examiner.com/weekly-standard/white-house-watch-the-fake-news-war-on-mcmaster.

152 **PJMedia.com, a conservative website:** David Steinberg, "EXCLUSIVE: Gen. McMaster Sparked a Row with the Israeli Delegation at a White House Meeting on Hezbollah," PJ Media, September 13, 2017, https://pjmedia.com/davidsteinberg/exclusive-gen -mcmaster-sparked-row-israeli-delegation-white-house-meeting-hezbollah/.

152 **Hannity and Laura Ingraham:** Rosie Gray, "The War Against H. R. McMaster," *The Atlantic*, August 4, 2017, https://www.theatlantic.com/politics/archive/2017/08/the-war -against-hr-mcmaster/536046/.

152 **anti-McMaster stories:** Gray, "The War Against H. R. McMaster."

153 **compelled to release a statement:** Julian Borger, "'A Good Man, Very Pro-Israel': Trump Defends McMaster from Far-Right Snipers," *Guardian*, August 5, 2017, https://www .theguardian.com/us-news/2017/aug/05/donald-trump-hr-mcmaster-israel-breitbart.

154 **Kelly took over:** Andrew Grandpre, "John Kelly, Trump's New Chief of Staff, 'Won't Suffer Idiots and Fools,'" *Washington Post*, July 29, 2017, https://www.washingtonpost .com/news/checkpoint/wp/2017/07/29/john-kelly-trumps-new-chief-of-staff-wont -suffer-idiots-and-fools/.

155 **protests in Charlottesville:** Sheryl Gay Stolberg and Brian M. Rosenthal, "Man Charged After White Nationalist Rally in Charlottesville Ends in Deadly Violence," *New York Times*, August 12, 2017, https://www.nytimes.com/2017/08/12/us/charlottesville-protest -white-nationalist.html.

155 **Trump asked Cohn:** Stephen J. Dubner, "A Free-Trade Democrat in the Trump White House (Ep. 371)," *Freakonomics*, March 13, 2019, http://freakonomics.com/podcast /cohn/.

156   **keeping Bannon on was untenable:** Jeremy W. Peters and Maggie Haberman, "Bannon Was Set for a Graceful Exit. Then Came Charlottesville," *New York Times*, August 20, 2017, https://www.nytimes.com/2017/08/20/us/politics/steve-bannon-fired-trump-departure.html.

156   **Mark Milley, tweeted:** Gen. Mark A. Milley (@ArmyChiefStaff), "The Army doesn't tolerate racism, extremism, or hatred in our ranks. It's against our Values and everything we've stood for since 1775," Twitter, August 16, 2017, 4:50 am, https://twitter.com/armychiefstaff/status/897742317897093121.

156   **Presenting a unified front:** Dave Philipps, "Inspired by Charlottesville, Military Chiefs Condemn Racism," *New York Times*, August 16, 2017, https://www.nytimes.com/2017/08/16/us/joint-chiefs-tweets-racism-charlottesville-veterans.html.

156   **"Just hold the line":** Pauline Shanks Kaurin, "Just Another Mattis Pep Talk?: How 'Hold the Line' Speaks to Civilian and Military Audiences," *Just Security* (blog), August 26, 2017, https://www.justsecurity.org/44518/mattis-pep-talk-hold-line-speaks-civilian-military-audiences/.

156   **Bannon helped to seal:** Robert Kuttner, "Steve Bannon, Unrepentant," *American Prospect*, August 16, 2017, https://prospect.org/article/steve-bannon-unrepentant.

157   **Bedminster golf club:** Andrew Rafferty and Kelly O'Donnell, "Trump Kicks Off 17-Day Stay at His New Jersey Golf Club," NBC News, August 4, 2017, https://www.nbcnews.com/politics/politics-news/trump-kicks-17-day-vacation-his-new-jersey-golf-club-n789371.

159   **prime-time address:** "Remarks by President Trump on the Strategy in Afghanistan and South Asia," White House, August 21, 2017, https://www.whitehouse.gov/briefings-statements/remarks-president-trump-strategy-afghanistan-south-asia/.

160   **kidnapped by the Taliban:** Jessica Murphy, "Joshua Boyle and Caitlan Coleman: The Couple Taken by the Taliban," BBC News, October 21, 2017, https://www.bbc.com/news/world-us-canada-41656159.

162   **Gorka told the BBC:** Aaron Blake, "More Drama in Trumpland: Gorka Publicly Shuns Tillerson's Effort to Scale Back North Korea Red Line," *Washington Post*, August 10, 2017, https://www.washingtonpost.com/news/the-fix/wp/2017/08/10/more-drama-in-trumpland-gorka-publicly-shuns-tillersons-effort-to-scale-back-north-korea-red-line/.

162   **Gorka tried to paint:** Mollie Hemingway, "Breaking: Sebastian Gorka Resigns from Trump Administration," *Federalist*, August 25, 2017, https://thefederalist.com/2017/08/25/breaking-sebastian-gorka-resigns-from-trump-administration/.

162   **The Secret Service issued:** Melissa Quinn, "Sebastian Gorka Was Barred from Entering the White House on Friday, Report Says," *Washington Examiner*, August 29, 2017, https://www.washingtonexaminer.com/sebastian-gorka-was-barred-from-entering-the-white-house-on-friday-report-says.

162   **he was fired:** Annie Karni, "White House Aide Sebastian Gorka Ousted from Post," *Politico*, August 25, 2017, https://www.politico.com/story/2017/08/25/white-house-aide-gorka-resigns-242054.

162   "ART [of] WAR": Jay Willis, "Seb Gorka Has Some Weird Shit in His Mustang Convertible," *GQ*, September 1, 2017, https://www.gq.com/story/seb-gorka-mustang-cleanout.

CHAPTER 8: HOUSE OF SAUD, HOUSE OF TRUMP

165   "I like them very much": Bernard Condon, Stephen Braun, and Tami Abdollah, "'I Love the Saudis': Trump Business Ties to Kingdom Run Deep," Associated Press, October 12, 2018, https://apnews.com/cafffbc8448e49329e04ef7941c2b85a.

165   "I couldn't care less": "Remarks by President Trump before Marine One Departure," White House, November 20, 2018, https://www.whitehouse.gov/briefings-statements/remarks-president-trump-marine-one-departure-25/.

167   a thousand flight cancellations: Christine Wang, "March Snowstorm Brings Flight Delays, Cancellations," CNBC, March 14, 2017, https://www.cnbc.com/2017/03/13/march-snowstorm-brings-flight-delays-cancellations.html.

169   "the worst deal ever": Peter Bergen, "How Donald Trump Created One Hell of a Mess with Iran," CNN, June 20, 2019, https://www.cnn.com/2019/06/20/opinions/us-iran-mess-trump-endgame-bergen/index.html.

172   this one was not: Chas Danner, "Beyond Russia: Understanding the New Trump Campaign Collusion Story," *New York*, May 20, 2018, http://nymag.com/intelligencer/2018/05/understanding-the-new-trump-campaign-collusion-story.html.

172   Trump intervened to say: Carol D. Leonnig et al., "How Jared Kushner Forged a Bond with the Saudi Crown Prince," *Washington Post*, March 19, 2018, https://www.washingtonpost.com/politics/how-jared-kushner-forged-a-bond-with-the-saudi-crown-prince/2018/03/19/2f2ce398-2181-11e8-badd-7c9f29a55815_story.html?utm_term=.56a303a6b1cf.

172   "an explosive remark": Maggie Haberman, interview by Jake Tapper, *The Lead with Jake Tapper*, CNN, May 19, 2017, http://transcripts.cnn.com/TRANSCRIPTS/1705/19/cg.01.html.

173   Trump was visiting Saudi Arabia: Peter Bergen, "Bergen: Saudi Women Driving a Sign Bigger Change Is Coming," CNN, September 27, 2017, https://www.cnn.com/2017/09/27/opinions/symbolism-of-saudi-women-driving/index.html.

173   days of $100-a-barrel oil: Peter Bergen, "Bergen: The Real Reason Saudis Rolled Out the Reddest of Red Carpets," CNN, May 22, 2017, https://www.cnn.com/2017/05/21/opinions/trump-riyadh-trip-opinion-bergen/index.html.

173   $40 a barrel: Hannah Breul, "Crude Oil Prices Started 2015 Relatively Low, Ended the Year Lower," US Energy Information Administration, January 6, 2016, https://www.eia.gov/todayinenergy/detail.php?id=24432.

173   called it "Vision 2030": Bergen, "Bergen: Saudi Women Driving."

174   harsh interpretation of Sunni Islam: Bergen, "Bergen: The Real Reason Saudis Rolled Out."

174   Committee for the Promotion of Virtue: Bergen, "Bergen: The Real Reason Saudis Rolled Out."

174   Fifteen of them perished: Bergen, "Bergen: The Real Reason Saudis Rolled Out."

174 **wings of the religious police:** Bergen, "Bergen: Saudi Women Driving."

175 **key conservative clerics:** Bergen, "Bergen: Saudi Women Driving."

176 **"my first sword dance":** Secretary of State Rex Tillerson, interview by Chris Wallace, *Fox News Sunday*, Fox News, May 21, 2017, https://www.state.gov/interview-with-chris-wallace-of-fox-news-sunday-3/.

176 **restore freedom of speech:** Yeganeh Torbati and Jonathan Landay, "U.S. Calls on Iran to Halt Support for 'Destabilizing Forces,'" Reuters, May 20, 2017, https://www.reuters.com/article/us-iran-election-usa-idUSKCN18G0PX.

176 **"Not one guy":** Jacob Pramuk, "Wilbur Ross Is Happy That the Saudis Didn't Protest Trump—but He Misses a Critical Point," CNBC, May 22, 2017, https://www.cnbc.com/2017/05/22/wilbur-ross-says-saudis-did-not-protest-trump-but-misses-key-point.html.

177 **Obama's Cairo remarks:** "Full Text: Donald Trump's Speech on Fighting Terrorism," *Politico*, August 15, 2016, https://www.politico.com/story/2016/08/donald-trump-terrorism-speech-227025.

177 **phrase "Islamic terrorism":** Mattathias Schwartz, "White House Blames Exhaustion for Donald Trump's 'Islamic Terrorism' Dog Whistle in Saudi Arabia," *The Intercept*, May 22, 2017, https://theintercept.com/2017/05/22/white-house-blames-exhaustion-for-donald-trumps-islamic-terrorism-dog-whistle-in-saudi-arabia/.

177 **"We are not here to lecture":** Ali Vitali, "Trump Speech to Muslims: 'We Are Not Here to Lecture,'" NBC News, May 21, 2017, https://www.cnbc.com/2017/05/21/trump-speech-to-muslims-we-are-not-here-to-lecture.html.

178 **millions of dollars of ransom:** Paul Wood, "Did Qatar Pay the World's Largest Ransom?," BBC News, July 17, 2018, https://www.bbc.com/news/world-middle-east-44660369.

178 **twelve thousand Qatari camels:** Declan Walsh, "Tiny, Wealthy Qatar Goes Its Own Way, and Pays for It," *New York Times*, January 22, 2018, https://www.nytimes.com/2018/01/22/world/middleeast/qatar-saudi-emir-boycott.html.

179 **implicated in the cyberattack:** Karen DeYoung and Ellen Nakashima, "UAE Orchestrated Hacking of Qatari Government Sites, Sparking Regional Upheaval, According to U.S. Intelligence Officials," *Washington Post*, July 16, 2017, https://www.washingtonpost.com/.

179 **Qatar sat on some:** Hadeel Al-Sayegh, "Qatar to Boost Gas Output in Sign of Strength amid Gulf Rift," Reuters, September 26, 2018, https://www.reuters.com/article/us-qatar-energy/qatar-to-boost-gas-output-in-sign-of-strength-amid-gulf-rift-idUSKCN1M62H8.

179 **Qatar had among the highest:** Beth Greenfield, "The World's Richest Countries," *Forbes*, February 22, 2012, https://www.forbes.com/sites/bethgreenfield/2012/02/22/the-worlds-richest-countries/#4c00b46a4627.

179 **Al Udeid Air Base:** Brad Lendon, "Qatar Hosts Largest US Military Base in Mideast," CNN, June 6, 2017, https://www.cnn.com/2017/06/05/middleeast/qatar-us-largest-base-in-mideast/index.html.

179 **The Qataris paid almost all:** Paul McLeary, "Can Trump Find a Better Deal Than the U.S. Air Base in Qatar?," *Foreign Policy*, July 20, 2017, https://foreignpolicy.com/2017/07/20/can-trump-find-a-better-deal-than-the-u-s-air-base-in-qatar/.

179 **Qatar also housed:** Nick Anderson, "In Qatar's Education City, U.S. Colleges Are Building an Academic Oasis," *Washington Post*, December 6, 2015, https://www.washington post.com/local/education/in-qatars-education-city-us-colleges-are-building-an-aca demic-oasis/2015/12/06/6b538702-8e01-11e5-ae1f-af46b7df8483_story.html.

179 **"the horror of terrorism":** Donald J. Trump (@realDonaldTrump), "So good to see the Saudi Arabia visit with the King and 50 countries already paying off. They said they would take a hard line on funding . . ." and ". . . extremism, and all reference was pointing to Qatar. Perhaps this will be the beginning of the end to the horror of terrorism!" Twitter, June 6, 2017, 9:36 am and 9:44 am, https://twitter.com/realdonaldtrump/status /872084870620520448 and https://twitter.com/realdonaldtrump/status/87208690680 4240384.

179 **meeting their counterparts in Australia:** Ali Harb, "Qatar Blockade: Tillerson Was Left in Dark as Kushner Met with Saudis," Middle East Eye, June 27, 2019, http://www .middleeasteye.net/news/qatar-crisis-tillerson-says-he-had-no-idea-about-blockade.

180 **eleven thousand American military servicemen:** Brad Lendon, "Qatar Hosts Largest US Military Base in Mideast," CNN, June 6, 2017, https://www.cnn.com/2017/06/05 /middleeast/qatar-us-largest-base-in-mideast/index.html.

181 **Qatar for $12 billion:** Ankit Ajmera, "Qatar Signs $12 Billion Deal to Buy F-15 Jets from U.S.," Reuters, June 15, 2017, https://www.reuters.com/article/us-gulf-qatar-boeing -idUSKBN19531Y.

181 **Nayef to step down:** Peter Bergen, "Trump's Uncritical Embrace of MBS Set the Stage for Khashoggi Crisis," CNN, November 15, 2018, sec. Opinion, https://www.cnn.com /2018/10/15/opinions/how-the-saudis-played-trump-bergen/index.html.

182 **interview with Bloomberg News:** "Mohammed bin Salman, Saudi Crown Prince Discusses Trump, Aramco, Arrests," Bloomberg News, October 5, 2018, https://www .bloomberg.com/news/articles/2018-10-05/saudi-crown-prince-discusses-trump-aramco -arrests-transcript.

182 **a half-billion-dollar yacht:** Grace Guarnieri, "Saudi Arabia's Crown Prince Bought the World's Most Expensive Mansion for $300 Million, and a $500 Million Yacht," *Newsweek*, December 18, 2017, https://www.newsweek.com/saudia-arabia-crown-prince-most -expensive-house-world-751128.

182 **more than $7 billion:** Rory Jones, Margherita Stancati, and Summer Said, "Saudi Arabia to Spend Billions to Revive Foreign Investment," *Wall Street Journal*, July 22, 2018, https://www.wsj.com/articles/saudi-arabia-to-spend-billions-to-revive-foreign-invest ment-1532260920.

182 **elections in the Saudi kingdom:** "Saudi 'Seeks Death Penalty' for Muslim Scholar Salman Al-Awdah," *Al Jazeera*, September 5, 2018, https://www.aljazeera.com/news /2018/09/saudi-seeks-death-penalty-muslim-scholar-salman-al-awdah-180905055 754018.html.

182 **Boys were arrested:** Muhammad Darwish, Tamara Qiblawi, and Ghazi Balkiz, "He Was Arrested at 13. Now Saudi Arabia Wants to Execute Him," CNN, June 2019, https://www.cnn.com/interactive/2019/06/middleeast/saudi-teen-death-penalty-intl/.

183 **leadership of the Saudi military:** "Saudi Arabia Fires Top Army Chiefs in Military Shake-Up," *Al Jazeera*, February 27, 2018, https://www.aljazeera.com/news/2018/02/saudi-arabia-fires-top-army-chiefs-military-shake-180227054218368.html.

183 **mother under house arrest:** Carol E. Lee and Courtney Kube, "Saudi Prince Hiding His Mother from Saudi King, Say U.S. Officials," NBC News, March 15, 2018, https://www.nbcnews.com/news/world/u-s-officials-saudi-crown-prince-has-hidden-his-mother-n847391.

183 **Beirut in 2005:** "Lebanon's Saad Hariri Demands 'Justice' for Slain Father at Trial," *Al Jazeera*, September 12, 2018, https://www.aljazeera.com/news/2018/09/lebanon-saad-hariri-demands-justice-slain-father-trial-180912083916681.html.

184 **The Houthis subsequently fired:** Caleb Weiss, "Analysis: Houthi Missiles against the Saudi-Led Coalition," *Long War Journal* (blog), August 2, 2019, https://www.longwarjournal.org/archives/2019/08/analysis-houthi-missiles-against-the-saudi-led-coalition.php.

184 **civilian casualties in Yemen:** Ryan Goodman, "Annotation of Sec. Pompeo's Certification of Yemen War: Civilian Casualties and Saudi-Led Coalition," *Just Security*, October 15, 2018, https://www.justsecurity.org/61053/annotation-sec-pompeos-certification-yemen-war-civilian-casualties-resulting-saudi-led-coalitions-operations/.

184 **The UN had earlier charged:** "Yemen: United Nations Experts Point to Possible War Crimes by Parties to the Conflict," United Nations Office of the High Commissioner for Human Rights, August 28, 2018, https://www.ohchr.org/EN/NewsEvents/Pages/DisplayNews.aspx?NewsID=23479.

185 **"sunset" provisions in the deal:** Ali Vaez, "The Iranian Nuclear Deal's Sunset Clauses" *Foreign Affairs*, October 3, 2017, https://www.foreignaffairs.com/articles/iran/2017-10-03/iranian-nuclear-deals-sunset-clauses.

185 **sticking to the agreement:** "Iran Sticking to Nuclear Deal, IAEA Says, amid New U.S. Sanctions," Reuters, November 22, 2018, https://www.reuters.com/article/us-iran-nuclear-iaea/iran-sticking-to-nuclear-deal-iaea-says-amid-new-us-sanctions-idUSKCN1NR1DL.

185 **Senate Armed Services Committee:** "Political and Security Situation in Afghanistan," Senate Committee on Armed Services, October 3, 2017, https://www.armed-services.senate.gov/imo/media/doc/17-82_10-03-17.pdf.

185 **"Yes, Senator, I do":** "Political and Security Situation in Afghanistan."

186 **General Joseph Votel:** "Hearing to Receive Testimony on United States Central Command and United States Africa Command," Senate Committee on Armed Services, March 9, 2017, https://www.armed-services.senate.gov/imo/media/doc/17-18_03-09-17.pdf.

188 **suffering from a stomach bug:** Asawin Suebsaeng and Lachlan Markay, "John Kelly: Rex Tillerson Was on the Toilet When I Told Him He'd Be Getting Fired," *Daily Beast*, March 16, 2018, https://www.thedailybeast.com/john-kelly-rex-tillerson-was-on-the-toilet-when-i-told-him-hed-be-getting-fired.

189 **"a fantastic job":** Donald J. Trump (@realDonaldTrump), "Mike Pompeo, Director of the CIA, will become our new Secretary of State. He will do a fantastic job! Thank

you to Rex Tillerson for his service! Gina Haspel will become the new Director of the CIA, and the first woman so chosen. Congratulations to all!," Twitter, March 13, 2018, 8:44 am, https://twitter.com/realdonaldtrump/status/973540316656623616.

189   **McMaster told the Munich audience:** Daniel W. Drezner, "The Munich Security Conference Is One of the Premier Global Forums, so What's with the Malaise?," *Washington Post*, February 18, 2018, https://www.washingtonpost.com/news/posteverything/wp/2018/02/18/the-munich-security-conference-in-winter/.

189   **"the Podesta Company":** Donald J. Trump (@realDonaldTrump), "General McMaster forgot to say that the results of the 2016 election were not impacted or changed by the Russians and that the only Collusion was between Russia and Crooked H, the DNC and the Dems. Remember the Dirty Dossier, Uranium, Speeches, Emails and the Podesta Company!," Twitter, February 17, 2018, 11:22 pm, https://twitter.com/realdonaldtrump/status/965079126829871104.

189   **John Bolton met with Trump:** Greg Jaffe and Josh Dawsey, "Trump Names Former Ambassador John Bolton as His New National Security Adviser," *Washington Post*, March 22, 2018, https://www.washingtonpost.com/world/national-security/trump-names-former-ambassador-john-bolton-as-his-new-national-security-adviser/2018/03/22/aa1d1 9e6-2e20-11e8-8ad6-fbc50284fce8_story.html.

190   **hundreds of cheering staffers:** Daniel Chaitin, "Departing National Security Adviser H. R. McMaster Gets 'Clap Out' from Large Group of Trump Staffers," *Washington Examiner*, April 6, 2018, https://www.washingtonexaminer.com/news/hr-mcmaster-gets -clap-out-from-large-group-of-trump-staffers.

190   **started in his new job:** Peter Bergen, "New Trump Adviser Is 'Not Much of a Carrot Man,'" CNN, April 9, 2018, https://www.cnn.com/2018/04/08/opinions/john-bolton -carrot-man-bergen/index.html.

191   **"overwhelmingly Democratic and liberal":** Bergen, "New Trump Adviser Is 'Not Much of a Carrot Man.'"

191   **America First guy:** Bergen, "New Trump Adviser Is 'Not Much of a Carrot Man.'"

191   **"unsigning" the agreement:** Bergen, "New Trump Adviser Is 'Not Much of a Carrot Man.'"

191   **a kid on Christmas Day:** Bergen, "New Trump Adviser Is 'Not Much of a Carrot Man.'"

191   **arms-control negotiations:** Bergen, "New Trump Adviser Is 'Not Much of a Carrot Man.'"

191   **"Iran will not negotiate":** John R. Bolton, "To Stop Iran's Bomb, Bomb Iran," *New York Times*, March 26, 2015, https://www.nytimes.com/2015/03/26/opinion/to-stop -irans-bomb-bomb-iran.html.

192   **bankruptcy lawyer, David Friedman:** David Remnick, "Trump's Daily Bankruptcy and the Ambassador to Israel," *New Yorker*, December 16, 2016, https://www.newyorker .com/news/news-desk/trump_daily_bankruptcy_israel_ambassador_david_friedman.

192   **"far worse than kapos":** David Friedman, "Read Peter Beinart and You'll Vote Donald Trump," Arutz Sheva, June 5, 2016, http://www.israelnationalnews.com/Articles/Article .aspx/18828.

192 **administration could support Israel:** David M. Halbfinger, "U.S. Ambassador Says Israel Has Right to Annex Parts of West Bank," *New York Times*, June 8, 2019, https://www
.nytimes.com/2019/06/08/world/middleeast/israel-west-bank-david-friedman.html.

193 **"Peace is within reach":** "'Time to Try Something Better': Kushner Says Peace 'Within
Reach' at Jerusalem Embassy Opening," *Fox News Insider*, May 14, 2018, https://insider
.foxnews.com/2018/05/14/jared-kushner-speaks-us-jerusalem-embassy-dedication
-ceremony-israel.

193 **simultaneously killing scores of Palestinians:** David M. Halbfinger, Isabel Kershner,
and Declan Walsh, "Israel Kills Dozens at Gaza Border as U.S. Embassy Opens in Jerusalem," *New York Times*, May 14, 2018, https://www.nytimes.com/2018/05/14/world
/middleeast/gaza-protests-palestinians-us-embassy.html.

193 **secure a top-secret clearance:** Peter Bergen, "Jared Kushner Just Joined a Really Big
Club," CNN, February 28, 2018, https://www.cnn.com/2018/02/28/opinions/jared
-kushner-just-joined-a-big-club-opinion-bergen/index.html.

194 **granting of clearances:** Brian Naylor and Tim Mak, "Whistleblower Says White House
Overturned 25 Denied Security Clearances," NPR, April 1, 2019, https://www.npr.org
/2019/04/01/708726227/whistle-blower-says-white-house-overturned-denials-of
-25-for-security-clearances.

195 **Palestinian Authority president:** Jack Khoury, "Abbas: Kushner's Anti-UNRWA Actions Prove U.S. Wants to Erase Palestinian Issue," *Haaretz*, August 4, 2018, https://
www.haaretz.com/middle-east-news/palestinians/.premium-abbas-kushner-report
-proves-u-s-wants-to-erase-palestinian-issue-1.6341547.

195 **United Nations Relief:** Clare Foran and Elise Labott, "US Ends All Funding to UN
Agency for Palestinian Refugees," CNN, September 1, 2018, https://www.cnn.com/2018
/08/31/politics/trump-administration-ending-funding-palestinian-refugees/index.html.

195 **vote at the UN:** Colum Lynch, "Haley Warns Diplomats on Jerusalem: Trump Is Watching You," *Foreign Policy*, December 19, 2017, https://foreignpolicy.com/2017/12/19/haley
-warns-diplomats-on-jerusalem-trump-is-watching-you/.

196 **$60 million to UNRWA:** Josh Rogin, "Tillerson Prevails over Haley in Palestinian
Funding Debate," *Washington Post*, January 16, 2018, https://www.washingtonpost
.com/news/josh-rogin/wp/2018/01/16/tillerson-prevails-over-haley-in-palestinian
-funding-debate/.

196 **condemned the US embassy move:** "Saudi King Slams Trump for Transferring US
Embassy to Jerusalem," *Times of Israel*, April 15, 2018, https://www.timesofisrael.com
/saudi-king-slams-trump-for-transferring-us-embassy-to-jerusalem/.

197 **Trump's Middle East envoy:** Noa Landau, "U.S. Mideast Envoy Greenblatt: We May
Postpone Publication of Peace Plan to November," *Haaretz*, June 16, 2019. https://www
.haaretz.com/israel-news/u-s-mideast-envoy-greenblatt-we-may-postpone-publication
-of-peace-plan-to-november-1.7373746.

197 **"a hot I.P.O":** David M. Halbfinger, "In Bahrain, Gaza Is Pitched as a 'Hot I.P.O.'
Many Palestinians Aren't Buying It.," *New York Times*, June 26, 2019, https://www
.nytimes.com/2019/06/26/world/middleeast/bahrain-kushner-palestinian-peace
.html.

CHAPTER 9: THE MURDER OF JAMAL KHASHOGGI

199 **"Will no one rid me"**: Olivia B. Waxman, "James Comey Makes Henry II, Thomas Becket Link" *Time*, June 8, 2017, https://time.com/4811148/comey-testimony-henry-ii -thomas-becket-will-no-one-rid-me-of-this-meddlesome-priest/.

199 **"There's not a smoking gun"**: Stephen Dinan, "Sen. Lindsey Graham: 'Smoking Saw' Ties Saudi Crown Prince to Khashoggi Killing," *Washington Times*, December 4, 2018, https://www.washingtontimes.com/news/2018/dec/4/lindsey-graham-sees-smoking -saw-khashoggi-killing/.

202 **recovered from the consulate**: This account is based on Carlotta Gall's *New York Times* story about a book about the murder, *Diplomatic Atrocity: The Dark Secrets of the Jamal Khashoggi Murder*, written by Turkish investigative journalists working for *Sabah*, a newspaper with close ties to Turkish intelligence.

202 **fiancée, who was still waiting**: Tuysuz Gul et al., "Surveillance Footage Shows Saudi 'Body Double' in Khashoggi's Clothes, Turkish Source Says," CNN, October 22, 2018, https://www.cnn.com/2018/10/22/middleeast/saudi-operative-jamal-khashoggi -clothes/index.html.

202 **"tell your boss"**: "Khashoggi Killing: 'Tell Your Boss Deed Is Done,'" *Al Jazeera*, November 12, 2018, https://www.aljazeera.com/news/2018/11/khashoggi-killing-boss-deed -nyt-181113033718617.html.

203 **"absolutely false, and baseless"**: "The Saudi Ambassador Lied Point-Blank about a Journalist's Murder. Now He Has the Gall to Come Back to D.C.," *Washington Post*, December 7, 2018, https://www.washingtonpost.com/opinions/global-opinions/khalid-bin -salman-took-part-in-the-coverup-of-jamal-khashoggis-killing-he-should-be-shunned /2018/12/07/7bcf51c2-fa48-11e8-8c9a-860ce2a8148f_story.html.

203 **result of "rogue killers"**: Summer Said, Rebecca Ballhaus, and David Gauthier-Villars, "Saudis Weigh Saying Journalist Was Killed by Mistake," *Wall Street Journal*, October 15, 2018, https://www.wsj.com/articles/turkey-to-inspect-saudi-consulate-where -khashoggi-went-missing-1539604362.

203 **labeled a terrorist group**: John Hudson, Souad Mekhennet, and Carol D. Leonnig, "Saudi Crown Prince Described Journalist as a Dangerous Islamist in Call with White House, Officials Say," *Washington Post*, November 1, 2018, https://www.washington post.com/world/national-security/saudi-crown-prince-described-slain-journalist-as-a -dangerous-islamist-in-call-with-white-house/2018/11/01/b4513e05-2d8e-4533-9cc8 -2cabf8bb2d0a_story.html.

203 **"connected to Osama bin Laden"**: Peter Bergen, "Jamal Khashoggi Was a Journalist, Not a Jihadist," CNN, October 22, 2018, https://www.cnn.com/2018/10/22/opinions /khashoggi-was-journalist-not-jihadist-bergen/index.html.

204 **"source of our strength"**: Peter Bergen, "The Awful Disappearance of Jamal Khashoggi," CNN, October 8, 2018, https://www.cnn.com/2018/10/08/opinions/the -awful-disappearance-of-jamal-khashoggi-bergen/index.html.

204 **war against the United States**: Bergen, "The Awful Disappearance of Jamal Khashoggi."

204 **adviser to Prince Turki**: Bergen, "The Awful Disappearance of Jamal Khashoggi."

204 **"It's a matter of choice":** Bergen, "Jamal Khashoggi Was a Journalist, Not a Jihadist."

206 **Qahtani was MBS's closest adviser:** "MBS in Touch with 'Former' Saudi Royal Adviser al-Qahtani: Report," *Al Jazeera*, January 11, 2019, https://www.aljazeera.com/news /2019/01/mbs-touch-saudi-royal-adviser-qahtani-wpost-190111120955535.html.

206 **Six weeks after Khashoggi's murder:** Mohammed Muslemany and Saphora Smith, "U.S. Treasury Slaps Sanctions on Saudi Officials over Khashoggi Killing," NBC News (Cairo), November 15, 2018, https://www.nbcnews.com/news/world/saudi-prosecutor -seeks-death-penalty-suspects-khashoggi-s-killing-n936496.

207 **CBS's *60 Minutes*:** Donald J. Trump, interview by Lesley Stahl, *60 Minutes*, CBS, October 13, 2018, https://www.cbsnews.com/news/president-donald-trump-vows-severe -punishment-if-saudi-arabia-is-behind-saudi-missing-journalist/.

207 **new arms sales:** "Fact Check: How Much Does Saudi Arabia Spend On Arms Deals With The U.S.?," *All Things Considered,* NPR, October 15, 2018, https://www.npr.org /2018/10/15/657588534/fact-check-how-much-does-saudi-arabia-spend-on-arms-deals -with-the-u-s.

207 **"I'm not going to destroy":** Josh Dawsey, Shane Harris, and Karen DeYoung, "Trump Calls Saudi Arabia a 'Great Ally,' Discounts Crown Prince's Responsibility for Khashoggi's Death," *Washington Post*, November 20, 2018, https://www.washingtonpost.com /politics/trump-defends-saudia-arabias-denial-about-the-planning-of-khashoggis-death /2018/11/20/b64d2cc6-eceb-11e8-9236-bb94154151d2_story.html.

207 **to do with the murder:** Samuel Chamberlain, "Trump Says 'I Don't Want to Hear the Tape' of Purported Khashoggi Killing," Fox News, November 18, 2018, https://www.fox news.com/politics/trump-says-i-dont-want-to-hear-the-tape-of-purported-khashoggi -killing.

207 **"it's a terrible tape":** Chamberlain, "Trump Says 'I Don't Want to Hear the Tape.'"

207 **hit was ordered by MBS:** Julian E. Barnes and Eric Schmitt, "Intercepts Solidify C.I.A. Assessment That Saudi Prince Ordered Khashoggi Killing," *New York Times*, December 2, 2018, https://www.nytimes.com/2018/12/02/us/politics/crown-prince-mohammed -qahtani-intercepts.html.

208 **"has got to go":** "'He Had This Guy Murdered': Graham Says 'Toxic' Saudi Crown Prince 'Has Got to Go,'" Fox News Insider, 2018, https://insider.foxnews.com/2018 /10/16/lindsey-graham-jamal-khashoggi-death-saudi-crown-prince-mohammed -bin-salman-must-go.

209 **Mattis called for a cease-fire:** Ryan Browne, "Mattis and Pompeo Call for Yemen Cease-fire 'within 30 Days,'" CNN, October 31, 2018, https://www.cnn.com/2018/10/30 /politics/jim-mattis-yemen-ceasefire/index.html.

209 **They charged eleven:** Jen Kirby, "Saudi Arabia Begins Trial for 11 Suspects in Khashoggi Murder," *Vox*, January 3, 2019, https://www.vox.com/2019/1/3/18166689/khashoggi -trial-saudi-arabia-mbs.

209 **Trump vetoed the resolution on April 16, 2019:** Allie Malloy, "Trump Vetoes Yemen War Powers Resolution, His 2nd Veto since Taking Office," CNN, April 17, 2019, https:// www.cnn.com/2019/04/16/politics/trump-vetoes-yemen-war-powers-resolution/index .html.

CHAPTER 10: FROM "FIRE AND FURY" TO "LOVE"

211   "To really understand": Cliff Sims, *Team of Vipers: My 500 Extraordinary Days in the Trump White House* (New York: Thomas Dunne, 2019).

214   Satellite imagery showed: Julian Ryall, "North Korea 'Preparing Another Nuclear Test', Satellite Images Suggest," *The Telegraph*, September 14, 2017, https://www.tele graph.co.uk/news/2017/09/14/north-korea-preparing-another-nuclear-test-satellite -images.

215   twenty-five million: Ann Babe, "South Korea Built a 'Master-Planned City' From Scratch. Now, Critics Disagree on Its Effectiveness," *US News & World Report*, June 4, 2019, https://www.usnews.com/news/cities/articles/2019-06-04/sejong-south-koreas -new-administrative-capital-city-draws-critics.

215   "their Independence Day": Daniela Cobos, "North Korea's Kim Jong Un Celebrates Missile Launch with Banquet," *International Business Times*, July 11, 2017, https://www .ibtimes.com/north-koreas-kim-jong-un-celebrates-missile-launch-banquet-2564238.

216   UN Security Council: Associated Press, "U.S. Says It Has U.N. Security Council Support for New Sanctions against North Korea," *PBS NewsHour*, March 30, 2018, https:// www.pbs.org/newshour/world/u-s-says-it-has-u-n-security-council-support-for-new -sanctions-against-north-korea.

216   "Save your energy Rex": Donald J. Trump (@realDonaldTrump), "I told Rex Tillerson, our wonderful Secretary of State, that he is wasting his time trying to negotiate with Little Rocket Man . . ." and ". . . Save your energy Rex, we'll do what has to be done!," Twitter, October 1, 2017, 10:30 am and 10:30 am, https://twitter.com/realdonaldtrump /status/914497877543735296.

216   "the calm before the storm": Mark Landler, "What Did President Trump Mean by 'Calm before the Storm'?," *New York Times*, October 6, 2017, https://www.nytimes.com /2017/10/06/us/politics/trump-calls-meeting-with-military-leaders-the-calm-before -the-storm.html.

217   "much faster pace": David Alexander, "Trump Declines to Explain 'Calm before the Storm' Remark," Reuters, October 6, 2017, https://uk.reuters.com/article/uk-usa-trump -military-idUKKBN1CB2G1.

217   Trump met with the generals: Bob Woodward, *Fear: Trump in the White House* (London: Simon and Schuster, 2018), 184.

217   "and my Button works": Donald J. Trump (@realDonaldTrump), "North Korean Leader Kim Jong Un just stated that the 'Nuclear Button is on his desk at all times.' Will someone from his depleted and food starved regime please inform him that I too have a Nuclear Button, but it is a much bigger & more powerful one than his, and my Button works!," Twitter, January 2, 2018, 7:49 pm, https://twitter.com/realdonaldtrump /status/948355557022420992.

217   "stop sending the military families": *Your World With Neil Cavuto*, Fox News, January 26, 2018, http://archive.org/details/FOXNEWSW_20180126_210000_Your_World _With_Neil_Cavuto.

218   an opening for Trump: Anna Fifield, "As Winter Games Close, North Korea Says It Is Willing to Talk to the U.S., According to Seoul," *Washington Post*, February 25, 2018,

https://www.washingtonpost.com/world/as-winter-games-close-olympics-chief-lauds
-diplomatic-thaw-between-the-koreas/2018/02/25/9eedf22a-18d1-11e8-930c-45838
ad0d77a_story.html.

218 **nuclear weapons and missile tests:** Anna Fifield, "North Korea Says It Will Suspend
Nuclear and Missile Tests, Shut Down Test Site," *Washington Post*, April 20, 2018,
https://www.washingtonpost.com/world/north-korean-leader-suspends-nuclear-and
-missile-tests-shuts-down-test-site/2018/04/20/71ff2eea-44e7-11e8-baaf-8b3c5a3da888
_story.html.

218 **Bolton had written:** John Bolton, "The Legal Case for Striking North Korea First,"
Wall Street Journal, February 28, 2018, https://www.wsj.com/articles/the-legal-case
-for-striking-north-Korea-first-1519862374.

219 **"Libya model for North Korea":** Megan Specia and David E. Sanger, "How the 'Libya
Model' Became a Sticking Point in North Korea Nuclear Talks," *New York Times*, May
16, 2018, https://www.nytimes.com/2018/05/16/world/asia/north-korea-libya-model
.html.

219 **"repugnance towards him":** "Full Text: North Korea Calls John Bolton Repugnant and
Threatens to Bail on Summit with Trump," *Quartz*, May 16, 2018, https://qz.com
/1279247/full-text-north-korea-calls-john-bolton-repugnant-and-threatens-to-bail
-on-summit-with-trump.

219 **"I'm not aware":** Specia and Sanger, "How the 'Libya Model' Became a Sticking Point."

219 **Trump met in Singapore:** "Trump and Kim Joint Statement from the Singapore Summit," *Washington Post*, June 12, 2018, https://www.washingtonpost.com/news/politics
/wp/2018/06/12/trump-and-kim-joint-statement-from-the-singapore-summit.

219 **US–South Korean military exercises:** Nancy Cook, Louis Nelson, and Nahal Toosi,
"Trump Pledges to End Military Exercises as Part of North Korea Talks," *Politico*,
June 12, 2018, https://www.politico.com/story/2018/06/12/trump-kim-meeting-press
-conference-637544.

220 **"Nuclear Threat from North Korea":** Donald J. Trump (@realDonaldTrump), "Just
landed—a long trip, but everybody can now feel much safer than the day I took office.
There is no longer a Nuclear Threat from North Korea. Meeting with Kim Jong Un was
an interesting and very positive experience. North Korea has great potential for the
future!," Twitter, June 13, 2018, 2:56 am, https://twitter.com/realdonaldtrump/status
/1006837823469735936.

220 **"we fell in love, okay?":** Roberta Rampton, "'We Fell in Love': Trump Swoons over
Letters from North Korea's Kim" Reuters, September 30, 2018, https://www.reuters
.com/article/us-northkorea-usa-trump/we-fell-in-love-trump-swoons-over-letters
-from-north-koreas-kim-idUSKCN1MA03Q.

220 **"critical to regime survival":** "North Korea Unlikely to Give up Nuclear Weapons:
U.S. Spy Chief Coats," Reuters, January 29, 2019, https://www.reuters.com/article
/us-usa-northkorea-nuclear-idUSKCN1PN1Y7.

221 **a "smart man":** Jill Colvin and Darlene Superville, "Trump in Japan: Trump Not
'Bothered' by North Korea Missile Tests," *USA Today*, May 27, 2019, https://www

.usatoday.com/story/news/world/2019/05/27/trump-japan-trump-not-bothered-north
-korea-missile-tests/1249177001.

221 **"fool of low IQ":** Ben Wescott and Jake Kwon, "North Korea Derides US Presidential Candidate Joe Biden as a 'Fool of Low IQ,'" CNN, May 22, 2019, https://www.cnn .com/2019/05/22/asia/north-korea-joe-biden-intl/index.html.

221 **"just to shake his hand":** Donald J. Trump (@realDonaldTrump), "After some very important meetings, including my meeting with President Xi of China, I will be leaving Japan for South Korea (with President Moon). While there, if Chairman Kim of North Korea sees this, I would meet him at the Border/DMZ just to shake his hand and say Hello(?)!," Twitter, June 28, 2019, 3:51 pm, https://twitter.com/realdonaldtrump/status /1144740178948493314.

221 **The tinpot dictator:** Jungah Lee and Brett Miller, "Spies and Satellites: Analyzing North Korea's Economy Isn't Easy," *Japan Times*, February 22, 2019, https://www .japantimes.co.jp/news/2019/02/22/asia-pacific/even-help-spies-satellites-analyzing -north-koreas-economy-isnt-easy/#.XVL1z-hKiM8.

221 **state of Vermont:** *Forbes*, accessed August 13, 2019, https://www.forbes.com/places/vt.

CHAPTER 11: PISSING OFF ALLIES, EMBRACING PUTIN

223 **"There is only one thing":** "Chequers, 1 April 1945," International Churchill Society, https://winstonchurchill.org/uncategorised/quotes-slider/2014-11-3-16-25-06.

223 **"We've had a president":** Ryan Teague Beckwith, "Read Donald Trump's 'America First' Foreign Policy Speech," *Time*, April 27, 2016, https://time.com/4309786/read-donald -trumps-america-first-foreign-policy-speech.

225 **Canadian master corporal:** Peter Bergen, "Trump's Way: Treating Allies Like Enemies and Enemies Like Allies," CNN, July 12, 2018, https://www.cnn.com/2018/07/11 /opinions/trump-treats-putin-like-a-buddy-and-allies-like-enemies-bergen/index.html.

225 **"still not paying what":** Peter Baker, "Trump Says NATO Allies Don't Pay Their Share. Is That True?," *New York Times*, May 28, 2017, https://www.nytimes.com/2017/05/26 /world/europe/nato-trump-spending.html.

226 **Obama had also pressed:** "Everything Obama Ever Asked For: But Alliance Members Leave Brussels Bruised and Confused," *New York Times*, July 12, 2018, https://www .nytimes.com/2018/07/12/opinion/editorials/trump-nato-obama.html.

226 **agreed-upon target:** Jim Techau, "The Politics of 2 Percent: NATO and the Security Vacuum in Europe," Carnegie Europe, September 2, 2015, https://carnegieeurope .eu/2015/09/02/politics-of-2-percent-nato-and-security-vacuum-in-europe-pub-61139.

226 **Merkel arrived in Washington:** Natalia Wojcik, "Trump Seems to Ignore Requests for Handshake with Merkel in the Oval Office," CNBC, March 17, 2017, https://www .cnbc.com/2017/03/17/trump-seems-to-ignore-requests-for-handshake-with-merkel-in -the-oval-office.html.

227 **"provide some degree of support":** Justin Rowlatt, "Russia 'Arming the Afghan Taliban,' Says US," BBC News, March 23, 2018, https://www.bbc.com/news/world-asia -43500299.

227 **died from exposure to Novichok:** "Novichok: Murder Inquiry after Dawn Sturgess Dies," BBC News, July 9, 2018, https://www.bbc.com/news/uk-44760875.

227 **"I have NATO":** Louis Nelson, "Trump Says Summit with Putin 'May Be the Easiest' of European Meetings," *Politico*, July 10, 2018, https://www.politico.com/story/2018 /07/10/trump-putin-meeting-2018-706141.

228 **making "false statements":** Donald J. Trump (@realDonaldTrump), "Based on Justin's false statements at his news conference, and the fact that Canada is charging massive Tariffs to our U.S. farmers, workers and companies, I have instructed our U.S. Reps not to endorse the Communique as we look at Tariffs on automobiles flooding the U.S. Market!," Twitter, June 9, 2018, 7:03 pm, https://twitter.com/realdonaldtrump/status /1005586152076689408.

228 **$360 billion a year:** "Canada U.S.-Canada Trade Facts," Office of the United States Trade Representative, accessed July 31, 2019, https://ustr.gov/countries-regions/americas /canada.

228 **piffling $12 billion:** "Russia: U.S.-Russia Trade Facts," Office of the United States Trade Representative, accessed July 31, 2019, https://ustr.gov/Russia.

228 **"Germany is totally controlled":** Meredith McGraw, "Trump Issues Blistering Attacks on Germany at NATO Breakfast: 'Germany Is Controlled by Russia,'" ABC News, July 11, 2018, https://abcnews.go.com/Politics/trump-issues-blistering-attacks-germany-nato -breakfast-germany/story?id=56504193.

228 **"was displeased because he was":** William Cummings, "Kelly Was Upset About the Food at NATO Breakfast, Not Trump Germany Remark, Sanders Says," *USA Today*, July 11, 2018, https://www.usatoday.com/story/news/politics/onpolitics/2018/07/11/john -kelly-upset-breakfast/777505002.

228 **"I have witnessed":** Jennifer Hansler, "Merkel Responds to Trump: 'I Have Witnessed' Germany under Soviet Control," CNN, July 11, 2018, https://www.cnn.com/2018/07 /11/politics/angela-merkel-east-germany-nato-trump/index.html.

228 **Trump turned his guns:** Jeff Mason and Michael Holden, "Trump Blasts UK PM May's Brexit Plan, Says It Puts Trade Deal in Doubt," Reuters, July 11, 2018, https:// www.reuters.com/article/us-usa-trump-britain/trump-blasts-uk-pm-mays-brexit-plan -says-it-puts-trade-deal-in-doubt-idUSKBN1K130C.

229 **Trump also dumped:** Palko Karasz, "Trump Targets London's Mayor, Sadiq Khan. How Fair Are His Criticisms?," *New York Times*, July 13, 2018, https://www.nytimes .com/2018/07/13/world/europe/trump-sadiq-khan-london.html.

229 **Trump slapped tariffs:** David J. Lynch, Josh Dawsey, and Damian Paletta, "Trump Imposes Steel and Aluminum Tariffs on the E.U., Canada and Mexico," *Washington Post*, May 31, 2018, https://www.washingtonpost.com/business/economy/trump-imposes -steel-and-aluminum-tariffs-on-the-european-union-canada-and-mexico/2018/05/31 /891bb452-64d3-11e8-a69c-b944de66d9e7_story.html.

229 **"We're all to blame":** Gillian Brassil and Spencer Kimball, "'The United States Has Been Foolish': Read the Full Transcript of Trump's Press Conference with Putin," CNBC, July 16, 2018, https://www.cnbc.com/2018/07/16/i-hold-both-countries-responsible-here -is-the-full-transcript-of-tr.html.

230 **"undermine our democracy"**: Kevin Breuninger, "Spy Chief Dan Coats Shoots Back at Trump for Refusing to Side with Him over Putin on Election Meddling," *CNBC*, July 16, 2018, https://www.cnbc.com/2018/07/16/dan-coats-shoots-back-at-trump-who-refused-to-side-with-him-over-putin.html.

230 **"stunning and disappointing"**: Henry Fernandez, "Trump Should Have Publicly Called Out Putin on US Election Meddling: Gen. Jack Keane," *Fox Business*, July 16, 2018, https://www.foxbusiness.com/politics/trump-should-have-publicly-called-out-putin-on-us-election-meddling-gen-jack-keane.

231 **"The sentence should have been"**: Matt Flegenheimer, "Would It or Wouldn't It Be Russia: Trump Goes Double Negative," *New York Times*, July 17, 2018, https://www.nytimes.com/2018/07/17/us/politics/trump-putin-russia.html.

231 **Mitchell interviewed Coats**: "A Look Over My Shoulder: The DNI Reflects and Foreshadows," Aspen Institute, July 19, 2018, https://aspensecurityforum.org/wp-content/uploads/2018/07/ASF-2018-A-Look-Over-My-Shoulder-The-DNI-Reflects-and-Foreshadows-3.pdf.

231 **number one threat**: Missy Ryan and Dan Lamothe, "Placing Russia First among Threats, Defense Nominee Warns of Kremlin Attempts to 'Break' NATO," *Washington Post*, January 12, 2017, https://www.washingtonpost.com/world/national-security/senate-set-to-question-trumps-pentagon-pick-veteran-marine-gen-james-mattis/2017/01/11/b3c6946a-d816-11e6-9a36-1d296534b31e_story.html.

231 **national security strategy**: "National Security Strategy of the United States of America," White House, December 2017, https://www.whitehouse.gov/wp-content/uploads/2017/12/NSS-Final-12-18-2017-0905.pdf; Peter Bergen, "Trump's New Strategy: Russia Is an Actual Threat," CNN, December 19, 2017, https://www.cnn.com/2017/12/18/opinions/trump-national-security-strategy-russia-china-peter-bergen-opinion/index.html.

232 **expelling sixty Russian diplomats**: Jeremy Diamond, Allie Malloy, and Angela Dewan, "Trump Expelling 60 Russian Diplomats in Wake of UK Nerve Agent Attack," CNN, March 26, 2018, https://www.cnn.com/2018/03/26/politics/us-expel-russian-diplomats/index.html.

232 **$40 million of arms sales**: Josh Rogin, "Trump Administration Approves Lethal Arms Sales to Ukraine," *Washington Post*, December 20, 2017, https://www.washingtonpost.com/news/josh-rogin/wp/2017/12/20/trump-administration-approves-lethal-arms-sales-to-ukraine.

232 **"He is wrong"**: "Remarks by LTG H.R. McMaster at Atlantic Council Baltic Summit Dinner," White House, April 3, 2018, https://www.whitehouse.gov/briefings-statements/remarks-ltg-h-r-mcmaster-atlantic-council-baltic-summit-dinner.

233 **suffered from "momentary confusion"**: Katie Reilly, "Nikki Haley's 'I Don't Get Confused' Comment Demonstrated Her Gift for the Clapback," *Time*, April 18, 2018, https://time.com/5245537/nikki-haley-i-dont-get-confused-larry-kudlow-spat.

233 **"she was in a box"**: Peter Baker, Julie Hirschfeld Davis, and Maggie Haberman, "Sanctions Flap Erupts into Open Conflict between Haley and White House," *New York Times*, April 17, 2018, https://www.nytimes.com/2018/04/17/world/europe/trump

-nikki-haley-russia-sanctions.html?hp&action=click&pgtype=Homepage&click
Source=story-heading&module=first-column-region&region=top-news&WT.nav
=top-news.

233 **not to meddle:** Jen Kirby, "Trump Jokes with Putin About Russian Election Meddling
and Getting 'Rid' of Journalists," *Vox*, June 28, 2019, https://www.vox.com/2019/6/28
/19102498/g20-trump-putin-election-meddling-fake-news.

233 **"a sense of his soul":** "Press Conference by President Bush and Russian Federation
President Putin," White House, Office of the Press Secretary, June 16, 2001, https://
georgewbush-whitehouse.archives.gov/news/releases/2001/06/20010618.html.

CHAPTER 12: REVOLT OF THE GENERALS

235 **"Through your actions":** William H. McRaven, "Revoke My Security Clearance, Too,
Mr. President," *Washington Post*, August 16, 2018, https://www.washingtonpost.com
/opinions/revoke-my-security-clearance-too-mr-president/2018/08/16/8b149b02-a178
-11e8-93e3-24d1703d2a7a_story.html.

237 **"'General' McChrystal":** Donald J. Trump (@realDonaldTrump), "'General' McChrystal got fired like a dog by Obama. Last assignment a total bust. Known for big, dumb
mouth. Hillary lover!," Twitter, January 1, 2019, 10:32 am, https://twitter.com
/realdonaldtrump/status/1080124615920373760.

237 **immoral and dishonest:** Roey Hadar, "Retired Army Gen. Stanley McChrystal: President Donald Trump Immoral, Doesn't Tell the Truth," ABC News, December 30, 2018,
https://abcnews.go.com/Politics/retired-army-gen-stanley-mcchrystal-president
-donald-trump/story?id=60065642.

237 **"pocket of Putin":** John O. Brennan (@JohnBrennan), "Donald Trump's press conference performance in Helsinki rises to & exceeds the threshold of 'high crimes & misdemeanors.' It was nothing short of treasonous. Not only were Trump's comments imbecilic,
he is wholly in the pocket of Putin. Republican Patriots: Where are you???," Twitter, July
16, 2018, 11:52 am, https://twitter.com/johnbrennan/status/1018885971104985093.

238 **"unfounded and outrageous allegations":** "Press Briefing by Press Secretary Sarah Sanders," White House, August 15, 2018, https://www.whitehouse.gov/briefings-statements
/press-briefing-press-secretary-sarah-sanders-081518.

238 **"divided us as a nation":** McRaven, "Revoke My Security Clearance, Too, Mr.
President."

239 **"I don't know McRaven":** Richard Sisk, "Trump Brushes Off Criticism from Adm.
McRaven: 'Don't Know Him,'" Military.com, August 17, 2018, https://www.military
.com/daily-news/2018/08/17/trump-brushes-criticism-adm-mcraven-dont-know-him
.html.

239 **Wallace of Fox News:** Andrew Kragie, "Everything's Political to Trump, Even Killing
Osama bin Laden," *The Atlantic*, November 19, 2018, https://www.theatlantic.com
/politics/archive/2018/11/trump-denigrates-retired-admiral-mcraven-hillary-fan/576157.

240 **outdid one another to flatter:** Tina Nguyen, "Trump Appointees Take Turns Praising
Him in Bizarre Cabinet Meeting," *Vanity Fair*, June 12, 2017, https://www.vanityfair
.com/news/2017/06/donald-trump-cabinet-meeting.

240 **"men and women"**: Adam Linehan, "Mattis Declines to Suck Up to Trump, Praises Troops Instead," *Task & Purpose*, June 13, 2017, https://taskandpurpose.com/mattis -declines-to-suck-up-to-trump-praises-troops-instead.

241 **blindsided by a Trump tweet**: Bob Woodward, *Fear: Trump in the White House* (London: Simon and Schuster, 2018), 202.

242 **"will be coming, nice"**: Donald Trump (@realDonalTrump), "Russia vows to shoot down any and all missiles fired at Syria. Get ready Russia, because they will be coming, nice and new and 'smart!' You shouldn't be partners with a Gas Killing Animal who kills his people and enjoys it!," Twitter, April 11, 2018, 3:57 am, https://twitter.com /realdonaldtrump/status/984022625440747520?lang=en.

244 **"We used a little"**: Anne Gearan and Missy Ryan, "U.S. and Allies Warn Syria of More Missile Strikes If Chemical Attacks Used Again," *Washington Post*, April 14, 2018, https://www.washingtonpost.com/world/national-security/us-launches-missile-strikes -in-syria/2018/04/13/c68e89d0-3f4a-11e8-974f-aacd97698cef_story.html; "Briefing by Secretary Mattis on U.S. Strikes in Syria," US Department of Defense, April 13, 2018, https://www.defense.gov/Newsroom/Transcripts/Transcript/Article/1493658/briefing -by-secretary-mattis-on-us-strikes-in-syria.

245 **Trump also feuded**: "Remarks by President Trump and NATO Secretary General Jens Stoltenberg at Bilateral Breakfast," White House, July 11, 2018, https://www.whitehouse .gov/briefings-statements/remarks-president-trump-nato-secretary-general-jens -stoltenberg-bilateral-breakfast.

245 **"the most successful"**: "To Conduct a Confirmation Hearing on the Expected Nomination of Mr. James N. Mattis to Be Secretary of Defense," Senate Committee on Armed Services, January 12, 2017, https://www.armed-services.senate.gov/imo/media /doc/17-03_01-12-17.pdf.

246 **made it a point**: Tom Vanden Brook, "Defense Secretary Mattis Emphasizes NATO Commitment on First Day," *USA Today*, January 23, 2017, https://www.usatoday.com /story/news/politics/2017/01/23/mattis-support-nato/96971878.

246 **"We simply cannot trust"**: "Remarks by Secretary Mattis on National Defense Strategy," US Department of Defense, December 1, 2018, https://dod.defense.gov/News /Transcripts/Transcript-View/Article/1702965/remarks-by-secretary-mattis-on-national -defense-strategy.

246 **summit in Singapore**: Roberta Rampton, "'We Fell in Love:' Trump Swoons over Letters from North Korea's Kim," Reuters, September 30, 2018, https://www.reuters.com /article/us-northkorea-usa-trump/we-fell-in-love-trump-swoons-over-letters-from -north-koreas-kim-idUSKCN1MA03Q.

246 **ballistic missile program**: David E. Saner et al., "New North Korea Concerns Flare as Trump's Signature Diplomacy Wilts," *New York Times*, May 9, 2019, https://www .nytimes.com/2019/05/09/world/asia/north-korea-missile.html.

246 **mortar attacks landed**: Dion Nissenbaum, "White House Sought Options to Strike Iran," *Wall Street Journal*, January 13, 2019, https://www.wsj.com/articles/white-house -sought-options-to-strike-iran-11547375404.

246 **Mattis blocked Bolton:** Peter Baker and Maggie Haberman, "Trump Undercuts Bolton on North Korea and Iran," *New York Times,* May 28, 2019, https://www.nytimes.com /2019/05/28/us/politics/trump-john-bolton-north-korea-iran.html.

247 **"invasion" of asylum seekers:** Zach Montague, "Pentagon to Send 2,100 More Troops to the Southwestern Border," *New York Times,* July 17, 2019, https://www.nytimes .com/2019/07/17/us/politics/troops-border-immigration.html.

247 **"Tomorrow is one week":** David Folkenflik, "Tensions Rise at Fox News over Coverage and Rhetoric Surrounding Migrant Caravan," NPR, October 30, 2018, https://www .npr.org/2018/10/30/662253600/tensions-rise-at-fox-news-over-coverage-and-rhetoric -surrounding-migrant-caravan.

247 **"sort of a Democrat":** "Trump on Prospect of Mattis' Departure: 'At Some Point, Everybody Leaves,'" CBS News, October 14, 2018, https://www.cbsnews.com/news/trump -60-minutes-interview-president-suggests-defense-secretary-james-mattis-could-be -next-to-leave-cabinet.

247 **off the mark:** Amanda Macias, "Defense Secretary Mattis: 'I've Never Registered for Any Political Party,'" CNBC, October 15, 2018, https://www.cnbc.com/2018/10/16/defense -secretary-mattis-never-registered-for-any-political-party.html.

248 **"We are done":** Jeremy Diamond and Elise Labott, "Trump Told Turkey's Erdogan in Dec. 14 Call about Syria, 'It's All Yours. We Are Done,'" CNN, December 24, 2018, https://www.cnn.com/2018/12/23/politics/donald-trump-erdogan-turkey/index.html.

249 **"period of years":** Peter Bergen, "Trump's Bizarre Decision on Syria," CNN, December 19, 2018, https://www.cnn.com/2018/12/19/opinions/trump-withdrawal-syria-bergen /index.html.

249 **"We have defeated ISIS":** Donald J. Trump (@realDonaldTrump), "We have defeated ISIS in Syria, my only reason for being there during the Trump Presidency," Twitter, December 19, 2018, 9:29 am, https://twitter.com/realdonaldtrump/status/1075397797929775105.

249 **"they're coming back now":** Courtney Kube, Carol E. Lee, and Josh Lederman, "U.S. Troops to Leave Syria as President Trump Declares Victory over ISIS," NBC News, December 20, 2018, https://www.nbcnews.com/news/us-news/u-s-troops-leave-syria -president-trump-declares-victory-over-n949806.

250 **see the president:** "Defense Secretary Jim Mattis Quits in Protest of Trump's Views," *Erin Burnett Outfront,* CNN, December 20, 2018, http://transcripts.cnn.com /TRANSCRIPTS/1812/20/ebo.01.html.

251 **two-page resignation letter:** "James Mattis' Resignation Letter," CNN, December 21, 2018, https://www.cnn.com/2018/12/20/politics/james-mattis-resignation-letter-doc /index.html.

251 **Trump called Secretary of State:** Dan Lamothe, "Trump's Explanation for Why Mattis Left as Defense Secretary Changes Again," *Washington Post,* February 1, 2019, https:// www.washingtonpost.com/national-security/2019/02/01/trumps-explanation-why -mattis-left-defense-secretary-changes-again.

252 **replaced by Patrick Shanahan:** Uri Friedman, "America, Meet Your (Acting) Secretary of Defense," *The Atlantic,* January 1, 2019, https://www.theatlantic.com/international

/archive/2019/01/acting-defense-secretary-shanahan-boeing-experience-trump
/579232.

252 **domestic violence dispute:** Zachary Cohen et al., "Shanahan Withdraws as Trump's
Defense Pick as Domestic Incidents Resurface," CNN, June 18, 2019, https://www
.cnn.com/2019/06/18/politics/shanahan-out-defense-secretary/index.html.

252 **"When President Obama":** Donald J. Trump (@realDonaldTrump), "When President
Obama ingloriously fired Jim Mattis, I gave him a second chance. Some thought I
shouldn't, I thought I should. Interesting relationship-but I also gave all of the resources
that he never really had. Allies are very important-but not when they take advantage
of U.S.," Twitter, December 22, 2018, 9:20 pm, https://twitter.com/realdonaldtrump
/status/1076663817831153664.

253 **"I am pleased":** Donald J. Trump (@realDonaldTrump), "I am pleased to inform you
that I have just named General/Secretary John F Kelly as White House Chief of Staff.
He is a Great American. . . . ," Twitter, July 28, 2017, 4:49 pm, https://twitter.com
/realdonaldtrump/status/891038014314598400.

253 **Kelly saw his tenure:** Molly O'Toole, "John F. Kelly Says His Tenure as Trump's Chief
of Staff Is Best Measured by What the President Did Not Do," *Los Angeles Times*, December 30, 2018, https://www.latimes.com/politics/la-na-pol-john-kelly-exit-interview
-20181230-story.html.

254 **John Bolton was dispatched:** David E. Sanger, Noah Weiland, and Eric Schmitt, "Bolton
Puts Conditions on Syria Withdrawal, Suggesting a Delay of Months or Years," *New
York Times*, January 6, 2019, https://www.nytimes.com/2019/01/06/world/middleeast
/bolton-syria-pullout.html.

254 **"Bolton's remarks in Israel":** Bianca Britton et al., "Turkey's Erdogan Slams Bolton, as
Trump Position on Syria Seems to Shift," CNN, January 8, 2019, https://www.cnn
.com/2019/01/08/politics/erdogan-bolton-syria-kurds-turkey-intl/index.html.

254 **"prudent and necessary":** Donald J. Trump (@realDonaldTrump), "The Failing New
York Times has knowingly written a very inaccurate story on my intentions on Syria. No
different from my original statements, we will be leaving at a proper pace while at the
same time continuing to fight ISIS and doing all else that is prudent and necessary!. . . .,"
Twitter, January 7, 2019, 9:55 am, https://twitter.com/realdonaldtrump/status/1082289
526339448832.

CHAPTER 13: WITHDRAWAL

257 **"There is no instance":** Sun Tzu, *Sun Tzu on the Art of War*, translated by Lionel Giles,
(Leicester, UK: Allandale Online Publishing, 2000), https://sites.ualberta.ca/~enoch
/Readings/The_Art_Of_War.pdf.

257 **"The worst thing":** Donald Trump and Tony Schwartz, *Trump: The Art of the Deal* (New
York: Ballantine Books, 2015), 53.

259 **"in the Middle East":** "Remarks by President Trump in State of the Union Address,"
White House, February 6, 2019, https://www.whitehouse.gov/briefings-statements
/remarks-president-trump-state-union-address-2.

260 **special representative for Afghanistan:** Peter Bergen, "Is the Trump Team Pulling Off a Diplomatic Coup to End America's Longest War?," CNN, January 29, 2019, https://www.cnn.com/2019/01/28/opinions/is-the-trump-team-pulling-off-a-diplomatic-coup-to-end-americas-longest-war-bergen/index.html.

261 **"terms of our surrender":** Ryan Crocker, "I Was Ambassador to Afghanistan. This Deal Is a Surrender," *Washington Post*, January 29, 2019, https://www.washingtonpost.com/opinions/i-was-ambassador-to-afghanistan-this-deal-is-a-surrender/2019/01/29/8700ed68-2409-11e9-ad53-824486280311_story.html.

262 **Khalilzad hadn't spoken:** Bergen, "Is the Trump Team Pulling Off a Diplomatic Coup?"

264 **Sher Mohammad Abbas Stanekzai:** Bergen, "Is the Trump Team Pulling Off a Diplomatic Coup?"

264 **Mohib told the reporters:** Jennifer Hansler and Kylie Atwood, "Senior Afghan Official Accuses US Envoy of 'Delegitimizing' Afghan Government," *CNN*, March 14, 2019, https://www.cnn.com/2019/03/14/politics/mohib-khalilzad-afghanistan-row/index.html.

264 **a supremely undiplomatic attack:** Hansler and Atwood, "Senior Afghan Official Accuses US Envoy."

266 **"it's very important":** "Exclusive Interview: Trump Sits Down with Tucker Carlson in Japan," Fox News, 2019, https://www.youtube.com/watch?v=mRQW675j6dM.

266 **"If we wanted to fight":** Quint Forgey, "Trump: I Could Win Afghanistan War 'in a Week,'" *Politico*, July 22, 2019, https://www.politico.com/story/2019/07/22/trump-afghanistan-war-1425692.

266 **"the kind of U.S. withdrawal":** David Petraeus and Vance Serchuk, "The U.S. Abandoned Iraq. Don't Repeat History in Afghanistan," *Wall Street Journal*, August 9, 2019, https://www.wsj.com/articles/the-u-s-abandoned-iraq-dont-repeat-history-in-afghanistan-11565385301.

CHAPTER 14: THE "INVASION"

269 **"The central image":** Richard Hofstadter, *The Paranoid Style in American Politics and Other Essays* (New York: Vintage Books, 2008), 29.

269 **"This attack is a response":** Peter Baker and Michael D. Shear, "El Paso Shooting Suspect's Manifesto Echoes Trump's Language," *New York Times*, August 4, 2019, https://www.nytimes.com/2019/08/04/us/politics/trump-mass-shootings.html.

271 **"unknown Middle Easterners":** Donald J. Trump (@realDonaldTrump), "Sadly, it looks like Mexico's Police and Military are unable to stop the Caravan heading to the Southern Border of the United States. Criminals and unknown Middle Easterners are mixed in. I have alerted Border Patrol and Military that this is a National Emergy. Must change laws!," Twitter, October 22, 2018, 8:37 am, https://twitter.com/realdonaldtrump/status/1054351078328885248.

271 **lethal terrorist attacks:** Peter Bergen et al., "Terrorism in America after 9/11," New America, accessed August 1, 2019, https://www.newamerica.org/in-depth/terrorism-in-america/who-are-terrorists.

271 **not one . . . southern border:** Peter Bergen, "There Is No National Emergency," CNN, February 14, 2019, https://www.cnn.com/2019/01/07/opinions/border-wall-would-do -nothing-to-stop-terrorism-bergen/index.html.

271 **"no credible information":** Philip Bump, "Key Parts of the Trump Administration's Border Rhetoric Are Wrong, According to the Trump Administration," *Washington Post*, January 8, 2019, https://www.washingtonpost.com/politics/2019/01/08/key-parts -trump-administrations-border-rhetoric-are-wrong-according-trump-administration.

272 **jihadist terrorism cases:** Bergen et al., "Terrorism in America after 9/11."

272 **The largest number:** Bergen et al., "Terrorism in America after 9/11."

272 **"more like an invasion":** "Fox News Host: Migrant Caravan Looks 'More Like an Invasion Than Anything Else,'" *Daily Beast*, November 2, 2018, https://www.thedailybeast .com/fox-news-host-migrant-caravan-looks-more-like-an-invasion-than-anything-else.

272 **"This is an invasion":** Donald J. Trump (@realDonaldTrump), "Many Gang Members and some very bad people are mixed into the Caravan heading to our Southern Border. Please go back, you will not be admitted into the United States unless you go through the legal process. This is an invasion of our Country and our Military is waiting for you!," Twitter, October 29, 2018, 10:41 am, https://twitter.com/realdonaldtrump/status /1056919064906469376.

272 **Robert Bowers murdered:** Julie Turkewitz and Kevin Roose, "Who Is Robert Bowers, the Suspect in the Pittsburgh Synagogue Shooting?," *New York Times*, October 27, 2018, https://www.nytimes.com/2018/10/27/us/robert-bowers-pittsburgh-synagogue-shooter .html.

272 **In early January 2019:** Peter Bergen, "There Is No National Emergency," CNN, February 14, 2019, https://www.cnn.com/2019/01/07/opinions/border-wall-would-do-nothing -to-stop-terrorism-bergen/index.html.

273 **"a big surprise":** Donald J. Trump (@realDonaldTrump), "Border rancher: 'We've found prayer rugs out here. It's unreal.' Washington Examiner People coming across the Southern Border from many countries, some of which would be a big surprise," Twitter, January 18, 2019, 8:22 am, https://twitter.com/realdonaldtrump/status/10862525880 88082432.

273 **no photos of the rugs:** For a recounting of this episode, see Tim Alberta, *American Carnage* (New York: Harper, 2019), 588.

274 **sixty miles of wall:** Lucy Rodgers and Dominic Bailey, "Trump Wall—All You Need to Know about US Border in Seven Charts," BBC News, June 26, 2019, https://www .bbc.com/news/world-us-canada-46824649.

274 **highest homicide rates:** Daniel F. Runde and Mark L Schneider, "A New Social Contract for the Northern Triangle," Center for Strategic and International Studies, May 2019, https://csis-prod.s3.amazonaws.com/s3fs-public/publication/190507_Rundeand Schneider_NTCA_pageproofs3.pdf.

274 **"long faced a persistent security threat":** Peter Bergen and David Sterman, "The Huge Threat to America That Trump Ignores," CNN, August 4, 2019, https://www.cnn.com /2019/08/04/opinions/el-paso-dayton-far-right-threat-bergen-sterman/index.html.

275 **lethal terrorist attack against Hispanics:** Baker and Shear, "El Paso Shooting Suspect's Manifesto."

275 **had predated Trump becoming president:** Bergen and Sterman, "The Huge Threat to America That Trump Ignores."

275 **with the 22 fatalities:** "Part IV. What Is the Threat to the United States Today?" New America, accessed August 13, 2019, https://www.newamerica.org/in-depth/terrorism-in -america/what-threat-united-states-today.

275 **"racism, bigotry and white supremacy":** Catherine Lucey, Rebecca Ballhaus, and Natalie Andrews, "Trump Condemns Racism, Bigotry and White Supremacy After Weekend Shootings," *Wall Street Journal*, August 5, 2019, https://www.wsj.com/articles/trump -suggests-lawmakers-could-combine-gun-background-check-legislation-with-immigra tion-reform-11565004350.

CHAPTER 15: THE PLANES WERE LEAVING

277 **"Everybody has a plan":** Mike Berardino, "Mike Tyson Explains One of His Most Famous Quotes," *South Florida Sun Sentinel*, November 9, 2012, https://www.sun -sentinel.com/sports/fl-xpm-2012-11-09-sfl-mike-tyson-explains-one-of-his-most -famous-quotes-20121109-story.html.

279 **"I stopped it":** Donald J. Trump (@realDonaldTrump), ". . . . On Monday they shot down an unmanned drone flying in International Waters. We were cocked & loaded to retaliate last night on 3 different sights when I asked, how many will die. 150 people, sir, was the answer from a General. 10 minutes before the strike I stopped it, not. . . . ," Twitter, June 21, 2019, 9:03 am, https://twitter.com/realdonaldtrump/status/11420553 88965212161.

279 **avoided service in Vietnam:** Michael Daly, "The Fallen Heroes Who Went to Vietnam in John Bolton's Place," *Daily Beast*, April 13, 2018, https://www.thedailybeast.com /the-fallen-heroes-who-went-to-vietnam-in-john-boltons-place.

280 **the nuclear deal:** Edward Wong, Helene Cooper, and Megan Specia, "Trump Adds Troops after Iran Says It Will Breach Nuclear Deal," *New York Times*, June 17, 2019, https://www.nytimes.com/2019/06/17/world/middleeast/iran-nuclear-deal-compliance .html.

281 **"I'm the one who tempers":** "Trump Says Bolton Doing a Good Job but Has to Temper Him," Reuters, May 9, 2019, https://www.reuters.com/article/us-usa-trump-bolton /trump-says-bolton-doing-a-good-job-but-has-to-temper-him-idUSKCN1SF2AI.

281 **Meanwhile, Bolton, who:** John Bolton (@AmbJohnBolton), "Delighted to be in Ulaanbaatar & looking forward to meeting with officials to find ways to harness Mongolia's capabilities in support of our shared economic & security objectives. Thank you for the warm welcome Secretary of State @davaasuren_d," Twitter, June 30, 2019, 7:12 am, https://twitter.com/ambjohnbolton/status/1145288948291440642.

281 **Colonel Douglas Macgregor:** "Tom Homan: Migrant Families Are Coming in at Record Numbers Because They Know We Can't Detain Them All," *Tucker Carlson Tonight*, Fox News, May 20, 2019, https://www.foxnews.com/transcript/tom-homan -migrant-families-are-coming-in-at-record-numbers-because-they-know-we-cant-detain -them-all.

282 **Oil prices jumped:** "Oil Jumps 3% Towards $64 as US Drone Downed in Gulf," *RTÉ*, June 20, 2019, https://www.rte.ie/news/business/2019/0620/1056413-world-oil -prices.

282 **troops to the Middle East:** "Statement from the National Security Adviser Ambassador John Bolton," White House, May 5, 2019, https://www.whitehouse.gov/briefings -statements/statement-national-security-adviser-ambassador-john-bolton-2.

282 **"the official end of Iran":** Donald J. Trump (@realDonaldTrump), "If Iran wants to fight, that will be the official end of Iran. Never threaten the United States again!," Twitter, May 19, 2019, 4:25 pm, https://twitter.com/realdonaldtrump/status /1130207891049332737.

282 **"a very big mistake":** Donald J. Trump (@realDonaldTrump), "Iran made a very big mistake!," Twitter, June 20, 2019, 10:15 am, https://twitter.com/realdonaldtrump/status /1141711064305983488.

282 **halved Iran's oil exports:** Alex Lawler, "Hit by Sanctions and Rising Tensions, Iran's Oil Exports Slide in July," Reuters, July 30, 2019, https://www.reuters.com/article/us -oil-iran-exports/hit-by-sanctions-and-rising-tensions-irans-oil-exports-slide-in-july -idUSKCN1UP1UD.

282 **reduce its support:** Liz Sly and Suzan Haidamous, "Trump's Sanctions on Iran Are Hitting Hezbollah, and It Hurts," *Washington Post*, May 18, 2019, https://www.wash ingtonpost.com/world/middle_east/trumps-sanctions-on-iran-are-hitting-hezbollah -hard/2019/05/18/970bc656-5d48-11e9-98d4-844088d135f2_story.html.

282 **Zarif told reporters:** David E. Sanger, "Iran's Foreign Minister Proposes Modest Deal to End Impasse with U.S.," *New York Times*, July 18, 2019, https://www.nytimes.com /2019/07/18/us/politics/zarif-iran-nuclear-deal.html.

283 **"not be shortsighted":** Farnaz Fassihi, "As Conflict with U.S. Grows, Some Iran Hard-Liners Suggest Talking to Trump," *New York Times*, July 19, 2019, https://www.nytimes .com/2019/07/19/world/middleeast/iran-hard-liners-trump-talks.html.

283 **above 4.5 percent:** Parisa Hafezi, "Iran to Lift Uranium Enrichment to 5%, above Level in 2015 Deal: Official," Reuters, July 6, 2019, https://www.reuters.com/article/us -mideast-iran-usa-announcement/iran-to-lift-uranium-enrichment-to-5-above-level-in -2015-deal-official-idUSKCN1U10HP.

CHAPTER 16: COMMANDER IN CHIEF

287 **It was a roll call:** Donald J. Trump, "Remarks by President Trump at a Salute to America," Speech, Washington, DC, January 4, 2019, https://www.whitehouse.gov/briefings -statements/remarks-president-trump-salute-america.

287 **Confounding his critics:** Madeleine Joung, "President Trump Has Planned a Controversial Fourth of July 'Salute to America,' Here's What to Know," *Time*, July 4, 2019, https://time.com/5619191/donald-trump-july-4-speech-controversy.

288 **Trump watched as dozens:** Jabeen Bhatti and Jane Onyanga-Omara, "President Trump Is Guest of Honor at Ornate Paris Bastille Day Celebrations," CNBC, July 14, 2017,

https://www.cnbc.com/2017/07/14/president-trump-is-guest-of-honor-at-ornate-paris
-bastille-day-celebrations.html.

288 **Initially, Trump planned:** Tamara Keith, "Trump's Military Parade Could Cost As
Much As $50 Million," NPR, February 15, 2018, https://www.npr.org/2018/02/15
/585924807/trumps-military-parade-could-cost-as-much-as-50-million.

288 **As a light rain fell:** Trump, "Remarks by President Trump at a Salute to America."

288 **Trump presided over substantial increases:** James N. Miller and Michael E. O'Hanlon,
"Quality over Quantity: U.S. Military Strategy and Spending in the Trump Years,"
Brookings, January 2019, https://www.brookings.edu/research/quality-over-quantity-u
-s-military-strategy-and-spending-in-the-trump-years.

291 **by Christmas 2020:** Gordon Lubold and Nancy A. Youssef, "Trump Says He Wants All
Troops in Afghanistan Home by Christmas, Going Further Than Security Adviser,"
Wall Street Journal, October 8, 2020, https://www.wsj.com/articles/trump-says-he-wants
-all-troops-in-afghanistan-home-by-christmas-going-further-than-security-adviser
-11602130656.

291 **2,500 troops in the country:** Robert Burns and Lolita C. Baldor, "Pentagon Says US
Has Dropped to 2,500 Troops in Afghanistan," Associated Press, January 15, 2021,
https://apnews.com/article/joe-biden-donald-trump-afghanistan-taliban-united
-states-16cc1dd5b2f74d463311d212ad0d215a.

291 **conflict in Gaza:** "Gaza-Israel Conflict in Pictures: 11 Days of Destruction," BBC,
May 21, 2021, https://www.bbc.com/news/world-middle-east-57205968.

291 **only six of the twenty-nine:** "Defence Expenditure of NATO Countries (2011-2018),"
North Atlantic Treaty Organization, News release, July 10, 2018, https://www.nato.int
/nato_static_fl2014/assets/pdf/pdf_2018_07/20180709_180710-pr2018-91-en.pdf.

292 **J-31 stealth fighter:** Jim Sciutto, *The Shadow War: Inside Russia's and China's Secret
Operations to Defeat America* (New York: Harper Collins, 2019), 54.

292 **Intellectual property theft:** Sherisse Pham, "How Much Has the US Lost from China's
IP Theft?," CNN, March 23, 2018, https://money.cnn.com/2018/03/23/technology
/china-us-trump-tariffs-ip-theft/index.html.

292 **During the campaign, Trump:** Michelle Ye Hee Lee, "Donald Trump's Claim That
China 'Will Enter' the Trans-Pacific Partnership 'at a Later Date,'" *Washington Post*,
June 30, 2016, https://www.washingtonpost.com/news/fact-checker/wp/2016/06/30
/donald-trumps-claim-that-china-will-enter-the-trans-pacific-partnership-at-a-later-date.

292 **In fact, China was not part:** James McBride and Andrew Chatzky, "What Is the Trans-
Pacific Partnership (TPP)?," Council on Foreign Relations, January 4, 2019, https://
www.cfr.org/backgrounder/what-trans-pacific-partnership-tpp.

292 **It was striking, then:** Idrees Ali, "U.S. Military Puts 'Great Power Competition' at
Heart of Strategy: Mattis," Reuters, January 19, 2018, https://www.reuters.com/article
/us-usa-military-china-russia/u-s-military-puts-great-power-competition-at-heart
-of-strategy-mattis-idUSKBN1F81TR.

292 **it was China:** "The World Bank in China Overview," The World Bank, April 8, 2019,
https://www.worldbank.org/en/country/china/overview.

293　**"building the most capable"**: "National Security Strategy of the United States of America," White House, December 2017, https://www.whitehouse.gov/wp-content/uploads /2017/12/NSS-Final-12-18-2017-0905-2.pdf.

293　**"a fight with a different civilization"**: Kiron Skinner, "What Does the State Department Think Will Be the Challenges of 2030?," New America, ASU Future Security Forum, April 29, 2019, https://www.youtube.com/watch?v=dZJL0NfJtaQ.

293　**"the first time that"**: "What Does the State Department Think Will Be the Challenges of 2030?," Interview by Anne-Marie Slaughter and Kiron Skinner, Future Security Forum 2019, April 29, 2019, https://www.youtube.com/watch?v=dZJL0NfJtaQ& t=21s.

293　**For Trump, the military aspirations**: Ben White and Aubree Eliza Weaver, "Trump Makes No Sense on Tariffs," *Politico*, September 18, 2018, https://www.politico.com /newsletters/morning-money/2018/09/18/trump-makes-no-sense-on-tariffs-344232.

293　**Trump imposed additional tariffs**: "USTR Announces Next Steps on Proposed 10 Percent Tariff on Imports from China," Office of the United States Trade Representative, August 13, 2019, https://ustr.gov/about-us/policy-offices/press-office/press-releases /2019/august/ustr-announces-next-steps-proposed.

293　**new tariffs would only be applied**: "USTR Announces Next Steps on Proposed 10 Percent Tariff on Imports from China."

294　**Trump presided over**: Teddy Ng, "US Steps up Freedom of Navigation Patrols in South China Sea to Counter Beijing's Ambitions," *South China Morning Post*, February 16, 2019.

295　**communications and operations**: For more on the Chinese militarization of space, see Jim Sciutto, *The Shadow War*, 163.

295　**Pentagon had considered climate change**: "Report on Effects of a Changing Climate to the Department of Defense," Department of Defense, Office of the Under Secretary of Defense for Acquisition and Sustainment, January 2019, https://climateandsecurity .files.wordpress.com/2019/01/sec_335_ndaa-report_effects_of_a_changing_climate _to_dod.pdf.

295　**Paris climate agreement**: Michael D. Shear, "Trump Will Withdraw U.S. from Paris Climate Agreement," *New York Times*, June 1, 2017, https://www.nytimes.com/2017 /06/01/climate/trump-paris-climate-agreement.html.

295　**"I was elected by voters"**: "Statement by President Trump on the Paris Climate Accord," White House, June 1, 2017, https://www.whitehouse.gov/briefings-statements /statement-president-trump-paris-climate-accord.

295　**as an "expensive hoax"**: Donald J. Trump (@realDonaldTrump), "We should be focused on magnificently clean and healthy air and not distracted by the expensive hoax that is global warming!," Twitter, December 6, 2013, 7:38 am, https://twitter .com/realDonaldTrump/status/408983789830815744?ref_src=twsrc%5Etfw%7 Ctwcamp%5Etweetembed%7Ctwterm%5E408983789830815744&ref_url=https %3A%2F%2Fwww.vox.com%2Fpolicy-and-politics%2F2017%2F6%2F1 %2F15726472%2Ftrump-tweets-global-warming-paris-climate-agreement.

295 **"the concept of global warming"**: Donald J. Trump (@realDonaldTrump), "The concept of global warming was created by and for the Chinese in order to make U.S. manufacturing non-competitive," Twitter, November 6, 2012, 11:15 am, https://twitter.com /realdonaldtrump/status/265895292191248385?lang=ca.

295 **"I'm not denying climate change"**: "Trump Says Climate Change Not a 'Hoax' but Questions If It's 'Manmade,'" CBS, October 15, 2018, https://www.cbsnews.com/news /trump-says-climate-change-not-a-hoax-but-questions-if-its-manmade.

295 **"Large parts of the Country"**: Donald J. Trump (@realDonaldTrump), "Be careful and try staying in your house. Large parts of the country are suffering from tremendous amounts of snow and near record setting cold. Amazing how big this system is. Wouldn't be bad to have a little of that good old fashioned Global Warming right now!," Twitter, January 20, 2019, 4:59 am, https://twitter.com/realdonaldtrump/status/108697149972 5160448?lang=en.

296 **"I believe that there is"**: "Interview: Piers Morgan Interviews Donald Trump on Good Morning Britain—July 16, 2018," *Good Morning Britain*, July 13, 2018, https://www .youtube.com/watch?v=Y8dzpol5D0Q.

297 **disagreed about the facts**: Zeke Miller, Eric Tucker, and Deb Riechmann, "Trump Says Coats Is Out as National Intelligence Director," Associated Press, July 29, 2019, https://www.apnews.com/6ad59c9104dc425bba166de4b9723612.

297 **"We continue to assess"**: Daniel R. Coats, "Statement for the Record: Worldwide Threat Assessment of the US Intelligence Senate Select Committee on Intelligence," January 29, 2019, https://www.dni.gov/files/ODNI/documents/2019-ATA-SFR ---SSCI.pdf.

297 **"Perhaps Intelligence should"**: Donald J. Trump (@realDonaldTrump), ". . . . a source of potential danger and conflict. They are testing Rockets (last week) and more, and are coming very close to the edge. There economy is now crashing, which is the only thing holding them back. Be careful of Iran. Perhaps Intelligence should go back to school!" Twitter, January 30, 2019, 5:56 am, https://twitter.com/realdonaldtrump/status/10906095 77006112769?lang=en.

297 **Ratcliffe, a three-term House member**: Peter Bergen, "Trump Clashes with a Truth Teller and Replaces Him with a Partisan Sycophant," CNN, July 29, 2019, https://www .cnn.com/2019/07/29/opinions/trump-clashes-with-truth-teller-bergen/index.html.

298 **"I think we need somebody"**: Jonathan Landay, "Defending Intelligence Pick, Trump Says U.S. Spy Agencies 'Run Amok,'" Reuters, July 30, 2019, https://www.reuters.com /article/us-usa-trump-intelligence/defending-intelligence-pick-trump-says-u-s-spy -agencies-run-amok-idUSKCN1UP2JX.

298 **together with his scant qualifications**: Paul Waldman and Greg Sargent, "Another Trump Nominee Goes Down in Flames. This Is a Big One," *Washington Post*, August 2, 2019, https://www.washingtonpost.com/opinions/2019/08/02/another-trump-nominee -goes-down-flames-this-is-big-one/.

298 **K. T. McFarland**: Adam Entous, "The Agonizingly Slow Downfall of K. T. McFarland," *New Yorker*, January 29, 2018, https://www.newyorker.com/news/news-desk /the-agonizingly-slow-downfall-of-k-t-mcfarland.

298 **Bill Shine:** Maggie Haberman, "Bill Shine, Ousted from Fox News in Scandal, Joins White House Communications Team," *New York Times,* July 5, 2018, https://www.nytimes .com/2018/07/05/us/politics/bill-shine-white-house-communications.html.

298 **Mercedes Schlapp:** "President Donald J. Trump Announces White House Appointments," White House, September 12, 2017, https://www.whitehouse.gov/presidential -actions/president-donald-j-trump-announces-white-house-appointments-2.

298 **Heather Nauert:** Emily Tamkin, "Trump Will Nominate a Former Fox News Host and State Department Spokesperson to the Top UN Job," *BuzzFeed News,* December 7, 2018, https://www.buzzfeednews.com/article/emilytamkin/heather-nauert-trump-fox -news-un-ambassador-nominate.

298 **Morgan Ortagus:** Samuel Chamberlain and John Roberts, "Morgan Ortagus to Be Named State Department Spokeswoman," Fox News, April 2, 2019, https://www .foxnews.com/politics/morgan-ortagus-to-be-named-state-department-spokeswoman.

299 **"You've got to be honest":** Nick Givas, "Tucker Carlson Says Trump 'Dominated' Kim as 'Wheezing' North Korean Dictator Struggled," Fox News, June 30, 2019, https:// www.foxnews.com/politics/trump-kim-north-korea-dominated-wheezing-dmz -tucker-carlson.

299 **"as dumb as a rock":** Allan Smith, "Trump Lashes Out at Rex Tillerson for Saying Putin Out-prepared Him," NBC News, May 23, 2019, https://www.nbcnews.com /politics/donald-trump/trump-lashes-out-rex-tillerson-saying-putin-out-prepared -him-n1009156.

299 **"What's he done for me?":** Leo Shane III, "Trump Insists He Fired Mattis, Says Former Defense Secretary Was 'Not Too Good' at the Job," *Military Times,* January 2, 2019, https://www.militarytimes.com/news/pentagon-congress/2019/01/02/trump-insists -he-fired-mattis-says-former-defense-secretary-was-not-too-good-at-the-job/.

299 **Trump so berated Homeland Security Secretary:** Michael D. Shear and Nicole Perl- roth, "Kirstjen Nielsen, Chief of Homeland Security, Almost Resigns After Trump Tirade," *New York Times,* May 10, 2018, https://www.nytimes.com/2018/05/10/us /politics/trump-homeland-security-secretary-resign.html.

299 **America's racial divisions:** Peter Baker, "Trump Fans the Flames of a Racial Fire," *New York Times*, July 14, 2019, https://www.nytimes.com/2019/07/14/us/politics/trump -twitter-race.html.

299 **baseless conspiracy theories:** Zachary B. Wolf, "How Trump's Paranoia and Conspir- acy Theories Become US Policy," CNN, August 12, 2019, https://www.cnn.com/2019 /08/12/politics/trump-conspiracy-theories-jeffrey-epstein/index.html.

299 **made false claims:** "100 Days of Trump Claims," *Washington Post,* https://www.wash ingtonpost.com/graphics/politics/trump-claims/?utm_term=.eafb5fb96211.

300 **grabbing an unfair share:** For a larger discussion of this point, see Arlie Russell Hoch- schild, *Strangers in Their Own Land: Anger and Mourning on the American Right* (New York: New Press, 2016).

300 **"We all share":** "Remarks by President Trump at a Salute to America," White House, July 5, 2019, https://www.whitehouse.gov/briefings-statements/remarks-president-trump -salute-america.

300 **"And from the banks"**: "Remarks by President Trump at a Salute to America."

301 **"Why don't they go back"**: Donald J. Trump (@realDonaldTrump), ". . . and viciously telling the people of the United States, the greatest and most powerful Nation on earth, how our government is to be run. Why don't they go back and help fix the totally broken and crime infested places from which they came. Then come back and show us how. . . . ," Twitter, July 14, 2019, 5:27 am, https://twitter.com/realdonaldtrump/status /1150381395078000643?lang=en.

302 **"locked and loaded"**: Donald J. Trump (@realDonaldTrump), https://twitter.com /realDonaldTrump/status/1173368423381962752.

CHAPTER 17: THE FINAL YEAR

305 **Jim Mattis launched:** Jim Mattis and Bing West, *Call Sign Chaos: Learning to Lead* (New York: Random House), 2019.

305 **Upper East Side:** "Distinguished Voices Series with Jim Mattis," Council on Foreign Relations, September 3, 2019, www.cfr.org/event/distinguished-voices-series-jim-mattis-0.

305 **"a truly consequential election":** "Distinguished Voices Series with Jim Mattis."

305 **"I'm old fashioned":** Mattis and West, *Call Sign Chaos*, xiii.

306 **sold for a reported $300 million:** David Carr, "Covering the World of Business, Digital Only," *New York Times*, September 23, 2012, www.nytimes.com/2012/09/24/business /media/with-digital-only-quartz-atlantic-to-cover-business-world.html.

306 **into a profitable enterprise:** "The Atlantic Announces Expansion," *The Atlantic*, February 21, 2018, www.theatlantic.com/press-releases/archive/2018/02/the-atlantic-announces -expansion/553871.

306 **for $100 million:** Lukas I. Alpert, "The Atlantic, Propped Up by Laurene Powell Jobs, Charts New Course," *Wall Street Journal*, August 24, 2019, www.wsj.com/articles/the -atlantic-propped-up-by-steve-jobss-widow-charts-new-course-11566651600.

308 **a "residual force":** Mattis and West, *Call Sign Chaos*, 206–8.

308 **"filled by Sunni terrorists":** Mattis and West, *Call Sign Chaos*, 206–8.

308 **egging on the president:** Bob Sellers, "Tariff Man: Behind Trump Economic Advisor Peter Navarro's Long Quest to Ratchet Up the Trade War With China," *Forbes*, August 27, 2019, https://fortune.com/2019/08/27/tariff-man-behind-trump-economic-advisor -peter-navarros-long-quest-to-ratchet-up-the-trade-war-with-china.

309 **"a heat-seeking missile":** Susan B. Glasser, "Mike Pompeo, The Secretary of Trump," *New Yorker*, August 19, 2019, www.newyorker.com/magazine/2019/08/26/mike-pompeo -the-secretary-of-trump.

309 **a call that he made:** "Read Trump's Phone Conversation with Volodymyr Zelensky," CNN, September 26, 2019, www.cnn.com/2019/09/25/politics/donald-trump-ukraine -transcript-call/index.html.

309 **Bolton had advised:** Carol E. Lee et al., "Bolton Criticizes Trump Policy on North Korea as Sources Say He Opposed Call to Ukraine," NBC, September 30, 2019, www .nbcnews.com/politics/national-security/john-bolton-says-north-korea-will-never-give -nuclear-weapons-n1060286.

309 **Pompeo listening in:** Jason Horowitz and Richard Pérez-Peña, "Pompeo Confirms He Listened to Trump's Call to Ukraine President," *New York Times*, October 2, 2019, www.nytimes.com/2019/10/02/world/europe/pompeo-trump-italy.html.

309 **general Keith Kellogg:** Greg Miller, Greg Jaffe, and Ashley Parker, "Trump Involved Pence in Efforts to Pressure Ukraine's Leader, Though Officials Say Vice President Was Unaware of Allegations in Whistleblower Complaint," *Washington Post*, October 2, 2019, https://washingtonpost.com/world/national-security/trump-involved-pence-in -efforts-to-pressure-ukraines-leader-though-aides-say-vice-president-was-unaware-of -pursuit-of-dirt-on-bidens/2019/10/02/263aa9e2-e4a7-11e9-b403-f738899982 d2_story.html.

309 **he continued to support:** Anton Troianovski and Ksenia Ivanova, "To Avoid Sanctions, Kremlin Goes off the Grid," *Washington Post*, November 21, 2018, www.washingtonpost .com/news/world/wp/2018/11/21/feature/how-russia-avoids-sanctions-and-supports -rebels-in-eastern-ukraine-using-a-financial-system.

309 **$400 million of military assistance:** Karoun Demirijian et al., "Trump Ordered Hold on Military Aid Days before Calling Ukrainian President, Officials Say," *Washington Post*, September 23, 2019, www.washingtonpost.com/national-security/trump-ordered -hold-on-military-aid-days-before-calling-ukrainian-president-officials-say/2019/09 /23/df93a6ca-de38-11e9-8dc8-498eabc129a0_story.html.

309 **Ukrainian investigators had concluded:** Will England, "Ukraine's New Chief Prosecu-tor to 'Audit' Biden Case," *Washington Post*, October 4, 2019, www.washingtonpost .com/world/europe/ukraines-new-chief-prosecutor-to-audit-biden-case/2019/10/04 /fce8d3fa-e68d-11e9-a6e8-8759c5c7f608_story.html.

309 **"I would like you to do us a favor":** "Read Trump's Phone Conversation with Volody-myr Zelensky."

310 **but here was the president:** Scott Shane, "How a Fringe Theory About Ukraine Took Root in the White House," *New York Times*, October 3, 2019, www.nytimes.com/2019 /10/03/us/politics/trump-ukraine-conspiracy.html.

310 **erratic and bombastic:** Adam K. Raymond and Matt Stieb, "The Wildest Moments From Rudy Giuliani's Ukraine Scandal Media Blitz," *New York Magazine*, October 3, 2019, http://nymag.com/intelligencer/2019/10/rudy-giuliani-ukraine-media-wild -moments.html.

310 **Trump doubled down:** Peter Baker and Eileen Sullivan, "Trump Publicly Urges China to Investigate the Bidens," *New York Times*, October 3, 2019, www.nytimes.com/2019 /10/03/us/politics/trump-china-bidens.html.

310 **moved House Speaker Nancy Pelosi:** Heather Caygle et al., "Why Pelosi and Her Party Finally Embraced Impeachment," *Politico*, September 26, 2019, www.politico.com /news/2019/09/26/nancy-pelosi-impeachment-trump-002118.

310 **an impeachment process:** Philip Ewing and Amita Kelly, "House Democrats Unveil 2 Articles Of Impeachment Against Trump," NPR, December 10, 2019, https://www .npr.org/2019/12/10/786569843/house-democrats-expected-to-unveil-articles-of -impeachment-tuesday.

310 **acquitted the president:** Nicholas Fandos, "Trump Acquitted of Two Impeachment Charges in Near Party-Line Vote," *New York Times*, February 5, 2020, https://www.nytimes.com/2020/02/05/us/politics/trump-acquitted-impeachment.html.

311 **murder of George Floyd:** Evan Hill et al., "How George Floyd Was Killed in Police Custody," *New York Times*, May 31, 2020, https://www.nytimes.com/2020/05/31/us/george-floyd-investigation.html.

311 **Trump threatened to send:** Dan Lamothe and Missy Ryan, "Trump Pulls Military into Political Fray of Minneapolis Unrest but Is Unlikely to Follow Through on Threat," *Washington Post*, May 29, 2020, https://www.washingtonpost.com/national-security/trump-unlikely-to-follow-through-on-threat-to-deploy-military-in-minneapolis-unrest-but-has-authority-to-do-so/2020/05/29/ac88c794-a1d1-11ea-9d96-c3f7c755fd6e_story.html.

311 **they were called up:** Paul Taylor and Carlos Sanchez, "Bush Orders Troops into Los Angeles," *Washington Post*, May 2, 1992, https://www.washingtonpost.com/archive/politics/1992/05/02/bush-orders-troops-into-los-angeles/4c4711a6-f18c-41ed-b796-6a8a50d6120d/. This section draws on Peter Bergen, "Trump Threatens to Unleash the Military in the US. When Will the Generals Speak Out?," CNN, June 2, 2020, https://www.cnn.com/2020/06/02/opinions/generals-must-speak-out-on-trump-bergen/index.html.

311 **More than fifty people:** Rich Connell and Ted Rohrlich, "Webster to Head Probe of Police Response to Riot," *Los Angeles Times*, May 12, 1992, https://www.latimes.com/archives/la-xpm-1992-05-12-mn-1690-story.html.

311 **invitation of California's governor:** Alicia Victoria Lozano, "The Insurrection Act Was Last Used in the 1992 Los Angeles Riots. Invoking It Again Could Undo Years of Police Reform, Some Warn," NBC News, June 4, 2020, https://www.nbcnews.com/news/us-news/insurrection-act-was-last-used-1992-los-angeles-riots-invoking-n1224356.

311 **"put him in charge":** Amanda Macias, "Trump Says the Top U.S. Military Officer Is 'In Charge' as George Floyd Protests Rock the Nation," CNBC, June 1, 2021, https://www.cnbc.com/2020/06/01/george-floyd-protests-trump-puts-top-us-military-officer-in-charge.html.

311 **not responsible for domestic:** Amanda Macias, "Pentagon Official Walks Back Trump Claim That Top Military Officer Is In Charge of Protest Response," CNBC, June 2, 2020, https://www.cnbc.com/2020/06/02/pentagon-official-walks-back-trump-claim-that-top-military-officer-is-in-charge-of-protest-response.html.

311 **"the battle space":** Missy Ryan and Dan Lamothe, "Trump Administration to Significantly Expand Military Response in Washington amid Unrest," *Washington Post*, June 1, 2020, https://www.washingtonpost.com/national-security/defense-secretary-pledges-pentagon-support-to-help-dominate-the-battlespace-amid-unrest/2020/06/01/7c5b4630-a449-11ea-8681-7d471bf20207_story.html.

311 **"If you don't dominate":** "President Trump's Call with US Governors over Protests," CNN, June 1, 2020, https://www.cnn.com/2020/06/01/politics/wh-governors-call-protests/index.html.

311 **protesters gathered outside:** "Police in D.C. Make Arrests after Sweeping Peaceful Protesters from Park with Gas, Shoving," *Washington Post*, June 1, 2020, https://www.washingtonpost.com/dc-md-va/2020/06/01/dc-protest-george-floyd-white-house.

311 **led a mounted charge:** Gordon F. Sander, "The Last Time the U.S. Army Cleared Demonstrators from Pennsylvania Avenue," *Politico*, June 7, 2020, https://www.politico.com/news/magazine/2020/06/07/us-army-demonstrations-washington-305913.

311 **flash grenades and tear gas:** Katie Rogers, "Protesters Dispersed with Tear Gas So Trump Could Pose at Church," *New York Times*, June 1, 2020, https://www.nytimes.com/2020/06/01/us/politics/trump-st-johns-church-bible.html.

312 **"church of the presidents":** *The History and Heritage of the Church of the Presidents*, 2010, video, https://www.loc.gov/item/webcast-4913.

312 **chairman Admiral Mike Mullen:** Mike Mullen, "I Cannot Remain Silent," *The Atlantic*, June 2, 2020, https://www.theatlantic.com/ideas/archive/2020/06/american-cities-are-not-battlespaces/612553.

312 **Jim Mattis evidently felt:** Jeffrey Goldberg, "James Mattis Denounces President Trump, Describes Him as a Threat to the Constitution," *The Atlantic*, June 3, 2020, https://www.theatlantic.com/politics/archive/2020/06/james-mattis-denounces-trump-protests-militarization/612640.

312 **Trump struck back:** Orion Rummler, "Trump Hits Back at Mattis, 'I Gave Him a New Life,'" *Axios*, June 4, 2020, https://www.axios.com/trump-james-mattis-twitter-b48287b9-e5db-47f0-aeb0-ebdfd5a5f831.html.

312 **General Martin Dempsey:** Steve Inskeep, "Former Joint Chiefs Chairman Condemns Trump's Threat to Use Military at Protests," NPR, June 4, 2020, https://www.npr.org/2020/06/04/870004024/former-joint-chiefs-chairman-condemns-trumps-threat-to-use-military-at-protests. This section draws on Peter Bergen, "The Elite Military Club That's Scorning Trump," CNN, June 8, 2020, https://www.cnn.com/2020/06/08/opinions/elite-military-club-scorning-trump-bergen/index.html.

312 **John Kelly, also weighed in:** Anthony Scaramucci, "General John F. Kelly: Inside the White House—SALT Talks," SALT, June 5, 2020, https://youtu.be/_zAu3cZdQVQ.

312 **Vincent Brooks, who had commanded:** Ret. Army Gen. Vincent K. Brooks, "Dismay and Disappointment—a Breach of Sacred Trust," *Army Times*, June 6, 2020, https://www.armytimes.com/opinion/2020/06/06/dismay-and-disappointmenta-breach-of-sacred-trust.

312 **Colin Powell, the chairman:** Devan Cole, "Colin Powell: Trump Has 'Drifted Away' from the Constitution," CNN, June 7, 2020, https://www.cnn.com/2020/06/07/politics/colin-powell-donald-trump-protests-cnntv/index.html.

313 **Even Mark Esper:** "Secretary of Defense Esper Addresses Reporters Regarding Civil Unrest," US Department of Defense, June 3, 2020, https://www.defense.gov/News/Transcripts/Transcript/Article/2206685/secretary-of-defense-esper-addresses-reporters-regarding-civil-unrest; Rebecca Kheel, "Pentagon Chief Breaks with Trump, Opposes Invoking Insurrection Act," *The Hill*, June 3, 2020, https://thehill.com/policy/defense/500877-us-defense-chief-does-not-support-invoking-insurrection-act.

313 **Esper had been "terminated":** Helene Cooper, Eric Schmitt, and Maggie Haberman, "Trump Fires Mark Esper, Defense Secretary Who Opposed Use of Troops on U.S. Streets," *New York Times*, November 9, 2020, https://www.nytimes.com/2020/11/09 /us/politics/esper-defense-secretary.html.

313 **idolizing World War II generals:** Hampton Sides, "Douglas MacArthur Is One of America's Most Famous Generals. He's Also the Most Overrated," *Time*, November 13, 2019, https://time.com/5724009/douglas-macarthur-is-one-of-americas-most-famous-gene rals-hes-also-the-most-overrated.

313 **US military budgets:** Jeff Stein and Aaron Gregg, "U.S. Military Spending Set to Increase for Fifth Consecutive Year, Nearing Levels during Height of Iraq War," *Washington Post*, April 18, 2019, https://www.washingtonpost.com/us-policy/2019/04/18 /us-military-spending-set-increase-fifth-consecutive-year-nearing-levels-during-height -iraq-war/.

313 **more than three hundred public:** Brianna Kablack et al., "The Military Speaks Out," New America, https://www.newamerica.org/international-security/blog/military-speaks -out.

313 **it was a "mistake":** David Welna, "Gen. Mark Milley Says Accompanying Trump to Church Photo-Op Was a Mistake," NPR, June 11, 2020, https://www.npr.org/sections /live-updates-protests-for-racial-justice/2020/06/11/875019346/gen-mark-milley-says -accompanying-trump-to-church-photo-op-was-a-mistake.

313 **Milley issued the apology:** "Gen. Mark Milley's Keynote Address to National Defense University Class of 2020 Graduates," Joint Staff Public Affairs, June 11, 2020, https:// youtu.be/7AKmmApwi0M.

314 **Occasionally Trump seemed to grasp:** "Members of the Coronavirus Task Force Hold a Press Briefing," US Department of State, March 29, 2020, https://youtu.be/_lkQhzK tUG4.

314 **Imperial College London:** Neil M. Ferguson et al., "Report 9: Impact of Non-pharmaceutical Interventions (NPIs) to Reduce Covid-19 Mortality and Healthcare Demand," Imperial College Covid-19 Response Team, March 16, 2020, https://doi.org/10.255 61/77482. This section draws on Peter Bergen, "Trump Finally Leveled with the American People," March 30, 2020, https://www.cnn.com/2020/03/30/opinions/trump-leveled -with-american-people-opinion-bergen/index.html.

314 **change in Trump's thinking:** William Booth, "A Chilling Scientific Paper Helped Upend U.S. and U.K. Coronavirus Strategies," *Washington Post*, March 17, 2020, https:// www.washingtonpost.com/world/europe/a-chilling-scientific-paper-helped-upend-us -and-uk-coronavirus-strategies/2020/03/17/aaa84116-6851-11ea-b199-3a9799c545 12_story.html.

314 **"Couple of weeks ago":** Berkeley Lovelace Jr. and Kevin Breuninger, "Trump Says He Takes Hydroxychloroquine to Prevent Coronavirus Infection Even Though It's an Unproven Treatment," CNBC, May 18, 2020, https://www.cnbc.com/2020/05/18/trump -says-he-takes-hydroxychloroquine-to-prevent-coronavirus-infection.html.

314 **Food and Drug Administration:** "Hydroxychloroquine or Chloroquine for COVID-19: Drug Safety Communication—FDA Cautions Against Use Outside of the Hospital Setting or a Clinical Trial Due to Risk of Heart Rhythm Problems," US Food and Drug

Administration, April 24, 2020, https://www.fda.gov/safety/medical-product-safety
-information/hydroxychloroquine-or-chloroquine-covid-19-drug-safety-communica
tion-fda-cautions-against-use. This section draws on Peter Bergen, "What's Behind the
Trumps' Covid Quackery?," CNN, May 20, 2020, https://lite.cnn.com/en/article/h_b995
24d3be8dc99726412fd4b93c4b27.

314 **News anchor Neil Cavuto:** Ursula Perano, "Stunned Fox News Host Reacts to Trump
Taking Hydroxychloroquine," *Axios*, May 19, 2020, https://www.axios.com/hydroxychlo
roquine-trump-fox-news-neil-cavuto-be0928c6-7313-407f-9d93-5fb16037b2b6.html.

314 **Eric Trump told Fox News:** Victor Garcia, "Eric Trump Says Democrats 'Trying to
Milk' Coronavirus Shutdown, Media 'Stoking Fear,'" Fox News, May 17, 2020, https://
www.foxnews.com/media/eric-trump-says-democrats-trying-to-milk-coronavirus-shut
down-media-stoking-fear.

315 **drive-through nationwide testing sites:** Yasmeen Abutaleb and Damian Paletta, *Nightmare Scenario: Inside the Trump Administration's Response to the Pandemic That Changed
History* (New York: Harper Collins, 2021), 257.

315 **At the end of April:** This section draws on Bergen, "What's Behind the Trumps' Covid
Quackery?"

315 **At the time:** Peter Baker, "Trump and Kushner Engage in Revisionist History in Boast-
ing of Success Over Virus," *New York Times*, April 29, 2020, https://www.nytimes
.com/2020/04/29/us/politics/trump-kushner-coronavirus-revisionist-history.html;
Hannah Lang and Bryan Mena, "U.S. Coronavirus Recession Lasted Two Months,
Ended in April 2020, Official Arbiter Says," *Wall Street Journal*, July 19, 2021, https://
www.wsj.com/articles/u-s-recession-lasted-two-months-ended-in-april-2020-official
-arbiter-says-11626715788.

315 **"be even more difficult":** Lena H. Sun, "CDC Director Warns Second Wave of Coronavirus Is Likely to Be Even More Devastating," *Washington Post*, April 21, 2020,
https://www.washingtonpost.com/health/2020/04/21/coronavirus-secondwave-cdc
director.

315 **Redfield was summoned:** "Trump Summons CDC Director to Clarify Remarks on
Second Virus Wave," Reuters, April 22, 2020, https://www.reuters.com/article/health
-coronavirus-usa-redfield/trump-summons-cdc-director-to-clarify-remarks-on-second
-virus-wave-idUSW1N2BU013.

315 **"There Isn't a Coronavirus 'Second Wave'":** Mike Pence, "There Isn't a Coronavirus
'Second Wave,'" *Wall Street Journal*, June 16, 2020, https://www.wsj.com/articles
/there-isnt-a-coronavirus-second-wave-11592327890.

315 *New York Times* **poll:** Margot Sanger-Katz, "On Coronavirus, Americans Still Trust
the Experts," *New York Times*, June 27, 2020, https://www.nytimes.com/2020/06/27
/upshot/coronavirus-americans-trust-experts.html.

316 **"a nice man":** Lawrence Wright, *The Plague Year: America in the Time of Covid* (New
York: Knopf, 2021), 191.

316 **The fastest vaccine:** Philip Ball, "The Lightning-Fast Quest for COVID Vaccines—
and What It Means for Other Diseases," *Nature*, December 18, 2020, https://www
.nature.com/articles/d41586-020-03626-1.

316 **by Election Day:** Caitlin Oprysko, "White House Aide Says Trump's Vaccine-by-Election Day Promise Was 'Arbitrary,'" *Politico*, October 30, 2020, https://www.politico.com/news/2020/10/30/white-house-aide-says-trumps-vaccine-by-election-day-promise-was-arbitrary-433670.

316 **logistics of vaccine distribution:** David Adler, "Inside Operation Warp Speed: A New Model for Industrial Policy," *American Affairs*, Summer 2021, https://americanaffairsjournal.org/2021/05/inside-operation-warp-speed-a-new-model-for-industrial-policy, provides an authoritative and thorough account of Operation Warp Speed.

316 **Operation Warp Speed:** Stephanie Baker and Cynthia Koons, "Inside Operation Warp Speed's $18 Billion Sprint for a Vaccine," *Bloomberg*, October 29, 2020, https://www.bloomberg.com/news/features/2020-10-29/inside-operation-warp-speed-s-18-billion-sprint-for-a-vaccine.

316 **only two months:** Baker and Koons, "Inside Operation Warp Speed's $18 Billion Sprint."

316 **threshold for approval:** "Coronavirus (COVID-19) Update: FDA Takes Action to Help Facilitate Timely Development of Safe, Effective COVID-19 Vaccines," US Food and Drug Administration, June 30, 2020, https://www.fda.gov/news-events/press-announcements/coronavirus-covid-19-update-fda-takes-action-help-facilitate-timely-development-safe-effective-covid.

317 **blood oxygen levels:** Noah Weiland et al., "Trump Was Sicker Than Acknowledged with Covid-19," *New York Times*, February 11, 2021, https://www.nytimes.com/2021/02/11/us/politics/trump-coronavirus.html.

317 **given oxygen twice:** Jim Acosta, "Trump Received Supplemental Oxygen on Friday, Source Says," CNN, October 3, 2020, https://www.cnn.com/politics/live-news/trump-covid-19-updates-saturday/h_1c9184f87a369cbaf032f8d7c33e26bc.

317 **best medical treatment:** Lenny Bernstein et al., "President Trump's Transfer to Walter Reed Reflects a Cautious Approach to Treating His Covid-19 Symptoms," *Washington Post*, October 3, 2020, https://www.washingtonpost.com/health/trump-health-risk-covid/2020/10/02/6e6f5af4-04b4-11eb-b7ed-141dd88560ea_story.html.

317 **Mark Meadows told:** Alexandra Alper, "After Mixed Messages from White House, Trump Says 'Real Test' Ahead in His COVID Fight," Reuters, October 3, 2020, https://www.reuters.com/article/health-coronavirus-trump/after-mixed-messages-from-white-house-trump-says-real-test-ahead-in-his-covid-fight-idUSKBN26P02B.

317 **Trump was furious:** Jim Acosta, "Trump Furious at Chief of Staff for Contradicting White House Physician, Sources Say," CNN, October 4, 2020, https://www.cnn.com/2020/10/04/politics/trump-mark-meadows-chief-of-staff/index.html.

317 **Trump staged a quick:** Barbara Sprunt, "Despite Risks to Others, Trump Leaves Hospital Suite to Greet Supporters," NPR, October 4, 2020, https://www.npr.org/sections/latest-updates-trump-covid-19-results/2020/10/04/920181116/in-brief-drive-by-trump-waves-to-supporters-outside-of-walter-reed.

317 **"don't let it dominate you":** "Trump: Don't Let Coronavirus Dominate You," *Bloomberg*, October 6, 2020, https://www.bloomberg.com/news/videos/2020-10-06/trump-don-t-let-coronavirus-dominate-you-video.

317 **What Trump didn't say:** Abutaleb and Paletta, *Nightmare Scenario*, 395.

317 **his coronavirus response coordinator:** Dan Diamond, "Election 'Distracted' Trump Team from Pandemic Response, Birx Tells Congress, Saying More Than 130,000 People Died Unnecessarily," *Washington Post*, October 26, 2021, https://www.washington post.com/health/2021/10/26/birx-testimony-congress-pandemic.

318 **told the conservative Newsmax:** Solange Reyner, "Michael Flynn to Newsmax TV: Trump Has Options to Secure Integrity of 2020 Election," Newsmax, December 17, 2020, https://www.newsmax.com/politics/trump-election-flynn-martiallaw/2020/12/17 /id/1002139.

318 **James McConville, the army chief:** Haley Britzky, "Army Leaders Push Back on Mike Flynn's Call for the Military to 'Re-run' the 2020 Election," *Task & Purpose*, December 18, 2020, https://taskandpurpose.com/news/army-secretary-chief-2020-election-mike-flynn.

318 **Flynn and his lawyer Sidney Powell:** Maggie Haberman and Zolan Kanno-Youngs, "Trump Weighed Naming Election Conspiracy Theorist as Special Counsel," *New York Times*, December 19, 2020, https://www.nytimes.com/2020/12/19/us/politics/trump -sidney-powell-voter-fraud.html.

318 **Dominion voting machines:** Haberman and Kanno-Youngs, "Trump Weighed"; see also Alan Feuer, "Dominion Demands That Sidney Powell Retract 'Baseless and False Allegations' about Voting Machines," *New York Times*, December 17, 2020, https:// www.nytimes.com/2020/12/17/us/dominion-demands-that-sidney-powell-retract -baseless-and-false-allegations-about-voting-machines.html.

318 **Trump then urged the mob:** Brian Naylor, "Read Trump's Jan. 6 Speech, a Key Part of Impeachment Trial," NPR, February 10, 2021, https://www.npr.org/2021/02/10/966396 848/read-trumps-jan-6-speech-a-key-part-of-impeachment-trial. This section draws on Peter Bergen, "Hold Trump Accountable for Incitement," CNN, January 8, 2021, https:// www.cnn.com/2021/01/07/opinions/inciting-terrorism-is-a-crime-bergen/index.html.

319 **"trial by combat":** "'Let's Have Trial by Combat' over Election—Giuliani," Reuters, January 6, 2021, https://www.reuters.com/video/watch/idOVDU2NS9R.

319 **"medieval battle scene":** Pierre Thomas, Luke Barr, and Quinn Owen, "'Like a Medieval Battle Scene': Officers Recount Being Attacked by Capitol Mob," ABC News, January 15, 2021, https://abcnews.go.com/Politics/medieval-battle-scene-officers-recount -attacked-capitol-mob/story?id=75284175.

319 **interrupted the election certification:** "Mob Attack, Incited by Trump, Delays Election Certification," *New York Times*, January 6, 2021, https://www.nytimes.com/live /2021/01/06/us/electoral-vote.

319 **resigned in protest:** "The Trump Administration Officials Who Resigned over Capitol Violence," *New York Times*, January 17, 2021, https://www.nytimes.com/article/trump -resignations.html.

319 **"The mob was fed lies":** "Sen. Mitch McConnell: 'The Mob Was Fed Lies. They Were Provoked by the President,'" C-SPAN, January 19, 2021, https://youtu.be/voMUpSp blB0.

319 **Joint Chiefs, General Milley:** Paul Sonne, "Joint Chiefs Call Riot a 'Direct Assault' on the Constitutional Process, Affirm Biden as Next Commander in Chief," *Washington*

Post, January 12, 2021, https://www.washingtonpost.com/national-security/military
-statement-biden-commander-in-chief/2021/01/12/9b722200-551a-11eb-89bc-7f5
1ceb6bd57_story.html.

320 **"An effort to subjugate"**: Lara Seligman, "Mattis Blames Trump for Inciting 'Mob Rule,'" *Politico*, January 6, 2021, https://www.politico.com/news/2021/01/06/mattis-trump -mob-rule-455675.

320 **"We are 100 percent steady"**: Bob Woodward and Robert Costa, *Peril* (Simon and Schuster, New York, 2021), xiii.

320 **to be impeached twice**: Tara Law, "What to Know about the U.S. Presidents Who've Been Impeached," *Time*, January 13, 2021, https://time.com/5552679/impeached-presi dents.

320 **with the result that**: "85% of Republicans Want Candidates to Agree with Trump, Quinnipiac University National Poll Finds; Americans Support Early Cut to Federal Jobless Benefit," Quinnipiac, May 25, 2021, https://poll.qu.edu/poll-release ?releaseid=3810.

320 **"We will be back"**: "Donald Trump Tells Supporters 'We Will Be Back in Some Form' in Last Speech as President," CNBC, January 20, 2021, https://youtu.be/hUmfcM LPw9Q.

INDEX

Abbas, Mahmoud, 195
ABC News, 37–38, 237
Abdi, Mazloum Kobani, 250
Abdullah, Abdullah, 130
Abdullah II of Jordan, 180
Abdulmutallab, Umar Farouk, 273
Abdul-Wahhab, Muhammad bin, 174
Abqaiq-Khurais attack, 302
"Abraham Accords," 291
Abrams, Elliott, 62–63
Abu Dhabi, 171
Academi (Blackwater), 140–41
Access Hollywood tape, 46, 82
Advisory Board, 306
Afghan Constitution of 2004, 264
Afghanistan, 125, 127–53. See also Kabul;
    Taliban
  al-Qaeda in, xvi–xvii, 129, 132, 133, 134,
    149, 158, 263
  Britain and, 143
  Camp David meeting of 2017, 157–59
  China and, 128
  CIA and, 129, 133, 143, 146, 154, 157–58
  McMaster and, 130–31, 132–37, 140,
    141–42, 144–46, 149–52, 153–54, 158–59
  meeting of May 2017, 135–37
  mineral resource wealth of, 127–28
  NATO support of, 225–26
  Obama and, 26–27, 55, 129–31, 131,
    158n, 159
  Pakistan and, 131, 132–33, 134, 150, 266

Prince's plan for use of contractors, 140–44
Russian support of Taliban, 226–27
"South Asia strategy" for, 158–60, 159n,
    161–62, 259
Soviet-Afghan War, 133, 264
Trump and. See Trump, Donald, and
    Afghanistan
U.S. withdrawal of troops, xi, xvi–xvii,
    260–68, 291
Agnew, Spiro, 190
Ahmadinejad, Mahmoud, 283
Air Force One, 82, 136, 172, 173, 175–76,
    228, 320
Ali, Javed, 151–52
Al Jazeera TV, 177, 181
Allen, John, 307
All Things Considered, 307
Al-Manar, 282
al-Qaeda, 28–29, 29, 36, 74–76, 273
  in Afghanistan, xvi–xvii, 129, 132, 133, 134,
    149, 158, 263
  in the Arabian Peninsula (AQAP), 75–78
  in Iraq, 26, 85–86, 102, 105, 115, 116,
    289–90
  in Saudi Arabia, 181
  in Syria, 250, 254–55
  in Yemen, 273
"alt-right" movement, 19
altruism, 294
Al Udeid Air Base, 179–81, 240
American Civil War, 14

American Prospect, 156–57
Andrews Air Force Base, 172, 189, 320
anti-Semitism, 272
Apprentice, The, 47–48, 253
Arab News, 204
Arab Spring, 20, 115, 168
arms sales, 191, 207
Artan, Abdul Razak Ali, 96
Art of the Deal, The (Trump), 257
Aspen Security Forum, 29, 123, 231
Aspen Strategy Group, 38–39
al-Assad, Bashar, 20, 96, 111–24, 169, 229,
    241–45
    chemical weapons use by, 111–15,
    241–44, 290
    Kellogg on bombing of Assad, 82–83
    Trump orders strikes, 113–16
Assange, Julian, 65
Atlantic, The, 306, 312
Atlantic Council, 232
Australia, 5, 152, 179, 214
"authoritarian model," 251
al-Awdah, Salman, 182
al-Awlaki, Anwar, 76
"axis of adults," 14, 16, 251, 290, 308–9
"axis of evil," 33

Baath Party, 74, 115
Badasch, Megan, 152
al-Baghdadi, Abu Bakr, 21–22, 118
Baghdad U.S. embassy of 2018, 246
Bagram Air Base, 26, 28
Bahrain, 291
Bannon, Steve
    Afghanistan and, 135, 140–41, 145–46, 150,
        151–52
    background of, 4, 6
    briefing of July 20, 2017, 3–9, 12–13, 14, 15
    as "chief strategist" in White House, 60–61
    departure of, 154–57, 162, 163
    election of 2016, 25, 39–40
    foreign policy views of, 4–6, 9
    "Javanka" and, 154
    Mattis and, 4–7
    McMaster and, 9, 145–46, 151–52, 153, 155
    on National Security Council, 70–71, 72, 88
    North Korea and, 213
    presidential transition and, 45–47, 59
    Special Initiatives Group, 72
    Syria and, 112, 113
    travel ban and, 98, 105
    Trump's inaugural address, 67–68

UAE and, 171–72
    Yemen and, 76–77
Baradar, Mullah, 265, 267
Barrack, Thomas, 170
Barrett, Amy Coney, xxi
Bash, Dana, 307
Bastille Day, 287–88
Battle of Midway, 287
Battle of Mosul, 118–19, 123
Battle of Raqqa, 118–19, 121, 122
Battle of 73 Easting, 85, 281
Battle of Tal Afar, 86, 104
BBC, 162, 226–27
Becket, Thomas, 199
Belgium, 103
Bell, Michael, 73–74
Bellinger, John, III, 38
Benghazi attack, 28, 60
Berlin Christmas market attack, 96
Biden, Hunter, 309
Biden, Joe, xv
    Afghanistan withdrawal, xvi–xvii, 291
    election of 2020, 221, 318
    Mattis and, 308
Biegun, Steve, 189
bin Laden, Osama, 32, 174, 241, 263
    Khashoggi and, 203–4
    raid and death of, 17, 28–29, 46, 74, 114,
        116, 160–61, 213, 238, 290
Birx, Deborah, 317
Blackwater (Academi), 140–41
Bloomberg News, 182, 202
Bolton, John
    Afghanistan and, 267
    background of, 83, 84, 190–91, 279
    as Fox News analyst, 34n, 84, 298
    Iran and, 84, 246, 279, 280–81, 282
    Iran nuclear deal, 191–92, 280
    Khashoggi's murder and, 203–4
    Mattis and, 189–90, 246–47
    national security adviser appointment, 83,
        84, 189–92, 218, 243, 280
    North Korea and, 84, 218–19, 221, 281
    Putin and Russia, 232
    resignation of, 309
    Syria and, 243, 248, 249, 254–55
    Trump's relationship with, 243, 281
    Ukraine phone call, 309
    Venezuela and, 281
border. *See* Mexico-United States border
Bossert, Tom, 119–20, 135, 146, 152, 190
Bossie, David, 47

Bowers, Robert, 272
"Bowling Green massacre," 101–2
Boxer, USS, 283
Boyle, Josh, 160–61
Bradley, David, 306–7
Breitbart News, 4, 72, 152
Brennan, John, 65–66, 69
   security clearance of, 237–38
Brennan, Margaret, 307
Brexit, 228, 300
Britain, 197, 291
   Afghanistan and, 135, 143
   Iran and, 185–87, 280, 283
   NATO and defense spending, 11, 225,
      226n, 291
   Putin and Russia, 227
   Trump's visit to, 228–29
Broadwell, Paula, 57, 82
Brookfield Properties, 193n
Brooks, Vincent, 312
Brown, Tina, 305
Bundy, McGeorge, 88
Bush, George H. W., 53–54, 183, 290, 312
Bush, George W., 239
   Afghanistan and, 27, 121–22
   "axis of evil," 33
   Iraq and, 53, 74, 289
   officials serving in administration of, 24, 38,
      57, 189, 190, 191, 305, 307
   Putin and, 233
   Saudi Arabia and, 240–41
   September 11 attacks, xv–xvi
Bush, John Ellis "Jeb," 22

Caddell, Pat, 40n
Call Sign Chaos (Mattis), 305–8
Camp David, 157–59, 216, 268
Canada, 225, 228, 273, 291
Capitol riots of 2021, xv–xvi, 318–20
Carlson, Tucker, 63, 266, 281, 298, 299
Carl Vinson, USS, 214
Caslen, Robert, 83–84
Cavuto, Neil, 314
CBS, 81, 207, 247, 307
Celebrity Apprentice, The, 65
Cengiz, Hatice, 201
Centers for Disease Control and Prevention
   (CDC), xx
Central American migrant caravans, 271, 272, 274
Central Command (CENTCOM), 8, 27, 51,
   52, 74, 81, 102, 114, 116, 128, 180, 185,
   186, 246, 248, 252

Central Intelligence Agency (CIA)
   Afghanistan and, 129, 133, 143, 146, 154,
      157–58
   ISIS and Syria, 111
   Khashoggi's murder and, 202–3, 207
   Putin and Russia, 227
   Russian interference in election of 2016 and,
      63–67
   Special Activities Division, 146
   Trump's attacks on, 296–98
   Trump's visit to, 68–69
Cernovich, Mike, 152
Chad, travel ban, 106
Chao, Elaine, 319
Charlottesville Unite the Right rally, 155–56
chemical weapons, 112, 115
   Russia's use of, 227, 232
   Syria's use of, 111–16, 232–33, 241–44,
      280, 290
Chemical Weapons Convention, 115
Cheney, Dick, 74
Chertoff, Michael, 24
China, 5, 11, 13, 40, 55, 66, 72, 73, 89, 169n,
   193, 207, 214, 231, 283, 291–95
   Afghanistan and, 128
   "clash of civilizations" and, 293
   cyber espionage, 292, 292n, 293
   global warming and, 295–96
   Iran and, 185, 186
   Kushner and, 61, 193, 194
   Mattis and, 241
   national security strategy on, 231
   North Korea and, 215–16
   Saudi Arabia and, 208
   South China Sea, 215, 294–95
   Space Force and, 295
   trade and tariffs, 293–94, 308
   trade deficit, 55, 292n
   Trans-Pacific Partnership, 7, 129, 292
"China virus," xxi
Christchurch, New Zealand, shooting, 275
Christie, Chris, 31, 45–47
Churchill, Winston, 223, 283
Clapper, James, 30, 65
Clausewitz, Carl von, 125
climate change, 7, 295–96
   Paris Climate Agreement, xix–xx, 7, 60, 193,
      295, 296
Clinton, Bill, xvii, 190, 247
Clinton, Hillary, 26, 190, 300
   election of 2016, 20, 23–24, 31–32, 39–40,
      41–42, 65–66, 100, 207, 239, 307

Clinton, Hillary (*cont.*)
  Libya and, 20
  Pizzagate conspiracy, 34, 152
  Russia and, 233
CNBC, 176
CNN, 29, 31, 66, 72, 78, 82, 115, 142, 172,
    203, 239, 251, 307, 312
Coats, Dan, 153, 296–98
  at Aspen Security Forum, 231
  ISIS and, 124
  Kim and North Korea, 220, 297
  Putin and Russian interference,
    229–30, 297
  resignation of, 296–97
  Senate Intelligence Committee testimony,
    220, 297
coercive interrogations, 289
Cohen, Eliot, 24, 51, 307
Cohen-Watnick, Ezra, 151
Cohn, Gary, 136–37, 251, 290, 308
  Afghanistan and, 145–46
  briefing of July 20, 2017, 3–4, 7–12, 15
  Charlottesville Unite the Right rally and,
    155–56
Cold War, 290
Coleman, Caitlan, 160–61
Colombia, 134
Comey, James, 65–66, 172
Conley, Sean, 317
conspiracy theories, 299–300
  election of 2020, 318–19
  Obama "birther," 17, 19
  Pizzagate, 34, 152
  Ukraine and election of 2016, 310
Constitution, U.S., 230
Conway, Kellyanne, 101–2
Cooper, Anderson, 82, 203
Corker, Bob, 57–58
Corvinus University, 34–35
Costa, Christopher, 75
Cotton, Tom, 62, 83
Council on Foreign Relations, 305–6
Counter-Terrorism Service (Iraq), 104, 117–18,
    123–24
COVID-19 pandemic, xx–xxii, 314–17
crime, 68, 100–101
Crocker, Ryan, 261
cross-border terrorism, 271–75
Cuba, 33
Cuban Missile Crisis, 279
Cursius, Patrick, 269, 275
cyber espionage, 292, 292*n*, 293

Daily Caller, 152
Damascus, 241–42
Daniels, Mitch, 46
Darwinism, 294
Dearborn, Rick, 47
"deep state," 71, 89, 91, 150–51, 255
Defeating Jihad (Gorka), 36
Defense Intelligence Agency (DIA), 27–29,
    30, 152
defense spending, 226, 245, 288
Democratic National Committee (DNC),
    63–64, 66, 189
Dempsey, Martin, 312
Denmark, 299
Dereliction of Duty (McMaster), 79, 86–87, 88,
    132–33, 308
devoir de réserve, 252
DeVos, Betsy, 141, 319
DHS. *See* Homeland Security, Department of
Dobbs, Lou, 298
Doha Forum, 249, 263
Dominican Republic, 144
Dominion Voting Systems, 318
Donnelly, Sally, 5
Dover Air Force Base, 77
Dunford, Joseph
  Afghanistan and, 13–14, 134–35, 147–48,
    149, 158, 267
  briefing of July 20, 2017, 7, 13–14
  Syria and, 242, 243–44, 249–50
  Yemen and, 76–77
DynCorp International, 142–43

Easterly, Jen, 75
East Germany, 228
East India Company, 143*n*
Egypt, 54, 62, 168, 187
Eisenhower, Dwight, 50, 214
elections. *See also* presidential election of 2016;
    presidential election of 2020
  of 2018, 246–47, 271, 272
electronics ban of 2017, 122
Ellis, Michael, 151
El Paso shooting, 269, 275
El Salvador, 274
Emiratis. *See* United Arab Emirates
Envoy, The (Khalilzad), 262
Erdogan, Recep Tayyip, 41, 201, 209, 248–49,
    254, 255
Esper, Mark, 309, 311, 313
European Union, 151, 229
  Brexit and, 228, 300

Evans, Harold, 305
evolution, 294
ExxonMobil, 13, 58–59, 176, 180, 187

Facebook, 21, 152
Faisal bin Turki al-Faisal, 201, 204
"fake news," 172, 233, 298, 307
Fallujah, 118, 123, 144
Fanone, Michael, 319
FARC (Revolutionary Armed Forces of
    Colombia), 134
Farook, Syed Rizwan, 21–22
Fauci, Anthony, xxi, 314, 315–16
Federal Bureau of Investigation (FBI), 152
    Flynn and, 81
    Gorka and, 35
    hostage-takers, 161n
    Russian interference in election of 2016 and,
        64–65
    travel ban and, 96–97
    Trump's attacks on, 230, 296–97
Federalist, 162
Feinberg, Stephen, 142–43
Field of Fight, The (Flynn), 32–33, 35–36
financial crisis of 2008, 289, 301
Fixing Failed States (Ghani), 262
Flournoy, Michèle, 61–62, 307
Flynn, Charlie, 27
Flynn, Lori, 27
Flynn, Michael, 66, 307
    background of, 25–30
    conspiracy theories of, 33–34, 318
    departure of, 81, 253
    as DIA head, 27–29, 30, 32
    election of 2016 and, 25–26, 30–34, 41–42,
        307
    election of 2020 fraud claims, 318
    ISIS and, 119, 120
    McChrystal and, 26–27, 32, 48–49
    national security advisor appointment, 42,
        46, 57, 70–73, 74, 81–82
    political lobbying of, 30–31
    Putin and Russia, 31, 66, 69–70
    Russia Today and, 31, 66
    Saudis and, 30, 171
    terrorism and, 28–30
    Trump's consideration as running mate, 31
    UAE and, 171–72
    Yemen and, 76–77, 149
Flynn, Michael, Jr., 34
"Flynn facts," 28
Flynn Intel Group, 30

Foley, James, 21, 117, 161n
Food and Drug Administration (FDA), xx, 316
Ford, Carl, 191
Fort Myer, 159
Fourth Armored Division (Syria), 243
Fourth Turning, The (Strauss and Howe), 6
Fox & Friends, 272
Fox News, 19, 25, 34, 63, 71, 77, 84, 176, 207,
    217, 233, 239, 247, 266, 272, 298–99,
    315, 316
France, 274, 291
    Afghanistan and, 225
    Bastille Day celebration in, 287–88
    Iran nuclear deal and, 185, 280
    ISIS and, 103
    NATO and defense spending, 11, 226,
        226n, 291
    terrorist attacks in, 21, 22, 23, 102
"freedom of navigation" exercises, 294–95
"free-riding," 11
Friedman, David, 192

Gates, Robert, 57–58
Gaza, 193, 197, 291
Geltzer, Joshua, 61, 77, 98
"Geographical Pivot of History, The"
    (Mackinder), 89
George Floyd protests, 310–12
Georgia, 231
Germany, 54, 274, 291
    Afghanistan and, 225
    Iran nuclear deal and, 185, 280
    NATO defense spending, 11, 226, 226n, 291
    Russia and, 228, 229
Ghani, Ashraf, 127, 130, 260–61, 262,
    264, 268
Gingrich, Newt, 31, 31n
Giuliani, Rudy, 56, 310, 319
Glasser, Susan, 307
Global Coalition to Defeat ISIS, 61, 119, 249
global warming. See climate change
Goldberg, Jeffrey, 306
Goldfein, David, 247
Goldman Sachs, 4, 8, 90
Goldwater, Barry, 190
Goodspeed, Tyler, 319
Gorka, Sebastian, 34–36, 298
    Afghanistan and, 142
    background of, 34–35
    departure of, 162–63
    Qatar blockade, 180
    "radical Islamic terrorism," 90

Gorka, Sebastian (*cont.*)
   Special Initiatives Group, 72
   travel ban and, 98
Graham, Lindsey, 22, 199, 208, 267
Greenblatt, Jason, 197
Greenland, 299
Greff, Byron, 225
Grisham, Stephanie, 319
GRIZZLY STEPPE, 64
Group of Seven (G7) summit, 227–28
Group of 20 (G20) summit, 221, 233
Guam, 214
Guantanamo Bay Detention Camp, 52, 107, 289
Gulen, Fethullah, 41
Gulf of Oman incident, 281–82
Gulf War, 85, 86, 183, 281, 290

Haass, Richard, 305, 306
Haberman, Maggie, 172
Hadley, Steve, 38–39
Haley, Nikki, 195–96, 215–16, 232–33
Hamas, 196
Hannity, Sean, 152, 298, 316
Haqqani network, xvii, 160–61
Hariri, Saad, 183
Harvey, Derek, 74, 113, 151, 180
Harward, Bob, 81–82
Haspel, Gina, 207, 267, 309
Hastings, Michael, 27
Hawaii, 106, 214
Hayden, Michael, 39
Hazaras, 262
Hegseth, Pete, 272
Helmsley, Leona, 17
Helsinki summit, 229–31, 237–38, 246, 290, 297
Henry II of England, 199
Heyer, Heather, 155
Hezbollah, 20, 152, 169, 171, 183, 282
Higgins, Rich, 150–51
Hill, Fiona, 74
Ho Chi Minh, 261
Hofstadter, Richard, 269
Homeland Security, Department of (DHS), 52–53
   Kelly's appointment, 52–53
   laptop ban and, 122
   Mexican border, 274, 299
   Russian interference in election of 2016, 64
   travel ban and, 96–101
Honduras, 274

Hook, Brian, 187
Hoover Institution, 186, 189, 252–53
Hostage Recovery Fusion Cell, 161*n*
House Intelligence Committee, 60, 151
Houthis, xix, 183–84, 282
Hundred-Year Marathon, The (Pillsbury), 5
Hussein, Saddam, 20, 36, 74, 85–86, 183
hydroxychloroquine, xx, 314–15

Ignatius, David, 307
immigrants, 40, 301, 307. *See also* Mexico-United States border
   crime and, 100–101
   cross-border terrorism and, 271–75
   in military, 307
Independence Day (2019), 287–88, 300–301
India, 5, 143*n*
Ingraham, Laura, 17, 152
Inhofe, James, 29
intellectual property theft, 292, 292*n*, 293
intelligence agencies, xviii, 63, 72–73. *See also specific agencies*
   Trump's attacks on, 230, 296–99
International Atomic Energy Agency, 185, 280
International Criminal Court, 191
International Monetary Fund (IMF), 173
Inter-Services Intelligence (ISI), 131, 160
iPhone, 195
Iran, 279–83, 302
   Bolton and, 191–92, 279–82
   calling off of air strikes, 279–80, 290, 299
   economic sanctions, 12, 185, 192, 255, 280, 281–83, 290
   Gulf of Oman incident, 281–82
   Mattis and, 51–52, 185–86, 187
   nuclear deal, xviii, 12–13, 52, 168–69, 184–88, 191–92, 297
   nuclear program of, 12–13, 52, 54, 60, 168–69, 184–88, 191–93, 280–83, 291, 297, 301
   oil in, 282
   Syria and, 169, 184–85, 254–55
   travel ban and, 97, 106
Iranian Revolution, 174
Iranian shooting down of American drone, 51–52
Iraq, 4–5, 24–27, 29–31, 36, 73–75, 191, 289–90
   al-Qaeda in, 26, 85–86, 102, 105, 115, 116, 289–90
   Bush and, 53, 74, 289

Counter-Terrorism Service of, 104, 117–18, 123–24
Flynn and, 26–27
ISIS in, 29–30, 36–37, 104, 117–19, 123–24, 134
McMaster in, 85–87, 104–5, 128, 138n
Obama and, 128–29, 130, 134, 159, 242, 250, 268, 308
oil of, 120–21
travel ban and, 97, 98, 103–5
U.S. withdrawal of troops, 128–30, 134, 159, 242, 250, 268, 308
weapons of mass destruction, 63–64
Iraq after America (Rayburn), 73–74
Iraqi refugees, 101–2
ISIS, 20–21, 23, 29–33, 36–37, 115–16, 119–24, 161n
in Afghanistan, 128, 130, 131–32, 134, 138, 158, 159
Foley murder, 21, 117, 161n
in Iraq, 29–30, 36–37, 104, 117–19, 123–24, 134
laptop bomb plot of, 122
Obama and, 20–21, 29–32, 118–23
Saipov and, 106–7
Saudi Arabia and, 179
Sri Lanka jihadi attack, 124
in Syria, 20–21, 41, 54, 90, 111, 115–17, 121–24, 138–39, 249–50, 254–55, 289–90
travel ban and, 96, 98, 103–6
U.S. withdrawal of troops from Syria and, 248–51, 254–55, 259, 290
Yazidis and, 116–17, 123
Islam (Muslims)
move of U.S. embassy to Jerusalem, 192–93, 195–96, 290
Muslim Brotherhood, 20, 54, 62, 177, 180, 181, 203–4
Obama on, 176–77
September 11 attacks and, 19–20, 38
sharia law and, 20, 33, 264
Wahhabi, 173–75
Islamic Revolutionary Guard Corps (IRGC), 169, 281–82
Islamic terrorism. *See also* terrorism
al-Qaeda. *See* al-Qaeda
ISIS. *See* ISIS
"Islamist" terrorism vs., 89–90, 177
September 11 attacks, 19–20, 174, 225
Taliban. *See* Taliban
travel ban and, 22, 23, 91, 93, 95–107

Islamophobia, 33, 35, 96
Obama allegations, 17, 19–20
Trump and, 19–20, 21–23, 37–38, 96, 100, 226, 271
use of "radical Islam," 25–26, 29–30, 33, 36, 55, 67, 89–90, 95, 177
Israel, 10, 55, 138, 152, 153, 171, 179, 195–97, 254
"Abraham Accords," 291
U.S. embassy move to Jerusalem, 192–93, 195–96, 290
Israeli-Palestinian conflict, 169–70, 172, 192–93, 195–97, 291

Jackson, Andrew, 69
Jackson, Thomas "Stonewall," 155
Japan, 5, 10, 11, 214
Jerusalem, 192–93, 195–96, 290
Jobs, Laurene Powell, 306
Jobs, Steve, 306
Johnson, Boris, 99, 228
Johnson, Jeh, 305
Johnson, Lyndon, 57, 79
McMaster's *Dereliction of Duty* and, 79, 86–87, 88, 132, 308
Johnson, Samuel, 285
Joint Special Operations Command (JSOC), 7, 13, 25, 26, 28, 48, 75, 116
Jones, Van, 78
Jordan, 156, 180, 187
al-Jubouri, Najim, 104–5
"Judeo-Christian civilization," 6
Justice Department, U.S., 100, 103, 296

Kabul, 27, 129, 132–33, 261–62
bombings, 132, 139, 225, 268
U.S. withdrawal, xvi–xvii
Karzai, Hamid, 264
Keane, Jack, 298
Afghanistan and, 55, 265–66
Iraq War and, 53
North Korea and, 217
Putin and Helsinki summit, 230–31
secretary of defense offer to, 251
Syria and, 254–55, 265, 299
Trump's relationship with, 53–55, 56
turning down secretary of defense, 49–50
Keane, Terry, 49
Kellogg, Keith, 24–25
acting national security advisor, 82–83, 83n
Afghanistan and, 135
ISIS and, 119
Pence's national security adviser, 83n, 309

Kelly, John
    Afghanistan and, 148–49
    "axis of adults," 251, 290
    Bannon and, 155
    as chief of staff, 52, 154
    criticism of Trump, 312
    departure of, 253
    DHS appointment, 52–53, 57
    Kushner's clearance and, 194
    Mattis and, 154, 253, 307
    McMaster and, 137
    Mexican border and, 274
    NATO and, 228
    North Korea and, 217–18
    Petraeus and, 57
    at SOUTHCOM, 52, 53, 274
    travel ban and, 98–99
    Trump's break with, 253
Kelly, Karen, 52
Kelly, Mary Louise, 307
Kelly, Ray, 305
Kelly, Robert, 148–49
Kennan, George, 36
Kennedy, John F., 19, 68, 279
KGB, 227, 230, 233, 264
Khalid bin Salman, 202–3
Khalid Sheikh Mohammed (KSM), 107
Khalilzad, Zalmay, 260–61, 262–65, 267–68
Khan, Humayun, 37
Khan, Imran, 266
Khan, Khizr, 37–38
Khan, Sadiq, 229
Khan Sheikhoun chemical weapon attack,
    111–15
Khashoggi, Jamal, 201–9
    bin Laden and, 203–4
    murder of, xix, 165, 201–9, 290
Khomeini, Ayatollah, 41
Kim Dong Chul, 161n
Kim Hak-song, 161n
Kim Jong Un, 161n, 207, 215–17, 218, 297. See
    also Trump, Donald, and Kim Jong Un
Kim Kye-gwan, 219
Kim Sang Duk, 161n
King, Angus, 185
King, Kevin, 161n
King, Martin Luther, Jr., 287, 300–301
King, Rodney, 311
Korean War, 219
Korkie, Pierre, 75
Kudlow, Larry, 308
Kunduz, 130

"kung flu," xxi
Kurdistan, 241
Kurds (Kurdish forces), 41, 90, 121–22, 124,
    241, 248, 250–51, 254, 255
Kushner, Charles, 47
Kushner, Jared, 193–95
    Bannon and, 154
    briefing of July 20, 2017, 8, 14
    Christie and presidential transition, 47
    COVID-19 pandemic and, 315
    Israeli-Palestinian conflict and, 169–70, 172,
        192–93, 195–97, 291
    as key foreign policy advisor, 308
    McFarland and NSC, 88–89
    McMaster and, 83–84, 90
    North Korea and, 213, 281
    presidential transition, 47, 56, 62
    Saudi Arabia and MBS, 168, 169–70,
        175–76, 181–83, 195, 203–4
    security clearance of, 193–95
    666 Fifth Avenue and, 193n
    Syria and, 113
    UAE and, 170–72
    Yemen and, 76–77
Kuwait, 10, 183, 289, 290

laptop ban of 2017, 122
Latvia, 292
Lebanon, 169, 183
Ledeen, Michael, 33
Lee, Robert E., 155, 156
LeFrak, Richard, 156
Lewandowski, Corey, 22, 25
Libya, 20, 31, 54, 180
    Benghazi attack, 28, 60
    travel ban and, 97, 106
"Libya model" for North Korea, 218–19
Lincoln, Abraham, 14, 301
Lincoln Memorial, 287, 288
Lockhart, Clare, 262
Lockheed Martin, 81
Lockheed Martin F-35s, 292
"Lock her up!" chants, 32, 307
London, 106, 229
Los Angeles riots of 1992, 311
Louis XIV of France, 285
Lowell, Abbe, 194

MacArthur, Douglas, 311, 313
McChrystal, Annie, 27
McChrystal, Stanley
    Afghanistan and, 48, 130–31, 237

Flynn and, 26–27, 32, 48–49
    Iraq War and, 26–27, 48
    resignation of, 27, 48–49, 237
    secretary of defense consideration of, 48–49
McConnell, Mitch, 319
McConville, James, 318
McCord, Mary, 103
MacDill Air Force Base, 120
McFarland, K. T., 71–72, 88–89, 298, 305
MacFarland, Sean, 36, 122–23
McGahn, Don, 194
McGurk, Brett, 61, 119–20, 249
Machiavelli, Niccolò, 285
Mackinder, Halford, 89
McMaster, H. R.
    Afghanistan and, xvi–xvii, 130–37, 140,
        141–42, 144–46, 149–52, 153–54,
        158–59, 186
    Ali and, 152
    background of, 85–87
    Bannon and, 9, 145–46, 151–53, 155
    briefing of July 20, 2017, 3, 8–9
    conservative attacks on, 152–53
    departure of, 189–90, 253
    Dereliction of Duty, 79, 86–87, 88, 132–33,
        308
    in Gulf War, 85, 86, 183, 281
    Iran nuclear deal and, 185, 187, 188
    in Iraq War, 85–87, 104–5, 128, 138n
    ISIS and, 121
    on Islamist terrorism, 89–90
    Jubouri and, 104–5
    Mattis and, 8, 253
    national security adviser appointment,
        83–84, 88–91, 138n
    North Korea and, 213, 214, 216
    Putin and Russia, 152–53, 231, 232
    Saudi Arabia and, 172, 185
    Syria and, 112–13, 121, 241
    travel ban and, 104–5, 106
    Trump's relationship with, 136–37,
        138–39, 138n
    war injury of, 138n
McMasterleaks.com, 152
McRaven, William H., 46, 235, 238–39
    open letter to Trump from, 238–39
Macron, Emmanuel, 287–88
Maduro, Nicolás, 281
Mahan, Alfred Thayer, 4
Malik, Tashfeen, 21–22
Manafort, Paul, 39

Mar-a-Lago, 83, 84–85, 96, 113, 136, 195, 251
Marcus Aurelius, 51
Marine Corps University, 35
Marshall, George C., 7, 50
Marxists, 151
Mateen, Omar, 22
Mattis, James "Mad Dog," 239–47
    Afghanistan and, 132–33, 139, 143–44, 145,
        147–50, 154, 158, 186
    "axis of adults," 14, 16, 251
    background of, 51–52
    Bolton and, 189–90, 246–47
    border wall and, 246–47
    briefing of July 20, 2017, 3, 7, 9–10, 13–15
    Call Sign Chaos, 305–8
    criticism of Trump, 312
    Iran and, 51–52, 185–86, 187
    in Iraq War, 4–5, 7, 51, 128
    ISIS and, 119
    NATO and, xix, 6, 50, 231, 245–46, 251
    North Korea and, 216–17, 219
    Petraeus and, 57
    Putin and Russia, 231
    Qatar blockade and, 179–81, 240
    resignation of, 239, 251–53, 299–300
    Saudi Arabia and, 179–81, 208
    secretary of defense appointment, 50–51,
        61–62, 68
    secretary of defense swearing in, 95–96, 95n
    South Korea and, 137–38, 249
    Syria and, 113–14, 241–45, 249, 250–51
    travel ban and, 95–96, 104, 105, 106
    Trump's break with, 239–40, 241,
        246–47, 253
    Yemen and, 76–77, 209
May, Theresa, 69–70, 228–29
MBS. See Mohammed bin Salman
Meadows, Mark, 317
Mecca, 174, 175
Medina, 175
Mencken, H. L., 93
mercantilism, 294
Merkel, Angela, 167, 226, 228
Mexico, 61, 152, 193, 291
Mexico–United States border, 33, 246–47,
    271–75
    active-duty soldiers deployed at, 246–47
    terrorism and migrants, 271–75
    Trump border wall, 56, 251, 271–72, 274
Mighty Wind, A, 137
military, 288, 302–3
    immigrants in, 307

Miller, Stephen
  anti-immigrant sentiments of, 100–101, 103
  background of, 67
  Tillerson and, 188
  travel ban and, 98, 99, 103
  Trump's inaugural address, 67–68
Milley, Mark
  appointment of, 247–48
  Capitol Hill riot and, 319–20
  Charlottesville Unite the Right rally and, 156
  Trump's photo op at St. John's Church, 311, 313
"misinformation conversation," xxi–xxii
Mitchell, Andrea, 231
Mnuchin, Steve, 7–8, 12–13, 197
MOABs (Massive Ordnance Air Blast bombs), 131–32, 217
Moderna, 316
Mohamed bin Zayed (MBZ), 171–72
Mohammed bin Salman (MBS), xix, 167–68, 173–75, 181–83, 195, 282
  Khashoggi's murder and, 201–9, 290
  purge in Saudi Arabia, 181–83
  Qahtani and, 206
  Qatar blockade and, 183
  White House lunch, 167–68, 172
  women's right to drive and, 175, 182
Mohib, Hamdullah, 264–65
Mongolia, 281
Moon Jae-in, 218
Morsi, Mohamed, 62
Mosul, 21, 118–19, 123
Moynihan, Daniel Patrick, 298
MSNBC, 101
Mubarak, Hosni, 54, 168
Mueller, Robert, 172, 229, 287
Muhammad, 177, 192
Mukasey, Michael, 24
Mullen, Mike, 312
Mulvaney, Mick, 309, 319
Munich Security Conference, 189
Muslim Brotherhood, 20, 54, 62, 177, 180, 181, 203–4
Muslims. See Islam
Muslim travel ban. See travel ban
Mutreb, Maher Abdulaziz, 202

Nagl, John, 139
National Counterterrorism Center, 29, 61
National Defense University, 35
National Geospatial-Intelligence Agency (NGA), 213–14

National Security Agency (NSA), 64–65
National Security Council (NSC), 8, 59–60, 70–74, 82, 88–91, 90–91, 194, 246
  Afghanistan and, 135–36, 144, 150–52, 259
  Bannon on, 70–71, 72, 88
  hostage-takers, 161n
  Kellogg and, 82–83
  McMaster and, 150, 151–52, 189, 190
  Syria and, 112–13
  travel ban and, 98
National Security Presidential Memorandum 3, 119–20
NATO (North Atlantic Treaty Organization)
  Afghanistan and, xvii, 4, 144, 147, 225–29, 323
  Article 5, 225
  defense spending, 11, 225–26, 226n, 245
  Mattis support of, xix, 6, 50, 231, 245–46, 251
  Syria and, 255
  Trump and. See Trump, Donald, and NATO
Nauert, Heather, 298
Navarro, Peter, 308, 315–16
Navy SEALs, 25, 32, 75–76, 105, 140, 146–47
Nayef, Mohammed bin, 181
Nazis, 35, 155, 192
NBC, 21, 69, 231, 307
neoconservatism, 32–33, 83
Netanyahu, Benjamin, 40, 192, 196–97
Never Trump movement, 24, 25, 38–39, 46, 48, 51, 61, 62, 307
Newsmax, 318
Newton-John, Olivia, 84
New York and New Jersey bombing of 2016, 23
New York City attack of 2001. See September 11 attacks
New York City attack of 2017, 106–7
New Yorker, 29, 305, 307, 309
New York Military Academy, 301–2
New York Post, 33, 47–48
New York Times, 10, 39, 65, 87, 172–73, 191, 233, 283, 315–16
New York Times Magazine, 240
Nicaragua, 144
Nice, terrorist attack in, 23
Nicholson, John "Mick," 130, 131–32, 147–48, 226–27, 307
Nielsen, Kirstjen, 299
9/11 attacks. See September 11 attacks
Nixon, Richard, 190, 283
Nobel Peace Prize, 220, 221

North Korea, 156–57, 185, 213–22, 246, 297.
    See also Kim Jong Un
  China and, 215–16
  economic sanctions, 213, 215–16, 220–21
  hostages in, 161*n*
  "Libya model" for, 218–19
  missile launches, 214–15
  nuclear program of, 157, 161*n*, 185, 213–22,
    246, 281, 297, 308
  travel ban and, 106
Novichok, 227
nuclear weapons, 10
  Iran and, 12–13, 52, 54, 60, 168–69,
    184–88, 191–93, 280–83, 291, 297, 301
  North Korea and, 157, 185, 213–22, 246,
    281, 297, 308
Nunes, Devin, 151

Obama, Barack, 26, 57
  "birther" conspiracy, 17, 19
  Cairo speech on Islam, 176–77
  China and, 294–95
  commander in chief role of, 288–89
  defense budgets of, 288
  hostage takers, 161*n*
  McChrystal and, 237
  Mattis and, 51–52, 252, 299–300, 308
  Merkel and, 226
  Muslim allegations against, 17, 19–20
  NATO and, 226
  North Korea and, 213
  Russia and, 233
  Russian interference in election of 2016 and,
    63, 64, 67, 81
  terrorism and, 29–31, 36–37
  Trump's meeting with, 59–61
Obama, Barack, and Middle East policy,
    20–21, 28–32, 168–69, 289
  Afghanistan and, 26–27, 55, 129–31, 131,
    158*n*, 159
  Bin Laden raid, 17, 28–29, 46, 114, 116, 213,
    238, 290
  Iran nuclear deal, xviii, 52, 168–69, 184–86,
    188
  Iraq, 128–29, 130, 134, 159, 242, 250, 268,
    308
  ISIS, 20–21, 29–32, 118–23
  Saudi Arabia, 168, 169, 170, 172, 176–77
  Syria, 20–21, 112, 116–17, 121–23, 161*n*
  Yemen, 75–76
Obamacare, 46
"Obama derangement syndrome," 32

O'Brien, Robert, 281
Ohio State University attack, 96
oil (oil prices), 120–21, 173, 254–55,
    282–83, 302
Oman, 120
"One Belt, One Road" policy, 5
Operation Green Sword, 131–32
Operation Warp Speed, 316
Orlando nightclub shooting, 22–23
Ortagus, Morgan, 298
al-Otaiba, Yousef, 170–71
Ottoman Empire, 9
Owens, Carryn, 78
Owens, Ryan, 105
Owens, William "Ryan," 76–78
Ozark Mountains of Missouri, 217

Pace, Peter, 46
Page, Carter, 24–25
Pakistan, 58, 267, 273, 289
  Afghanistan and, 131, 132–33, 134, 150, 266
  capture of KSM, 107
  hostages in, 160–61
  Inter-Services Intelligence, 131, 160
  "South Asia strategy," 159*n*
  travel ban and, 97–98
Palestinian Brotherhood, 180
Palestinians. *See* Israeli-Palestinian conflict
Papadopoulos, George, 24–25
Paris
  Bastille Day celebration in, 287–88
  terrorist attacks in, 21, 22, 102
Paris Climate Agreement, xix–xx, 7, 60, 193,
    295, 296
Paris Peace Accords, 261
Patriot missiles, 137, 186
Patterson, Anne, 62
Patton, George, 51, 252, 313
Paul, Rand, 63
Pelosi, Nancy, 310
Pence, Mike
  Afghanistan and, 153–54
  briefing of July 20, 2017, 13, 14–15
  COVID-19 pandemic and, 315
  election of 2016 and, 31
  Kellogg as national security adviser, 83*n*, 309
  Mattis' swearing in, 95–96
  North Korea and, 216
  presidential transition and, 46–47, 49, 50,
    58, 81
Perez, Evan, 29
Peshmerga. *See* Kurds

Petraeus, David
  in Afghanistan, 130–31, 266
  in Iraq War, 27, 51, 53, 56, 73–74, 74, 87
  national security adviser consideration,
    81–82
  secretary of state consideration, 56–57
Pfizer, 316
Phares, Walid, 24–25
Pillsbury, Michael, 5
Pittsburgh synagogue shooting, 272
Pizzagate conspiracy, 34, 152
PJMedia.com, 152
Podesta, John, 34, 65, 189
"political correctness," 33, 36
Politico, 139
Pompeo, Mike
  Afghanistan and, xvi–xvii, 143, 146, 153–54,
    157–58, 262, 267
  Benghazi attack, 60
  at CIA, 60, 146, 230
  Mattis and, 251
  North Korea and, 218
  Saudi Arabia and, 184
  secretary of state appointment, 189, 218, 309
  Syria and, 249
  Yemen and, 209
Posse Comitatus Act of 1878, 311
Pottinger, Matthew, 72–73, 319
Powell, Colin, 84, 312
Powell, Dina, 90
Powell, Sidney, 318
Presidential Command (Rodman), 89
presidential election of 2016
  Russian interference in, 63–67, 207,
    229–31, 232
  Trump and. *See* Trump, Donald, and
    election of 2016
presidential election of 2020, 221, 316–17, 318
  fraud claims, xv, 318–19
President's Daily Brief, 82, 194
Priebus, Reince
  Afghanistan and, 140–41
  briefing of July 20, 2017, 14
  chief of staff, 52, 60–61, 154
  firing of, 240*n*
  Syria and, 113
Prince, Erik, 140–44
Prince Sultan Air Base, 240–41
Putin, Vladimir, 227–33, 300
  Afghanistan and, 264–65
  Flynn and, 31, 66, 69–70
  G20 meeting, 233

Helsinki summit, 229–31, 237–38, 246,
    290, 297
  Hill and, 74
  NATO and, xviii–xix, 227–29, 238
  Russia and U.S. election of 2016, 65–66,
    207, 310
  Syria and, 112, 232–33, 250
  Tillerson and, 58–59
  Trump and. *See* Trump, Donald, and Putin
Pyeongchang Winter Olympics, 218

el-Qaddafi, Muammar, 20, 54, 219
al-Qahtani, Saud, 206
Qatar, 177–79, 249, 265
  blockade and diplomatic crisis, 140, 178–81,
    183, 240, 242
  Khashoggi's murder and, 204–5
  Kushner and real estate, 193*n*
Qatar News Agency, 178, 179

"radical Islam" ("radical Islamic terrorism"),
    25–26, 29–30, 33, 36, 55, 67, 89–90,
    95, 177
Rahami, Ahmad Khan, 23
Ramadi, 118, 123
Raqqa, 118–19, 121, 122
Rasmussen, Nick, 29, 61
Ratcliffe, John, 297–98
Rayburn, Joel, 73–74
Reagan, Ronald, 38, 62, 67, 71, 83, 84, 190,
    231, 290
Reagan Defense Forum, 246
"reciprocal altruism," 294
Redfield, Robert, 315
Regeneron, 317
Reince, Staff, 240
Remnick, David, 29
Republican National Convention (2016),
    31–32, 307
Republican Party, 57, 187, 294, 301, 306
  Never Trump movement in, 24, 25, 38–39,
    46, 48, 51, 61, 62, 307
  travel ban and, 101
Ressam, Ahmed, 273
Rice, Condoleezza, 58, 86
Rice, Susan, 59–60, 129
Ricks, Tom, 139
Riyadh, 172–77, 178–79, 201–2, 207
Rodman, Peter, 89
Rodriguez, Leon, 97
Rogers, Mike, 60, 65
Rolling Stone, 27, 48

Rollins, Ed, 31*n*
Romney, Mitt, 48
Roosevelt, Franklin Delano, 7, 12
Ross, Wilbur, 127–28, 176
Russia, 226–33. *See also* Putin, Vladimir
    Afghanistan and, 264–65
    economic sanctions, 64, 81–82, 232–33
    Germany and, 228, 229
    GRU in, 229
    McMaster and, 152–53, 231, 232
    Syria and, 112–15, 138–39, 232–33
    Ukraine and, 67, 228, 231, 232
    U.S. national security strategy document,
        231–32
Russian interference in election of 2016, 63–67,
    207, 229–31, 232
Russia Today (RT), 31, 66

al-Saadi, Abdul-Wahab, 117–18, 123
Sageman, Marc, 35
Saipov, Sayfullo, 106–7
Salman, King of Saudi Arabia, 168, 175–76,
    183, 196, 205, 208, 248
Salman, Mohammed bin. *See* Mohammed bin
    Salman
San Bernardino attack, 21–22
Sanders, Sarah, 84, 219, 228, 238, 272–73
Saudi Arabia, 10, 167–84, 240–41
    Abqaiq-Khurais attack, 302
    China and, 208
    Gulf of Oman incident, 281–82
    Khashoggi's murder, xix, 165, 201–9, 291
    Kushner and, 168, 169–70, 175–76, 181–83,
        195, 203–4
    MBS's purge, 181–83
    Qatar blockade, 178–81, 183, 240, 242
    Syria and, 178, 205, 248
    Trump and. *See* Trump, Donald, and Saudi
        Arabia
    Trump's state visit, 172–73, 175–77, 207, 290
    U.S. aid and arms sales to, 175, 176, 207,
        208, 209
    Wahhabism in, 173–75
    women's right to drive in, 175, 182
    Yemen and, xix, 169, 183–84, 208–9
Saudi Aramco, 173
Saunders, Thomas A., III, 35
Schadlow, Nadia, 90
Schlapp, Mercedes, 298
Schmitz, Joe, 24–25
Schwarzenegger, Arnold, 65
Scowcroft, Brent, 70, 89

Senate Armed Services Committee, 130,
    144, 185
Senate Homeland Security Committee, 97
Senate Intelligence Committee, 36, 220, 297
Sensitive Compartmented Information Facility
    (SCIF), 113–14
Seoul, 214–15
September 11 attacks, 19–20, 174, 225
    twentieth anniversary, xv–xvi
Sessions, Jeff, 47, 144–45
    Afghanistan and, 144–45, 153–54
    travel ban and, 103–5
Shaghati, Talib, 104
Shahzad, Faisal, 273
Shanahan, Patrick, 252
sharia law, 20, 33, 264
Shia Islam, 28, 74, 115, 117, 174, 178, 182,
    246, 302
Shine, Bill, 298
Sims, Cliff, 211
Singapore summit, xvii, 219–21, 246
60 Minutes, 207, 247, 295
Skinner, Kiron, 293
Smith, Dana Shell, 180
Smith, Shepard, 247
Soleimani, Qasem, 302
Somalia, 31, 96, 289
    travel ban and, 97, 106
Somers, Luke, 75
Soros, George, 152, 272
South China Sea, 215, 294–95
Southern Command (SOUTHCOM), 52,
    53, 274
South Korea, 10, 137–38, 157, 214, 217–18,
    221, 246, 253, 299
    Korean War, 219
Soviet-Afghan War, 133, 204, 264
Soviet Union. *See also* Russia
    Cold War, 290
    Korean War and, 219
Space Force, 295
Special Initiatives Group (SIG), 72
Special Operations Command (SOCOM), 120
Spicer, Sean, 76–77
"Squad, the," 301
Sri Lanka jihadi attack, 124
Stahl, Lesley, 247
Stalin, Joseph, 208
Stanekzai, Sher Mohammad Abbas, 264
Stern, Howard, 37
Stewart, Corey, 203
Stitt, Kevin, xx

Strait of Hormuz, 281–82, 283

Sturgess, Dawn, 227

Sudan, travel ban, 97, 106

Sunni Islam, 28, 74, 115, 117, 173–75, 308

Sun Tzu, 162–63, 257

Surrender Is Not an Option (Bolton), 190–91

Sweeney, Kevin, 5

Syria (Syrian Civil War), 64, 241–45, 254–55, 289–90
  chemical weapons use, 111–16, 232–33, 241–44, 280, 290
  hostages in, 161*n*
  ISIS in, 20–21, 41, 54, 90, 111, 115–17, 121–24, 138–39, 249–50, 254–55, 289–90
  Kellogg on bombing of Assad, 82–83
  Kurdish forces in, 41, 121–22, 124, 248, 250, 254, 255
  Obama and, 20–21, 112, 116–17, 121–23, 161*n*
  travel ban and, 96–97, 106
  Trump orders strikes, 113–16
  U.S. aid to, 196
  U.S. military forces in, 122, 123
  U.S. military strikes against, 242–45, 280, 290
  U.S. withdrawal of troops, 248–51, 254–55, 259, 260, 289, 290, 299

Syrian Democratic Forces (SDF), 124, 248–51

Syrian refugees, 23, 96–97, 107, 226

Taiwan, 73

Tal Afar, 86, 104

Taliban, 4, 55, 128, 130–34, 161–62, 226–27
  Haqqani network, xvii, 160–61
  Quetta Shura of, 267
  Russia and, 226–27
  takeover of Afghanistan, xvi–xvii
  Trump administration's negotiations with, xvi–xvii, 259–68, 283, 291

tariffs, 193, 228, 229, 293–94

taxes, 46, 155

Tel Aviv, 192, 290

terrorism (terrorist attacks), 21–24, 29–30, 41, 229, 289. *See also* Islamic terrorism; and specific attacks
  alleged cross-border, 271–75
  media coverage of, 101–3
  travel ban and, 97–98, 100–107
  by U.S. citizens, 97–98, 101, 105–6, 271, 272, 274–75

THAAD (Terminal High Altitude Area Defense), 137–38

al-Thani, Tamim bin Hamad, 178–79, 242

Thomas, Raymond "Tony," 120, 123

Thucydides, 109

Tillerson, Rex, 179–81, 299
  Abrams and, 62–63
  Afghanistan and, 133, 140, 145, 150
  "axis of adults," 14, 16, 251
  background of, 13, 58–59
  briefing of July 20, 2017, 3, 7, 12–15
  "Club of Two," 8, 9–10
  at Exxon, 13, 58–59, 176, 180, 187
  firing of, 188–89
  Iran nuclear deal and, 185, 187, 188
  lack of focus of, 140
  North Korea and, 162, 216
  Qatar blockade and, 178–81
  Saudi Arabia and, 58, 172, 176, 178–81
  secretary of state appointment, 58–59, 62–63
  Syria and, 112–13, 140
  travel ban and, 105
  UNRWA and, 196

Todd, Chuck, 43

Townsend, Frances, 24, 48

trade, 4, 7–8, 14, 56, 62, 310
  China and tariffs, 73, 203, 292*n*, 293–94, 308
  Trans-Pacific Partnership (TPP), 7, 129, 292

trade deficit, 10, 11–12, 15, 55, 292n

transgender military ban, 241

Trans-Pacific Partnership (TPP), 7, 129, 292

travel ban, xxi, 23, 93, 95–105
  "dissent channel" cable, 99–100
  execution of, 97–100
  Syrian refugees and, 96–97, 107
  terrorism and, 97–98, 100–107

Trudeau, Justin, 228

Truman, Harry, 36, 77–78, 115

Trump, Donald
  Access Hollywood tape, 46, 82
  Afghanistan policy. See Trump, Donald, and Afghanistan
  America First policy of (Trump Doctrine), 4, 9, 10–11, 13, 15, 68, 71, 128, 138, 150, 163, 191, 207, 245, 253–54, 289, 300
  attacks on intelligence agencies, 230, 296–99
  briefing of July 20, 2017, 3–16
  bullying of, 299–300
  cavalier approach to national security, 194–95
  Charlottesville Unite the Right rally and, 155–56
  China and trade, 73, 207, 291–95, 308
  CIA visit, 68–69
  climate change and, xix–xx, 7, 295–96
  commander in chief role, 287–302

Trump, Donald (*cont.*)
  conspiracy theories of, 17, 19, 299–300, 310,
    318–19
  COVID-19 pandemic and, xx–xxii,
    314–17
  defense budget of, 288
  election of 2016. *See* Trump, Donald, and
    election of 2016
  election of 2020, 316–17
  election of 2020 fraud claims, xv, 318–19
  embrace of dictators, xix, 207, 291
  ending America's foreign wars, 259–68
  hostage-takers and, 160–61, 161*n*
  impeachment of, 309–11
  inaugural address of, 67–68
  Independence Day speech of 2019, 287–88,
    300–301
  Iran and, 281–83, 302
  Iran nuclear deal, 12–13, 184–89, 191–92
  ISIS and, 109, 115–16, 119–24
  Islamophobia of, 19–20, 21–23, 37–38, 96,
    100, 226, 271
  last year in office, 313–20
  "misinformation conversation," xxi–xxii
  national security strategy of, 24–25,
    231–32, 293
  NATO and. *See* Trump, Donald, and NATO
  North Korea and, 213–22. *See also* Trump,
    Donald, and Kim Jong Un
  photo op at St. John's Church, 311–13
  presidential transition of. *See* Trump,
    Donald, presidential transition of
  revolt of the generals, 237–55
  Russia and, 226–33. *See also* Trump, Donald,
    and Putin
  September 11 attacks, xv–xvi, 19, 20
  South Korea and THAAD, 137–38
  State of the Union (2019), 259–60
  Syria policy. See Trump, Donald, and Syria
  terrorism and the border, 271–75
  travel ban of. *See* travel ban
  Ukraine phone call, 309–10
Trump, Donald, and Afghanistan, 13–14, 125,
    127–53, 259–60, 289
  Biden's withdrawal, xvi–xvii
  Camp David meeting, 157–59
  meeting of May 2017, 135–37
  meeting of July 19, 2017, 147–50
  meeting of July 26, 2017, 153–54
  meeting with veterans, 146–47, 148
  Prince plan, 140–44
  rules of engagement, 139–40

skepticism about war, 127, 129, 130,
    134–36, 150
  "South Asia strategy," 158–60, 159*n*,
    161–62, 259
  Taliban peace negotiations, xvi–xvii
  U.S. withdrawal of troops, 260–68
Trump, Donald, and 2016 election, 20, 21–25,
    35–43, 96, 100, 109, 115–16, 127, 169,
    176–77, 207, 223, 301
  Flynn and, 25–26, 30–31
  Gold Star family controversy, 37–38
  Russian interference, 63–67, 207, 229–31, 232
Trump, Donald, and Kim Jong Un, xvii–xviii,
    42, 216, 217, 218, 219–21, 245, 246, 289,
    291, 297
  DMZ meeting, xvii, 221, 290, 299
  Hanoi meeting, xvii, 220–21
  "love letters," xviii
  Singapore summit, xvii, 219–21, 246
Trump, Donald, and NATO, xviii–xix, 4, 11,
    188, 226–29, 245–46, 300
  Brussels July 2018 summit, 228–29, 245
  defense spending, 11, 225–26, 226*n*, 245
  disdain and interest in withdrawal, 10, 50,
    67, 147, 228, 248, 253–54, 291, 301
Trump, Donald, and Obama, 41–42, 288–89
  "birther" conspiracy, 17, 19
  presidential transition meeting, 41–42
Trump, Donald, and Putin, xviii–xix, 67,
    69–70, 207, 227–30, 291, 300
  G20 meeting, 233
  Helsinki summit, 229–31, 237–38, 246,
    290, 297
  White House invitation, 231
Trump, Donald, and Saudi Arabia, xix, 10, 165,
    167–81, 192, 205, 208–9, 242, 282
  Khashoggi's murder, 165, 203–4, 205–8
  MBS, xix, 167–68, 172, 282, 291
  Qatar blockade, 178–81
  state visit, 172–73, 175–77, 207
Trump, Donald, and Syria, 205, 241–42, 280,
    289–90
  Kellogg on bombing of Assad, 82–83
  orders strikes, 113–16
  presidential transition and, 121–22
  sharing of intelligence with Russia, 138–39
  U.S. withdrawal of troops, 24–251, 254–55,
    259, 260
Trump, Donald, presidential transition of, 45–67
  cabinet picks, 48–67
  chaos of, 59–61
  Christie and, 45–47

Trump, Donald, presidential transition of (*cont.*)
   Russian interference in election of 2016 and,
     63–67
   secretary of defense, 49–51
   secretary of state, 56–59
Trump, Donald, Jr., 107
Trump, Eric, 314–15
Trump, Fred, 107
Trump, Ivanka, 90, 154, 192, 194, 281
Trump, Mary Anne MacLeod, 107
Trump Bedminster Golf Club, 50, 157, 267
Trump border wall, 56, 251, 271–72, 274
Trump rallies, xx, 96, 165, 220
Tsai Ing-wen, 73
Tubaigy, Salah Mohammed, 201–2
Tumulty, Karen, 238
Turkey, 121, 201, 204, 248–50
   coup attempt of 2016, 41
   Syria and, 248–49, 254–55
Tyson, Mike, 277

Ukraine
   Manafort and, 39
   Russia annexation, 228, 231, 309
   Trump phone call and impeachment, 309–10
Understanding Terror Networks (Sageman), 35
"underwear bomb," 75
United Arab Emirates (UAE), 76, 81, 170–72,
    178, 179, 204, 291
United Kingdom. *See* Britain
United Nations, 151, 184, 190
   General Assembly (UNGA), 39–40
   North Korea and, 215–16, 220–21
   Relief and Works Agency (UNRWA), 195–96
   Security Council, 115, 216, 221
Unrestricted Warfare (Qiao and Wang), 5
U.S. Agency for International Development
    (USAID), 190
USA Today, 142
"usufruct," 306
Uzbekistan, 106

Vatican, 6, 14
VBIEDs (vehicle-borne improvised explosive
    devices), 118
Venezuela, 33, 106, 281
Vickers, Michael, 30
Vietnam War, 37, 79, 261
   McMaster's *Dereliction of Duty* on, 79,
    86–87, 88, 132, 308
   Paris Peace Accords, 261

Vision 2030, 173–74
Vitézi Rend, 35
Votel, Joseph, 116–17, 118, 120, 186, 248–50

Waddell, Ricky, 151, 158
Wahhabi Islam, 173–75
Walker, Scott, 46
Wallace, Chris, 176, 239, 272
Wall Street Journal, 21, 72, 141, 218, 266, 315
Walmart shooting, 269, 275
War and the Art of Governance (Schadlow), 90
War Powers Act of 1973, 279
Washington, George, 287
Washington Examiner, 191, 273
Washington Post, 24, 31, 201, 261, 307, 315
   McRaven's open letter to Trump, 238–39
weapons of mass destruction (WMD), 63–64,
    219. *See also* chemical weapons; nuclear
    weapons
Webb, Jamie, 225
Weekly Standard, 62
Weeks, Timothy, 161*n*
Welch, Edgar, 34
WhatsApp, 195
WikiLeaks, 63, 65, 66
"winning without fighting" strategy, 294–95
Wolff, Terry, 119–20
Wollman Ice Rink (Central Park), 142
Woodward, Bob, 307
World War I, 4, 112, 156, 274
World War II, 4, 7, 9, 11, 35, 53, 54, 62, 291
"Wuhan virus," xxi

Xi Jinping, 55, 113, 114

Yakla raid, 76–78
Yale Law School, 190
Yang Jiechi, 73
Yates, Sally, 100
Yazidis, 116–17, 123
Yemen (Yemeni Civil War), xix, 37, 75–78, 169,
    280, 289
   Houthi rebels in, xix, 183–84, 282
   Saudi Arabia and, xix, 169, 183–84, 208–9
   travel ban and, 97, 103, 106
   Yakla raid, 76–78

Zakaria, Fareed, 115
Zarif, Mohammad, 282–83
Zazi, Najibullah, 273
Zelensky, Volodymyr, 309–10